IMPERIALISM

IMPERIALISM

*The Story and Significance of a
Political Word, 1840-1960*

BY

RICHARD KOEBNER
AND
HELMUT DAN SCHMIDT

CAMBRIDGE
AT THE UNIVERSITY PRESS
1964

PUBLISHED BY

THE SYNDICS OF THE CAMBRIDGE UNIVERSITY PRESS

Bentley House, 200 Euston Road, London, N.W.1

American Branch: 32 East 57th Street, New York 22, N.Y.

West African Office: P.O. Box 33, Ibadan, Nigeria

CAMBRIDGE UNIVERSITY PRESS

1964

Printed in Great Britain by
Spottiswoode, Ballantyne and Co., Ltd.
London and Colchester

RICHARD KOEBNER

Professor Koebner had established a European reputation for himself before Hitler's expulsion of non-Aryan academic teachers put an end to his tenure of the professorship through which he had added to the distinction of Breslau University. Till that time he had been known as a medieval historian. Apart from many scholarly articles, he had published *Die Anfänge des Gemeinwesens der Stadt Köln*, *Zur Entstehung und ältesten Geschichte des deutschen Städtewesens*, *Venantius Fortunatus*, *Seine Persönlichkeit und seine Stellung in der geistigen Kultur des Merowinger-Reiches*, *Der Dictatus Papae*.

From 1934 until 1955 he held the Chair of Modern History at the Hebrew University of Jerusalem. His removal from the sources so essential to him in his former fields of study necessitated a change in the direction of his interests. He supervised the translation into Hebrew of H. A. L. Fisher's *History of Europe* and wrote a supplementary chapter for that book. His name became a household word not only amongst senior scholars but also amongst younger students in England when he wrote for the *Cambridge Economic History* his famous chapter on 'The Settlement and Colonisation of Europe'. His interests became gradually concentrated, however, on the history of the changing use and connotations of words involving concepts of great significance for historians. Though he never succeeded in speaking English without a strong foreign accent, he could charm and fascinate bodies of English scholars when, during his frequent visits to this country, he expounded his views and described his work in the field of semantics. Minute inquiries in literature, that covered large areas and long periods, enabled him to throw unexpected light on the use of a word like 'tyranny', or a term like 'Western Civilization'. Finally, these researches came to be concentrated on the changing meanings of concepts like 'empire' and 'imperialism' and resulted in an important work which adds a new dimension to our study of these matters.

It was remarkable that an historian so technical in his work during the first half of his career, and still so minute in his researches during the

Richard Koebner

second half of his career, should have had also an extraordinary interest in art and in philosophy. Throughout his life he was drawn to the study of aesthetics, and in 1957 he published in Germany a book, written in collaboration with his wife, Gertrud Koebner, *Vom Schönen und seiner Wahrheit, Eine Analyse aesthetischer Erlebnisse*, which reflects this aspect of his mind. The resulting combination of qualities made him an inspiring teacher whose pupils have been distinguished by their devotion to him, and also enabled him to be a constant fascination and stimulus to his colleagues in the historical profession. He was deeply attached to England, to English institutions, and to the history of English political life. And he was attached by rare and peculiar bonds to his English friends.

HERBERT BUTTERFIELD

PREFACE

Richard Koebner planned to continue his comprehensive study of Empire beyond the beginning of the nineteenth century where his written work ended. He hoped to give a detailed account of the attitude of the British people towards their Empire and of the evolution of imperial ideas up to the Statute of Westminster of 1931. He also intended to link that study with an investigation of imperialism as a political slogan. When he died in April 1958 he had collected for that purpose several thousand excerpts and notes and had published two articles on the slogan of imperialism.[1] Soon after his death Mrs Koebner permitted me to examine his papers. Since 1936 I had been associated with Professor Koebner, first as his pupil and later as his first assistant in the Hebrew University of Jerusalem. I remained in close contact with him in Britain and knew that death had prevented him from bestowing some of his best thoughts on future generations of historians. I, therefore, offered to suspend my own research work in order to preserve and develop his last historical study as quickly as possible. My undertaking was greatly facilitated when Sir Llewellyn Woodward and Dr Robert Oppenheimer enabled me to carry out my work at the Institute for Advanced Study in Princeton, N.J., during the academic year 1959/60. There I translated and deciphered some of his shorthand notes, supplemented the excerpts where necessary, and on that basis wrote the book in accordance with Koebner's original plan.

Koebner's semantic method and his way of reporting in detail controversial views concerning the British Empire and the notion of imperialism have been fully incorporated together with his drafts and published articles. In writing this book I decided to make the story of imperialism the main theme, which, indeed, had been the starting-point of Koebner's inquiry. Two major works dealing with concepts of Empire have been published after Koebner's death, A. P. Thornton's *The Imperial Idea and its Enemies* and the third volume of the *Cambridge History of the British Empire*. They dealt with some aspects of the subject which made another full treatment appear less worthwhile. Having decided to write the story of imperialism rather than the story of Empire I found I could still use Koebner's notes to the fullest extent. Professor Koebner had collected those notes with the help of his devoted wife, who in the preparation for this book, as for his book on *Empire*, was his indispensable amanuensis. I was obliged, however, to add a good deal of the twentieth-century material in order to make imperialism a more coherent story. To give that story a link with the present time I wrote the last chapters as an epilogue, although Koebner himself would have been content to conclude this study with the tenth chapter, strict and scrupulous historian as he was. His style was carefully polished, his writing cautious and weighed. I could not hope to emulate it. It is inevitable that in such a case of joint authorship the language lacks uniformity. As many of his ideas and thoughtful analyses as possible have been preserved. Some, alas, we have lost with him. I sincerely hope, however, that this service of love will contribute to the memory of a great historical mind and to a field of studies to which he gave many working years of his life. I am indebted to Professor L. E. Woodward and to Dr Ronald E. Robinson for suggestions and points of criticism which encouraged and assisted me in my work, and to Professor Norman Bentwich for his assistance in reading the proofs.

H. D. SCHMIDT

PRINCETON
March 1960

Cumque ab eo domestici quaererent, cur tristis in adoptionem regiam transiret, disputavit quae mala in se contineret imperium.

VITA MARCI ANTONINI IV, 5: 4

CONTENTS

INTRODUCTION

This is the biography of a political word and its rise to world power status. From its early beginnings in the 1840's until today it has changed its meaning no less than twelve times, and nobody of the present generation is aware of its first meaning or of subsequent meanings which that term possessed in the days of Palmerston and Disraeli. Few people realize how the word spread and what circumstances promoted its diffusion. Generations come into the possession of words and ideas as they come into the possession of public buildings. They call them 'their own' and no longer remember who built them and for what purpose. Sometimes those buildings are put to new uses and their public function is altered. The fate of ideas and words often tells a similar story. Their use and function reveal the mind of each generation. Words do not change their meanings fortuitously; they often acquire specific connotations in connexion with specific events and situations. And, just as words have an impact upon actions, so there is an impact of actions upon words which is of particular interest to the historian. There is probably no period in history which may not be enlightened by a pursuit of semantic inquiries; the semantic approach to history has something to reveal in all periods. But it may be observed that the reciprocal impact of social situations and events upon words, and of words upon actions and attitudes, has been increasing in frequency and force during the last two centuries, and consequently the semantic approach to history is of particular interest to the historian of modern times.[1]

Of all the words and expressions which may interest the historian, there is one class which is recognized to be of conspicuous importance. These are the words which, in the discussion of public affairs, are the means of swaying the moods and attitudes of hearers and readers: catchwords, watchwords, or slogans. In politics slogans are often the means of bringing people together in self-assertion or self-defence: they create solidarity. They are at work when people engage to co-operate in maintaining old institutions or in creating new ones. They inspire enthusiasm for common causes. They provoke love and loyalty; or alternatively they instigate disgust and hatred. And the object of these emotions may be institutions, communities, or individuals. Moreover, it is clear that political and other slogans are increasingly important in proportion to the numbers to be enlisted in the common cause.

Not words only but also particles of words have careers of historical importance. Ancient Greek has provided the language of the modern world with the suffix *ismos*. Originally it referred to actions which are at the same time denoted by the cognate suffix *izein* making a verb; the suffix *istes* denoting a person active in the appropriate *ismos*. All these three suffixes have taken part in the formation of modern languages; they have become international links between national vernaculars. In the case of *ism*—and to a lesser degree also of *ist*—this interconnexion is not only a feature of grammar and lexicography, but is at the same time a manifestation of highly important interrelations in public life. The suffix *ism* has come to denote not so much the action in progress (as it did in Greek words like *ostracismos* and *baptismos*) as principles of action or intentions. In this meaning it makes the word to which it is attached understood far beyond the country of its birth, the more so because in most cases the root of the word, like the suffix, is of classical origin. There is *atheism*, *dogmatism*, and *rationalism* in religion, *idealism* and *materialism* in philosophy, *impressionism* in art. But the *isms* which have had the strongest emotional appeal are those which signify topics of political conflict: *liberalism*, *conservatism*, *nationalism*, *capitalism*, *socialism*, *communism*, *colonialism*, and *imperialism*. Indeed, the *ism* suffix has won a leading position in shaping modern political slogans. It has developed in two directions. The suffix serves the purpose of denoting the principle which a party or, more generally, a section of society, accepts as representing its belief in matters of public interest: *liberalism*, *socialism*, and *communism*. But at the same time the suffix *ism* itself has added a note of derogation to the words to which it is attached: *despotism*, when used in France before and during the Revolution, became an early example of this sort, and *imperialism* has today acquired a sharply derogatory meaning. Indeed, this suffix has served to concentrate great blocks of political emotion which would otherwise have remained dispersed and consequently less effective.

Introduction

The semantic approach to history is not, of course, new. It has shown
remarkable results in the study of institutions. For institutions are
inseparable from the legal expressions used in acts of legislation or
administrative orders. In the investigation of 'historical consciousness',
that is, of the understanding men have had of their place in history and
the political beliefs that have been expressed in this manner, the value of
the semantic method is pre-eminent. Indeed, most of the evidence we
have in this matter is 'semantic'. The study of the expressions of a
political vocabulary, however, presents peculiar difficulties.

Like the expressions of a legal vocabulary, they are instruments in the
handling of social affairs and represent themselves as susceptible of
definition. But while the meaning of a legal term can often be ascertained
with some precision, and while its range of movement is usually narrow
and its transformation slow and orderly, the meaning of political terms
is subject to no authority but its acceptance by the public which uses it,
or to which it is addressed. The expressions of our political vocabulary,
and among them those denoting 'historical consciousness', are unavoidably ambiguous: their meaning is in perpetual movement and one
meaning constantly overlaps another. These expressions spring from
vague emotions, and are often more powerful than precise. In them
social organizations become articulate to ordinary people who have,
from generation to generation, to adjust their lives to them. The individual inherits a language which soon teaches him that he is moving in
a world governed by collective personalities, old and young, friends
and foes, each of which has a distinct character. These personalities bear
the names of nations, religions, classes, interests, movements, powers,
races, civilizations, and generations. Represented by their names they
are co-ordinated to one another and form the social world into which
the individual is born. But since these names are always coloured by
emotion, and are voiced with approval or disapproval, they at the same
time suggest to the individual what his own place shall be in that world.
Injunctions of solidarity and commands of enmity radiate from them.
They determine the attitude of a child towards social groups at a very
early age.[1] In that way political sentiment and emotive slogans are
passed on to subsequent generations reinforced by literature and new
historical crises. We shall see that the life of *imperialism* as a political

slogan has so far lasted for more than eighty years without showing any signs of senility. Nor can that period be regarded as exceptionally long. *Perfidious Albion* as a slogan has so far had a career spanning nearly 150 years.[1]

The semantic approach to history may then begin with what a dictionary can supply. There some of the vicissitudes of the words and expressions the historian is concerned with are to be discovered; and even the dates at which changes of meaning earliest manifested them-selves may be given. But the part played by a word in the history of a society does not become apparent in the context of exemplary phrases and quotations which dictionaries offer. Even a very full enumeration of applications, such as is represented in concordances of the vocabulary of individual authors and works, does not bring to the surface the social and political realities to which the word was allied. Where the object of the historian is to discover the manner in which human action and the words of a political vocabulary are interrelated, the dictionary is only a beginning.

A sentence which presents the immediate context of the word has to be seen in its own larger context: it is part of a speech or a written argument; the speech or the argument is an episode in the progress of a discussion; the discussion is aroused by problems in which a smaller or larger group of contemporaries is passionately engaged. The political or historical expression is aimed to make people realize what is at stake for them. The historical moment is, as it were, condensed in its sound. And not until the historian succeeds in seeing the expression in this inter-relation with facts which matter for society can he understand the historical consciousness which is propagated by the concept. From interpreting words in the context of specific situations, he passes to inquire what these situations have meant to the men concerned in them, and from there he must go on to show how the word became a partner of the action which grappled with the situation, what objectives the men had in mind who uttered the word, what future world they hoped to create, what new age to enter. Thereby historical consciousness is revealed and social motives become more intelligible.

What is new in recent historical consciousness is the specific meaning which the word *modern* has acquired since about the middle of the eighteenth century. The term has come to emphasize the conviction that the present age is one of incessant crises leading on to new developments which are not comparable with any of the past. To understand the present age as a time heavy with impending catastrophe is an attitude that can look back to a long tradition. It has often derived fresh inspiration from the Hebrew prophets and from apocalyptic literature. It has had its secular varieties, from classical visions of human decadence to Hamlet's discovery that 'the time is out of joint'. But what is new in the recent understanding of the *modern* age is the belief that the critical present is at the same time the beginning of an unprecedented new period in human history. The present is understood to be creative to the same degree as it is catastrophic. The conviction of being *modern* is assertive. It commits man to a scientific outlook, to social improvement, and economic development. Their path must not be blocked by holy cows, the fast of Ramadan, tribal traditions, the veil, or purdah. The new era demands for itself a new allegiance. This conviction, then, is common to all the modern assertive ideologies, all the party slogans, and to all the *isms* of the last two centuries. They aspire to be both modern and assertive, even where they appear to be negative watchwords, such as *despotism* in the eighteenth century and *imperialism* in the present.

Though the following chapters will deal with the detailed political discussions and controversies which called forth the evocation of the names of Empire and Imperialism in changing circumstances and content, the careful reader will perceive beneath the expression of conflicting opinions the deeper current of historical thought. He will notice how a generation of Englishmen becomes alive to the existence of an oversea Empire about whose meaning and future there is considerable doubt. He will observe how the English outlook expands, and in doing so perceives the growth of Anglo-Saxon settlements in other parts of the world and the spreading of parliamentary democracy. The belief in that process was becoming popular when the advance of Russia in Asia posed new problems, as did the rise of German military might. We shall see the impact of Africa on the British interpretation of the Anglo-Saxon's place and mission in history, and watch the dawn of the global rivalries prior to the outbreak of the First World War with its crop of anti-imperialist theories. Once again a world, tired of the 'age of imperialism', hoped for a better age of peace and social progress, only to be bitterly disappointed. Three simultaneous global struggles are now in progress and imperialism is claimed to be the main issue in all three of them, a word growing more ambiguous in meaning as it grows in emotive strength and gains in geographical diffusion.

Today the word may be found applied to systems of control maintained by densely settled colonists of the dominant people, but also to political influence which is exerted through military and administrative agencies, or even mainly through the influence of business concerns which have managed to domicile themselves in the dependent country. The dominance called 'imperialistic' may have originated in conquest or in treaties concluded with indigenous rulers. The practical value of the dominance appears in most cases to materialize in financial returns. But *imperialism* may also be thought constantly concerned with securing strategic outposts. The sections of the dominant nation to whom these interests apply may or may not be the same.

The word not only refers to systems of rule and interests of dominance very different from one another; it is also made characteristic of most varied habits of policy. It may be primarily applied to the obstinacy with which existent control is maintained. But it may also hint at a supposed tendency of the 'imperialist' power to extend its sway. High-handed action and the reckless use of brute force may be branded by the name as emphatically as subtle, conspiratory tactics by which the rulers and exploiters ingratiate themselves with certain sections of the dependent population. All these ambiguities, however, have not prevented *imperialism* from becoming an immensely powerful term of abuse on every continent. It is now so frequently employed by the radio and the press communicating in almost any spoken tongue on earth that in February 1960 a frequency count, including the press and radio of America, Europe, Asia, and Africa, showed that *imperialism* was used at a rate of at least one in every ten political broadcasts. The term was most often used in the Middle East, in Central and North Africa, and in communist countries. The bias which makes its popularity is directed against something more elementary than frameworks of rule or ways of policy, or even the attainment of economic or strategic advantages. It evokes the imagination of a mental disposition supposed to be ingrained in the character of the sets of people which have sent a nation on its imperialistic career. It assumes a consistent, calculated master-plot guided by an evil spirit of acquisitiveness and expansion. The evil spirit is alleged to be responsive to the prospects of widespread command and of obtaining riches from subject peoples and the lands in which they dwell. It is regarded as passionately adventurous, instinctively attracted by the difficulties it may have to overcome in unfamiliar environments. It is ruthless and unscrupulous; morally supported by an unshakeable belief in the innate mastership of the nation. Its self-reliance is, indeed, qualified by ceaseless apprehension of antagonistic forces from without and from within. Because of this disquietude and because of its natural aggressiveness *imperialism* cannot but be bellicose.

That construction includes an element whose origin needs a special explanation; the name *imperialism* itself. It has been loaded with an emotive force eluding all demands for precise definition. One way of retracing it which has been suggested is on first impression very plausible, but it leads to untenable assumptions. The word recalls the *imperium* of ancient Rome—and in some respects the collective spirit to which it alludes may appear to have directed Roman conquerors and governors. The term 'empire' was in any case applicable to modern states whose aggrandizement by the acquisition of dependencies was within fresh memory. Comparisons between such systems and the *Imperium Romanum* have often enough provided a subject for rhetorical flourish as well as for sedate reflexion, and for praise as well as for warning comment. The word *imperialism* has frequently entered this context. But can we really believe that it took its origin from scholarly reflexions, and was from them copied by the organs of public opinion which gave it currency around the globe? For the public addressed by these organs in 1900 and in subsequent years classical reminiscenses were certainly not very persuasive. They were not at all appropriate to give a name to one of the most precarious issues of the present age. This was not the way how historical consciousness could be given shape in the mind of many peoples.

The intimation of the Roman analogy was only an after-effect of the popularity already attained by the word in its topical significance. The same is necessarily true of a broadly generalizing application, to which it has been harnessed in innumerable writings on matters of history and politics. The word has been found convenient for typifying any system of extended rule from the days of Nineveh down to the Soviet Union. World history has appeared studded with 'imperialisms'. The inclusion of various empires which vanished long ago has given to the word the appearance of representing a definable category of political science, an assumption which enhanced its prestige in political literature of a controversial character. A term accepted for dispassionate argument in doctrine and description easily seems to retain its 'scientific' character when it serves the purposes of incrimination. This renown can, however, do nothing to explain the emergence of the word. 'Imperialism' cannot possibly have originally served unbiased needs of classification, and only afterwards descended into the arena of politics. Its career was clearly the other way round. This is best witnessed by those historical and sociological authors who have not been content with a perfunctory application of the term, but tried to give account of its usefulness for the scrutiny of various instances of political and economic dominance. They have either confessed to being baffled by the ambiguity of the word, or been compelled to allow for so many varieties of its application that its comprehensive meaning dwindled into vagueness. In their critical inquiry the philosopher and the historian pull in a different direction from the politician: concerned with a common vocabulary, the former try to remove from its expressions just that ambiguity which (in so far as it can be concealed) makes them valuable and effective in the eyes of the latter.

The 'semantic' approach to history calls our attention to these tensions; it puts both politician and philosopher on their guard and shows the manner in which they can profitably go into partnership—the politician as the interpreter of the situation, and the philosopher together with the historian as the critic of his excesses. It may be true that the materials of philosophical analysis are nothing more than the expressions which belong to a popular vocabulary, and that scientific history is never more than a comment upon that popular consciousness which is misrepresented as history; but the analysis and the comment have their effect. They make us less ready victims of destructive ambiguities and less liable to mistake the expressions of popular historical consciousness for historical realities. Every people unavoidably seeks a place for itself in history; it interprets the past in order to be at home in the present. The service of the scientific historian is to keep that interpretation from becoming so remote from what the evidence obliges us to believe that it no longer retains the plausibility upon which its power depends. Politics is a battle of ambiguities: the service of the philosopher is to keep ambiguity within bounds and to prevent it from engendering useless illusions.

Growth and expansion of power there has always been. The rise and decline of realms which extended their rule over dependencies had been a commonplace theme of historical reflexion long before *imperialism* was heard of. The foundations and prospects together with the rights and wrongs of imperial structures became subjects of animated discussion under the new name, because they presented themselves as having a specific bearing on problems of contemporary society. The new name was primarily understood to emphasize this urgency. Its rapid career signified that it took its place among the concepts which were felt to embody the signature of the present age in general. As an item in the language of history it purported to have a direct reference to the crossroads of most modern history.

In spite of being construed upon *imperium*—the emblem of antique glories—the word appealed to an historical consciousness which was acutely aware of characteristics of the modern age, unprecedented and only born with it. The aspirations for extended power, on which the word commented ought, indeed, to have roots in inveterate habits; they were nevertheless assumed to rely on energies, which only the aggregate wealth and the technical accomplishment of modern society could have provided. The concept added to the series of the self-assertive attitudes of mind to which Western society seemed to have given birth by its autonomous growth in the nineteenth century. It formed a parallel to such notions as *individualism, capitalism, socialism, liberalism,* and *nationalism.* Like any one of those it focused upon sectional interest which was conditioned by an incessant growth of material resources, but also tended to monopolize the right of leadership in the further organization of social energies. Almost all of these one-sided claims were known to be raised with a full confidence in their rightfulness—and some of them would not be afraid of asserting themselves by those very names. Their respective opponents, on the other hand, would not fail to invest the name in question with the quality of indicating a danger to the future destinies of society. Each such denomination, therefore, indicated one particular aspect of a constant crisis inherent in contemporary history. *Imperialism*, in a way, rounded off this picture by enlarging the area for which it was valid. There was even proof of its being pronounced at one time not only in a hostile but also in an assertive mood. The word could denote a belief in extending the blessings of modern progress to the untapped resources of Asia and Africa, to the backward peoples inhabiting these continents. If voiced in abhorrence, however, it meant illegitimate encroachment on the indigenous rights of these peoples and, moreover, pointed at a precarious enlargement of the sphere in which conflicting interests of the European nations could lead to war.

The divergent interpretations of the effects of *imperialism* are naturally bound up with incompatible attitudes towards the moral energies behind it. They appear to be all devotion to noble causes in one reading, all self-seeking and demonic in the other. There is no doubt regarding the conception which has prevailed in the long run. The appreciative handling of the word *imperialism* has always been on the defensive against its derogatory use, and the latter has conquered the world in the course of our century. As a term of abuse that word has become a cosmopolitan member of the language of history. It enables many peoples in distant regions of the earth, living without any traditions in common, to feel united in fighting a joint enemy. Americans prided themselves in repudiating *imperialism* in Europe, while the word was at the same time hurled at all the Western nations by the communists. That was the situation after the First World War. In our days Indians, Arabs, Malayans, and Africans fully believe they know its meaning and are on the alert against what it depicts. Having only just emerged from colonial rule and attained the status of national independence for the first time in their history as a Westernized nation, with all the paraphernalia of a modern state, their overriding fear is of becoming dependent again on one of the world powers such as the United States or the Soviet Union. In October 1959 the President of the United Arab Republic, Gamal Abdul Nasser, was approached and requested to define *imperialism*. He approved of the following definition: 'Imperialism has meant different things at different times. More recently, it has come to mean, in both the East and the West, the subjugation of small nations to the interest of the bigger ones. It is in this sense that H.E. the President, like many other political leaders of our time, uses this word.' Other leaders and publicists of small nations would probably agree with that definition. In South America, Africa, and in Asia the *imperialist* is the twentieth-century version of the devil, a political devil, who has constant designs on the newly-won national independence of Asians and Africans and on the economic growth and independence of Latin America. In communist countries the devil wears a top hat and carries a dollar and an atomic bomb signifying the combination of economic and military conquest; in West Europe and North America the devil is red, at present carrying hammer and sickle. Before the last war, however, many Europeans believed they saw the devil loom in the West, speaking English but looking Jewish. That image has by no means disappeared from European minds, and was deliberately invoked by German papers in East Germany in the early 1950's.

The world-wide acceptance of *imperialism* as a partisan slogan sends us back to the question of its emergence. It has been adopted—or shall we say parroted?—by millions of people to whom the notion of 'imperial' matters has been a stranger. *Imperialism* could not possibly have been adopted as a stereotyped war-cry by Russians and Orientals, if the word had not before become tellingly indicative of present-day problems in the language of public opinion in the West.

We must go back a step farther. We cannot assume that several Western languages should have co-operated in providing the word with its penetrating sound. It must have obtained its characteristic note, together with the many ambiguities of its interpretation, in the internal controversies of one single nation. It was originally expressive of divided views which members of that nation took when passing judgement on its recent history. It flattered not a few of them; but these voices were counteracted by divergent opinions to which it signified objectionable courses of politics and grave issues of the national conscience. This attitude had won firm ground before the term was heeded by the world outside and given universal currency in condemnatory meaning. The nation in which it first took root would be particularly prepared for it, if the title of Empire had already a recognized place within the orbit of its institutions and political interests.

To raise these suppositions is already to speak of one nation and its empire—of England and the British Empire. *Imperialism* rose to the status of a main topic in the language of history in connexion with events in British politics which made English statesmen and English public opinion dwell on the recent history of the British Empire and on the implications of its growth. This origin has remained visible. It has left its mark on the career of the word. In English political usage at home and abroad it has added to its ambiguities. *Imperialism* has been understood as denoting the aim to maintain and to strengthen the solidarity of the constituent parts of the British Empire. This interpretation of the word has a special bearing on the relations between Great Britain and her self-governing colonies, the 'dominions' or Commonwealth countries, as they are now called—and this application is sometimes endorsed even today. On the other hand, the derogatory use of the term has always proved most acrimonious and most inflammatory when it was pointing at Britain and the British Empire. Many people in the world who have cried out against *imperialism* have added the adjective British. As a result *imperialism* was given a British connotation to such an extent that, in the minds of many, oppression of neighbouring peoples on the same continent was not considered to constitute a policy of *imperialism*, but the control of a people across the sea was. The anti-Western use of the slogan has been more popular, more widely adopted, and has had a longer past than its use against an Eastern or Asian power.

To throw more light on the still obscure past of that political word we must give special attention to the initial stage of its career, which was entirely British; and to the matrix of Empire notions out of which it arose. It was of seminal significance for all the meanings in which the word attained an international status later on, including the concept of 'the age of imperialism', into which the whole world was said to have drifted. We must, therefore, go back to the early Victorian period. We shall end this story in 1960, when *imperialism* as an alarm cry and partisan slogan carries a deeper significance. It has become an expression of a fundamental global problem of world order and limited sovereignty; it often expresses paradoxical attitudes. On the surface of politics three camps have seized it today. It serves in the main as a battle-cry in the cold war, chiefly in the political warfare of the communists, but also in anti-communist utterances voiced in the West; it plays an important part in the struggle for political emancipation which is being waged by the peoples of Asia and Africa; thirdly, it is used in attacks against Anglo-American power in Latin America, and was popular in that connexion among Europeans a short time ago.,

We shall begin our story with the new reign of the young Queen Victoria. If an imaginary reporter had approached some politically-minded men of letters in the late 1830's or early 1840's with the request to define the terms *Empire* and *imperialism*, clear answers would not have been readily obtained. Some might have come forward with the startling reply that Empire was just another name for the British Isles or, perhaps, a more fanciful name for England. As for imperialism well-informed Englishmen would, with some disdain, utter Bonapartism as nearest approximation to a precise definition, meaning the alien and happily banished system of Napoleon's ill-omened *empire*. Thus to begin our biography of imperialism proper we must cross the English Channel and meet the 'parti impérialiste', which rose to prominence at about that time.

THE IMPERIALISM OF LOUIS NAPOLEON

The word *imperialism* was introduced into the English language as a gloss on a regime which had been established in France. It indicated the various—and in English eyes often dubious—ways by which the *Empire* of Napoleon maintained its hold on the French during the period 1852–70. Among the political systems which for any reason have been called 'imperial' the Second French Empire left the least conspicuous mark on historical memory. The principles in whose name it had been established by the self-styled renovator of the Napoleonic Empire were after seventeen years abandoned by that ruler himself. However, as long as that system was maintained it meant a challenge to political thought. In England the term *imperialism* came into use as an answer to this challenge. This ephemeral fact is memorable for two reasons. It implies a testimony about its own time and it has unobtrusively bestowed a heritage on the later career of the term.

In English the term *imperialism* could never have been originally identified with an alien system of government, if at that time the word had had even the remotest connexion with the British Empire. The manifold problems attached to the government of the British Empire never failed to arouse lively discussion, but the public was not conscious of the idea that the problems of British rule could be surveyed or made the subject of criticism on the basis of so comprehensive a notion as the term *imperialism* implied. Imperialism at first meant a foreign system of domestic politics, the way the Emperor of the French cast the public mind in a specific mould and educated the nation to look up to his authority as the mainspring of public benefaction. He posed as the popular leader and he discouraged the belief in liberal institutions. Napoleon III bought allegiance to the monarchy by impressing the people with the semblance of growing wealth at home and success abroad. He developed military prestige, let the army outshine civilian honours, and endeavoured to make the French a docile people basking in the imagination of national glory. This system of sentimental bondage was stigmatized as 'Imperialism'. When later on English liberals warned their nation against being bewitched by imperialism they rarely evoked the shadow of Napoleon III and referred to notions of 'imperial' affairs which had arisen in England itself, but in the interpretation which they gave to these notions the original meaning and its connexion with Napoleon III was a noticeable ingredient.

'Ismes' denoting not only partisanship but also ideologies were great favourites of public controversies among the French living under the July Monarchy. The word *impérialisme* became known as a neology side by side with *bonapartisme*. It did not have the same significance. Instead of expressing allegiance to the dynasty of Napoleon it could refer to the desire for restoring to France the glories bound up with this name.[1] The name *parti impérialiste* in this sense became prominent in 1840. It had by then little to do with Prince Louis Napoleon, who had just prejudiced the Bonapartiste cause by his ill-starred raid on Boulogne. But Louis-Philippe and Adolphe Thiers had seen reason to demonstrate that the spirit of the Emperor was still with the nation. They had made him symbolically present in the nation's midst by having his body transferred from St Helena to the Invalides. While this ceremony was in preparation, hopes were aroused that in the Levant France could break loose from dependence on England and secure success for her protégé, the Pasha of Egypt. Popular yearnings for regaining the frontier of the Rhine were countenanced and the French army was ostensibly prepared for mobilization. With the downfall of Thiers this militancy proved abortive, but it gave substance to the notion that France could still recover the 'imperialist' spirit. After all the disappointments of the year 1840, *La Quotidienne*, the paper of the small legitimist minority, strongly appealed to the army veterans to take a leading part in this cause. They were the men, the paper declared, 'qui unissent à merveille les vieux souvenirs de la monarchie avec les souvenirs récents de la gloire impériale. . . . Le parti bonapartiste n'est plus rien. Le parti impérialiste reste puissant. . . . Le parti impérialiste, c'est le parti militaire de l'Empire, . . . le parti de l'epée, le parti de l'honneur.'[2]

The 'imperialist party' of this tirade was a quixotic construction, but the journalistic hotspur who posed as its herald was not wrong when he felt that the name of *l'Empire* was about to regain its place among the conflicting symbols of French national causes. He was also right in stating what it meant at that moment. Its appeal lay in the association with military glories. On their account the concept could be construed as bearing no reference to the 'imperial dynasty' and none in particular to the adventurous Prince Louis.

The process of dissociating *imperialist* from the compromised *bonapartist* as political attributes in 1840 is also evident in the writings of the exiled German poet Heinrich Heine. In June the two terms were still synonymous to him but in October he registered the trial of Prince Louis as a defeat of *bonapartisme* and transferred the attribute of 'imperialistisch' to the policy of Thiers.[1]

There was some irony in the fact that Prince Louis, the vociferous claimant of the Napoleonic heritage, had always made the same vow—to stand for *les idées napoléoniennes, le système impérial, la cause de l'Empire* without being prompted by any personal ambition of 'une restauration impériale'.[2] This assurance was not only insincere; it could not have been realized in any case in those days. A policy which pretended to renew the 'Empire' needed a leader who had some title to being trusted with the inherited belief in the imperial legacy. The colours in which the imperial cause appeared in the excitement of 1840 were illusive in yet another respect.

Military glory and triumphs abroad did not figure foremost in the imaginations which sanctified the memory of the Emperor and the Empire. Stability of internal conditions, the common man's security against social feuds and subversive conspiracies counted far more. This was what Louis Bonaparte understood at an early date. What he promised in the name of *Idée Napoléonienne* was always the conciliation of order and liberty, of authority and popular rights, the 'hierarchy' in the democracy. These specious pledges of impregnable harmony—not less premonitory of Fascist assumptions than reminiscent of the first Napoleon—culminated in the image of *un colosse pyramidal à base large et à tête haute*.[3] It was on the realities illustrating this image of 'the pyramid' that English critics were to build their concept of French 'Imperialism' when Louis Napoleon's Empire had come into its own.

During the last years of the July Monarchy the 'Napoleonic idea' remained as far out of sight as the man who proclaimed it. Together with him it regained publicity in the autumn of 1848. He cared for its being widely advertised after the Revolution had been transformed into a movement towards stability and he as a seemingly harmless abettor of this development had been admitted to the Constitutional Assembly of the Republic. Making democracy safe for order and authority—could anything be more in keeping with the wants of the ordinary citizen than proclaiming this postulate as the mission which the heir of the name of Napoleon Bonaparte held in pledge? He dedicated himself to this duty in the manifesto by which he presented himself to the nation as a candidate for the presidency. He also knew that to the great majority of the electors who had not studied the fine phrases of his political meditations his name would convey the same message. 'Mon nom se présente à vous comme symbole d'ordre et sécurité. . . . Plus la mémoire de l'Empereur me protège et inspire vos suffrages, plus je me sens obligé de vous faire connaître mes sentiments et mes principes.' His feeling proved right. As Tocqueville was to state three years later after the *coup d'état*, Louis Napoleon had 'the merit or the luck to discover what a few suspected, the latent Bonapartism of the nation. The 10th December showed that the memory of the Emperor, vague and indefinite, but therefore the more imposing, still dwelt like an heroic legend in the imaginations of the peasantry.'[1]

There were only few people who suspected the power of those memories; but Lamartine had been among those few. When addressing the National Assembly on the question of the popular vote in the presidential election he expressed his fear that the people might easily be tempted to abdicate their security, dignity, and liberty for the sake of the mere reminiscence of the Empire, 'a reminiscence of despotism'.[2] If we compare those premonitions with the afterthought of Tocqueville, we might easily assume that from 10 December 'imperialism' was a latent idea which was leading to an autocratic regime. The term, however, though occasionally on the lips of speakers in the debate, did not become a central topic of controversy while the conflicts between the President and the Assembly proved that the constitutional problem of France had not found a solution. Louis Napoleon on more than one occasion demonstratively recalled that he embodied the legacy of *l'Empereur.* On one occasion he went so far as to compare the 'national manifestation', which had made him President, with the declaration that had established the Empire in 1804. Both acts had been intended to stabilize and to save the great principles of the French Revolution. Others besides the Austrian Ambassador must have heard his friends boast: 'L'Empire se fera, ou plutôt il est fait.' By editing his writings and compiling a political dictionary of Louis Napoleon's aphorisms members of his circle had taken care to prove that the names of Empire and *système impérial* such as used by him embodied an idea—'a political code . . . from whose application we must expect a new era of grandeur and glory'.[1] In the face of these demonstrations the guardians of the Republic found no other words of abuse but *bonapartisme* and *despotisme* —the first pronounced in derision, the other as a warning. Why did they not comment on the idea of *imperialism*? Had they used that term, it would have brought out even more the abhorred prospects invoked by the other two. It would have indicated an intention on the part of the President to reinstate the constitution of the Empire and an inclination on the part of large sections of the nation to throw in their lot with the 'Napoleonic idea'. Both issues, however, seemed remote. No Napoleonic party had emerged in the elections to the legislative assembly. The President was, by the Constitution, prevented from running for a second period of office. He had no legal opportunity of presenting a popular mandate in favour of his political leadership. The Assembly, devoid though it was of a solid republican majority, finally stood firm on the constitutional *status quo* in the 'great parliamentary week' of July 1851. Three months later Lamartine declared himself satisfied that the forthcoming elections would show popular opinion siding with the majority of the legislature. Louis Napoleon Bonaparte would abide by the decision; he would see an advantage in being no longer president but 'one of the men of the people, . . . a great citizen'. The *Revue des Deux Mondes* in those days assured its readers that the name of this man, in the minds of those who voted for him on 10 December 1848, had been far from signifying 'a taste for the imperial form of government'. It had only expressed defiance of that republic which had immediately issued from the Revolution of February.[2] Complacent retrospects soon proved delusive.

The fact that the party-ridden assembly had, for once, found a majority in confirmation of its authority, did nothing to allay the widespread fear of social upheavals. As a safeguard of social stability that assembly wielded no confidence. Popular opinion could now be expected to accept the refuge of a strong executive which the 'Napoleonic idea' appeared to offer. During the following weeks the 'Chronicler' of the *Revue* showed himself incessantly haunted by this vision of a growing distrust in parliamentary guidance. His apprehension is mirrored in the terms he used for the description of the political crisis. There was, he wrote, dangerous naïvety in the demand of the *bourgeois absolutistes* to give them 'administration' instead of 'politics'. Who did not remember, he asked, the promise of marvels expected to result from the marriage of the Napoleonic idea with democracy? The President ought to be seriously warned against dreaming of such a marriage; it was a phantom. Regrettably, however, the Napoleonic regime, which had so often undergone the 'transfigurations' of deceitful poetry, was about to change its appearance once more and to assume an indefinable 'aspect of humanitarian dictatorship'.[1] A fortnight later the same journal again inveighed against the 'indefatigable detractors of free institutions and of deliberating assemblies'. These people were only too conscious of the fact that they wished to make the ruins of those assemblies the 'pedestal of their idol'. They imagined that having recourse to that refuge they were saving appearances and making their pettiness become greatness. It was a mere disguise for 'counter-revolution'. The Chronicler was reminded of an aphorism used by the great Republican Royer-Collard, who had said a long time before: 'Theocracy recommends itself by having a counter-revolutionary look.' Perhaps for the same reason, the journal concluded, the attempt is now made to revive *Imperialism*.[2]

That was the word; but it had only a fortnight to live. Once more the *Revue* desperately entreated the majority of the Assembly 'to prevent as energetically as it still had the power to do so the fatal consequences of either too close an intimacy or too personal a strife between those two principles of which one could not exactly say whether they were enemies or allies—the imperialist idea and the radical idea'. However, the majority to which this warning was addressed had just virtually abdicated. The Republicans had refused to trust the Assembly with its constitutional power to ensure its military protection.[1] Three days later Louis Napoleon had removed all doubts. He had needed no help from the 'radical idea'. He had given short shrift to the Assembly and established his power with the active assistance of the army and the connivance of the bourgeoisie. The cause for which he stood in the *coup d'état* of 2 December 1851 was, he proclaimed, that of 'France regenerated by the Revolution of 1789 and organized by the Emperor'. Though he demanded only the mandate for himself of a ten years' presidency, he had virtually heralded the Empire as a definite form of government. On the last day of the year Comte Vieil-Castel noted in his diary:

His henchmen press for l'empire; there is a general flutter, ambitions are stirring. . . . Poor French nation! Vainglorious whore who turns from one love affair to the next . . . decorations and titles, that is what now replaces the *panem et circenses* of ancient Rome. . . . Begone, miserable year that has made us long for a dictatorship and repudiate our liberties excessively used before. People who only a month ago declared Louis Napoleon an idiot now proclaim him a great man.

This comment was made by a man who was by no means a democrat. His loyalty to the Bonaparte dynasty had lately been rewarded by an administrative post at the Louvre. It says much that he could not speak of a sincere 'imperialist' enthusiasm which had been manifest in Paris. He did not know of the word as a slogan of protest murmured by the suppressed opposition. Only the most hackneyed term of abuse reached him from such quarters, the saying 'anarchy has been happily delivered of *despotism*; mother and child are well'.[2]

In the eyes of the Austrian Ambassador, who summed up the situation in April 1852, there was only one pre-occupying question: 'When shall we have the Empire?' In September, after Louis Napoleon's pronunciamento at Bordeaux, the answer was a foregone conclusion—and now Comte Huebner reported of the *élans impérialistes* which had hailed the President in the Midi.[3] In choosing this word, however, he scarcely echoed a term which had become popular. The words *impérialiste* and *impérialisme*, it is true, were well understood in Imperial France. But, together with *Césarisme*,[4] they had to be treated with caution and were better not used at all as they were suspect of being treasonable comment. In 1863 the 'Impressions' of an English *Flâneur* in Paris, of which we shall have to say more, were translated into French under the title *Dix ans d'Impérialisme en France*. It was an exact replica of the English heading. The translator, who pretended to dissociate himself completely from every criticism voiced by the author, declared that he had conformed to the English title only to prove the scrupulous exactness of his literal rendering. He knew, he declared, that the title was 'ironical and almost injurious'. Implicitly he gave in the text further proof of its odious character by suppressing the word and replacing it by the term *régime impérial, gouvernement impérial* or *Empire* at every place where *imperialism* occurred in the original. *Imperialism* is preserved in the text only at the beginning of the fifth chapter, which deals with the question why French imperialism could not, like Roman imperialism before, inaugurate a golden age of literature. A few pages after that the word *Imperialists* of the original is rendered by the translator as *Ultra-Impérialistes*. This transformation also betrays a consciousness that the term as such was capable of giving offence.[1]

Though the 'obnoxious' expression could not sound so strange to French ears, the translator gave the impression he had every reason to present it as a genuinely English growth. It mirrored the feelings with which uncompromising believers in British constitutional traditions regarded the Second French Empire. It had come into existence before that empire was constituted. By then quite openly, as it did clandestinely in France, it referred to the portentous shadows of the First Empire and to the man who visibly longed to be accepted as its restorer. The President's hopes and prospects for 'an ascent step by step ... to the distant grandeur of the empire' were coolly noticed by English observers in 1850–1.[2] It seemed natural to call his adherents *imperialists*. The word was no neologism. As long as the framework of the Holy Roman Empire was maintained amidst its ceaseless distractions it had often been applied to the partisans of its nominal head. After the fall of that political edifice in Central Europe the word was disposable for any cause of an emperor or pretender to emperorship in a foreign country.[3] The *North British Review* of Edinburgh in an article on 'France since 1848', inserted in its issue of May 1851, felt entitled to alternate *Imperialists* with

Bonapartists. Both names appeared equally characteristic of the people who in the election of 10 December 1848 had shown they were 'attached to anything that bore the name or the impress of Napoleon' —recruited from the army, the peasantry, and also to a degree from the middle-class elements 'who remembered that Napoleon had restored order and stability'. In the course of that article, however, the mentality of the French people in general came in for a censorious scrutiny, which resulted in bestowing on *imperialism* a significance outranging that of *imperialist*, its literal counterpart. The French had proved unregenerate in many respects. Religion had ceased to be a formative element in its character; it was for that reason that France—in contradistinction to England—had been exposed to violent political convulsions and had after every one of them remained morally vulnerable in her attitude to public interests. 'Appetite for material felicity' was unrestrained. French literature was showing itself 'allied not only with democracy'—however recommendable that might be in itself—'but also with the lowest and most envious passions of the mob'. These moral defects caused the people to be 'unqualified' for representative institutions. These were, therefore, in France particularly exposed to corruption. The French, in the last resort, failed to understand what such institutions meant. 'The idea of ruling themselves is one which has not yet reached the French understanding. The idea of choosing those who are to rule them is the only one they have hitherto been able to conceive.' By 'corruption' the author of the article meant the enormous size of the French centralized administration. It numbered 535,000 officials while Britain was content with 23,000. To obtain a government post was one of the strongest interests of French families; patronage for such places was the main activity one expected from deputies elected for the Assembly. At the same time the complacent submission to this bureaucracy was basically at variance with the claim for self-government. France was 'in a radically false position, and she has not yet found it out; she is endeavouring unconsciously to unite two incompatibilities. Her government has all the finished and scientific organization of a despotism, with the political institutions which belong to freedom.' That organization had been created by Napoleon, by the Empire. When recalling this origin the author could not but arrive at

9

a prognostication which, in the end, made him hit on a special expression concurrent with 'despotism' but more directly adapted to French history. 'The republic of today may wake and find itself an empire to-morrow—scarcely an individual Frenchman would feel the difference —and not one iota of the administration need be changed. As it exists now, it was the child and may be the parent of *imperialism*.'[1]

The writer did not make much of the word; he was, it appears, not conscious of being its inventor. Whether this was in fact its first appearance or not—we cannot but find it strikingly tinged with connotations which were to return to it again and again when the aims and sentiments to which it referred were stigmatized as imperialism in connexion with British foreign and colonial politics. Forming, as it does, the keystone of an argument written in the spirit of moral indignation the word denotes an attitude to public affairs imaginable only on the basis of moral perversity. Imperialism is the 'false position' into which a nation is led when it has lost sight of the principles of the gospel as well as of those of civil liberty. The judgement passed on it takes it for granted that these sets of principles are inseparable. Imperialism is nurtured by unmanly deference to authority, by inordinate greed, by social habits distinctly vulgar. This diagnosis was here pronounced by a staunch British Protestant on the Frenchmen born and bred in the traditions of the Napoleonic 'Empire'. Later it was recognized by critics, sometimes equally religious, to fit Englishmen allured by the 'imperial' prospects which had been opened to them by a Disraeli or a Chamberlain or a Cecil Rhodes, whom hostile spectators of a later age regarded as overbearing politicians, militant adventurers, or capitalist speculators.

To the editors of the *North British Review* not only these horizons were necessarily closed; they did not anticipate, as they frankly confessed after the *coup d'état*, that their warning of the French Republic 'waking and finding itself an empire' could literally come true 'in seven short months'.[2] Up to December 1851 English public opinion, like that of France, took a legalistic view of the situation. Serious observers were scared by the question how the disunited republic would survive the elections due in the following May; they did not credit Louis Napoleon with such bravery and faithlessness as was necessary in order to forestall the result. Therefore, when the blow fell, it came as an offensive surprise, and that attitude grew into ardent revulsion when details of its truculent execution were made known by *The Times*, whose secret informant was Tocqueville. Palmerston, to whom the surprise meant a relief deserving the expression of approval, found himself for once out of touch with his high-minded compatriots and had to resign office as Foreign Secretary. The infuriated protest of public opinion—in which *The Times* took the lead and was seconded even by publications habitually tuned to sedateness such as the *Quarterly Review* and the *Annual Register*—was unanimous in proclaiming 'the abhorrence which such acts as these must excite among a free nation'. And in view of the violent and careful suppression of free French opinion by which the Act of 2 December was completed, it was now taken for granted that the better part of the French nation, in their heart of hearts, did not feel differently. Louis Napoleon had 'extinguished all freedom among the most advanced nation of the Continent'. His act was one of 'military absolutism', of 'treason', of 'usurpation', a 'despotic revolution', the establishment of 'autocracy' pure and simple. *The Times*, dimly remembering Montesquieu, set store by the axiom that 'despotism has no true principle of government but fear'. This attitude of disgust at political developments in France, mingled with pity for the French nation, prevented public opinion from giving at once serious thought to the question of the possible rebirth of *l'Empire* supported by a wide section of that nation. The possibility of imperial revival was treated with contempt, its popularity with disbelief. 'We fear that the lofty idea of a transcendental empire will soon turn out to be neither other nor better than the old devices and oppressions of vulgar despotism', *The Times* wrote; and the *Annual Register* predicted that the Prince President 'must march forward in the fatal path of arbitrary power until France rises to free herself from the yoke of bondage by another revolution.[1]

This purely negative verdict, however, could not long remain unqualified. Louis Napoleon's presidency had, when it still conformed to constitutional principles, been thought suggestive of genuine imperial sympathies cherished in France. Now, when he had so quickly disposed of the constitution, this subject necessarily came in for discussion again

—and the term *imperialism* became its denominator. In its issue of February 1852 the *North British Review* rose to the occasion of resuming and amplifying its reflexions of the preceding May. It now had even more reason to dwell on 'this singular union of what seem to Englishmen two opposed and mutually excluding conditions of polity—Republican institutions and Imperial sway'. A 'nominal constitution with arbitrary despotism' was definitely to be regarded as that system which 'satisfies a Frenchman's confused and misty ideal'. For, as the writer then found out, that ideal was ultimately based on the desire for equality which had animated the 'prolific principles established in 1789'. 'A Frenchman's notion of liberty is not personal freedom, but political equality; . . . his bugbear, his bête noire, his pious abomination is not a chief or master, but a privileged order. His dislikes and dreads an aristocracy, not an autocracy.' It was therefore that the first Napoleon could profess 'to complete the idea of a Republic and to govern in its name'. That claim had found a fitting symbol in his five-franc coins which bore the inscription of *République Française* on the one side, *Napoléon Empereur* on the other. The *Review* paralleled that juxtaposition by the page-heading it gave to these explanations: *Democracy and Imperialism combined.*[1]

Sporadic occurrences in a Scottish journal can scarcely be assumed to have been decisive for the acceptance of a term into common English usage. It cannot be accidental, however, that, within two months from the appearance of that headline, we find the word freely used by a German refugee in London and by a literary critic in America, both taking their cue from the action of Louis Napoleon. It seems fairly certain that the word imperialism spontaneously suggested itself by that time to many people who in speech or writing discussed the *coup d'état*. The German testimony is *The 18th Brumaire of Louis Bonaparte*, the pamphlet written by Karl Marx for the socialist monthly which his friend Weidemeyer was about to launch in New York. Its dominant intention was to show how contemporary France with its frequent changes of constitutional principle provided an object lesson for the dependence of political history on class struggle. Seen in this light Louis' victory appeared as deadly impaired by the intrinsic weakness of the economic forces which had brought it about. His uncle had been the idol of the small peasants liberated by the Revolution. Those had transferred their veneration to his nephew. *Die Parzelle*, the plot, as the prophet of the industrial proletariat derisively dubbed them, had outlived economic reality. Encumbered with mortgages they turned Napoleonic ideas into 'hallucinations' of their 'agonies. . . . Yet the parody of imperialism was necessary in order to set the mass of the French nation free of the dead-weight of tradition and consummately to demonstrate the contrast between the political system and the realities of society.'[1] When these spiteful dialectics reached New York, an American 'Whig' had just been inspired by the *coup d'état* to compose an ideological construction very different in outlook, but no less grim, and expatiating emphatically on the concept of imperialism. This author discovered that Louis Napoleon was nothing but the hero in action whose ideal portrait had been impressed on the English-speaking public by Thomas Carlyle. 'A greater and more dangerous enemy of political freedom there cannot be than the imperialist whose Scottish scepticism demolishes the *forms* while his servile reverence erects the *man*. It is heathenism in politics. By this new and absolute imperialism the State is best governed when some Louis Napoleon or Doctor Francia *is* the state.' Carlyle's intense hatred of America was well founded; it ought to be reciprocated by a rejection of his hero-worship and the imperialism implied in it. 'If there be a system or a doctrine utterly hideous and detestable to an American, it is imperialism. . . . Deriving its powers from the ambition of an army and the fear and admiration of an ignorant multitude, it ignores the liberty of the individual and of the state.' Being possessed by even stronger idiosyncrasies than the un-Carlylian Scotsman who wrote in the *North British Review*, the critic traces the parallel between Louis Napoleon and Carlyle back to the simultaneous appearance of the first Napoleon and Goethe. Those two joined in corrupting the morals of the old world outside the British islands. 'Pantheism and Imperialism, the two forms of modern heathenism, have since then held paramount sway over the educated intellect of Europe.'[2]

Each of the single applications in which we have seen the term emerge in 1851-2 relied on its being generally understood. In each case it was appealed to in the interpretation of current political events. If from these interpretations we elicit what made its appeal, we see that it lay in its historical reference to the Napoleonic tradition in France together with the general meaning of autocracy, an autocracy based on an obedient army on the one hand and on the acclamation of a credulous multitude on the other. These had been the facts which constituted imperialism as the living force enabling Louis Napoleon to establish autocratic leadership. Soon popular acclamation and the President's response to it followed their expected course. By the end of 1852 he was *l'Empereur* under the name of Napoleon III. Once that goal had been reached the concept of French imperialism was in keeping with the new realities. It could signify the personal character which Napoleon III impressed on his emperorship and the methods by which he secured his rule together with the characteristic features of popular acclaim, which implied an apparent promise that those methods would achieve a lasting success. The career reserved for the concept in this respect was cut short, however, before long. For some time, indeed, the 'imperial' regime to which it alluded went on to be treated with horror in English public opinion—the more so because, notwithstanding the new Napoleon's solemn assurances, it seemed suspect of aggressive intentions and raised anxious questions concerning the adequacy of Britain's naval defences. Cobden—whom abhorrence of warlike activities, then as before and afterwards, easily made forget every liberal principle except free trade—stood rather alone in expressing confidence in Napoleon. Within one year, however, greater tolerance towards the regime can be observed in Britain, for the grudgingly acknowledged ruler of France became the ally in the war against Russia, in the Crimean War. This war was countenanced by Liberal opinion—with Cobden and Bright as isolated dissidents—as being waged against that other Emperor whose preponderance was looked at as the bane of liberty on the Continent and likely to remain so unless immediately challenged.[1] The government which joined Britain in the sacred cause of fighting the tyranny of the Tsar deserved to be spared harsh comments and criticisms of its own autocracy. The truce was observed by British political journalists during the war and for some time after the common victory.

For Napoleon III this victory meant a personal triumph at home. He had proved the sagacious leader who would restore national glory without endangering the national frontiers. Among the many observers whom that triumph sent thinking one at once hit on the concept of *Imperialism*—not an Englishman, but a German essayist, Theodor Mundt. The *Sketches of Imperial Paris*, which he published in 1857, have their point in manners and morals rather than in politics. They claim to demonstrate, however, that Parisian life owed all its salient traits to the imperial court and government. To this observation the author had felt inspired by 'every step on the imperialistic pavement of Paris'. 'Imperialism', he insists, 'is the thread which runs through all the walks of life and lends them their character.' The author was manifestly proud of teaching the German public a new word.[1] He gave it prominence in his sensationalist diction—a diction once acquired in the licentious preachings of 'Young Germany', but now in the guise of offended morality put to the uses of a vulgarly pompous sociology which combined the lurid with the doctrinaire. Whether he originally picked up the term in French conversation or owed it all to spontaneous inspiration cannot be clearly decided. He failed to make a lasting impression on German writing.[2] He was scarcely read in England. More-over, in his zeal he made the new imperialism of Napoleon III re-sponsible for aspects of cultural life at which, as we have seen, English moralists had taken offence in earlier days. Still, some elements of his argument deserve mentioning. They stress facts which in English eyes constituted the problematic character of a system on whose attractive power the Second French Empire relied. Mundt sees this 'imperialism' exhibit itself in the pageantry of the court and the army. He finds it in league with stock-jobbing and maintained, in so many words, that 'by its whole nature and all its aims the new imperialism has stimulated the immense rush for the stock-exchange which means an excitement to all the classes'. He emphasizes the studied courtship with which the Emperor appears to woo the socialists. At this point, however, a snag is seen in the system. 'Imperialistic socialism' can demonstrate its merit only by offering good white bread to the masses, by providing work and rebuilding the capital. 'Imperialistic liberty' has already proved a dead failure. Imperialism does not dare to be parliamentarism. Iso-lating itself in its stronghold of violence it becomes unable to live up to the claim of embodying the principles of the Revolution. 'The victorious banners of imperialism are moving in the country over nothing but intellectual and moral defeats', the author sums up the position, yet he hopes for its improvement. Imperialism may be comparable to the 'braggarts of vice' who now flourish in Paris—people boasting of more immorality than they really practise.[1]

In England the truce observed by journalists and politicians which had restrained such comments was harshly brought to an end in 1858 by the repercussions which Orsini's attempt on the life of the Emperor had in England. The publicity given by the *Moniteur* to the army demonstrations which demanded strong measures against the 'den of assassins' led to the angry debates in the House of Commons which baffled Palmerston's attempt to propitiate France and enforced his second eclipse. Critics of the 'Conspiracy to Murder Bill' not only found it outrageous that control over the British 'asylum of all oppressed people' should now be demanded in the name of a man who once had been sheltered by it himself, but also had this man again ranged among the 'despots' of the present age. It was with him, the 'great god' behind the utterings of French sentiment, in mind, that, as John A. Roebuck said, the British nations had now to be conscious of being 'in the proud position—though I will say that it is for the human race a lamentable one—of being the sole depositories of liberty in Europe'. Gladstone and others joined in these protestations.[2] The newly aroused animosity was prevented from affecting the mutual relations of the two governments. But English public opinion had again reason to concern itself with the realities and potentialities of the French regime. Had not 'the grenades of 14th January, followed by a series of most astounding explosions' indicated dangerous tensions underneath the calm surface of Imperial France? Might not these tensions discharge themselves in adventures abroad? It is with these questions in mind that in the autumn of that year imperialism was declared by one of the leading journals, the *Westminster Review*, to embody the crucial problem of present and future French politics.

The author of the inquisitive study *France under Louis Napoleon* lays stress on his attitude of a dispassionate observer who is ultimately concerned with the possible repercussions of French domestic politics on Europe in general. He makes no mention of specific British interests; he professes detachment from any party's and any government's cause.

Introduced under such auspices, imperialism assumes the character of a definable form of government whose potentialities can be objectively scrutinized. It is the form of government to which contemporary France has submitted. Experience has shown, however, that 'France affects the whole world by her convulsions'. Therefore, 'the present' must be thought 'pregnant with consequences'—'whether Imperialism prove permanent or not'. So far Louis Napoleon has mastered the external position of France by his diplomacy. But his artfulness in this field which made him appreciate the alliance with Britain will not suffice to ensure further success. He needs stability at home. Hence, the actual question is 'whether the Imperialist form of government will last, or at least elaborate itself into a satisfactory settlement'. It must not be examined with regard to 'the facts of its being objectionable in parts'. Its prospects depend 'upon how far, in spite of such drawbacks, it still responds to the real requirements of the French people'.[1]

Among the practices which in the author's eyes embody imperialism those which affect the intellectual and political life of the nation are expounded at greater length than is found in the German study. The reader obtains a detailed—and in its result certainly not dispassionate—view of the strict control to which public opinion is submitted in Imperial France. Such newspapers as are still allowed to exist are prevented from mentioning any 'occurrence which might cast discredit on an Imperial establishment'. The government supervises the book-trade and devotes special attention to the educational effects of learning. Classical studies are regarded as dangerous, we are told; history has to be taught in conformity with imperial instructions; the *Collège de France* is governed by tyrannical regulations. Close collaboration with the clergy has been secured. The suppression of self-government has been made complete by the dissolution of municipal councils. Thereby the unbridgeable gulf between the government and the still existing liberal parties has become manifest. These parties cannot but insist on 'the necessity of loosening the administrative fetters'. No regeneration is possible without such radical reform; for on it depends 'the achievement of the Revolution of 1789, which is viewed by the nation as its Bill of Rights and is adopted by Imperialism as its pretended code'.[2]

Imperialism

In view of this discrepancy the economic and social politics of the Empire are to be understood as devices 'for entangling the nation at large into an indissoluble alliance' with the government of the Emperor. The overriding principle is here again interference at every place. This practice conforms to 'the all-devouring appetite involved by the exigencies of a government whose nature fears everything not subject to its inspection'. Napoleon, however, is giving a special flavour to this interference. It witnesses 'the supreme value set by his mind on the influence exercised by material interests on mankind; and the desire of palming off Imperialism as practically solving those questions of labour and prosperity which, under the name of Socialism, had become a feature in modern politics'. Here the remarks of the author are identical with those made by Theodor Mundt. Like Mundt he underlines the favours granted to 'stock-jobbers', and the enormous expenses imposed by the regime on the tax-payers for the embellishment of the capital. The reviewer cannot suppress a shudder at the sight of this prodigality. 'At the cost of upwards of twelve million francs a year spent on interest by the town of Paris, Imperialism has already purchased "panem et circenses", with which its vanity flattered itself to be able to drug disaffection.' This is not the only point in which Imperialism has proved economically unsound. Louis Napoleon would have chosen to help the nation first of all by leading it towards Free Trade. But when deciding in favour of that principle he had not been aware of 'the incongruity between its unshackled disposition and the strict discipline of Imperialism'. He began to fear depression in certain trades. He had to consider that 'it was indispensable for the success of Imperialism that it should captivate public opinion with the same rapidity as that with which it had been jerked into existence on the bayonets of the soldiery'. For this reason the unhealthy way was preferred to the sound, stock-jobbing to Free Trade.

In conclusion the author cannot but abandon his professed dispassionateness and dismiss the system with whole-hearted condemnation. Self-preservation appears as its only aim, and perversion of the public spirit as its unrelenting method. 'To lower the intellectual vigour of the nation by breaking up the volume of its thought and diverting its flow into isolated and scanty rills of such slender current as to be

easily kept within bounds—to exhibit to the world how the wayward-
ness of mind will yield beneath the compression of a stern resolution—
these are the tasks set itself by Imperialism.'[1] In his elaborate description
the reviewer has made the term suggestive of a political system which
must always appeal to the basest instincts and discourage upright
morality while it professes to be the fountain-head of universal welfare.
The moral interpretation follows the same line as had been indicated by
the *North British* reviewer seven years earlier. The assumption, however,
that the system had genuine roots in French national tradition is rejected.
The alleged harmony with the ideas of 1789 is considered a flimsy
pretence. Such scepticism was in keeping with the opinions which
independent Frenchmen confided to English visitors.[2] Though the
concept of imperialism as delineated by the *Westminster Review* did not
directly imply an adventurous and aggressive foreign policy, suspicion
in that direction was warranted by Napoleon's intervention in Italy.
When in the spring of 1859 he made himself a champion of the Italian
cause and set out to help Victor Emanuel and Cavour against Austria,
a wave of anxiety swept the country—later to be castigated by Richard
Cobden as 'the third panic'. The reinforcement of the navy and the
strengthening of the coastal defences became the topics of the day.
Volunteer units of 'riflemen' were formed; Alfred Tennyson thought
fit to impress on them:

> Be not gull'd by a despot's plea! . . .
> How can a despot feel with the Free? . . .
> True we have got—*such* a faithful ally
> That only the Devil can tell what he means.

Alarmists in more responsible positions such as the members of the
House of Lords would, in public at any rate, impute the intention of
invading England not to the Emperor but to the nation whose ambition
he had to satisfy and eventually would voice their conviction 'that every
Frenchman living dreamt both by day and by night of humiliating this
country'. But the more cool-headed Earl of Clarendon, who had been
Foreign Secretary during the Crimean War, was prepared to think the
worst of Louis Napoleon whom he assumed to have concluded a coalition against 'that stupid ass John Bull', who was now at long last

ceasing 'to invite attack by total unpreparedness'. The government, headed by Palmerston since June that year, deprecated 'language not well calculated to promote the object of unbroken friendly alliance'. Britain and France, in fact, soon after acted as allies along the Chinese coast. Napoleon, too, showed himself intent on buying English confidence by negotiating with Cobden the commercial treaty which matured in the course of 1860. He thereby enabled Cobden to reiterate the axiom of the *Westminster Review* in the opposite meaning and to declare wherever he could do so 'that the Emperor whose great intelligence no one disputed' could not be credited with 'pursuing, in his own person, the uncompatible career of the first Napoleon and Sir Robert Peel'. This argument might have been convincing in the eyes of strict believers in the moral power of Free Trade; but the autocratic power of Napoleon continued to be regarded as a disquieting factor which ought to be watched with caution. Persons of the highest as well as of the most simple-minded section of the population shared that sentiment of fear.[1]

Against the background of that sentiment the concept of imperialism was kept alive. As the term retained its primary reference to the internal conditions of a foreign country there was occasion for using it at intervals only. But where we find it used during the following years we see that its ominous meaning was taken for granted. At the same time the conditions underlying the efficiency of the political system denoted by the word remained subject to debate. Goldwin Smith, Professor of History at Oxford and a faithful disciple of Cobden, desired to reconcile himself to the assumption that there was 'a strong tendency to what is called Imperialism' inherent in the 'Keltic race'. It was 'opposed to the Constitutionalism to which the Teutonic races tend'. It was apparently making 'even the highly civilized Kelt of France, familiar as he is with theories of political liberty, almost incapable of sustaining free institutions'. 'A similar attachment to the rule of persons rather than that of institutions' was—it was the historian's main thesis—characteristic of the Irish.[2] 'Rather unsettled ideas about Imperialism', which could have been exemplified by this sweeping statement, but had their real motive in a 'considerable attention' focused of late on 'the internal state of France', were noticed by an experienced observer at about the same time

(1862), who again thought it necessary to bring English opinion nearer to French realities. He undertook this task in the two-hundred-odd pages of his retrospect *Ten Years of Imperialism in France*. Its subtitle *Impressions of a Flâneur* does an injustice to the author himself—who might have had reasons for concealing his identity and minimizing the truly methodical character of the studies on which his 'impressions' were based.[1] They broadly cover the same ground as the 'sketches' collected on the 'imperialist pavement' by Theodor Mundt five years earlier, but are substantiated far more solidly. One of their main interests is to determine as exactly as possible the extent to which imperialism has remained faithful to the policies of the July Monarchy and to indicate deviations. He draws renewed attention to the original stronghold of the regime, the French army. The *coup d'état*, 'the beginning of Imperialism', the author explained, had meant an encouragement to all the traditional incitements of military prestige. The July Monarchy had created a new army animated with a high spirit of splendour and victory through continual campaigns in Algeria. 'No changes external or internal in organisation can affect the power of such traditions. . . . Imperialism has not been slow in supplying these plentifully.' This, of course, referred to Louis Napoleon's three wars, the Russian, the Italian, and the Chinese. A new 'imperial army' had emerged from those that looked up to the dynasty and—whatever the future of the new loyalty — 'a magnificent legacy which Imperialism will leave to France'.

The author goes on to inquire into the workings of the system on the civilian side—the vast bureaucratic machinery whose potentialities had been so appalling to the 'Reviewer' of 1851 and whose successes so doubtful to the other 'reviewer' of 1858. To him it means a 'terrestrial providence', whose documentation by the 'hundreds of decrees and laws', registered every year in the *Bulletin des Lois*, 'will be the astonishment of future generations and an invaluable source of information for the historian of Imperialism'. It has its drawbacks, though its advantages are more prominent. It has acted in keeping with established tradition by spending large sums on national enterprise and the promotion of prosperity. But while using up a smaller 'leaven', the 'Imperial Fertilising system' has produced a higher 'rise'. 'The system of public works in France is old, but the application of it as a poor-law system is due to Imperialism; and, if we are to judge by recent events, the application must be said to have been successful.'[1]

At this point of the study the old question arises of how far the system has succeeded in winning national confidence. Flâneur begins with a very assertive statement but ends with a serious question-mark. In relying entirely on *panem et circenses* the government has been assisted by the political apathy of the nation. 'The more we examine and the better we know this psychological phenomenon, the milder are we inclined to judge Imperialism. Whatever the opinion be about the origin of it, never did power understand better the temper of the people it has to deal with.' In the author's view the antagonism between property and labour has been at the bottom of all political unrest in France—and 'the social side of the struggle must be always kept in mind if we wish to understand the real character of Imperialism. . . . The ten years of Imperialism has been a time of truce between the two adversaries.' An outward sign of the resulting complacency is the extensive use publicly made of comparing Imperial France with Imperial Rome. 'Of all the incense offered up by officious writers on the shrine of Imperialism none is so much relished as those effusions in prose and verse which choose for their theme the resemblance between French and Roman Imperialism.' Flâneur could not know that Napoleon himself was preparing to give personal sanction to the analogy by writing a 'History of Julius Caesar'. However, he soon reaches the point where comparison becomes invidious. Material satisfaction has not been accompanied by artistic and intellectual inspiration. In this respect 'Imperialism in Paris has not been able to learn the secret from Imperialism in Rome'. An 'intellectual dearth . . . has come over France under the iron pressure of the last ten years'. And, at the same time, the fact that the whole system is based on 'iron pressure' lets the author fall back upon the old assertion of a 'false position', a 'vicious circle'. Many dissidents are biding their time in a forcible 'armed neutrality'. Besides, there are antagonists 'who, for one or another reason, can never be reconciled with Imperialism. Their number is exceedingly small, but their activity is so much the greater.' Wanting a voluntary response where it would be needed most, 'Imperialism lives day by day'.

The Imperialism of Louis Napoleon

A thorough transformation of the French national character still remains the 'task which Imperialism has to perform'.[1]

Flâneur did not emulate the tone of moral reprobation which had loomed large in English comments on Imperial France, and, whether willingly or not, had given colour to the term by which he denoted the theme of his argument. However, he could not interpret this concept without making use of the same connotations which carried the habitual undertone of an adverse judgement. While substantiating his analysis of the French system by a wealth of graphic description, he provided, at the same time, strong evidence of the systematic spirit which made it run its fateful path. More convincingly than ever before imperialism was shown to be the daring attempt to mould the temper of a nation so that it might merge its happiness in the glorification of its leader. This idea could not be separated from the name of *empire*; but it could be transferred from that particular empire in which it had been seen alive to another political system which, for whatever reason, was called an empire, too. Flâneur's appreciation of the alliance between Napoleonic imperialism and French national prestige, together with his comments on imperialism as a form of managing public sentiment, must be particularly impressive to a reader who bears in mind what was said about British imperialism in the days of Lord Beaconsfield and again in 1898 and during the following period. He is confronted with a striking similarity of portraiture and questioning. We shall later see that the similarity is not accidental. The concept of imperialism as developed by the critics of Louis Napoleon's regime became posthumously effective in criticisms launched against 'imperial policies' of Great Britain—different though outward circumstances were. The possibility of transferring its application to British problems of contemporary history became apparent while it still had a living object in the French Emperor. In individual cases the word suggested itself to writers who commented on British politics. Their utterings carried too little weight to pass into general usage; they were nevertheless characteristic straws in the wind.

The word obtruded itself to the young Charles Dilke when in a chapter of his *Greater Britain* he digested his impressions of British government in India. With questionable justification he assumed that it was steering towards a deliberate humbling of indigenous aristocracy for the benefit of uniform British rule. When this interpretation occurred first Dilke made a rather harsh use of the new concept. 'Virtually, in annexing any Eastern country, we destroy the ruling class, and reduce the government to a mere imperialism, where one man rules and the rest are slaves.'[1] Later, in commenting on the complaints of a noble Mohammedan, he subtly qualified that statement.

It is not likely that our rule will ever have much hold on the class that Asudulla represents, for not only is our government in India a despotism, but its tendency is to become an imperialism, or despotism exercised over a democratic people, such as we see in France. . . .[2] All this is very modern, and full of 'progress', no doubt; but it is progress towards imperialism, or equality under paternal despotism.

The warning is soon supplemented by the no less high-handed and not so new judgement that in any case 'freedom exists only in the homes of the English race'.

To another Radical writer of the later 1860's 'imperialism' appeared the most fitting by-word for any influence wielded by people in power which would 'stifle the atmosphere' of free thought—such atmosphere as England happily enjoyed.[3] There was one Liberal journal, however, which by then desired to elicit other meanings, meanings denoting true national aims, from the much abused word. This was the *Spectator*, the paper which had backed Edward Gibbon Wakefield and the Colonial Reformers to whom the *Empire* had been a hallowed term. It is with that cause in mind that in its issue of 11 January 1868, commenting on an intended candidature of Goldwin Smith for the House of Commons, the journal confessed it had 'not been the lot of this journal . . . ever to agree cordially' with him and declared that Smith 'always appears to us to lack Imperialism in its best sense'. The stricture obviously alludes to Goldwin Smith's advocacy of an abrogation of Great Britain's responsibility for her colonies; the collection of essays on which six years earlier he had propounded political separation bore the title *The Empire*. However, interest in the Colonial Empire did not constitute the full meaning of 'Imperialism in its best sense' as understood by the journal. The expression is explained as 'the consciousness that it is sometimes a binding duty to perform highly irksome or offensive tasks, such as the defence of Canada or the government of Ireland.¹ Here a note of militancy is sounded which at that time was unusual in references to the British Empire. This note was contained in the term imperialism itself, which had become established already in English public opinion in a sense originally applied to the spirit of Imperial France. The writer intended to convey that 'in its best sense' imperialism was a virtue which Goldwin Smith and the group of Radicals to which he belonged shunned but which Britain needed, a willingness to sacrifice blood and money for the sake of causes in which the national honour was at stake.

The *Spectator* maintained its ambiguous interpretation of the term and made its militant connotation more explicit on another occasion. Late in 1869 it declared the discontinuance of two Radical newspapers to be a symptom of 'the extinction of that group of Middle-Class Radicals, which, under the name of the Manchester School, threatened at one time to absorb the Liberal party of Great Britain'. The group had enjoyed—and in the personality of John Bright was still possessed of— great leadership; why was it now in decay? It was because 'the majority of his school ... were men totally destitute of intellectual sympathy, of any political emotion which we can describe by the word heart'. That defect had been conspicuous in their lack of sympathy for foreign champions of political liberty such as Kossuth, Karl Blind, and Louis Blanc. Moreover, 'the Manchester men ... did not sympathize with their own people. They could not comprehend what Englishmen meant in 1854 by hungering for a war; or see why, being in it, they should want to win; or understand how men could be such fools as to prefer an idea to comfort.' What was the idea whose validity for the British nation had escaped the Manchester men? It was a particular brand of that 'emotion' to which the article had referred before. 'The emotion which we call Imperialism, which is as strong in America as in England, and which once stirred is absolutely irresistible,—which, for instance, swept down Lord Palmerston in the zenith of his power, and would, in a week, sweep down Mr Gladstone,—was to them a caprice, a humour, almost a mark of lunacy.'²

This was preposterous boasting in more than one respect. Manchester Liberalism was not yet a spent force. Mr Gladstone had more than four years to prove that his attitude to national concerns abroad would not lose him popular favour to such an extent as to bring about his resignation. And what evidence was there to prove that responsiveness to national honour was in fact 'the emotion which we call Imperialism'? That reading of the word was wholly the *Spectator*'s own. However, like the contrarious and in its way also arbitrary interpretation applied to it by Charles Dilke, it goes far to prove that the term had become colourful enough for applications to problems on whose behalf British parties would join issue. The time to prove that capacity to the full had still to come; indeed, while the *Spectator* mused about the question what Imperialism could mean to the English nation, the word was about to lose its significance to France. The forces of opposition whose potential energy Flâneur had considered as being far in excess of their small numbers had grown so much as to frighten Napoleon and hasten fundamental reforms. If the Liberal Empire became a reality, the term imperialism lost its meaning. *The Times* confirmed this trend by implication just in those days; it warned 'Red Republicanism' and Socialism in France that a repetition of February 1848 would only bring back 'Imperialism' and with a vengeance. The issue was not permitted to be pursued to the end. The Empire fell with Sedan before it could show its new character. Still, in the eyes of some English Radicals it remained the creation of imperialism to the very end.[1]

II

THE NAME OF THE BRITISH EMPIRE IN THE FIRST DECADES OF QUEEN VICTORIA'S REIGN

The paradoxical fact that in the early stage of its career the word imperialism was unequivocally understood by Englishmen to refer to the *Empire* of Louis Napoleon arouses perplexing questions concerning the attitude of the nation to its own world-wide Empire. When the French autocrat embarked on the experiment which came under the name of *Imperialism*, the British system of dependencies to which, in whatever different shades of application, the title of Empire could not be denied had just been exposed to various experiments of reconstruction. These were to no small extent bound up with ventures of territorial aggrandizement. Of the annexations in question the Indian Empire, the sub-continent still administered by the East India Company, had a considerable share. The Colonial Empire, the multitude of countries whose very diversified affairs were handled by the Colonial Office, was, while likewise growing in size, deeply affected by reforms. Those reforms went far to disengage its component parts from the commercial and administrative ties which were traditionally considered to be inseparable from the status of colonies. The principles of Free Trade and, in special cases, those of Responsible Government, were about to subvert the whole colonial system. This development had been subject to lively discussion. It was by many a public man in Britain considered to be preparatory to a dissolution of the imperial connexion. The spectre of such dissolution was a heritage of the American Revolution; the rise of Great Britain to industrial supremacy in the world at large had added the question whether colonies could still be regarded as national economic assets. On the other hand, Edward Gibbon Wakefield and the whole school of Colonial Reformers had emphatically advocated and actively promoted the systematic enlargement and organization of dense colonial settlement, first of all in Australia and New Zealand. The growth of the Indian Empire by conquest and, temporarily, the commercial opening up of China, which led to the establishment of the British colony of Hong Kong, had not failed to arouse criticism. The unremitting opposition of Richard Cobden and his 'Manchester School' towards all ventures of aggrandizement, especially when accompanied by militancy, was notorious enough. Since its spectacular victory in the Repeal of the Corn Laws Cobdenism had to be considered as a powerful ferment of public opinion. Those topics, especially the prospects and the usefulness of the Colonial Empire, were left over for political debate at the time when Napoleon III established his Empire and gave proof of its stability. A few years later the Indian Empire was exposed to the severe crisis of the Mutiny, which could not but arouse disquieting questions concerning its management when the British Government and Parliament had made it their direct responsibility. The idea of the Free Trade Empire was set at naught in 1859 by Canada when she submitted British imports to custom duties. This disappointing move was followed by troubles in Anglo-American relations, which revived the fear that wayward Canada might become an actual military liability to the imperial realm. During all that time, when speaking of imperialism, people referred to the internal conditions of a foreign state which was styled an *empire*. Was the very existence of the word not suggestive of relating it to issues nearer home—the specifically imperial concerns of the imperial government and parliament of Great Britain? There would, it appears, have been ample opportunity for relating the word imperialism to any policy which asserted the responsibilities of the British Empire in the face of all the doubtful ventures to which it had exposed itself. As that word had a decisively abusive ring it would, one might think, have recommended itself to the critics as an abuse directed against those statesmen and publicists who still believed that the imperial structure could last in its entirety and was worth maintaining. It could also have been applied when judgement was passed on expensive and often atrocious warfare waged in an exotic region of the world, be it India, the Far East, South Africa, or New Zealand. Nothing of the kind happened.

When in 1868 the *Spectator* hit upon the idea that the word imperialism was 'in its best sense' appropriate to denoting 'a binding duty to perform highly irksome or offensive tasks', this aphorism was launched without precedent. It is an implicit testimony to the fact that the expression had never been used in comments which found fault with the commitments of the British Empire. Modern historians have disregarded this fact when dealing with these comments. They have expanded either on the anti-imperialism proclaimed in them or on the imperialism of their opponents. This phraseology, as we shall see later, took its cue from political criticism passed on those sceptics in retrospect by advocates of closer imperial connexions from the 1870's onward. It did not base itself on earlier usage. To do justice to the scholars who have applied those terms to controversies antedating the 1870's, it must be acknowledged that they conscientiously abstained from contaminating the words with connotations which made them political slogans thereafter under new conditions.[1] However, the retroactive application of slogans is always precarious, and becomes a dubious device when it neglects the fact that the word in question was at the time under discussion well known and used with reference to matters completely outside the range of any later application. When neglecting this fact, the historian exposes himself to the danger of suggesting a distorted view of the public mind. The fact that what came into mind whenever the word imperialism was heard or remembered between 1852 and 1870 was always the French Empire and never the British serves to indicate that the latter lacked the quality which made the former subject to criticism under that term—the quality of representing a challenge to the public mind by its very existence. Most critics of British imperial affairs did not seem to consider the name of the British Empire a provocation against which their moral or political conscience was bound to react. This negative inference implies another one. The name of the British Empire was not, as a rule, raised in boastful rhetoric. There were no statesmen or publicists prominent in English public life for whom, on the ground of attitude or public utterances concerning the imperial position of Great Britain, the term 'imperialism' or 'imperialist' would have been characteristic.

Can these inferences be confirmed by actual evidence of a more positive nature? At first sight they seem to conflict with utterances made by two notable adversaries of British colonial and imperial activities, Richard Cobden and Goldwin Smith. These men harboured a genuine aversion for the notion of empire. On certain occasions, moreover, they appear to have assumed that this notion and the ambition which it implied were faithfully cherished by the nation at large. There is no doubt that they would have been happy, if there had been no British oversea Empire and no people who valued it. The statements, however, in which they immediately joined issue with the concept show by their very sparseness and by other circumstances in which they were made that both authors found it by no means easy to make political capital out of the hateful word. Cobden's most violent denunciation of the political morality to which the British Empire owed its world-wide extent formed part of one of the pamphlets by which in 1835 and 1836 he introduced himself to the public as a fighter against the moral, economic, and political self-deceptions which prevented the nation from reaping the fruits of its industry. One of those fallacies which Cobden endeavoured to expose was the doctrine that England had to obviate the 'aggrandizing' tendencies of Russia in the Near East. In that attitude, he stated, unfounded scares were mingled with misplaced self-righteousness. Those who found fault with the territorial 'robberies' of Russia would do well to remember what was in the case of Great Britain with hypocritical politeness styled as enlarging 'the bounds of his Majesty's dominions'.

Surely we who are staggering under the embarrassing weight of our colonies, with one foot on the rock of Gibraltar and the other at the Cape of Good Hope—with Canada, Australia and the peninsula of India, forming Cerberus-like the heads of our monstrous empire—and with the hundred minor acquisitions scattered so widely over the earth's surface as to present an unanswerable proof of our wholesome appetite for boundless dominion—surely we are not exactly the nation to preach homilies to other people in favour of the national observance of the eighth commandment.[1]

'Monstrous Empire', 'appetite for boundless dominion'—Cobden would never have recanted those bitter indictments. When he had risen to the stature of a popular leader in matters of commercial policy and financial reforms, he never forgot and rarely concealed his conviction that those interests were subordinate to the higher aim of purifying political morals. He desired to cure the nation of an inveterate perversity which allowed the instincts of inordinate greed to seek satisfaction in the forcible expansions of British rule, and he found this task very difficult. 'It will take time . . . to play off John Bull's acquisitiveness against his combativeness. He will not be easily persuaded that all his reliance upon brute force and courage has been a losing speculation.' Thus Cobden wrote to John Bright in 1848. Later on official acquiescence in Lord Dalhousie's Burmese war and annexation made him publicly bewail the fact that 'all classes are ready to hail with approbation every fresh acquisition of territory'; discontent with British rule in India and Chinese affairs stirred him to utter the same complaint in a private letter in 1860.[1]

However, the notion of 'empire' played no major part in all those indictments and the name of British Empire none at all. The only sentence in the Burma pamphlet which borders on vilifying the concept of empire is contained in its peroration which voices the hope 'that the national conscience which has before averted from England, by timely atonement and reparation, the punishment due for imperial crimes, will be roused ere it be too late from its lethargy. . . .' In this entreaty, whose religious tenor was wholly sincere, the reference to 'imperial crimes' can hardly be taken as a comment on the name of the British Empire. It is preceded by a no less sermonizing appeal to 'the supremacy of that moral law which mysteriously sways the fate of empires', and by the warning to remember the penalties which fell on the conquerors of Mexico, Peru, and—Algeria. Cobden's antipathy to the imperial position of Britain overseas came into the open only as a regret that she had allowed herself to be enticed by such immoral allurements of conquest and military prestige as had proved pernicious in the case of other empires. It was, on other occasions again, by declaring that 'empires' in general were the unwholesome heritage of a benighted past of mankind, that Cobden gave vent to his abhorrence of what the concept might imply in relation to his own country. 'I believe that the desire and the motive for large and mighty empires, for gigantic armies and great navies . . . will die away.' 'I may seem Utopian; but I don't feel sympathy for a great nation, or for those who desire the greatness of a people by the vast extension of empire . . . We have had great empires at all times—Syria, Persia, and the rest. What trace have they left of the individual man?'[1]

None of these utterings can be considered as reaction to a grandiloquent use which attached to the name of the British Empire. The famous book written by his disciple Goldwin Smith has by its very title *The Empire* given rise to a different impression. It seems to have been intended as a rebuttal of boisterous provocation. That title, however, was the outcome of an afterthought and, as we shall soon see, a rather arbitrary one. The book was a compilation of eighteen articles published by the author in the *Daily News* from January 1862 to March 1863. None of those articles had the name Empire in its title—and in none of them had the author quarrelled with political phraseology. The first of the articles states no more than the mere existence of the name and its reference to the British dominions in general. '. . . I do say, that since what we call the Empire was formed the world is changed and that we ought to take practical note of the change. I say, too, that the greatness of England really lies not in her Empire, but in herself.' Soon Goldwin Smith shows so little embarrassment at the word that, commenting on India, he confesses: 'It is indeed something—it is much—to have displayed on that great theatre the qualities of an Imperial race.' Later on he defames the concept by putting it into the context of a truly Cobdenite denunciation, asserting that only the aristocratic parasites of the nation really take advantage of the Empire. 'If the advantages of the Colonial Empire were real, all the people would share them. . . . But the mere pride of empire, and the pleasure of indulging it, belong only to the imperial class.' He adds a stricture on 'the general character of ostentation and wastefulness which the Empire gives to our Government'.[2] These malicious hints were rather unsubstantiated; but the author decided to make more out of them when he arranged for the articles to be published in book form. In its preface he explained the choice of its title by a long definition. It is worth quoting that definition at length. In its beginning it shows that, by making the name of Empire the comprehensive headline of a critical survey of colonial, Indian, and certain external affairs, the author was not so much referring to an established terminology as intending to create such usage on his own account. In its closing sentence the definition provides the concept proclaimed by it with a stigma extending to all the interests to which it refers.

The term Empire is here taken in a wide sense, as including all that the nation holds beyond its own shores and waters by arms or in the way of dominion, as opposed to that natural influence which a great power, though confining itself to its own territories, always exercises in the world. In the case of our Empire this definition will embrace a motley mass of British Colonies, conquered Colonies of other European nations, conquered territories in India, military and maritime stations, and protectorates, including our practical protectorate of Turkey, as well as our legal protectorate of the Ionian Islands.

These various dependencies stand in the most various relations to the Imperial country. . . . The reasons, or alleged reasons, for retaining them are also of the most various kinds. . . . The pride of Empire, however, runs through the whole and so does the notion that extent of territory is the extent of power.

The beginning and the end of this statement are scarcely reconcilable. By explaining circumstantially what the term Empire is *here* to mean, the author betrays some apprehension lest an untutored reader might relate it not to British dominions 'beyond the shores' but to the United Kingdom itself. This apprehension was well founded. The identification of the 'empire' with the 'natural' influence of Great Britain was by no means extinct in English usage. Therefore, it seems rather arbitrary that in the end a specific 'pride of Empire' is attributed to dominion overseas, even including the alleged 'practical protectorate of Turkey'. If the reader expects to find this 'pride of Empire' to become exemplified in the body of the work by authoritative evidence —speeches made by ministers or leading politicians, testimonies of public opinion—he must feel disappointed. After the publication of the author's first article *The Times* asked him to consider that even 'the possession of a merely apparent power', such as embodied in the Colonies and India, was presenting to the world an 'air of grandeur' which was politically valuable. This remark, on which Goldwin Smith sarcastically commented in his second letter,[1] was probably the only quotation by which the reader could be satisfied that some 'pride of Empire' existed, and it was not very impressive in this respect. In the last resort this notion did not mirror an experience; it was nothing but a construction—or, in the eyes of Goldwin Smith himself, a self-evident postulate. He had stated that, for the costs and risks which the nation incurred because of its dependencies, nothing palpable was given to it in return. If so, what motive could be imagined to prevail with all those people who still valued the maintenance of the imperial connexion? Obviously some irrational impulse—and as 'mere sentiment' could not be believed to count in political relations, the motive must needs be what politicians sometimes called by the nebulous, imported word *prestige*—a nauseating concept both to Goldwin Smith and to Cobden—'a blind and tyrannical passion'.[1] This was the 'pride of Empire' of which all advocates of the overseas Empire were assumed to be possessed even in cases where there was no evidence.

The British legislators and the British public were not used to being addressed on behalf of 'the Empire' when there was an occasion for 'talking big'. This is proved by a parliamentary incident which only a few years earlier, in 1857, had obliged Lord Palmerston to call for the verdict of the electorate on his Far Eastern policy. Cobden and all his followers considered Palmerston to be the very embodiment of that old-fashioned and vainglorious statesmanship which still induced far too many Englishmen to hanker after the semblance of greatness, world-wide dominion, and reckless self-assertion.

It is not to be expected [Goldwin Smith originally said in the first of his articles], that an inch of the Empire will be given up by the present Premier. Though youthful in bodily vigour, he is old in ideas, and unconscious of the great moral and material changes which have taken place in Europe since he first entered public life.[2]

If Palmerston had been in the habit of making frequent and conspicuous use of the term *British Empire*, his Radical opponents would not have failed to notice and challenge the use of that expression. As it happened, on that particular occasion he for once had recourse to the term but the choice of his expression passed almost unnoticed.

The British representative in Hong Kong, Sir John Bowring, had by warlike action sought retribution of the alleged offence committed by the Chinese governor against the British flag in the case of the *British* ship *Arrow*. Sir John had also demanded the admission of British merchants to the town of Canton as had been promised in earlier treaties. Palmerston and his Cabinet had countenanced Sir John's steps and were about to support them by a strong naval and military demonstration off the Chinese coast. These measures aroused violent protests in both Houses of Parliament. Conservatives joined hands with Radicals and found followers among conscientious Whigs such as Lord John Russell. The speakers moving votes of censure, Lord Derby in the Lords and Cobden in the Commons, vied in professions of abhorrence and shame. The Earl declared himself 'an advocate for weakness against power, for perplexed and bewildered barbarism against the arrogant demands of overweening, self-styled civilization, . . . for the feeble defencelessness of China against the overpowering might of Great Britain'. Cobden differed from him in that he thought the Chinese not at all barbarians. He asked ironically: 'Is not so venerable an Empire as that deserving of some sympathy—at least of some justice—at the hands of conservative England?' He withheld his strong suspicion that Englishmen were habitually given to truculence. He declared the case to be exceptional; but this allowed him to speak all the more strongly in 'defence of our own honour'.

We have had the character of being sometimes a little arrogant, a little over-bearing, and of having a tendency to pick a quarrel; but we never yet acquired the character of being bullies to the weak and cowards to the strong. Let us consider the case precisely as if we were dealing with America instead of China.

Russell (as severely as Cobden could have done) expressed suspicion that the matter was handled by the government as a matter of *prestige*, of which 'we have heard much of late—a great deal too much, I think. . . . ' He proclaimed that if such prestige was 'separate from the character, from the reputation, and from the honour of our country . . . then I, for one, have no wish to maintain it.'[1] Here the general theme was indicated to which, between 24 February and 3 March 1857, the two Houses devoted seven debates. What were the true morals, the true dictates of British national honour to be applied to such an incident?

Replying to Cobden the Colonial Secretary H. Labouchere for a moment varied the theme. The events in China, he declared, 'deeply concern most important commercial interests in this country—they

affect still more deeply interests which are much more considerable—
the reputation and credit of the British Empire'.[1] He did not repeat this
phrase and it was lost on the orators who spoke after him. Palmerston
revived it in the fourth night of the debate in the Commons when he
rose to deprecate the vote of censure.

I do say that this House has now in its keeping not only the interests, the
property, and the lives of many of our fellow-countrymen, but that it has also
in its keeping the honour, the welfare, the reputation—expressions which
my noble Friend, the Member for the City of London (Lord John Russell),
justly preferred to the foreign term 'prestige'—of this great empire. That is
a sacred and a holy trust, and to many minds it will be a sacred duty, the way
in which they discharge it.

This time the challenge implied in the word was taken up by the
Conservative leader, Disraeli, who had to wind up the debate besides
Cobden. He restricted his retort to a short peroration. 'I hope that
honourable Members . . . will dare to vindicate the cause of justice and
to lay down a principle, without the observance of which the empire
of which we are so proud may soon be questioned.'[2] In the ensuing
division the motion of the Opposition was carried by a majority of
fourteen. Parliament was dissolved; elections were held in April and
resulted in a glaring triumph of Palmerston. Cobden, Bright, and some
of their adherents lost their seats. This victory, however, was not
achieved by Palmerston's plea for 'this great empire'. The fact that he
had used this phrase and that it had been challenged by Disraeli passed
unnoticed outside Parliament. *Punch*, strongly pro-*Pam*, summarized
both speeches without mentioning the word empire at all.[3]

Demonstrative use of power and insistence on the national honour of
the flag had in the *Arrow* case been combined with an enforcement of
commercial interests.[4] The heated dispute over the case in Britain would
have been profusely interspersed with comments on 'Imperialism', had
it occurred forty years later. In 1857 nobody knew of such terminology
—and even the short references to 'the Empire' which escaped the lips
of some politicians cut no ice. This is what we had to expect when we
saw what the word imperialism meant at that time. However, those
references also imply another lesson. They show that the name of the
Empire, though lacking any provocative ring, held a dignified place in

the political language of that time. Disraeli had actually declared the Empire to be an object of 'pride'—only in a meaning different from that incriminated by Goldwin Smith.

Such occasional side-glances point to a notion of unquestioned respectability. The question arises what was in the mind of men when they referred to it. This question, remarkably enough, cannot be answered by an invariable definition. The honours paid to the Empire or the British Empire were neither always addressed to the same entity nor always evoked by the same distinctive attributes. One meaning, indeed, has to be taken out of account for the time preceding Goldwin Smith. *The Empire*, such as defined by him, as comprising 'all that the nation holds beyond its own shores and waters', to the *exclusion* of the United Kingdom itself, was entirely the invention of his bias. What he called 'the Empire' was in common usage called by different names. One would speak of the British dominions or possessions in general (and, of course, not include such areas as the Ionian Islands). Applied to British possessions the concept of 'empire' did not denote an undivided domain. There were two great complexes of oversea dominion, each administered by a specific department—the *Colonial Empire* and the *Indian Empire* ('our Empire in the East'). For *the British Empire* or *the Empire* there remained two basic interpretations. It was possible and sometimes thought necessary to let those names stand for the whole comprehensive system constituted by the United Kingdom and all its dependencies. One could, on the other hand, without denying the applicability of this broadest interpretation, use the name in a more restricted sense to mean only the United Kingdom, so that the Colonies and the Indian Empire were regarded as dependent on the British Empire rather than being parts of it. This reading of the name had a stronger emotional appeal than the first, more comprehensive notion. Taken literally it was only an ornate alternative expression for the United Kingdom, even for Great Britain or England. Its *raison d'être* was ultimately just what Goldwin Smith wished to see excluded from the meaning of the word—'that natural influence which a great power ... *always* exercises in the world'. The island empire was, indeed, not 'confining itself to its own territories'; but, undoubtedly, its world-wide power was rooted in them.

Between the interpretation which stressed the dominion over dependencies and the other which looked to the greatness of the native country there was still room for yet a third. It dwelt on the connexion between Great Britain and those dependent countries which had been completely or to a large extent built up by settlers originating from her soil. It focused its attention on the relation between the 'Mother-country' and the 'Colonies'. This was a topic for discussion in the early Victorian Age. The discussion was understood to concern essential problems of what was called the British Empire. In some way this mode of thinking and speaking revived the language which had been established during the critical decade preceding the American Revolution. The similarity was by no means fortuitous. The phraseology in question gained ground in close connexion with the developments of expansion, the constitutional frictions, and the revolutions of commercial policy, which from the late 1830's down to the 1850's gave rise to the impression that England had to face a new colonial problem, the possible emergence of new disrupting conflicts. Though the situation was in fact very different from that of 1774-5, the maintenance of the Colonial Empire was for a time providing the topic in whose context the name of the British Empire was not prominent. To those who valued the tie between the mother country and the colonies its preservation became virtually identical with the integrity of the British Empire itself. Not all public men, however, were of that opinion.

The diversity of interpretations, or at least accentuations, to which the name of the Empire was exposed in the early Victorian Age left a fateful heritage. It lived on in the incongruous meanings and the shrill contrasts of valuation which clung to the watchword *Imperialism* when it became related to the British Empire in the later decades of the Queen's reign. In none of the three applications did the name of the British Empire figure officially as a term of legal nomenclature. Their difference, therefore, did not give rise to serious dispute. They all, moreover, had an ancestry going as far back at least as the reign of King George III. It remains to ascertain in what contexts of political interest each figured in public life. We shall witness how, from the late 1830's onward, the crises of the colonial system led to a competition between the second interpretation, which identified the Empire with the United Kingdom, and the third, which applied the term to the system of links between Britain and her colonies.

As to the first and most comprehensive interpretation of the name *The British Empire*, it suffices to state that occasions for dwelling on it occurred very rarely. Nobody doubted that Great Britain and Malta, Canada and India, Jamaica and New South Wales could be regarded as parts of one and the same empire, that the British Empire, thus understood, filled a wide space and claimed numerous isolated parts in all the regions of the globe. Yet the subjects of the young Queen were not used to hearing this elementary fact advertised in everyday life. A writer, who in 1847 tried his hand at a comprehensive guide-book[1] on British possessions in the eastern hemisphere, defined the countries he reviewed not as the British *Empire* but as the British *World* in the East. Political language sometimes used the phrase 'imperial interests' in order to distinguish them from the interests of a single colony; but this term was most often simply related to the responsibility incurred by the central authorities in their widely extended engagements. The title of Imperial Parliament was bestowed on the Houses of Parliament in keeping with the more limiting interpretation of the word imperial. In 1800, in fact, it meant that there was no longer a separate Parliament in Dublin but only one sovereign legislature of the United Kingdom of Great Britain and Ireland. That this legislature together with the Imperial Crown was also the ultimate authority for all oversea dependencies needed no emphasis at that time. Forty years later people felt differently about it because of the existence of numerous 'imperial' problems overseas. George Cornewall Lewis, in his *Essay on the Government of Dependencies* (1841), was in the position roundly to declare:

The entire territory subject to a supreme government possessing several dependencies (that is to say, a territory formed of a dominant country together with its dependencies) is sometimes styled an *empire*; as when we speak of the British empire. Agreeably with this acceptation of the word empire, the supreme government of a nation, considered with reference to its dependencies, is called the imperial government, and the English Parliament is called the imperial parliament as distinguished from the provincial parliament of a dependency.[2]

The closing sentence was manifestly inspired by the fact that the British Parliament had a short time before (1837-9) asserted its authority in serious conflicts with the legislative assemblies of Canada and Jamaica. The preceding definition of the British Empire in its deliberate drabness emphasizes the generic character of *empire* spelt with a small letter e. This is not only a specimen of the didactic mind of a writer who in 1832 had published *Remarks on the use and abuse of some political terms*, but also reflects his uneasy attitude towards the Canadian issue of his time. It militates against the style of Lord Durham's Report on Canada in which the British Empire prominently figured as the name of a venerable entity. Such veneration in Lewis' eyes implied a precarious commitment. It could give colour to the irrational belief that the imperial tie must be maintained even when it put the 'dominant country' under an irksome obligation. The author desired to invalidate that belief; the whole argument of his essay was intended to support the case which he developed towards the end—the conditions which might arise 'if a dependency is considered as in training for ultimate independence'.[1] This, in Lewis' firm opinion (which he never expressed in so many words), was the case of Canada. Englishmen had to be weaned from harbouring sentiments which stood in the way of applying such 'training' to that colony. The seemingly colourless definition of 'empire', which appears in the first chapter of the inquiry, was meant to contribute to this educational purpose. It stressed the elements of 'dominant country' and 'dependency', mainly because it seemed certain that the dependent status of Canada could not be maintained for long. The history of that colony clearly pointed to self-government; and 'a self-governing dependency', he roundly declared, was 'a contradiction in terms'.[2] There was, the reader was given to understand, little to be made of the term Empire in the case of the connexion between Great Britain and Canada. Lewis did not care for the term at all; it was for him—as for Cobden—tinged with unsavoury associations. After having been juridically defined the word vanishes from his argument and only towards the end reappears for a moment in a sorrowful aside on 'the prevailing opinions concerning the advantages of extensive empire', which seem to prevent Englishmen from taking the case of 'a dependency training for independence as seriously as they should'. Thus this much respected commentator defined the whole complex of countries looking up to the Imperial Parliament as the British Empire in a style deprecating all enthusiasm.

It would be difficult to find within the limits of our period a pronouncement which based itself on the same attributes, made itself equally well known, but referred to the system with unqualified pride. One utterance of such character, however, deserves mention, though it was probably quickly forgotten. It occurred in the context of an argument not primarily concerned with British affairs. When in the spring of 1859 Cavour and Napoleon III were expected to undertake the liberation of Italy from Austrian dominance, the *Edinburgh Review* published an article commenting on the general principle which was proclaimed to be at issue in that continental conflict. The 'theory of nationality' was supposed to mean that 'each political unity constituting a state is to be commensurate with one of those branches of the human family which have the same language, race, national character, and that the rule of any of these branches over fractions of another branch is to be regarded as an intolerable oppression . . .'. If that interpretation was correct, the journal concluded, it would in the case of Italy be bound up with claims not only on Austria but also on Switzerland, France, and England (with regard to the Ticino, Corsica, and Malta). The application of that principle would have even wider consequences. It would 'lead to the entire dissolution of the multifarious states which are properly called empires and in particular of those of Russia, Austria, and Great Britain'. This possible world-wide result was by no means hidden from the view of the radical advocates of the nation-state doctrine, as we learn from the article. 'The Abbé Gioberti, one of the lights of modern Italy, argues that these composite states are monstrous anomalies, which must be of short duration.'

This challenge roused the author to a vehement protest. The theory of nationality was 'of modern growth and uncertain application'. It was at variance with historical experience. 'No state ever realised this condition.' Gioberti's assertion was 'contradicted by the entire history of mankind, and by facts of irresistible authority'. Among those irrefutable counter-arguments one counted for the writer in particular. The record of the British Empire gave the lie to the theory of nationality.

The 'majestic edifice raised by the . . . authority of England' connected 'scattered dependencies with one great whole infinitely more powerful, civilised, free than any separate fragment could be'. It was based on 'the subordination of national or provincial independence'; but this abrogation had issued in 'the true citizenship of these realms'. The author referred to two recent applications of the 'rights' inherent in the majestic edifice—one, the crushing of the Indian Mutiny, the other, the rejection of the demands of people living on the Ionian Islands for union with Greece, 'though they indeed do not even owe allegiance to the British Crown'. The writer was apparently aware of the fact that the two episodes to which he alluded had each met with strong criticism in England. He stood up, however, to any objection on the strength of two further arguments. One was the history of the Island Kingdom itself: 'In the name of that right, we have formed the people of these islands into a United Kingdom, though that union has cost us a secular contest with the disaffection of Ireland, and has not always been accepted on this side of our northern border.' The other argument ran that it was 'the glory of England' not only 'to have constituted such an empire' but also 'to govern it, in the main, on just and tolerant principles, as long as her imperial rights are not assailed'. The author dwelt a little more on those principles by claiming that England could, indeed, teach other states a lesson, could remind the world of the fact that 'this heterogeneous empire is not so much held together by the force of England, as by the respect she has ever professed for national usages, the desire she feels to carry self-government to the furthest practicable limits, and to attach her possessions to the Crown, not by the severity, but by the lightness of her control'.

Between these eulogies the statement that 'the people of England have never shown much forbearance in the defence' of their imperial rights, whenever they found them assailed, leads on to a blunt declaration on the national principle and British policy. 'It is utterly repugnant to the first principles of our own policy and to every page in our history, to lend encouragement to that separation of nationalities from other empires which we fiercely resist when it threatens to dismember our own.'[1] However, an ideological co-ordination of 'imperial' and foreign policy, such as was postulated here, had actually never been characteristic of British statesmanship. The article made that assertion at a time when a Conservative ministry, benevolent towards the Austrian monarchy, was committed to a policy of non-interference in Italian affairs. One may call it a misfortune that at this juncture the exertions of the Cabinet for a diplomatic arrangement were frustrated by Austria herself, who decided on sending an ultimatum. It was certainly an unforeseen coincidence that two months later Lord Derby and Lord Malmesbury had to go out of office just as Austria lost Lombardy in battle. Had they, however, remained in command, they would scarcely have taken the view that the common cause of empires was at stake.

Still less could the maxim of a co-ordinated imperial and foreign policy have meant anything to their successors, the Whig Lords Palmerston and John Russell. Their painstaking endeavours to maintain the balance of European power in the diplomatic tangle which accompanied Italian events in 1859–60 finally changed to a demonstrative attitude, which came precariously near the commitment abhorred by the *Edinburgh Review* in April 1859.[1] When Victor Emanuel and Cavour had openly joined hands with the rebels in the Papal States and with Garibaldi in Naples, the British Government, unlike the Continental Powers, came out with an unqualified declaration in favour of the unification of Italy. Russell's famous despatch of 27 October 1860 not only proclaimed 'that the people in question are themselves the best judges of their own affairs', but also prejudiced more far-reaching issues by sympathizing with the 'conviction . . . that the only manner in which Italians could secure their independence of foreign control was by forming one strong Government for the whole of Italy'.[2] The makers of British policy were manifestly far from apprehending that such principles, once conceded to an old European nation, could ever become a danger to the British Empire. Nor could they, at that time, expect doctrinary objections against the rightfulness of British imperial rule over exotic nations, particularly in India. John Stuart Mill, the philosopher of consistent liberalism, had just declared: 'The sacred duties which civilized nations owe to the independence and nationality of each other, are not binding towards those to whom nationality and independence are a certain evil, or at best a questionable good.' Mill applied that maxim explicitly to 'the relations of the British Government with the native States of India'.[1]

Seen in retrospect the demand for a co-ordination between European and British imperial causes in that article published by the *Edinburgh Review* assumes the appearance of the warning-cry of a lone Cassandra. Its fears were mitigated, though, by the complacent conviction that the cause of 'empires' had in the case of England been vindicated by her 'just and tolerant principles' and by her aim 'to carry self-government to the furthest practicable limits'. The juxtaposition of self-governing colonies and Indian affairs in a paragraph dealing with the merits of the British Empire is another point where the author's argument took an uncommon turn. In accounting for it—this is by no means a pedantic reflexion—we have to consider that he wrote on 'empires' in general and so (like G. C. Lewis but in a very different spirit) handled the term 'the British empire' as the specimen of a class, not as the proper name of a political entity. He, too, we might say, thought of the British 'empire' as spelt with a small letter. Whenever it entered the discussion as a term pronounced with any emphasis, India was rarely the topic in question. Conversely, problems of the British Empire in India rarely prompted writers, Goldwin Smith's *Letters* being an exception,[2] to discuss the British Empire in general or mention it by that name. Henry Kilgour's plan to include representatives of the Indian administration in his 'Proposed Institution of a Joint Committee of the Legislatures and Governments of the British Empire', written in 1858 and motivated by the rebellion in India, caused no wide echo. The 'Eastern Empire' was considered to be an Empire in its own right and in this sense its servants referred to it when they sent their reports home.[3] In that sense, too, the name figured venerably in John William Kaye's *History of Indian Progress*, in which the author tried to give an adequate account of the activities of the East India Company, five years before it had to surrender its power. 'During the sixty years of which I speak', he wrote, 'we have been building up our present enormous empire . . . We had all that time to do with an empire inchoate and imperfect, calling for measures . . . of defence . . . of aggression, which have left neither leisure to consider, nor money to provide the means of domestic improvement.'[4] In those and similar solemn sentences the author endeavoured to impress the public at home with the magnitude of the task which Providence had bestowed on the British in the Indian Empire. Twenty-five years were to pass before the two entities, the British and the Indian Empire, became a closely linked pair in English political rhetoric. It was Disraeli who took the lead in heralding such language later in the century. His attitude to the notion of empire was rooted, however, in a different tradition.

If we ask what significance was applied to the name of the British Empire at the time of Queen Victoria's accession, the answer must be that it was governed by the interpretation which related the name to the United Kingdom of the British Isles and to England in particular. We may add at once that this reading remained applicable until about 1860. At an earlier stage of our inquiry we have shown how this conception, which harked back to the idea of the Imperial Crown, regained palpable reality in the era of the Napoleonic wars, when Englishmen began to realize that their industrial and maritime vigour enabled them to stand up to any great power in the world. We showed earlier how the 'insular' interpretation of empire remained a living memory for Goldwin Smith's contemporary, E. A. Freeman. It freely entered the style of writers who came to the fore in the 1830's. Thomas Carlyle—in *Chartism*, 1837—wanted his unheroic countrymen to remember their noble, toiling, and wise ancestors who lived long before Albion with its other Tin Islands 'became a British Empire'.[1] His prosaic antipode, J. R. McCulloch, in the same year for the first time published his *Statistical Account of the British Empire*, intending to give 'a fair representation of the present condition of the United Kingdom'. He explicitly restricted his survey to 'the British Empire exclusive of its foreign dependencies'. A short supplement added some statistical data of the latter 'only in those respects in which they may be supposed to contribute to or diminish our wealth and prosperity'. There was a clear purpose in that restriction. The author wanted his readers to look at those foreign dependencies with the eyes of Adam Smith, to keep in mind 'that the advantages supposed peculiarly to belong to the colonial trade are in a great degree imaginary'.[2] This was the reason why any questions concerning the internal development of the oversea territories under British rule were excluded. McCulloch's *Account* saw a number of new editions, unaltered in this point, during the following two decades.[1]

Among the rising politicians of the day Benjamin Disraeli stood out as manifesting a personal allegiance to the name of empire, which cannot but appear remarkable in view of what it came to signify to the aged statesman in later years, but it failed to impress the public which he wooed in his early struggles. In election addresses, pamphlets, and letters he gave incessant promise of defending 'the glory of this country as a great empire', 'the unparalleled empire raised by the energies of your fathers' against the 'domestic oligarchy of the Whigs', who by their 'rash and experimental legislation' were 'lounging it away'. Dangers menacing the colonies occupied only a subordinate place in those invectives. Empire was a name which was used in homage to such feeling of English greatness as had been substantiated by the political history of the country. This allusion was still in Disraeli's mind when in 1851, having risen to leadership in the Conservative Party, he took a motion on agricultural distress as an occasion for regaling the House of Commons with his doubtful classical reference to 'imperium et libertas'.[2]

The identification of the British Empire with the United Kingdom can still be found as taken for granted in 1859.[3] The term was rarely used in connexion with topical issues of foreign affairs. It played no part in the discussion of the rights and wrongs of the Crimean War. It had, as we saw, no place in Palmerston's vocabulary before he adopted it in the *Arrow* debate of March 1857. On that occasion he chose it in order to enhance the reputation of strength and self-respect of Great Britain amongst the peoples of Asia.[4] Disraeli's short retort connecting 'the empire of which we are so proud' with 'the cause of justice' likewise touched on the aspect of reputation.

Six years later, in another improvisation, he for the first time gave the notion of the British Empire a more comprehensive and central character with regard to British interests in the East. Palmerston and Russell had just paid the Ionian Islands as the price for having declared a European nation 'the best judges of their own affairs'. Russell's despatch of 27 October 1860 had provided the spokesmen of the Islands and public opinion in Greece with a useful argument in favour of their old demand that Britain abandon her rights of overlordship in the archipelago, granted to her in the European peace settlements of 1815. Union with Greece had become an object of political agitation. For many years British governments had refused to listen; one reason, though not officially admitted, was the strategic value of the island of Corfu. The popular demand for union with Greece grew stronger by its combination with a constitutional crisis in Greece where a new dynasty had to be established. The Palmerston administration felt no longer able to stand in the way and decided to hand over the islands to Greece before Parliament assembled early in 1863. Whether with sincere conviction or not, the Tory Opposition protested in both Houses against the surrender of the naval stronghold of Corfu.[1] Disraeli, leading the opposition in the Commons, widened the scope of that argument in a sequence of memorable sentences:

Within the last twenty-five years the route to our Indian possessions has been changed; and, whatever the intention of the treaties of 1815, the country has been constantly congratulated on having a chain of Mediterranean garrisons, which secured our Indian empire. I am perfectly aware that there is a school of politicians—I do not believe they are rising politicians—who are hostile to the very principle of a British empire. But I have yet to learn that Her Majesty's ministers have adopted the wild opinions which have been prevalent of late. Professors and rhetoricians find a system for every contingency and a principle for every chance; but you are not going, I hope, to leave the destinies of the British empire to prigs and pedants. The statesmen who construct and the warriors who achieve are only influenced by the instinct of power and animated by the love of country. Those are the feelings and those the methods which form empires.[2]

Disraeli's invective at this point implied a taunting criticism of Lord Palmerston as being virtually in league with Goldwin Smith, the author of the Letters to the *Daily News* and Regius Professor of History in the University of Oxford, one prominent member of the group derided as 'professors and rhetoricians, prigs and pedants'. Goldwin Smith's enthusiasm for curtailing British dominion had just turned on the Ionian Islands. He had expressed his conviction in his latest *Letters* that in view of the impending triumph of Free Trade, 'we have no need now to post ourselves in arms all over the globe'. He believed that in the

Mediterranean 'a revived Spain, a revived Italy and, in course of time, a revived Greece will take good care' of any potential encroachment on the part of France.[1] Goldwin Smith's extreme distrust in Palmerston was as well known as was Palmerston's disbelief in such dreams. The alleged detection of a sympathy between the two antagonists was not meant to be taken seriously. Disraeli's attack testifies, however, to a singular effect which Goldwin Smith's heresies had had on him. They had stirred his old sympathy for the notion of empire as a symbol of British power in the world. The issue of the Ionian Islands inspired him to formulate a close connexion between the British Empire, power in the Mediterranean, and the safety of the Indian Empire. We shall later see that this co-ordination of interests was, at that time, the only way in which the notion of the British Empire could, in his view, be related to a topical issue arising out of British policy. We may doubt, however, whether it had the force of a convincing argument in the eyes of Disraeli himself. It failed, at all events, to impress either his listeners or public opinion in general. His assertion that the Mediterranean had increasingly become a vital link in the communication between Britain and India was irrefutable. P. and O. steamships plied the sea between Britain and Egypt meeting the vehicles for the overland route to the Red Sea in Alexandria.[2] Palmerston's opposition to the Suez Canal project proved his own apprehension of future interference with this line of communication. That negative attitude had already proved to be an unpleasant irritant in Britain's foreign policy.[3] It was difficult to add another troublesome burden on Britain's foreign relations by maintaining a grip on the Ionian Islands for the sake of British sea-power. Thus Disraeli's appeal to the 'instinct of power'—a phrase uncommon in the mouth of an English politician in any case—was particularly ill-placed, combined, as it was, with an attempt to declare the Mediterranean a sphere of British imperial interest.

Disraeli had not the reputation of being a competent judge of world affairs. His manner of developing the concept of empire was not understood even by his own party. One Conservative member contested the right of the Government 'to contract the landmarks of the Empire', which prompted Palmerston to point out in self-defence that the islands were not 'part of the dominion of the British Crown'. The *Spectator* commented on Disraeli's speech, discovered elementary mistakes in his interpretation of the relation between wealth and power but ignored his reference to the Empire.[1] In fact, in those days the concept of empire usually occurred in a different context.

III

COLONIAL CRISES AND THE NEW MEANING OF EMPIRE

Between 1840 and the early 1870's the name of the British Empire was evoked in a tone of high seriousness in connexion with a distinct group of colonies. Problems had arisen concerning the responsibilities of the United Kingdom towards those dominions for which it was not only the seat of authority and the protecting power, but also the 'mother-country' in the strictest sense of the word, the country from which the settlers had come and from which a steady stream of new immigrants was expected to swell the already existing urban and rural communities. In that sense the United Kingdom was the mother country to a limited number of colonies in relation to which the name of the British Empire—as distinct from that of the Colonial Empire—had an emotional appeal. West Indian planters and merchants counted least in this respect, despite the fact that among the English oversea settlements theirs was the oldest. They still occupied an important place in British trade and their clamorous protests against being sacrificed to the ill will of philanthropists and free-trade doctrinaires were not without success, but they could not in any case attract many British immigrants in their state of economic difficulties.[1] Other territories which originally seemed to be capable of providing new homes for destitute or adventurous Britons and Irishmen proved disappointing. Thus the colonies at the Cape of Good Hope and on the Swan River in West Australia, whose foundation had been prompted by strategic and naval interests, remained stagnant for decades. On the other hand, one group of settlements had a record of steady development from the end of the eighteenth century onwards. The British population of Canada and the Maritime Provinces of British North America was on the increase. The nucleus of British settlers was constituted by the Loyalists of the old American colonies, whose descendants still remembered that they were entitled to the letters U.E.—United Empire—after their names. Originally there had been less than 100,000 Empire Loyalists in Canada but almost five times that number had come to that country between 1815–40.[1] Since 1820 another colony appeared to be a new land of promise for British settlers. South East Australia, i.e. New South Wales with its extensions in Van Diemen's Land and Port Philip-Melbourne was a dumping ground for convicts until 1840 (Van Diemen's Land even until 1852), but its pastoral wealth had attracted thousands of small 'emancipists' and free settlers. Finally, there was a third group of settlements in South Australia and New Zealand, which were energetically developed after 1840.

The history of these three groups of colonies, Canada, New South Wales, and South Australia with New Zealand, became closely linked with the activities of Edward Gibbon Wakefield and his political followers, the Colonial Reformers. The anarchic occupation of land in New South Wales and the ceaseless frictions which emerged in this region between settlers and government officials inspired the prisoner of Newgate to write his imaginary *Letters from Sydney*. They culminated in the two demands for systematic colonization and self-government. They displayed the vision of colonies which 'would no longer be new societies' but 'so many extensions of an old society'. Wakefield and his adept, Charles Buller, the parliamentary agent of an Australian Patriotic Association, were advisers of Lord Durham on his mission to Canada in 1838 and influenced the Report which outlined a new constitution for the British colonies of North America. The agitation of the Reformers likewise gave rise to the South Australia Act of 1834, which was a compromise between their aims and the demands of the Colonial Office. On the initiative of the Reformers a company was formed which forced the hands of the Government and resulted in the foundation of an organized colony in New Zealand. The carefully prepared settlements of Otago and Canterbury provinces nine and eleven years later were again the work of associations built up under the auspices of Wakefield.

In 1829 the *Letters from Sydney* had concluded with the prediction that, if colonies were organized in accordance with its principles, 'Britain would become the centre of the most extensive, the most civilized, and, above all, the happiest empire in the world'. When in February 1850 the constitutional aims of the Reformers were about to take definite legal shape in the Australian Government Bill, Sir William Molesworth, their parliamentary protagonist, proclaimed: 'We ought to look upon our colonies as integral portions of the British Empire, inhabited by men who ought to enjoy in their own localities all the rights and privileges that Englishmen do in England.'[1] Between those two dates the name of the British Empire acquired a new meaning connoting a federal relationship between Great Britain and her self-governing colonies. The Colonial Reformers had an important share in the development of this connotation, directly by their contribution to the Durham Report, indirectly by their active, critical contributions to the reconstruction of the colonial system which emerged during this period. Though only intermittently emphasized and never growing into an exclusive definition, that idea was to have a career of its own. It meant a spontaneous revival of that interpretation of the British Empire which had been offered to the mother country by many a patriot in the old American colonies during the conflicts which Britain finally failed in solving.

The beginnings of that career may be dated from the time when British legislators and statesmen were confronted with the grave constitutional problem of Canada after the rebellion in 1837. The problem was not only how to restore authority but also how to secure allegiance to the Crown. In the parliamentary debates of January 1838, which confirmed the discretionary powers granted to Lord Durham's governorship, the notion of Empire was frequently used to emphasize the one or the other aspect of the problem. The concept was used in a way that testifies to the ambiguity of the term as it then still existed, it being applied to the whole complex of dominions under the Crown as well as to the United Kingdom alone without anybody objecting. Sir Robert Peel, in the course of a speech against the abandonment of sovereignty, used empire to mean the dominions under the Crown, while Sir William Molesworth vindicated the basic loyalty of the restive Canadians by calling them the people 'firmly attached to the dominion of this empire'. Yet it would be hasty to take their different interpretations of empire as characteristic of their opposed political attitudes. Lord John Russell as government representative laid stress on the conciliatory intentions of Lord Durham's mission. Speaking for himself he indulged in liberal speculations on the eventual 'alliance' between Britain and Canada and in doing so actually managed to use the term Empire first in the one sense and later in the other.[1] The lack of clear distinction between the two meanings of empire can also be found in the great state-paper which Lord Durham submitted to the Government after the abrupt termination of his mission. His *Report on the Affairs of British North America* expressed criticism of previous policy for having been directed against the 'dismemberment of the Empire' and for planning to oppose 'resistance to the Empire'. In another stricture ministers were reproached in the Report for having felt only 'remotely and slightly affected by the good or bad legislation of these portions of the Empire', or for having been of the opinion that Canadian affairs were 'too petty to attract the due attention of the Empire'.[2] It is clear that the term Empire is not used consistently and is without specific significance. A closer examination of the language of Lord Durham's Report, however, reveals a highly interesting feature for the purpose of our study. The name of the British Empire is used for the United Kingdom in passages which are meant to emphasize the author's main cause—the lasting attachment of the Canadians to Great Britain. The report is dedicated to the Queen with the recommendation: '... a connexion secured by the link of kindred origin and mutual benefits may continue to bind to the British Empire the ample territories of the North American Provinces and the large and flourishing population by which they will assuredly be filled'. This is more than an ornamental phrase. It discloses nothing of the policies suggested for the promotion of the proposed link, but it clearly hints at the main intention of the whole Report. In the concluding section this intention is made explicit by a solemn warning and a courteous prayer. The author hopes 'that the Imperial Government and Legislation will appreciate the actual crisis in the affairs of these colonies and will not shrink from any exertion that may be necessary to preserve them to the Empire'; he confesses to have been moved 'by the earnest desire to perpetuate and strengthen the connexion between this Empire and the North American Colonies which would then form one of the brightest ornaments in Your Majesty's Imperial Crown'.[3]

In the body of the Report this style of accentuating the link between the Empire and the colonies is applied to the interpretation of the 'predominant feeling of all the English population of the North American Colonies' and to the inferences drawn from this feeling with regard to the constitutional future of those colonies. Lord Durham was impressed by the strength of the national sentiment which still prevailed among the British North Americans. He became convinced that the national sentiment and self-respect were rooted in an attachment to the mother country but also in an 'attachment constantly exhibited by the people of these provinces towards the British Crown and Empire'.[1] This conviction underlay the well-known three major principles of the Report, responsible government, the reconstitution of a united Canada incorporating the French province of Lower Canada, and, lastly, an extension of the legislative union to the Maritime Provinces and even Newfoundland in the East. Responsible government was the national pride of a society of British origin, a sentiment, which 'may, if rightly appreciated, be made the link of an enduring and advantageous connection'.[2] Such rights of self-government cannot be conceded to a separate province of mainly French character. In this context Lord Durham asserts his basic tenet that the feud between English and French settlers, the cause of the disorders in Lower Canada, can be healed only by a consistent assimilation of the French: 'I entertain no doubts as to the national character which must be given to Lower Canada; it must be that of the British Empire; that of the majority of the population of British America; that of the great race which must, in the lapse of no long period of time, be predominant over the whole North American Continent.'[3] Responsible government and the union of the two Canadas together would have the effect of giving to the loyal colonists the power and consciousness of 'having some objects of a national importance'. Such a prospect would be brightened still further by the Maritime Provinces joining the union. In this context the ultimate aim of promoting the 'connexion with the Empire' is most persuasively stressed. 'The full establishment of responsible government can only be permanently secured by giving these Colonies an increased importance in the politics of the Empire.' Other statements become even more pronounced about the ultimate, political effect of such a union, which would embrace a great and powerful people and '...under the protection of the British Empire, might in some measure counterbalance the preponderant and increasing influence of the United States....' As to the future development of an imperial sentiment Lord Durham felt optimistic.

I am, in truth, so far from believing that the increased power and weight that would be given to these Colonies by union would endanger their connexion with the Empire, that I look to it as the only means of fostering such a national feeling throughout them as would effectually counterbalance whatever tendencies may now exist towards separation.[1]

Like other public men who looked at the map and had studied the history of North America, Lord Durham could not escape the haunting question whether that fateful word—separation—did not embody the ultimate end of the British Colonies. How could the 'strong allegiance to the British Empire' of whose prevalence he had no doubt, be preserved from being 'sapped' by physical pressure and spiritual attraction which were menacing it from across the border of the United States? Durham's answer to that problem was based on the allegiance and attachment 'to British as distinguished from French institutions'. On those terms that loyalty could be lost as well as saved. It could be lost, if the precarious attraction to the U.S.A. was strengthened by the feeling that the Republican neighbours enjoyed more of the old British liberties than her Majesty's loyal subjects in Canada. In that case disaffection was bound 'to give an enemy a certain means of inflicting injury and humiliation on the Empire'. British North Americans could not possibly 'long feel contented with a political system which places them . . . in a position of inferiority to their neighbours'. 'The colonist of Great Britain', as Lord Durham sees and interprets him, knows himself to be 'linked, it is true, to a mighty empire . . . but he feels, also, that his link to that empire is one of remote dependence . . . he knows that in its government he and his own countrymen have no voice'.[2] Such sentiments of inferiority must be removed; and the Report aims at securing the conditions for their removal.

Lord Durham insisted that 'a colonial legislature, thus strong and self-governing', would not feel inclined to abandon the link with

Great Britain but would become more durable and advantageous under the new auspices. Like other statesmen before him—like William Huskisson when introducing his final reforms and like Lord John Russell when introducing the bill which authorized his late mission,[1] Lord Durham could not suppress a reflexion that one day history might ordain different decrees. 'In the hidden decrees of that wisdom by which this world is ruled', it might be written that after all 'these countries are not for ever to remain portions of the Empire'. Such fatalism, he shrewdly warned, could not but issue in the same maxims of policy as would, in his opinion, make for lasting allegiance. Should Providence have decided on final separation 'we owe it to our honour to take good care that, when they separate from us, they should be not the only countries on the American continent in which the Anglo-Saxon race shall be found unfit to govern itself'. In that precautionary aside the phrase 'connexion with the Empire' was, as in other places, for reasons of stylistic expediency, abandoned in favour of the phrase 'portions of the Empire'.[2] It was restored to its prominent place in the provisos made for the 'authority of the Imperial Legislature' and in matters 'absolutely involving the few imperial interests, which it is necessary to remove from the jurisdiction of Colonial legislation'.[3] The transition from one phrase to another gives only more prominence to the meaning of the concept of Empire as it is impressed on the readers of Lord Durham's Report. The preservation of a lasting allegiance on the part of those colonies who were ripe for a high degree of self-government was to be considered as the most vital point in the maintenance of the British Empire. In whatever sense the name of this Empire was raised—whether the strength of the United Kingdom was stressed or the extent of its overseas dominions was surveyed—the strong appeal to national dignity implied in it was bound up with the certainty that those colonies would remain firm in their allegiance.

To have disseminated this idea was perhaps the most far-reaching effect of Lord Durham's state-paper, both as regards the diffusion of its teaching in Britain and the Colonies and as regards its lasting influence. The plan of a unified and self-governing British North America, with which in its author's mind the future of the British Empire in those regions was vitally linked, was not implemented. Its constitutional principle, the maxim of Responsible Government, was not endorsed by the imperial authorities. It was, in the course of ten years, to materialize along the winding path of trial and error. The union of the two Canadas became law in 1841 but completely failed to achieve the assimilation of the French Canadians. No attempt was made to include the Maritime Provinces in the union from which Lord Durham had expected a good deal in the achievement of 'objects of national importance', beginning with a railway connecting Halifax with Quebec. The problem, how-ever, of making the autonomous growth of colonial societies compatible with the maintenance of an imperial federation was in the Report so eloquently co-ordinated with the exposition of its organic demands that it could not fail to impress any person who took an interest in colonial questions. Only from this time on was the development of colonies which grew by immigration from Britain understood to constitute the crucial problem of the future of the Empire. Only from this time on was 'the Empire', in this context of a tie uniting self-governing Britons overseas with the mother country, made a topic of debate. The debate had begun, indeed, when Lord Durham was sent to Canada, but he expanded on it in a language particularly serious and emphatic. This language came to be adopted by politicians who either refused to accept his conclusions or welcomed the promotion of colonial loyalty. The two phrases of the Report, 'connexion with the Empire' and 'portions of the Empire', found their way into political usage. Gradually 'portions of the Empire' became the predominant phrase, while 'connexion with the mother country' and 'Colonial Empire', though used less often, served the purpose as well.

An example for the suggestiveness of Lord Durham's language is apparent in the missive in which Lord John Russell, the Colonial Secretary on whom the reconstruction of the Canadian constitution devolved, explained to the new Governor, Charles Poulett Thomson, that the principle of Responsible Government was not acceptable. Russell declared his agreement with 'the practical views of colonial government recommended by Lord Durham' and the aim to gain the 'affectionate attachment of her (the Queen's) people in North America', but at the same time he advised the Governor to use the language of his predecessor in order to stress the limits of that conciliatory practice.

The minister had 'the Queen's commands ... to protest against any declaration at variance with the honour of the Crown and the unity of the Empire'. The example of England taught the wisdom of mutual forbearance and moderation. Thus the Governor was advised only to 'oppose the wishes of the Assembly where the honour of the Crown, or the interests of the Empire are deeply concerned'.[1] It is not quite clear what the expressions 'the unity of the Empire' and 'the interests of the Empire' exactly mean. Their use, as at times Lord Russell's rhetoric, betray rather than cover up an underlying uncertainty about forthcoming issues. For the above ceremonial phrasing Lord Durham's Report had provided the model. Moreover, the Report could strengthen Lord Russell's confidence that the invocation of the imperial cause would find some resonance in the colonies where the traditions of the United Empire Loyalists were still alive.

This statesman, at all events, brought to his office a belief in the growth of the Empire by colonization. In the short time of his term of office—little more than two years—he took a manifest interest in the occupation of Australia and New Zealand by British settlers and in this respect was sympathetic towards the aims of the Colonial Reformers.[2] The Reformers themselves did not excel in passionate declarations concerning the future of the Empire during the following years. It had been congenial to Lord Durham to dwell so much and with solemnity on that point. He felt himself the creative arbiter of national destinies. In his mission and report he seized the opportunity of presenting the public with the fruits of his sovereign mind. But Durham died in 1840. As Wakefield's writings show, the founder of the colonial reform movement was by no means averse to making sweeping statements about the inherent connexion between imperial greatness and colonial development, but he was distracted from literary activities by agitation related first with Canadian affairs and later with New Zealand. Afterwards a stroke disabled him for a time. The most devoted collaborator of Durham as well as of Wakefield was Charles Buller. He spent the energy of the few years still left to him in virulent attacks against the bureaucracy of the Colonial Office, whose permanent under-secretary, James Stephen, was rather unfairly ridiculed by him as 'Mr. Mother-country'. The style of his writings disproves the slander which declared him, rather than Lord Durham, to have been the author of the most decisive sections of the Report.[1] Among the other parliamentary spokesmen of the group the most fiery, Sir William Molesworth, was a 'Philosophical Radical', who believed it his duty to join Cobden and other financial reformers in their disparagement of colonial expenditure. The proud name of Empire could not easily appeal to such a man. This name, however, assumed new overtones during the administration of Sir Robert Peel, 1842–6, when the transformation of commerce and trade in the direction of free trade occupied the foreground of British politics.

The commercial system of Britain included what was called 'the colonial system'. Owing to the reforms promoted by William Huskisson in the 1820's, the system was no longer dominated by subservience to the monopoly of the British 'shopkeeper', although Molesworth in flippant abuse denounced it as still being liable to Adam Smith's proverbial sarcasm.[2] Its only feature which almost exclusively preferred British economic interests to those of the colonies was a small residue of the Navigation Laws. In every other respect the principle of British monopoly had given way to that of reciprocity between British and colonial import regulations. Colonial produce was granted preferential duties in British ports. Colonial interests, therefore, were bound to be adversely affected by the adoption of Free Trade. Reform would hit colonial monopoly in the main. The first steps towards commercial reform affected only a small number of such items—Canadian wheat and timber, West Indian sugar, and Australian wool. Those items were vital enough and Free Traders attacked the principle of colonial preference with full vigour. On that point the Colonial Reformers were in full agreement with them. Lord Henry Howick (later the 3rd Earl Grey), one of their representatives in the House of Commons, was also one of the most outspoken advocates of the abolition of colonial preference. It was thought that the colonists, in order to be on an equal footing with the citizens of the mother country, ought to rely on their own economic energy and not seek shelter behind British commercial privilege.

Such an attitude could not easily be represented as compatible with the promotion of closer ties between the mother country and the colonies. The utmost that could be said of Free Trade in this respect was that its inherent soundness would in the long run leave those ties intact. That expectation could not be defended with the vigour with which it could be attacked from the opposite point of view. It could be claimed that the abrogation or even curtailment of colonial preference would utterly prejudice colonial loyalty and the preservation of the Empire. Colonial producers might begin to ask themselves whether there was still a valid reason justifying the continued connexion with the mother country. That was what Peel and his Colonial Secretary, Edward Stanley, feared when they decided to adhere staunchly to the principle of colonial preferences in the reformed tariff of 1842. In some cases the discrimination in favour of colonial goods was even greater than it had been before. As was to be expected in view of the rising demands for Free Trade, the government was criticized for allowing the colonies to rely on an artificial system of commerce which might expose them to even greater harm later on when the commercial policy of Great Britain might be changed in accordance with the principles of Free Trade.[1] This warning roused Stanley to a vehement protest and a glowing eulogy of the wider issues implicated in the colonial trade. The whole system and strength of Britain's colonial ties was at stake, the empire. It was Colonial trade, he declared,

which more than any other employed our shipping, consumed the produce of our manufactures, and gave encouragement to native and to colonial industry —and, more than all that, which kept entire that strong, that beneficial tie of nationality, that tie of mutual connection between the different parts of this great empire, which constituted its protection from war and its strength and glory in peace. . . . With that strength only which arose from union could that empire be maintained. But if they deprived the colonies of the sense of mutual commercial advantage, they would diminish the strength arising from union, and if they abandoned the colonies and commerce with the colonies, they would diminish their national power and glory, and sink into the condition of a second-rate power.[2]

Such language, associating the glories of the Empire with the demand for economic solidarity within its confines, had not been heard from a British minister since William Pitt had solicited the Commons to accept his Irish treaty project. It was not to be heard from such quarters again until Joseph Chamberlain agitated for his tariff reform. Under the Old Colonial System there had been no need for making imperial greatness a point in determining commercial policy. Colonies were by definition parts of a system of mutual intercourse. Huskisson only in passing referred to the 'great interests of the British Empire'.[1] The principle of mutual relationship such as it was understood by the government and the parliamentary majority had not yet changed. However, the language of the Colonial Secretary was inspired by the Durham Report. This is shown by the emphatic reference to the 'beneficial tie of nationality'. Peel confirmed that it was Canada by whose future relation to Great Britain the whole structure of the Empire would be judged. He seconded Stanley with an equally anxious appeal:

I am now protesting against that unqualified and exceptionless doctrine— namely, that you ought to treat Canada in respect to colonial and commercial intercourse on the same footing as other countries. If such a proposition be entertained, there is an end at once to our colonial empire, and to maintain it will only be to place a useless burden on ourselves. If you sanction this proposition, then you ought also to say let the colonies assert their own independence and provide for their own maintenance.

The colonial preferences were passed by a large majority in the House. For that result, however, the fact that they did not signify a major change in traditional policies was more responsible than the emphatic appeals made by the two ministers to the imperial sentiment and duties of the House.[2] Their idea of making the unity of the Empire a leading principle of economic policy was bound to remain barren of any result. There were two reasons why that idea was incapable of holding its own against the rising tide of Free Trade. One reason was that the group of politicians who believed whole-heartedly in the national mission of the Colonial Empire, the Colonial Reformers, were not prepared to interpret that mission in terms of a commercial super-structure to be imposed and maintained by force. Such paternal care for the new colonies as they demanded from the imperial authorities should materialize rather in the encouragement of self-reliance than in the offer of economic protection. The man who had objected to an 'artificial system of commerce' and who had been so strongly answered by Peel and Stanley in the name of imperial unity, was no other than Lord Howick, the brother-in-law of Lord Durham and one of the Whigs whom the Colonial Reformers had won over for their ideas. He spoke for the whole group when he declared tariff preferences to be incompatible with self-reliance. Such a policy, far from weakening the link with the colonies, would make it 'permanent and mutually beneficial'.[1] The assumption that colonial preferences could be treated as a consolidated and agreed imperial cause proved illusory soon enough. Already in 1843 Canada obtained an improvement of the trading conditions granted to her in Peel's first Corn Law only the year before. This Canada Corn Law, doing away with the sliding scale and substituting it by a nominal uniform duty, caused Lord Howick to renew his warnings in the strongest terms. It also made other grain-exporting colonies wonder why they should not obtain a similar concession. Such a demand, combined with the resentment over the fact that the favourable terms granted to the import of wool had been withdrawn, was voiced in New South Wales. There colonial self-government was about to assert itself on a more democratic basis. In 1842 colonial wool was admitted to Britain duty-free, while foreign wool was subject to a small duty. In the budget of 1844 that latter duty was abolished so that Australian wool lost its privileged position. The loss of preference suffered by Australian wool glaringly contrasted with the discriminating treatment applied to Canadian and Australian grain. The manifest injustice, a member of the Legislative Council of New South Wales complained, was all the more offensive as 'in Australia there was a whole population of British origin', while 'the greater part of the Canadian population was alien in language and in blood', a population conspicuous for its rebellion against Britain. Australia, on the other hand, was loyal. 'If England,' the speech concluded dramatically, 'persisted in this Joseph-and-his-brethren sort of system, she would retain perhaps numerous dependencies, but she would never become the vast united empire which she ought.'[2] The critic who spoke in such visionary terms of the Empire was Robert Lowe, who at that time devoted his energy to the promotion of colonial settlement and education in Australia and whose impressive language was soon to be heard in London and will, at a later stage, attract our attention again for the purpose of our study—

curiously enough as directed against all imperial phrases. In those years Lowe's contention that the whole principle of 'United Empire' was to be tested over the issue of colonial preference found vociferous assistance in the British Parliament. In May 1845 a motion was brought into the House conceding to Australian produce the same terms as had been granted to Canada. The language of that motion combined old and more recent ideas about the scope and purpose of the Empire and the colonizing effort. In connexion with the measures envisaged the motion asserted that their tendency would be 'to spread British colonisation over the most distant regions of the globe', and continued 'it will also unite and knit together the various dominions of our wide-spread Empire in the bonds of mutual interest and mutual goodwill'. In the following debate at least one Conservative member proved responsive to that view. Free Traders, prominently represented by John Bright, welcomed the motion as a step in their direction, and, therefore, Lord Howick, too, could, for once, challenge the Government to live up to their pledge to promote 'the common advantage of the Empire'. Peel had nothing to say in reply to those remonstrances but the motion was rejected by the House.[1] Neither he nor the defenders of the cause realized how soon the question of corn would demonstrate that the economic unity of the Empire could not be presented to the nation by any party as a major political principle. The Irish famine effected what the agitation of the Free Traders, despite their massive popular influence, had so far failed to achieve. It provided a terrible object lesson on the result of restrictions imposed on the basic needs of a growing population. It compelled the parliamentary leaders of both parties, first Lord John Russell and later Sir Robert Peel, to bow to Cobden's demand for the repeal of the Corn Laws.

This revolutionary measure affected the export of Canada. To the majority of the Conservatives who did not follow the Prime Minister in his defection, Canadian export meant little compared with the destruction of the privileges enjoyed by the British landed gentry. Nevertheless, the issue of Canadian export and colonial preference figured prominently in the debates of both Houses. Canadian wheat-growers and millers had every reason to believe they were let down. The exceptionally favourable terms offered to them by Britain in 1843 had given rise to considerable capital investment and expansion of grain farming in Canada. The set-back now suffered through the Repeal of the Corn Laws greatly annoyed Canadian farmers and revived the old doubts on the reliability of their allegiance to the mother country. The decision in favour of a free import of corn could not but be understood as heralding the final victory of Free Trade and the abolition of the principle of colonial preferences. A pointer to that effect was provided by an item in the budget of 1846. The duties on foreign timber were reduced, thereby making it harder for Canadian timber to compete in the British market.

When introducing his legislative proposals for the repeal of the Corn Laws, Peel tried to avoid a debate on the colonial system in general asserting that a liberal policy in one respect did not mean the total abolition of colonial preferences. He could not, however, prevent the issue of Canadian loyalty and the future of the Colonial Empire from playing a conspicuous part in the passionate debates which were occasioned by the third reading of the Bill in May 1846. Challenged by Lord George Bentinck and Disraeli, Russell openly confirmed that the Repeal signified a fundamental change in the whole system of the Empire. 'I think we run no risk with regard to our Colonies. I think they have great advantages, setting apart the one which they enjoy of differential duties; the trade of our Colonies, if it is to be changed, I think, ought to be changed more gradually and with more caution than that of the great people of whom we are the representatives; but I think, united with this great Empire, forming a part of it, they will not be sorry to see our restrictive system abrogated.' Lord Russell as he spoke was not aware of the fact that every major change in the restrictive system of Great Britain was likely to lead to a similar change in the system of colonial preference, but he realized—and said so—that the days of that system were numbered. Lord Stanley, a staunch protectionist and champion of the imperial connexion, not only understood the Repeal of the Corn Laws in those terms, but also restated his conviction that commercial preferences were an integral factor in the preservation of colonial loyalties. He brought that idea home to the Lords in whose midst he rose to speak in terms more glowing than those he had used when addressing the Commons four years earlier:

Now destroy this principle of protection, and I tell you in this place that you destroy the whole basis upon which your colonial system rests . . . it is to your colonies that you owe that there is not a sea in which the flag of England does not float . . . that there is no zone in either hemisphere in which there are not thousands who recognise the sovereignty of Britain—to whom that language and that flag speak of a home, dear, though distant, of common interests, of common affection—men who share in your glories—men who sympathize in your adversities, men who are proud to bear their share of your burden, to be embraced within the arms of your commercial policy and to feel that they are members of your great and imperial *Zollverein.*

He was not alone in using that German word for the definition of the colonial system. He went on rebuking Cobden, who had denounced that system as 'mutual robbery'; it was, Stanley assured the Lords, mutual insurance devised for the 'sustainment of the strength of the Empire'. Again, Lord Stanley had to face the bitter fact that the liberal promoters of colonial development had no use for mutual insurance and sided with Cobden, who had so little love for colonies, in matters of commercial policy. His old antagonist, Lord Howick, now in the Lords as Earl Grey, retorted that the only way to strengthen the imperial connexion was 'to direct labour in the Colonies to its natural and most productive channels'.[1]

Two months later the Repeal had become law and Earl Grey was Colonial Secretary in Lord John Russell's cabinet. That these men were in earnest about the new policy was immediately proved by an open attack on the 'bulwark of colonial preference', the sugar of the West Indian planters, who constituted the oldest colonial society. Their virtual monopoly—shared by East Indian possessions, Mauritius in particular—had been sanctioned under Peel's administration as a moral commitment of the nation. The planters, whose gains had become more precarious by the abolition of slavery, were protected against foreign, especially Brazilian, competitors by a high import duty imposed on foreign sugar. The government now proposed to absolve the British consumer's conscience from taking into account either the economic position of the English planters or the demands of philanthropy. As a result the problem of the imperial connexion once again became the topic of heated debates. Russell was accused of ruining Jamaica and heading for the dissolution of the Empire. In reply he reiterated the doctrine that the 'immense advantage' which 'this Empire had ... in the loyalty, the strength, and the assistance of the colonists' would grow even more solidly secure, if the 'limited and restricted system of former days' was definitely 'acknowledged to be erroneous'. In the end the planters obtained a further period of grace together with a large number of other colonial preferences. Wholesale abolition was made an immediate issue only when Gladstone had become certain of general assent in 1853.[1]

If Free Trade was to be established step by step the first blows at the system of colonial preferences in 1846 logically led to the abolition of commitments binding the colonies to Great Britain. Permission for the colonies to abrogate protective duties which favoured British goods had to be legislated as well as the abolition of what still remained of the Navigation Laws, the most time-honoured national monopoly. Both measures were particularly urgent for setting Canada at rest and facilitating her commercial relations with the United States so as to counter the constantly dreaded political attraction which might issue from Canada's neighbour. Accordingly, Russell in 1846 implemented the abolition of duties discriminating in favour of British goods on the Canadian market, and in 1849 the abolition of the Navigation Laws came into effect. Those measures aroused new debates and pronouncements about the future of the Empire. Prognostications were often contradictory. 'It would be a question of time, and of money, how long political connexion would survive commercial independence,' a protectionist warned when the abolition of British monopolies in the colonies was discussed. Earl Grey deplored such objections by giving the assurance—quite mistakenly as it turned out—that Parliament was still left in possession of the authority to regulate the general trade of the colonies and the mother country 'in the manner most conducive to the welfare and prosperity of the Empire'. In November 1847 the Queen's speech foreshadowed a reconsideration of the Navigation Laws by announcing the government's intention 'to ascertain whether any changes can be adopted, which, without danger to our maritime strength, may promote the commercial and colonial interests of the Empire'. British ship-builders, however, could not easily be persuaded that those imperial interests could be promoted otherwise than by insuring their preferential share in maritime strength. A similar opinion prevailed in Canada where such interests were vital. From St John, New Brunswick, a petition was issued in 1848 warning the Queen that the projected abrogation of the Navigation Laws would prove 'generally prejudicial to the British Empire, and particularly to this loyal colony'.[1]

The Queen's speech of November 1847 was remarkable in that it gave official sanction to the interests of the Empire as defined by the declaration made by Lord John Russell. Russell had come round to the principles of Free Trade, and his idea of Empire implied an economic interpretation of the imperial connexion which resembled the con-constitutional interpretation established by the Durham Report. Underlying that idea there was the confidence that liberal institutions would go far to strengthening the ties of loyalty. Actually, Russell became converted also to Lord Durham's constitutional doctrine of Responsible Government. Earl Grey had not been Colonial Secretary for long when he authorized an instruction to the Governor of Nova Scotia that the principle of Responsible Government was upheld by the Government.[2]

The new concept of Empire which the Durham Report helped to develop can be detected in the reply given by Sir Howard Douglas, a Conservative member of the House of Commons, to criticism of colonial management in New Zealand. In the New Zealand Debate of June 1845 Sir Howard gave the word Empire a ring in which solemn and powerful notes blend with ideas of geographical expansion and visions of systematic colonization. ' ... My opinions,' Sir Howard Douglas claimed, 'are as old as the days in which the foundations of this great Empire were laid in those well-known establishments by which these little islands have become the centre of a mighty Empire, and those opinions are as firm as that Empire is, I trust, enduring.' [3] Here the Colonial System is conceived as sustaining and defending the Empire. Such a belief, however, was anything but traditional. Its elements were new and less widely or firmly defended than the speaker seemed to admit.

Another point of interest concerns the personality and background of the man who voiced his belief in the British Empire. Sir Howard Douglas had been connected with service in Canada since the end of the eighteenth century. In Britain he had made a name for himself as an authority on military engineering, but in Canada his name was associated with his term of office as Governor of New Brunswick between the years 1823–31. He became the founder of the University of Fredericton. When he delivered his eulogy of the Empire, he echoed a sentiment which came from Canada. We find that a strong empire-consciousness emanated from the colonies and from the men who championed their cause in Britain.

The liquidation of commercial laws which had operated in favour of Canadian export to Britain gave rise to heated debates about the future connexion between Canada, Britain, and the United States. In 1849 agitation in favour of federation with the United States had reached such a pitch that officers of the militia became disaffected, and public demonstrations in favour of federation called forth counter-demonstrations of loyalists. In their passionate declarations Empire, always spelt with a capital letter, was a highly emotive word which stood for the continued connexion with the mother country. At one such meeting one motion was worded: 'That it is the opinion of this meeting that, from the loyal and patriotic feeling displayed by the inhabitants of the Province upon former trying occasions, to preserve the integrity of the Empire, the same spirit would again be exerted if necessary for the same purpose. . . .' Other motions expressed the hope for a close co-operation between Provincial and Imperial legislature, and the confidence that Canada stood to gain more from her continued connexion with the 'greatest Empire of the Earth'.[1] The Governor of Canada, Lord Elgin, was highly sympathetic to those sentiments and knew how to bring them to the notice of the Government in England, as we see from the Elgin-Grey Papers. He pointed out to the Colonial Minister, Lord Grey, that the strongest argument in favour of severing Canada's connexion with Britain was Britain's own indifference towards that connexion.[2]

Free Trade and the policy of 1846 were liable to opposite interpretations. This is the crux of the matter. It was possible to regard Free Trade as a principle upon which a new, essentially federal, system of imperial relationships was to be built. On the other hand, it was also possible to view the introduction of Free Trade and the gradual liquidation of the Colonial System as the initial step towards the final dismemberment of the Empire. The second interpretation gained support from the fact that the policy of Free Trade had been championed by Cobden and that Cobden appeared as an ally of Wakefield and Molesworth cavilling at the Colonial Office and demanding drastic economies in oversea expenditure. Neither Wakefield nor Molesworth cared much for the ulterior ends of their allies provided they assisted them in their immediate political aims. Godley seemed quite ignorant of being virtually allied to the self-same 'material spirit' which, he complained, was driving the colonies out of the Empire. Nor did the Colonial Reformers make the clarification of their concept of Empire easier by being expansionist in Australia but restrictionist in South Africa, as was the case of Molesworth, their main parliamentary spokesman.

Lord John Russell, the Prime Minister, was more circumspect. In his mind the idea of Empire had also become more definite in the 1840's. In the New Zealand Debate of June 1845 he spoke of the future colony as 'a branch of this mighty Empire'. Four years later, in a private letter to the Duke of Bedford in which he argued in favour of a policy of Free Trade, he drew a sharp division between his policy and Cobden's plans. 'But while I am decided against returning to protection on food, I am quite averse to giving any countenance to the plans of Hume and Cobden. I think them destructive of the Empire.'[1] Empire in that context could only mean the connexion between the mother country and the colonies. At the same time Russell's words betray a fear of the final dissolution of the Empire.

In that winter of 1849/50 imperial connexion was an issue which was prominently aired in public, not only in connexion with the curtailment of public expenditure and the liberalization of trade, but also with the principle of self-government. That principle, too, like Free Trade was liable to contradictory interpretations, dissolution or new imperial development. At Bradford Cobden 'fired a broadside that must have made every pane of glass in the Colonial Office tingle, and the red tape dance upon its tables' in the words of the *London Daily News*. The nation, Cobden maintained, was asked to foot the bill for vast army and navy expenditure on account of the colonies. If the idea was to build up a vast Downing Street Empire governing and protecting Canada, Australia, New Zealand, the Cape, and the West Indies, it would, no doubt, adversely affect the house-keeping money at the disposal of every family in the United Kingdom. If, on the other hand, British colonies received the right of self-government together with the duties of self-support and self-protection, there would be more money left in the pocket of every Briton. Canadian opinion discussed that speech as well as the reaction of British papers to Cobden's thesis. It was hard to escape the conclusion that Britain viewed the eventual dissolution of the Empire with equanimity. Even *The Times* gave its support to Cobden's suggestions about the future development of the link between Britain and her dependencies, while the London *Morning Chronicle*, though agreeing in principle with Cobden's contention, commented: 'He will get his millions saved all the sooner if he thinks something less about the mere money saving, and a vast deal more about the welfare of colonial communities, the progress of colonial enterprise, and the honour and stability of the Empire. . . .' The paper then went on to say that self-government was not necessarily tantamount to the dissolution of the Empire, a way of getting rid of colonies that were not worth keeping, but, on the contrary, possibly the only way of keeping colonies that were worth keeping.[1] The public debate on the future of the colonial connexion reached its climax in February 1850 when the Prime Minister made his great speech on colonial policy and introduced a bill extending the principle of self-government to Australia.

Russell must have felt in the course of the debates and uncertainties of the preceding months that a major government declaration on colonial policy was due. The speech was given particular significance and solemnity by the wealth of historical documents and statistical data which the speaker presented to the public. A lengthy retrospect led on to the recent abrogation of the Navigation Laws, the last remnant of the Old Colonial System. That step together with the new constitutional venture of self-government posed the decisive question 'which has been much agitated, and which has found supporters of very considerable ability—namely, that we should no longer think it worth our while to maintain our colonial empire'. Russell then justified the continued British responsibility for the Empire on grounds of a contribution

towards the civilizing of distant portions of the world, imperial
strength, responsibility for the welfare of native races like those of New
Zealand and Natal, the security offered by colonial ports to British
shipping 'most useful in time of peace, but . . . absolutely necessary in
time of war', and, finally, the inability of the colonies to defend themselves. The argument of defence requirements could not sound too
convincing in those days when it was difficult to visualize circumstances
which would make the possession of colonies vital to British security.
Russell must have anticipated two objections to his line of argument.
He would be told that the new commercial and constitutional principles
supported by his government would lead to final separation in any case,
that all the sums spent on the so-called imperial responsibilities were,
therefore, utterly wasted. He would have to face the other school of
thought who would contend that Britain's imperial responsibilities
brooked no more concessions to the colonies. To forestall objections to
his policy from either side he hit upon the time-honoured formula of
stoic self-satisfaction. Should the time come when a colony attained
such a standard of self-government, wealth, and power that it could
stand on its own feet and maintain its independence without Britain,
when such a colony began to look upon the old connexion with Britain
as onerous 'whatever may happen, we of this great empire shall have
the consolation of saying that we have contributed to the happiness of
the world'.[1]

The debate which followed Russell's speech brought forth another
attempt to clarify the meaning of Empire. Molesworth, now that the
victory of Colonial Reform seemed secured, interpreted that name in
a different vein. He adapted Burke's concept to the new conditions. He
restricted the name of colony to places settled by and suitable for Englishmen. Imperial power would extend its protection to all the British
colonies around the globe, colonies in that restricted sense. Such imperial
powers 'ought to be strictly reserved to the Imperial Government;
and they ought to be reserved, because they are indispensable for the
maintenance of the unity of the empire, and for the management of the
common concerns of the whole empire'. Such powers ought not to be
delegated to the colonies. Local powers and administration, on the other
hand, ought to be left in the hands of the English settlers on the spot, who

must not be subjected to the arbitrary authority of a distant Colonial Office. 'Then the colonists, relieved from the hated tyranny of the Colonial Office; enjoying all the rights and privileges of British citizens; bearing true allegiance to the Monarch of these realms; willingly obeying the laws made by the Imperial Parliament . . . would be bound to the empire by the strong ties of race, language, and self-interest.' Government by the Colonial Office was not a source of strength but a source of weakness in an empire composed of free Englishmen. Molesworth underlined that view again ten days later when the Bill was read for the second time. British colonists, Molesworth hoped, 'would cease to be subjects of that office, and would become true citizens of the empire. They ought to look upon their colonies, properly so called, as integral portions of the British empire, inhabited by men who ought to enjoy in their own localities all the rights and privileges that Englishmen do in England.' Molesworth concluded his speech by the vision of imperial representation in an imperial parliament of the future.[1]

He was neither the first nor the last to indulge in the dream which Franklin had once called 'union'.[2] Disraeli had discussed it with Derby a short time before. In any case Molesworth's triumph could not obliterate the fact that the future constitution of the Empire together with its future stability had been question-marked by the Prime Minister. Lord Elgin felt he had been painfully crossed in his endeavour to lend all his support to the loyalists of Canada. To demonstrate the defeatist effect of the Prime Minister's hint at a possible separation of the wealthy and strong colonies from the mother country, Elgin quoted Robert Baldwin, the Canadian statesman, who said to Elgin in dismay: ' . . . is it not hard upon us while we are labouring through good and evil report to thwart the designs of those who would dismember the Empire that our adversaries should be informed that the difference between them and the Prime Minister of England is only one of time?' Elgin could only assure Baldwin that Russell was not favouring the dissolution of the Empire by any means; and as for himself that it was his firm conviction it was dangerous to hold political maturity of a colony to be incompatible with Empire membership. A momentous question would have to be answered sooner or later. Elgin formulated that question boldly and bluntly.

Is the Queen of England to be the Sovereign of an Empire, growing, expanding, strengthening itself from age to age—striking its roots deep into fresh earth and drawing new supplies of vitality from virgin soils?—Or is she to be for all essential purposes of might and power monarch of Great Britain and Ireland merely—Her place & that of Her line in the World's History determined by the productiveness of 12,000 square miles of a coal formation which is being rapidly exhausted, and the duration of the social and political organization over which She presides dependant on the annual expatriation with a view to its eventual alienization of the surplus swarm of Her born subjects?[1]

Again it is on the colonial soil that a language thrives which pronounces the name of the British Empire with unrestrained enthusiasm such as was rarely heard in the mother country. Comments on the Prime Minister's speech were more pensive, even when confident in the permanence of the colonial tie.[2] In April 1851 The *Edinburgh Review* surveyed the whole issue in an article called: *Shall we retain our Colonies?* The Cobdenites proposed to abandon the Empire as a measure of economy. The article first dealt with Cobden's clear, logical, and bold arguments but concluded that cheap government was not the only criterion and price not the only argument. Another flaw in Cobden's logic was the analogy with private limited income. The income of a nation like Britain could be increased if an effort was called for in the interest of national safety and honour. Income was not a major consideration and it was not true to say that the British Empire was to be dissolved because the nation could not afford it. On the other hand, the 'rhetorical flourish' that wishes to link the Empire with the glory and might of England's name—a stricture pronounced on Wakefield and his *View of the Art of Colonisation*—was no telling argument in a debate with the 'advocates for cheap government at any cost'. The magisterial style of distributing reprimands to both sides forced the assertion of 'broadly imperial' politics down to meticulous, concrete reasoning. Dismissing the military argument as one for the War Office or the Commons to debate when Army or Navy Estimates came up for discussion or when Britain's security had to be mapped out, the author thought it was necessary to distinguish between the cost of the colonies and the cost of military and naval stations. It could be proved that the expenses bewailed by Cobden (and by Molesworth) were bound up with the maintenance of indispensable military outposts and that the nation was perfectly able to meet the cost. In the eyes of the *Edinburgh Review* all those considerations, economic as well as military, were not relevant to the issue. Much more important were Britain's obligations towards the natives and the white settlers as exemplified in South Africa. With the colonies left to themselves, who could prevent white settlers from enslaving the natives or vice versa? In the latter case the white settlers would have no option but to seek the protection of another white power, possibly that of the United States. Where the colonists were predominantly British, the element of sentiment was a far more important factor than the cool, calculating Cobdenites had realized. Whatever colonists might feel about the arbitrary decisions of the Colonial Office

we feel certain that the very first peril they encountered from without, the very first time they were menaced either with insult or with conquest by a foreign Power, they would instinctively and undoubtingly appeal to England for assistance and protection; and England would respond to their confidence with the most prompt and generous aid.

The natural attachment of British settlers to their kith and kin was no calculable item of statistics but it had to be reckoned with, the article insisted. Finally, returning to the level of cool, rational economics, what if Cobden's dream did come true but the new, independent colonies found their revenues to be insufficient? Would they not have recourse to new tariffs and close the markets 'we ourselves have planted in the wilderness, one after another, to the produce of our spindles and our looms'? So the author reached the same conclusion which Russell had already outlined in his Australia Speech. To miss that unique opportunity which Providence had granted to man for the development of civilization, for the sake of saving two million pounds was a thought worthy of shop-keepers but not of statesmen, not of British tradition.[1] The author can be seen to be in a defensive position. He must plead moral reasons because he cannot make out a strong political case for the retention of the Empire.

It remained for Lord Grey, Russell's Colonial Secretary—always at loggerheads with his erstwhile friends, the Reformers—to define the interest of Britain in the Colonial Empire—and thereby in the British

Empire—in terms more precise than those used by Russell and at the same time less meticulously scraped together than those presented by the *Edinburgh Review*. They constitute, as it were, the conclusion of a long public debate. Lord Grey's concept of the meaning of Empire is developed mainly in the Preliminary Remarks and Concluding Observations of his work on *The Colonial Policy of Lord John Russell's Administration*, the great self-vindication, written by him directly after the resignation of the Government in 1852. He stressed the same moral obligations as the Reviewer before him, but frankly confessed that there was a 'moral' motive of a different kind—national self-respect. In Parliament and outside the colonial debate had usually been confined to the relations between Britain and one particular colony. Therefore, the problem of the Empire as a whole had often been ignored and no coherent view or policy been presented. The abolition of the old system of colonial trade had given rise to a review of the colonial empire and a discussion about its future. Earl Grey then explained the reasons why he believed the British Colonial Empire ought to be maintained. Colonial possessions had given Britain a responsibility which the country could not shirk together with power and influence. She had gained steady and faithful allies in various parts of the world. She had acquired a great moral influence which was likewise beneficial to the country's security. British power would be diminished by the loss of the colonies. Mother country and colonies derived greater protection from the existence of the mutual tie. '. . . It seems to follow, that the tie which binds together all the different and distant portions of the British Empire, so that their united strength may be wielded for their common protection, must be regarded as an object of extreme importance to the interests of the Mother country and her dependencies.' Self-interest apart, the British Crown was the most powerful civilizing and pacifying instrument on earth. Britain's withdrawal would spell the end of peace and civilization in some colonies. Providence had entrusted Britain with greater power, which implied the duty of advancing the welfare of mankind. Even in the white colonies Britain's withdrawal would endanger the internal peace. Grey used the name of British Empire and Colonial Empire indiscriminately as he defended its continued existence against 'the views of those who wish to dismember the British

Empire by abandoning the Colonies'. Such a policy of dismemberment would be unworthy of a great nation.[1] In his concluding remarks Grey freely admitted errors committed in the past yet asserted 'that, taking our Colonial Empire as a whole, I greatly doubt whether any other period of equal length can be pointed out in our history in which that Empire has prospered so much, and has made such large strides towards future greatness, as during the years of which I have been speaking'. Grey knew that Adam Smith and the emergence of the United States were strong arguments in favour of eventual dissolution of the Empire. He remained opposed to the formal surrender of all power from Britain to her colonies. It would lead to frequent contests of authority, he thought. He did not believe the eventual loss of her colonies would be fatal to Britain but was inclined to regard such a development as a grievous calamity. 'You,' he finally appealed to the reading public, 'I am persuaded, will concur with me in this opinion, and will feel no less strongly than myself the desire that the great British Empire may to a long futurity be held together, and preserve its station among the principal Powers of the earth.'[2] With all his earnest endeavour to defend the idea of the Empire and to outline practices of Colonial Policy which would preserve that Empire, Grey was not able to make the concept of Empire an operative idea which could serve as a guide to future colonial administration. He failed in reconciling the tradition of Adam Smith with that of Edmund Burke, the principal thinkers from whom he had derived his main thesis.

Grey's book in 1853 concluded the debate which had begun in 1839 about the future of the connexion between Great Britain and her colonies. Colonial government in Canada, the abolition of the old colonial system of preferential trade, and the future government of Australia had occasioned the debate in the course of which the name of Empire assumed the particular connotation of *the global union which linked the mother country with her children in the colonies*. While the use of Empire as a name for the United Kingdom was dying out, the debate about the future of the imperial connexion was resumed in the 1860's. It kept the new idea of Empire alive. Once again it was Canada that touched off a new exchange of arguments for and against imperial ties.

The American Civil War brought about an increase in international tensions along the southern border of Canada and the prospect of military action. In 1861 Canadians had reason to fear aggressive actions perpetrated by those Americans who hoped to restore national unity by means of an external war. Later in the year the British vessel *Trent* was boarded by American marines, who removed two agents bound for Europe on a mission for the Confederate States. Already in summer 1861 British troops were ordered to reinforce Canadian garrisons. The war scare passed; but it demonstrated the danger of Britain being drawn into a war for the defence of her Empire in America. While the debate about the nature of the colonial empire had centred round the problem of imperial economy, the problem of imperial defence now came to the fore. Should the colonies become not only self-governing, self-support-ing, but also capable of self-defence against all aggressors? If so, what was the meaning of Empire to be, if such an Empire was to remain in existence at all? Thus the American Civil War started the discussion as to the rights and duties of the colonies, in particular the connexion of Canada with Britain, afresh. 'I think the present war . . . will draw a good deal of attention to the question of a colonial empire', Robert Cecil wrote to Adderley, adding in a pensive mood, 'whether it be worth having, or at what price.'[1] Sir Charles Bowyer Adderley, one of the active Colonial Reformers, thought so, too, and published his own ideas in an open letter addressed to Disraeli on the *Present Relations of England with the Colonies*. The letter had been motivated by the problem of Canadian defence and by the debate in the Commons on the occasion of the despatch of British forces to Canada in June 1861. Palmerston defended the action as a measure of ordinary routine precaution. Disraeli did not accept that reply. Even if the Canadian border was violated in the course of the American conflict, 'are there no inhabitants in Canada—are there not a numerous and gallant people there, accus-tomed to military discipline?' he asked. He thought Britain's over-readiness to rush reinforcements to Canada might lessen the military ardour of the Canadians to protect their own homes.[2]

Adderley thereupon wrote:

Dear Disraeli, I address myself to you . . . because you are the last leading statesman there (in the House of Commons), who has openly shown a due appreciation of the naked and disastrous truth . . . that England has lost the right estimation of her special art, the vital interest in colonisation, and has substituted for her former offspring a semi-dependency, looking to her for protection, instead of sharing with her in universal empire.

Such an empire of equal partners would require the active contribution of all its members also in the field of defence. Adderley, therefore, welcomed Disraeli's question in the House: 'Are there no inhabitants in Canada?' 'If the time is near when the strength of the empire must be brought to their support, doubly requisite is it that the Colonists should have put forth their own strength.' Adderley and his friends had spent many years in Parliament in order to restore self-government to the Colonies but the colonies received it without the correlative responsibilities. The Colonies thus obtained the control of their own taxation and the use of British taxation as well. Adderley felt assured that Disraeli's approach was the only sound one and that 'the interests of the Crown in a great colonial empire will not be trifled with by you'. After that dedicatory introduction Adderley explained his idea of imperial partnership, common citizenship, and colonial self-defence. '... Every part of the Empire should raise its own means of defence at home, and at the sound of danger all should be ready to rally round the threatened power.' The enemy should know that a temporary success gained in any quarter would bring down the vengeance of the whole imperial might.[1]

The problem of imperial defence had occupied the Government ever since the Crimean War when troops were needed in Europe and in the Colonies. During that time a Canadian militia was established. The question of colonial military expenditure became particularly irritating when in that period the Colonial Office was separated from the War Office. Already in 1859 an interdepartmental committee studied the expenditure and policy of colonial defence and found—the representative of the Colonial Office disagreeing—that the burden placed on Britain by the colonies in terms of manpower and money was too heavy and that the defence spirit of the colonies was hampered by such a policy. In its suggestions the report distinguished between imperial defence and local defence. Nor was that committee the only official inquiry into imperial defence conducted prior to the American conflict and the emergence of a danger to the Canadian border. A select committee of the House of Commons inquired into the defence of the British dependencies in spring 1861. The witnesses called by the committee agreed that self-government ought to go together with responsibility for military defence.[1]

The House of Commons Debate on British Troops in Canada in June 1864 endorsed the ideas underlying the resolution of 1862. Canada was expected to develop and improve her own military force but at the same time was reassured that an attack against her by the United States would not remain a localized Canadian affair but would expose the whole length of the American coast and all American commerce to the attack of the British fleet. The most important debate on the subject of Canadian security, and imperial defence, however, took place in March 1865. There was general agreement in the House that the main security for Canada lay in friendly relations between Britain and the United States and also that in the case of an American-British conflict 'the main defence of Canada would lie in the fact that the power of the British Empire would be exerted not only in America but all over the world'. At the same time it was emphasized that the Canadians, while relying on the power of Great Britain to defend them, ought to make a contribution towards their defence. In that debate the phrase 'the power of the British Empire' meant the combined forces and resources of all British possessions, and a plea for the improvement of the fortifications of Quebec could be made in the name of 'the honour and interest, as well as the welfare of the whole British Empire'.[2] Bright opposed the motion in favour of a contribution to Canadian defence to be made out of British funds and proposed Canadian independence as the better solution, indeed, the only solution to the problem of Canadian defence. He thought Britain could never defend Canada against the United States and was over-committed in America. He developed his view, characteristically enough, because he, too, wished to maintain and strengthen the Empire. ' . . . A great Empire', he argued 'may be lessened territorially, and yet the Empire itself may not be diminished in its power and authority in the world.' Support of the idea of Canadian separation, like support of the idea of free trade in the 1840's, was by no means identical with rejection of the Empire.

Between 1839 and 1865 the three major issues affecting the relations between Great Britain and her colonies—self-government, the abolition of the old colonial system of trade, and colonial defence—gave the term Empire a new prominence and a more definite meaning in the minds of statesmen, politicians, and colonial administrators who debated them. Denoting a complex and heterogeneous system of colonial links with the mother country, a new connotation of Empire had emerged. When people referred to China as an Empire, to the Roman Empire, or to the German Empire of the past, the massive compactness of one block was a determining element of the concept. There was no precedent for a notion of Empire as it began to emerge in the British debates. As yet there was little evidence to show that the wider public showed an interest either in the new meaning of Empire or in its substance. The concept remained confined to a small group of public men, whose classical and historical education was, undoubtedly, a factor which guided their minds to a fresh interpretation of an ancient political term. There is, on the other hand, just as little evidence that 'separatist' views enjoyed a wide popularity. It was only during the twelve years which followed the debate on colonial defence in 1865 that the nation showed a greater response to the name of Empire. That process was brought about by the literary discussion at home and by the outbreak of a new colonial crisis overseas.

IV

THE RISE OF EMPIRE SENTIMENT 1865–1872

In 1865 it was only the religious eccentric in Britain whose mind, reared in the long apocalyptic tradition of Christian sectarianism, would envisage a great and spiritual destiny of the British Empire. A pamphlet, entitled *Destiny of the British Empire*, endeavoured to prove that the Empire was identical with the everlasting kingdom prophesied in the Bible, and predicted that British ascendancy in India not only required the integrity of the Ottoman Empire but also necessitated the development of the Holy Land, to which under the auspices and in the ships of Britain the Jews would return.[1] The cool, reflecting political writers of that day imagined no spectacular future or destiny of the Empire but a gradual transition of all the colonies from British rule to independence, which would have the blessing of the Government and the British tax-payer alike.

Disraeli believed the idea of a Colonial Empire to be popular, because people erroneously regarded it as a source of profit and power and had not yet adjusted themselves to the altered relations existing between the metropolis and the colonies.[2] Cobden had coined the damning phrase, the 'bloodstained fetish of Empire'. In a less agitating spirit the political literature of 1865 not only discussed colonial reform against the background of Canadian strategy but also reflected the frustration suffered in the Maori War, which had been renewed in 1863. Henry Thring's *Suggestions for Colonial Reform*[3] listed in its preface all the colonial problems which in 1865 were still awaiting a satisfactory solution. Each problem, whether it had arisen in Canada, Australia, Natal, or New Zealand, had a bearing on the question of colonial connexion with the mother country. Thring stated that the connexion was neither well understood nor established on a sound footing. He repeated the earlier findings of the Select Committee of the House of Commons when he stated that a distinction had to be made between colonies and military and naval posts. He did not include

India, Gibraltar, Malta, or other military dependencies in his draft for the regularization of colonial development and, like the members of the Select Committee, he was firmly convinced that self-government implied rights as well as duties. Colonies did not pay, but, the author emphasized, they were not a question of the pocket. No Englishman could be indifferent to the part taken by his country in peopling vacant places of the earth, disseminating English laws, liberty, and religious values, '... he cannot but earnestly desire the establishment, throughout that empire on which the sun never sets, of copies of English institutions, rather than the examples of French centralization or of Russian despotism'. Thring then formulated a procedure—as legal draughtsman of the Government he was particularly qualified for such an undertaking—which offered a uniform scheme of constitutional development of colonial government in four stages:

1. Occupation of new territory and Colonial Office rule,
2. Colonial status and the establishment of local government,
3. Division of local and imperial powers as representative self-government develops,
4. Independence.

Once independence had been proclaimed, the new state was envisaged by the author as bound to Britain by no other obligation except an undertaking not to discriminate against her economically and to preserve the continuity of British law. Thus an author in those days could combine in his political treatise an unashamed pride taken in the Empire with perfect equanimity as to the formal steps that would lead towards its dissolution.

Viscount Bury's *Exodus of the Western Nations*, the work of a man who had close ties with Canada, was published in the same year as Thring's pamphlet. It agreed with the latter as to the unsatisfactory state of the relations between England and her dependencies and the need for a more realistic appraisal of the change that had taken place in those colonies which were *de facto* independent. Bury demanded that the *de jure* recognition of independence should be the outcome of mutual agreement, not the outcome of a quarrel. But there was a characteristic disagreement between the approach of the legal draughtsman who observed the situation from Whitehall and that of the member of Parliament who knew Canada from practical, personal experience. Viscount Bury shared the Canadian dislike for the term of colony and their sentimental attachment to the mother country. He, therefore, did not think Thring's formulation of the future relations between Great Britain and her independent ex-colonies was adequate. With the future Confederation of British North America in his mind he drafted articles of alliance, which provided for British defence of her ex-colony in case of attack, for close trading and cultural relations, and common citizenship.[1] Not many officials of the Colonial Office would have gone so far as Sir Henry Taylor, who demanded a policy of separation facilities, but there was a good reason for John Bright to suspect that there was no objection to Canadian independence in official circles of the Government. Bright welcomed statements to that effect as signs of progress in sound political opinions.[2] The year 1865, perhaps, was the nadir in the political thought about the Empire. In a spirit of dejection Matthew Arnold composed his poem, *Heine's Grave*. He sympathized with Heine's upbraidings of England and admitted woefully Britain's decline.

> Yes, we arraign her! but she
> The weary Titan! with deaf
> Ears and labour-dimmed eyes,
> Regarding neither to right
> Nor left, goes passively by,
> Staggering on to her goal;
> Bearing on shoulders immense,
> Atlantëan, the load,
> Wellnigh not to be borne,
> Of the too vast orb of her fate.[3]

Whether they hailed the development as a sign of progress or watched it with gloom, most thinking men in those days had little doubt about the impending dissolution of the British Empire. The factor which was not always visible and never calculable was the strength of empire sentiment among the workers of Britain and the feeling of loyalty and attachment among the colonists. Such emotions showed only in times of distress and danger. A ripple of empire emotion ran through Britain soon after. It was caused by the unrest which broke out in Jamaica in October 1865. Neither trade nor defence was involved in the dispute so much as the status of Her Majesty's subjects whatever their colour or race.

The immediate cause of the unrest was not political. It led to racial riots in the course of which some twenty civilians, including whites, were killed. Martial law was proclaimed in some areas, and in the course of prompt military action ordered by Edward Eyre, the Governor, several hundred negroes were executed with and without trial. The unrest was nipped in the bud but the Governor's action came in for severe criticism at home. Eyre was called to London, and an Enquiry Commission was sent to Jamaica upon whose findings the British press took up a strong position for and against the Governor. Would a governor have taken the same action if the population had been white, it was asked. Were negroes a different class of citizens? John Bright addressed a meeting at Rochdale which had been convened in support of Parliamentary Reform. A sentence significant for its emotive style and content drew the applause of his listeners. It implied a strong condemnation of the 'legal putting to death of subjects of the Queen and citizens of the empire'.[1]

The Governor was eventually replaced and became involved in legal action. In 1868 he was charged at the Old Bailey with misdemeanour in connexion with the execution of a negro leader. The case was dismissed. Commenting on the judgement the *Spectator* wrote that the Governor's error had been pardoned because it involved negro blood. The supporters of the Governor assumed that coloured rebels could not expect the same treatment as Anglo-Saxon or Celtic rebels. The *Spectator* admitted the difficulty which the Governor faced. It deplored the sentimental outcry at home in support of 'strong government' and the middle-class fury over the demand to treat negroes in distant colonies exactly like the Irish, the Scots, and the English. Such a spirit, such a temper was at variance with British institutions, with English law and the religious values of the country. '... A partial, a vulgar, and an insolent temper still lurks in our hearts, utterly inconsistent with the equity, magnanimity, and self-restraint needful to a people wielding a great empire which they can only extend by moral and religious virtue of a high order, and which they cannot lose without bringing down anarchy upon the earth.'[2] So the name of Empire remained a name to be used in solemn appeal, this time on behalf of the equal rights to be enjoyed by all its citizens.

Are political institutions the result of drift, accident, good fortune, or are they the result of intelligent discussion, foresight, vision, and planning? In the 1860's such a question was not out of place. There was a vague feeling in the air that the British Empire, in the sense of traditional colonial links, had reached a point where new roads opened up and that its leaders and its citizens lacked as yet a sense of directiveness. Empire-conscious observers felt that the colonies were faced either with the prospect of planned, institutionalized independence or the hazards of planless drifting. The problem of Empire was essentially taken as a problem of the colonies and was more keenly felt in the colonies than in Britain. In 1866 Joseph Howe hoped to make a contribution to the debate by publishing a pamphlet, entitled *The Organization of Empire*. The pamphlet endeavoured to breathe into the concept of Empire the spirit of power and strength with which it was associated in the minds of the humbler people and the colonists. The writer of the pamphlet was a prominent citizen and statesman of Halifax. In Nova Scotia he had made a name for himself as a champion of free trade and self-government. If we found earlier on that free trade and self-government were by no means ideas that spelt Empire defeatism, we could have held up Joseph Howe as an illustration for the new content that began to fill the old term. The pamphlet was prefaced by the solemn language which so often characterized mid-Victorian evocations of Empire.

Under the Providence of God, after centuries of laborious cultivation, the sacrifice of much heroic blood, the expenditure of a vast amount of treasure, the British Empire, as it stands, has been got together, and the question, which is presented to us, in some form of Parliamentary or newspaper disputation almost every week is, what is now to be done with it.

Howe opposed drift and presented his utopian ideas about the future structure of the Empire. He foresaw the development of responsible government in the colonies and their representation in the House of Commons at Westminster, a 'Parliament of the Empire'. That scheme did not include Crown colonies inhabited by alien populations, because none of those had a responsible government, but there was no objection in principle to their evolution towards self-government and representation in the Parliament of the Empire. Backward portions of the Empire were to be administered much in the same way as territories were treated in the U.S.A. Defence policy and finance must be uniform so as to pool the strength and resources of all empire possessions for the benefit of all empire members.[1]

After Cobden's death in 1865 the recognized principal advocate of his ideas was Louis Mallet, who was a leading authority in the field of commercial policy. In an essay on the political opinions of Cobden, written for the *North British Review* in 1867 and reprinted as Introduction to *The Political Writings of Richard Cobden* in 1869, Mallet endeavoured to restate Cobden's political principles and relate them to the political and economic problems of the day. Unlike his fellow-champion of free trade, Howe, he showed no enthusiasm for the British Empire as such. It was not his problem. He was at pains to explain that Cobden had not been opposed to British rule in other countries, not even in India. There the British helped to spread the great ideas of their own country such as free press, trial by jury, the abolition of slavery, and the representative system of government. Free trade, Cobden had hoped, and the peaceful interdependence of nations would one day be added to that noble array and find their expression in British administration. As for the contemporary problems of India, Mallet contended that Cobden would have urged a stern abstinence from any return to a policy of conquests and the loyal application of liberal economic and financial principles. The topic of India led Mallet on to the problem of foreign policy. Cobden, he explained, battled against the false conception of British power and wealth. Those were not derived from monopoly, colonial servitude, the maintenance of numerous armed services, and a 'spirited foreign policy', but from free trade, colonial self-government, and a policy of non-intervention. Some people in England were ready to admit Cobden's economic principles but refused to accept their political implications 'and indulge the illusion that England may yet secure the moral and material fruits of the Free Trade policy without renouncing the pursuit of an Empire of Force, in futile rivalry with nations the sources of whose military power must always be far greater than her own'. Mallet chose the expression 'Empire of Force' in order to distinguish, no doubt, between what he regarded as the evil concept of Empire and the desirable one, the Empire of free-trading, self-governing colonies. In an Empire of Force the financial burden imposed on the people would remain so heavy that the English workers could never hope to attain a decent standard of living. They would labour under the constant strain 'on the productive energies of the country required to enable it to play the part of a great military Empire for ever extending its dominion over alien races'. Such a policy could only lead to another page added to the dismal record of the fall of empires.[1] Mallet's restatement of Cobden's principles, therefore, was by no means a rejection of the British Empire as it began to be understood in the 1860's, but a fervent agitation in favour of an Empire which bore the stamp of Cobden's views. In substance Mallet's imperial hopes were not greatly different from those of the Colonial Reformers.

The travel-record written by a brilliant young Cambridge graduate made a lasting impact on the minds of political thinkers in England as well as on the Continent. Charles Dilke's trip round the English-speaking world in the years 1866–7 was presented as an interesting account of a global trip. As such it for the first time enabled the English reader at home and in the colonies to visualize the nature of the British Empire in all its variety and complexity, a thing which had been impossible before in an age when very few people travelled extensively in many directions, and communication was still slow outside Europe and America. In addition to his interesting travel account Dilke offered definite and new ideas, which had sprouted in the 1850's. He combined a fervent English nationalism with radical sentiments and incorporated Gobineau's idea of racial inequality along with Darwin's biological principle of natural selection. Surveying the English-speaking world in 1867, Dilke agreed with most thinking Englishmen of his time that the English Government in its relation with the colonies was faced with the alternatives of either drift or separation. To such a small degree was the maintenance of formal imperial ties with the colonies a national objective in Britain that the leading champion of British expansion in 1868 could extol its record and hail its future without insisting on a political connexion. He could bestow the name of 'Greater Britain' on the race which he had seen in the ascendant in many parts of the world, yet fervently advocate the emancipation of Canada and Australia.

Dilke made his readers conscious of the fact that Great Britain had extended round the world into a Greater Britain which was held together by the bonds of race, language, and law. Through Greater Britain England was speaking to the world and was absorbing other nations of the world, particularly in America. As Dilke walked through the American cities he observed racial characteristics and pondered over their racial future. He rejoiced at the thought of mighty America 'imposing English institutions on the world' and observed that 'the true moral of America is the vigour of the English race—the defeat of the cheaper by the dearer peoples, the victory of the man whose food costs four shillings a day over the man whose food costs four pence'. Dilke found a bitter racial struggle being waged in the English-speaking world. The struggle was caused, he believed, by the inferior races impeding the progress of the English people to universal dominion. He was confident that Saxondom would triumph. Nearly ten million square miles containing three hundred million people were ruled by the Anglo-Saxons. Those controlled a surface four and a half times as large as the Roman Empire at its greatest extent. They would prove more than a match for the remaining nations of the world. In conquest and colonization the Saxon would outstrip the Muscovite, his nearest rival.

Next to race, language and institutions formed the strongest binding forces of Greater Britain. English was the chief instrument in civilizing natives. It was the language of good government, of political and physical science and true learning. It was the tongue of the ruling race in India where the development of free institutions was the ultimate justification for British rule. As yet freedom existed only, according to Dilke, 'in the homes of the English race' in America, Australia, and in Britain. Eventually, Dilke hoped, other peoples like the Indians would accept and defend the free institutions and the rule of law which the British had taught them.[1]

As yet India, Ceylon, and Mauritius were incapable of independence. Dilke thought they would relapse into anarchy, if Britain withdrew. The maintenance of British rule in those dependencies, as Dilke called them, was beneficial to both. For Britain those countries constituted a nursery of statesmen and warriors. In the case of English colonies, i.e. countries settled by Anglo-Saxons, Dilke favoured ultimate separation. He did not believe that Britain could benefit from paying Canadian or Australian defence bills or that Australians and Canadians would be inclined to pay British bills in the future when Britain would have to defend Luxembourg or Serbia. The formal connexion between Britain and Canada did more harm than good, for it hampered good relations with the United States. Formal political ties did not matter in trade either. 'Common institutions, common freedom, and common tongue have evidently far more to do with trade than union has; and for purposes of commerce and civilization, America is a truer colony of Britain than is Canada.' In that way Dilke disposed of the idea of Empire as an organized system of political relations between Britain and the colonies. 'Mother of free nations' was in Dilke's eyes a prouder word than prestige and Empire. 'The strongest of the arguments in favour of separation is the somewhat paradoxical one that it would bring us a step nearer to the virtual confederation of the English race.[1]'

The book was bound to become popular. It combined a forceful, suggestive language with a strong appeal to the pride and values of the mid-Victorian Englishman. It opened up new vistas to an English world and new directions of progress. It purged the idea of separation from the spirit of resignation and instilled it with expansive vitality. The book, published in 1868, made its strong appeal in the name of the English race, not in the name of Empire. However, the notion of the Anglo-Saxon race, so eloquently proclaimed, is not free from ambiguity. In most cases the word 'civilization' could be substituted for race, since it is to laws and principles of government, to language and institutions that he refers. Yet the belief in the power of 'blood', which recalls Carlyle and Disraeli, is not missing; on occasion Dilke professes to prefer 'aiding our Teutonic brethren in their struggle for unity' to 'assisting Imperial France'. Small wonder that Dilke could still stir the imagination of Teutonic racialists in the twentieth century.

'Greater Britain', as distinct from Empire, seems to have undergone during the global trip a development of which the young author himself was not fully aware. His 'separatist' attitude towards the settlement colonies is so obviously influenced by the literary campaign of

Goldwin Smith that it must have been fixed in Dilke's mind before his global voyage. What he observes about the separation of Canada and the retention of Australia, on condition that she learn to look after her own needs, he could have stated without seeing those countries. His journey led to the experience of the great industrial power of the Anglo-Saxon 'race', a quality displayed in the economic exploitation of backward countries and quite unsentimentally applauded by the author. Another conviction gained by observation on the spot was that British dominion in India and in the 'dependencies' (i.e. colonies populated by backward races) was a lasting benefit to the dominated peoples and a noble task incumbent on the British people. The first of these beliefs resounds with that boisterous pride which was so much disparaged by the Radical tradition and by Goldwin Smith. The second, moreover, is tantamount to an acquiescence, not only in the existence of the Empire, but in its expansion by new annexations. We saw that Dilke's use of the word *Imperialism* had no reference to the British Empire. There was, nevertheless, an element in his work which foreshadowed the meaning of imperialism in later years—the belief in domination over alien races as an educational mission, and the acceptance of 'vastness' of Empire as a demand of 'the age'. Apart from this, and in spite of the highly individual character of the book, it may be thought typical of a change in the climate of opinion. It emerged after the debate on the structure and future of the Empire had gone on for some years. At the start of the debate account was taken of the precarious nature of imperial commitments which became first apparent in the Canadian problem. It led to the conviction that they were not only precarious, but precious, too, a view particularly stressed among organs of public opinion by the *Spectator*. However, in 1868 there was little evidence as yet that the unity and integrity of the British Empire was a cause which could count on many supporters. Dilke's marked separatist views were not singled out for criticism when the British press reviewed his book.[1]

The feeling that something ought to be done in order to propagate interest in the Empire made progress, indeed. In the same year in which Dilke's book was published, a preliminary meeting of men interested in colonial affairs was convened with a view to founding a colonial society.

The society was formally launched in March 1869. Its motto was to be 'United Empire'. Among its sponsors were members of Parliament of great renown, belonging to both parties. Associated with them were some lesser-known men who had the advantage of either having been born in a colony or knowing parts of the Empire from long experience. The office of president was accepted by Lord Bury, who only three years earlier had dwelt on the peaceful secession of Canada, but now severely denounced the doctrines of Goldwin Smith and expressed the hope that the Society would become instrumental in undoing their influence. Such a hope was not shared by other members such as Sir Frederic Rogers, who continued to believe in separation as the ultimate result of sound colonial policy. The inaugural dinner of the Society was honoured by the presence of the new Prime Minister, Gladstone, who —evidently under the strong impact of Dilke's ideas—laid stress on the unity of the British race, the unity of the Empire, which rested on the basis of freedom. Lord Granville, the Colonial Secretary, on that occasion referred to the Order of St Michael and St George as 'the gracious mark of the Sovereign's favour to those who have done real and great service to the Empire'. During the early debates on the purpose and nature of the colonial society, Mr Chichester Fortescue, who like Viscount Bury had moved away from the idea of separation, said that it was the function of a society like that to serve the integrity of the Empire.[1]

Dilke's review of the English-speaking world was followed by another review of the colonies and their recent achievements and fortunes by the author of the open letter addressed to Disraeli in 1861. In 1869 Adderley published a *Review of 'The Colonial Policy of Lord J. Russell's Administration' by Earl Grey and of Subsequent Colonial History*. The author had in the preceding years been under-secretary for the colonies in Derby's administration and helped to carry through the House of Commons the legal establishment of the Dominion of Canada. He wished to make a contribution to the theory of colonial government as well as to continue the description of the historical development in the colonies. Adderley disagreed with Grey about the nature of the colonial connexion. He opposed the view, prevalent in Grey's time, that paternal control exercised by the Colonial Office was an adequate form of government of English settlements. Such a state of affairs was incompatible with constitutional principles enjoyed by the English at home, fatal to the vigour and prosperity of the settlers, and exposing colonies to the party-struggles of the mother country. To deny English colonists the same measure of liberty as they enjoyed at home could only lead to another lamentable conflict as broke out in America in the eighteenth century. 'How powerful an empire our connexion with such fellow-subjects, free as ourselves, and only bound together by a common Head, might have produced, if we had not violated the conditions of success, and forced them to escape from us for their life as a separate nation, . . . we can only regretfully conjecture.' Holding up the American War of Independence as a warning example, Adderley developed his suggestions for an empire of self-governing dominions. Lord Grey demanded too much power for the metropolis, he explained. 'The unity of aggregate power, and consistency of general policy, which would result from a community of rights and co-operative sympathy throughout the Empire, which would make the living whole too large to attack, and too cosmopolitan to be aggressive, is lost by the assumption of such dictation from the centre, however sparingly resorted to, based, as it must be, on the abdication of citizenship by all the rest, and coupled with the vain undertaking from one small heart of empire to furnish men and money everywhere to maintain and defend the inert mass.' In that compact sentence of criticism, Adderley gave his readers an idea of his own view of empire. The Empire would be characterized by a combination of power so big as to deter would-be attackers. It would possess a consistent overall policy as a result of common rights and sentiments. The nature of that policy would be peace-loving because of the cosmopolitan outlook of the Empire. Local aggression would of necessity be restrained by the global interests of the other dominions. A common citizenship would guarantee identical rights and duties to all Empire citizens.[1]

Adderley's classical models were ancient Greece and Edmund Burke's view of Englishmen carrying their liberty with them into the colonies. He did not, therefore, include Crown Colonies settled by alien peoples and military stations in the same category. Racist evaluation had influenced his judgement, and he justified the continued denial of self-government to the Crown Colonies on grounds of military expedience and racial inferiority. Those colonies and dependencies, however, were not subject to the English people but their allegiance was to the Crown in common with the English people. The Crown was bound to give those colonies the best local government that could be devised and locally paid for.

The empire-consciousness of the writer led him to the anomaly of the connotation implied in the word *imperial*, which was so different from what he wanted *Empire* to mean and from what, in fact, it had already begun to mean. The former term was still being used in the sense where it could be equated with British and often in contradistinction to the adjective *local* when administrative matters were discussed. Adderley felt the use of *imperial* was symptomatic for the metropolitan outlook which he desired to replace by the concept of genuine partnership. 'But what, after all, is the meaning of the word "Imperial"? The phrase has come to be used convertibly with "English", as if everything in which the honour or interests of the metropolis of the Empire are concerned should be undertaken solely by the metropolis, free of cost to the rest of the Empire.'[1] It was a result of the wrong concept of *imperial* that England was expected to furnish both troops and money whenever the integrity of the Empire was threatened. The other extreme was separation, but between dependence and separation 'lies the real secret of a lasting connexion—that of common partnership'. Adderley's concept of Empire did not include new imperial institutions. He did not think an Imperial Parliament—Imperial in his sense—was possible. Lord Russell thought otherwise.

Introducing the publication of his speeches in 1869, he eloquently defended the view that the Crown should support and defend the colonies everywhere, but conceded that the cost of naval and military expenses should be shared. Such a sharing-out could only be carried out in an assembly in which the mother country as well as the dependencies were represented, and for that purpose Russell proposed a Congress or Assembly to sit in autumn and make the financial and military decisions of policy which the Empire demanded. To those who regarded such a scheme as impracticable Earl Russell replied that many other political innovations had at first looked impracticable, such as the Reform Act of 1832 and the repeal of the Corn Laws. Great changes were about to be made.

Amid these changes, there is no greater benefit to mankind, that a statesman can propose to himself, than the consolidation of the British Empire. In my eyes it would be a sad spectacle, it would be a spectacle for gods and men to weep at, to see this brilliant luminary cut up into spangles,—to behold Nova Scotia, the Cape of Good Hope, Jamaica and New Zealand, try each its little spasm of independence, while France, the United States, and Russia would be looking on, each and all willing to annex one or more of the broken fragments to the nearest portion of their dominions.

What made the British Empire greater and more beneficial to mankind than other Empires Russell had no doubt. It was what he called 'our free institutions'. His empire-sentiment had been kindled in the preceding years by the same factor which, undoubtedly, affected the thinking of other British minds. Aggregation of power and new empires could be observed looming largely all round the horizon. Italy, Germany, Russia, France, and, above all, the United States had been building up political, economic, and military power. Russell clearly foresaw a development of keen competition for new colonies and territorial expansion. He did not think Britain could abdicate her imperial part in history. 'There was a time when we might have stood alone as the United Kingdom of England, Scotland, and Ireland. That time has passed. We conquered and peopled Canada, we took possession of the whole of Australia, Van Diemen's Land and New Zealand. We have annexed India to the Crown. There is no going back.—

Tu regere imperio populos, Romane, memento.

For my part, I delight in observing the imitation of our free institutions, and even our habits and manners in Colonies, at a distance of 3,000 or 4,000 miles from the Palace of Westminster.'[1] The historian J. A. Froude voiced similar views in his Rectorial Address delivered at the University of St. Andrews in March 1869. Alluding to Dilke's *Greater Britain* he pointed out that narrow Britain had become the breeding place and nursery of a race that was spreading over the world and hoped many more young men would go out and people the new lands. 'Britain may have yet a future before it grander than its past; instead of a country standing alone, complete in itself, it may become the metropolis of an enormous and coherent empire.' Such a desirable turn of history depended on the condition that Britain's children would continue to look to their mother country with affection unlike the Irish who had gone to America. British boys should feel that there was a place for them in the world wherever the British flag was flying. They would be good Britons still in Canada and in New Zealand. Thus the American tragedy would be avoided, for Britain had sent to America her convicts and undesirables, who left our shores with a sense of burning wrong and bitterness. As a result 'we have raised up against us a mighty empire to be the rival, it may be the successful rival, of our power'.[1] There must have been a correlation between the military growth of rival empires and the increase in empire sentiment that speaks out of the many lines spoken and printed which we quoted as evidence for the new Empire feeling. In those years the ideas of Goldwin Smith lost ground. It was in this changing climate of opinion that the *Spectator* for the first time, it seems, could enunciate the term *Imperialism* in a new form, as we already noted in the first chapter.[2] The term did not catch on in the new sense in which it was used as expressing a consciousness of a duty to perform an often unpleasant military task in the defence of the integrity of the Empire. As late as 1878 Lord Carnarvon could say: 'Imperialism is a newly-coined word to me.' But the new interest in seeking ways of preserving and modernizing the Empire was clearly reflected in the new tone of political literature dealing with colonial problems as well as in a writer's ability to regard imperialism in a new light. The New Zealand crisis and Empire scare of the years 1869–70 went another step in the same direction and proved that such sentiments as were expressed by a growing number of writers and politicians had found a ready echo in the country.

The Gladstone Ministry inherited from their predecessors the unpleasant task of winding up the Maori Wars in New Zealand. Neither the British Liberals nor the Conservatives liked the policy adopted by the Colony towards the Maoris, because as a result military support from the mother country was called for. Organized resistance was no longer encountered. The British Government had prevailed on the colonists to reduce claims to native lands and to provide the Maoris with judicial and constitutional safeguards. What remained was to extricate the British Government from further responsibility and to leave the final settlement to the New Zealanders themselves. In accordance with the general resolution of the House of Commons of 1862 the British garrison was to be withdrawn. The Duke of Buckingham, Colonial Secretary in Disraeli's administration, had insisted on that measure all the more strictly, because the costs of the Maori War incurred by the British Exchequer could not be recovered. The Earl of Granville, Colonial Secretary to Gladstone, could not but maintain the same demand for the withdrawal of British forces, but he encountered a new financial request. The New Zealand Government professed to be unable to provide for defence against the Maoris, unless the British Government granted a loan of one and a half million pounds. In a despatch which left the office only a few days after he and Gladstone had welcomed the Colonial Society, Granville declined the request. His refusal was adorned with sharp recriminations. In its short history, it alleged, the colony had unceasingly brought embarrassment, moral as well as material, upon the mother country. New Zealand was not entitled to ask anything from Britain; on the contrary, there was substantial reason for 'a very heavy claim, if we thought proper to urge it, on the part of the mother country against the colony'. Most probably this rigid lecture flowed from the pen of Sir Frederic Rogers, whose exasperation after ten years of epistolary quarrels with New Zealand is easily understood. But Lord Granville signed it, so the responsibility for the despatch devolved upon the Cabinet.[1]

Whatever the dismay wrought upon the recipients of the note, it was nothing in comparison with the repercussion it had in England when it became known there in early summer 1869. Sir George Grey, the guardian of the young dominion, joined with some New Zealanders in a letter to *The Times* declaring: '. . . that the policy which is being pursued towards New Zealand would have the effect of alienating the affections of His Majesty's loyal subjects in that country, and was calculated to drive the colony out of the Empire.' This alarm-cry started a movement of protest which engendered pronunciamentos of different kinds almost incessantly for about a year. The *Spectator* was the first to give the indictment a wider scope. In its issue of 24 July, the paper asserted that the harsh handling of New Zealand by English officials reflected contempt and insolence. New Zealand was treated in the same despicable way as the Thirteen Colonies were once treated, in a spirit 'which converts them rapidly into bitter opponents of the Imperial connection'. The *Spectator* maintained that it was all part of a consistent policy which extended to other colonies as well. The Government was completely converted to the principles of Goldwin Smith.

It is not only New Zealand which is to be dismissed, but Australia, not only Australia, but the Canadian Dominion, all that ring of Anglo-Saxon States which . . . might be converted into a chain of faithful and most powerful allies. With the exception of India, Ceylon, the Mauritius, and the costly Crown colonies retained as military stations, the Empire is to be surrendered as a burden too heavy to be borne.[1]

A horrifying spectre appeared. The Empire was in danger. It was being broken up by narrow-minded, haughty officials of the Colonial Office.

The opinions brought out in the ensuing press campaign were not arrayed according to party lines. With the radical *Spectator*, which returned to the subject indefatigably, there sided such a conservative paper as the *Standard*, while *The Times* gave unqualified editorial support to Lord Granville and even deemed it appropriate to mention the possibility of peaceful separation and the beneficent effects which might result from it. Such was its comment upon a move taken in August by some members of the Colonial Society. These, in order to check the alleged destructive policy of the Government, issued a circular inviting the colonies to agree to a conference of representatives, which was to be held in London the following February. Pending the reaction of the colonies to the circular, a series of discussions was arranged by the sponsors of the move. In September the National Association for the Promotion of Social Science, meeting at Bristol, had on its agenda 'the legal and constitutional relations between England and the colonies'. The President, Sir Stafford Northcote, delivered the opening address. His speech reflected the feeling that a crucial point had been reached in the relationship between the mother country and her colonies and that the country was faced with the choice between separation and Empire.

One school among us, animated by much the same narrow spirit as that which dictated the old Colonial restrictive system, considers that in the interests of the mother country we ought now to cast off our Colonies, as useless, costly, and embarrassing to keep. Another school considers that, although the Colonies ought not to be retained against their will, and ought, if they desire to remain connected with us, to contribute a fair share of the expense of their own defence, it is as yet for the general advantage of the whole empire that it should remain entire.[1]

The strongest Empire sentiment was expressed by the Australian F. P. Labilliere, who claimed to speak for the other Australians as well when he maintained that no good colonist or Englishman should ever contemplate the breaking up of the Empire. 'The union of the empire is a sentiment, or rather a sacred principle, in devoted loyalty to which we should all vie with one another.' The advantages of the mutual bond were numerous in peace and war, Labilliere argued. The self-governing colonies would come to the aid of the mother country in times of war. There was greater strength in union. There would be fewer wars in the world, 'if the integrity of the British Empire is preserved'. God had conferred upon the British Isles an unparalleled destiny. English language, literature, ideas, trade, laws, institutions, and liberties had spread round the globe and borne fruit in different soils and climates. The future promised an even more glorious empire than the one existing in the present.[2]

From the end of November a campaign of weekly meetings was conducted at the Cannon Street Hotel in London which went on until the beginning of the New Year. Some resolutions were passed which emphasized the value of the colonies to the mother country and of the Imperial connexion to the colonies. Displeasure was expressed about Lord Granville's despatches. At the same time agitation was rife for a petition to the Queen requesting governmental promotion of emigration to the colonies. That movement was not related to the New Zealand affair; but both agitations were headed by the same men, and the petitioners did not fail to point to 'the prosperity of the whole Empire'. State-aided emigration to the colonies had once been a favourite topic of Thomas Carlyle. He now remained silent but his place was taken by two other prominent authors—John Ruskin and James Anthony

Froude. Ruskin, the new Professor of Fine Art at Oxford, went out of his way in his inaugural lecture to join forces with the other Empire-minded men of letters who expressed and deliberately disseminated Empire sentiment. So Ruskin spoke in appealing terms of England's destiny, of her pure race 'mingled of the best northern blood' and told his students that they ought to make their 'country again a royal throne of kings, a sceptred isle, for all the world a source of light, a centre of peace' by becoming colonists, by founding colonies as fast and far as possible. England ought to teach her colonists that their chief virtue was fidelity to their country and their first aim to advance the power of England by land and sea.[1] In January 1870 Froude started a series of articles in *Fraser's Magazine*, all of them fulminating against the materialist spirit of the Manchester School, which prevailed in England, and against its alleged lack of interest in the colonies. The awkward consequence of that short-sightedness was, he pointed out, that the bulk of emigrants turned to the United States, were lost to England, and strengthened her 'greatest rival' . England was becoming a country of bankers, merchants, manufacturers, and workmen, the latter living in unhealthy conditions, which could not but demoralize them and destroy the mettle of the nation. The only remedy was the preservation of a vigorous peasant population, a return to the land in the form of state-aided emigration to the colonies. Froude appealed to Disraeli and the Conservative Party to take up the cause of colonization on a large scale. Finally, Froude argued in favour of a united and expanding empire on the basis of power. The political future, he thought, belonged to powers with wider territories than those of Western Europe. Unless Britain desired to sink to the position of Holland, yielding her place to others, she must plant many more English homes on other continents, she must make it clear that an Englishman emigrating to Canada or Australia was still on English soil as much as if he was still in Yorkshire or Devonshire 'and would remain an Englishman while the English empire lasted'. Two million Britons, settled in the colonies, would contribute more to British power than all the wars Britain had to fight. Fresh nations of Englishmen would spring up, self-supporting and unconquerable. 'With our roots thus struck so deeply into the earth, it is hard to see what dangers, internal or external, we should have cause to fear, or what impediments could then check the indefinite and magnificent expansion of the English Empire.'[1]

From the tribune of the press and public opinion the matter passed on to that of Parliament. In the House of Lords the answer to the Queen's speech was made an occasion for a protest by the Earl of Carnarvon, the expert on colonial affairs among the Conservatives. On 14 February he expressed the deepest distrust of the intentions of the Government and challenged the administration bluntly to state whether they were about to 'dismember the Empire' or not. Finally, he voiced his 'humble and earnest protest against a course which I conceive to be ruinous to the honour and fatal to the best interests of the empire'.[2] Granville's reply did little to alleviate Carnarvon's suspicion. He stated, indeed, that a policy of separation would at present not meet with general consent, but laid even more stress on the necessity not to attempt the retention of an unwilling colony by force. Anxiety spread to Government benches. On 26 April the Liberal R. R. Torrens moved the appointment of a Select Committee on colonial policy. Such a motion was an innovation. Before that session of 1870 relations with the colonies in general, apart from specific questions, had not been a topic for debate on the parliamentary agenda. Torrens desired an inquiry into the political relations between the self-governing colonies and Britain 'with a view to the maintenance of common nationality'. He also wanted an investigation of the modes of communication between the colonies and Britain, because some channels of communication were patently defective, and those unsatisfactory conditions were exploited by 'men of great ability to propagate opinions adverse to the integrity of the Empire'. Torrens then attacked the ideas of Goldwin Smith and defended the Empire on grounds of the growing overpopulation of Great Britain and Ireland, the vital need for the command of the seas, the attachment of the colonies, and the obligation to defend them against attack. Other members in the course of the debate pronounced the Colonial Office unfit to conduct 'the affairs of a great Empire'. Viscount Sandon added another reason why the idea of separation of the colonies had to be opposed. The historical trend was in the opposite direction everywhere. Italy, Germany, and the races in the North endeavoured to group themselves into larger states. 'Why should we, at such a moment, in obedience to the opinions of any set of men, however enlightened, crumble up that great Empire which Providence had placed in our hands?'[1]

The motion of Torrens gave an opportunity to Gladstone to define his attitude to the colonies in more specific terms. He strongly denied that there was any new policy afoot. The Government was loyal to that policy which had been followed for some decades, and their only guiding maxim was 'the successive development and application of admitted principles to one colony after another, according as circumstances allow and invite the application'. In his explanation of what those principles were Gladstone went remarkably far in the direction abhorred by the new champions of the Imperial connexion. Torrens had asserted that the official policy was now passing from the period of Responsible Government into a new one, 'in which separation is openly avowed as the rule of policy'. Gladstone claimed that it had always been the essence of Responsible Government to secure a peaceful separation, 'if it should occur', and it had been the 'secret of our policy with regard to colonial reform'. He gave that interpretation a rather cumbrous historical introduction to prove his point that the development of Transatlantic possessions had 'in obedience to laws stronger than the will of man' made separation inevitable. Unhappily separation had always been brought about by war and bloodshed, but Britain had learnt the lesson that violent separation was the reaction to and result of a policy of restraint.

The discourse goes a long way to show the difference of emotional approach to Empire matters, which held and was to hold Gladstone apart from those who were in search of a new inspiration. Maybe it shows, too, that he gave sympathetic attention to those who advised a policy of preparing the ground for peaceful separation. But the effect upon him of their doctrine must not be judged by his readiness to accept some of their arguments. Acquiescence in the prospect of dismemberment was neither the last word of Gladstone on the Imperial connexion nor his answer to the New Zealand problem. In both respects he spoke his mind only after having finished his historical retrospect. He declared that the policy followed so far 'while securing the greatest likelihood of a perfect, peaceable separation, whenever separation may arrive, gives the best chance of an indefinitely long continuance of a free and voluntary connexion'. This remark, though unduly cursory, proved him to have remained the true disciple of the Colonial Reformers and was in keeping with his address at the Colonial Society dinner in the previous year. He then turned to the root of the trouble, the New Zealand question, dealing with it by general allusions to 'pecuniary matters' and 'colonial defence' and sermonizing with truly Gladstonian high-mindedness. The Government had behaved faultlessly in dealing with that question. They were neither ready to sacrifice the interests of the tax-payer nor for the sake of economy prepared to abandon honour and duty, but the real issue was not the pecuniary burden. It was the 'evil done ... to the colonies themselves'. Here the Prime Minister touched upon a point which he had found objectionable in traditional policy. Britain had failed to teach her colonies to rely upon themselves but led them to rely on the belief that 'come what would, they would be defended by a power thousands of miles away'. Such a policy was mistaken. 'Unless men are taught to rely upon themselves, they can never be truly worthy of the name of free-men.'

This was a veracious statement, no doubt. Quarrelling with the New Zealanders, refusing the defence loan, and maintaining this refusal in the face of newspaper criticism and protest meetings, showing provocative composure towards the angry incriminations of the new paladins of Empire unity—all this had been done by Gladstone only for one reason, only for giving better effect to the morals of Responsible Government. He did not wish to become a bad educator by giving in to the demand of a spoiled child. But while making this avowal after a year of resistance, he was already prepared to relax his rigid morality and content himself with a gentle compromise. After a few weeks a loan to the New Zealand Government, although on a reduced scale, was granted by the Government and eloquently welcomed by the recipients. The conflict, which had been immediately responsible for the Empire scare, was thereby settled. Soon afterwards Lord Granville, whose unmistakable detachment had not a little contributed to the fury of the Empire champions, exchanged the Colonial for the Foreign Office and was replaced by Lord Kimberley. Of the topics brought up by the heated debates one at least remained a matter for further discussion—closer union.

Side by side with *Fraser's Magazine* and the Colonial Society the radical reformer, Edward Jenkins, embarked on a fierce Empire agitation. In 1871 in two articles, published in the *Contemporary Review*, he introduced the watchword of 'Imperial Confederation'. The debate opened by him was to continue for many decades and may be considered still in progress today. While the cause of Empire was now leading to the problem of imperial federation, speculation about separation died out; it was kept in mind as a portent of the past. In the years 1871–2 angry refutation of separation and of the countenance allegedly given to it by the Gladstone Ministry was expressed by Froude, by Tennyson in his Epilogue to the *Idylls of the King*, and also by Disraeli in his Crystal Palace Speech. Up to then Disraeli had withheld the expression of any opinion on that subject.

Taking a comprehensive view of the Empire debates of the years 1869–71 one can hardly fail to notice a manifold disproportion between causes and effects, sentimental vision and reality. The critics not only misunderstood the Government; they were not in accord with Colonial opinion either and not entitled to speak in the name of the colonists overseas. The *Spectator* maintained that, had the request for peaceable separation really come, the ministry would have been doomed. But there were no signs of such a request on the part of the colonies. The case against the Government was not greatly advanced by dramatization such as Disraeli attempted in his Crystal Palace Speech. 'What has been', he asked, 'the result of this attempt during the reign of Liberalism for the disintegration of the Empire? It has entirely failed. But how has it failed? Through the sympathy of the Colonies for the Mother Country. They have decided that the Empire shall not be destroyed.'[1] That was to fabricate a legend; the rescue of the Empire attributed to the colonies was as fictitious as the sinister plans imputed to the Government. It was misleading, first of all, to speak of 'the colonies' as a co-operating political group. The sister-colonies had not even interceded for New Zealand in her struggle with the Colonial Office. The authors of the circular of August 1869 who tried to mobilize colonial action and opinion earned rebuff from all quarters. In Australia they received a particularly rough handling. The Legislative Assembly of New South Wales called them 'presumptuous busybodies', while the Council of

Queensland expressed their dissatisfaction with the mischievous interference 'of those self-constituted Colonial Societies and other pretended representatives of the Colonies in England'.[1]

As a matter of fact, the Australasian Colonies strove for more independence just when the men who stood up for them in England asked for greater unity. To the great annoyance of Gladstone and Kimberley they wanted to raise preferential duties in order to overcome the fiscal quarrels which were dragging on among themselves. An Inter-Colonial conference convened in Melbourne in 1871 accepted a resolution, formulated by the Prime Minister of Victoria, to the effect that 'Imperial interference with inter-colonial fiscal legislation should finally and absolutely cease'. Julius Vogel, treasurer of New Zealand, mentioned some time later, it is true, 'imperial federation in some form' as a possible alternative to 'full fiscal independence as regards tariffs'; but it was clear that 'federation in some form' implied a system of tariff protection for the whole Empire, a step that was not acceptable to the British electorate. When Disraeli's Crystal Palace Speech became known in New Zealand, Vogel availed himself of this plea for Imperial consolidation only to press still more urgently the demand for fiscal independence of his country. During the dispute it fell to Gladstone to defend the existing conditions of Empire unity against the wish of the colonies to have their own way. Kimberley, who was more prepared to be lenient from the beginning, became afraid in the end that the colonies might seriously consider steps leading to the dissolution of the Empire, unless fiscal independence was conceded. He prevailed over his reluctant chief; and in 1873 Parliament had to pass the 'Australian Colonies Duties Act', which endowed the countries of that continent with 'power to make commercial arrangements among themselves in favour of their own produce'. Again, the Australian Customs Bill of 1873 stimulated debate inside and outside Parliament about the nature of imperial union.

When this Act was passed, the closer union of the Empire had been a topic of debate in England for more than two years. The campaign for the unity of the Empire, however, was by no means an imperial campaign, in which the colonies had taken a leading part; the assent, shrewdly given to it by Julius Vogel, was only an exception. One might wonder, indeed, whether the advocates of imperial unity in Britain did not notice the listlessness of their clients in the colonies. It is this lack of a sense of realism that helps us to understand the fundamentally emotional character of the whole Empire movement. Those people who declared the Empire to be in danger, and afterwards to be in need of closer integration, might have misread the historical and actual conditions. They acted not on the basis of factual information and survey but under the impulse of a deep sentiment which nourished an idea and a strong desire to translate that idea into reality. We saw that the sentiment and the idea of Empire had been gaining ground and a more definite meaning in England from the second half of the 1860's. We noted the admiration for the possibilities of 'so vast an Empire as our own' flashing through the mind of young Charles Dilke; we saw the *Spectator* asking for 'Imperialism in its best sense', the Colonial Society choosing 'United Empire' as its motto, and Froude's vision of Britain as the metropolis of an enormous Empire. For him and for others the New Zealand affair served to strengthen an attachment to the Empire as a cherished national symbol. Warm and eloquent expressions of devotion towards it played a prominent part in the manifestos of Government critics. 'What have you done with the British Empire?' the *Spectator* asked the Government in July 1869 and added it did not dare to decide how far the lassitude that paralysed public men 'may be spreading among the electors, how far the spirit of imperialism has died out of Englishmen'. Here the two words Empire and Imperialism were joined to each other in veneration.[1] It was a style still peculiar to the *Spectator*, but the term 'Empire' had attained unmatched dignity by then and the attribute 'Imperial' occasionally shared it. 'Sentiment', 'sacred principle', that was what Labilliere of the Colonial Society had called the newly discovered symbol. 'Dissolving the Empire', 'dismembering the Empire'—those were the common reproaches launched against the Government. Some years earlier such phrases would not necessarily have implied a reproach; now it was like speaking of Atreus or Medea. The longer the debate went on, the more splendid the concept appeared. There rose the vision of an Empire, settled by self-governing Britons, united by the common bond of race, language, trade, and political institutions. 'Let the Canadian Dominion, let

Australia, the Cape, and New Zealand be occupied by subjects of the British Crown—be consolidated by a common cord of patriotism, equal members all of them of a splendid Empire', Froude wrote in the last of his articles of 1870/1, which we already mentioned earlier. At the same time Edward Jenkins in his project of 'Imperial Confederation' introduced his plan with the high-sounding assertion: 'The Briton, who ... encloses in one view the magnificent cordon of Empire, that British might and prowess have drawn about the globe,' might soon begin to realize the significance of his imperial destiny.[1]

> Is this the tone of Empire? here the faith
> That made us rulers?. . .

Tennyson indignantly asked those who told the Canadians, 'your love is but a burden' adding:

> The loyal to their crown
> Are loyal to their own far sons, who love
> Our ocean-empire with her boundless homes
> For ever-broadening England. . . .[2]

Such language would have been denounced as inordinately boastful a few years earlier. The new Credo of Empire was proclaimed, like all credos in the initial stage, by a small group of intellectuals and former colonials, dubbed 'busybodies' in Australia, not by the representatives of the great social interests and only to a smaller extent by party leaders. But those sentiments were capable of gaining ground and winning wider popular appeal. That was the belief of Benjamin Disraeli, the leader of the opposition, a man who excelled in the vigilance of public opinion. He, who for some decades had shown little attachment to the name of the British Empire and still less to the colonies, now stood up for them and made them the key-notes of his great speeches of 1872.

V

THE SIGNIFICANCE OF DISRAELI'S IMPACT—
LEGEND AND REALITY

In 1872 Empire had become the symbol of two political aspirations—
a desire to strengthen the bonds between the self-governing British
settlements and the mother country and a belief in the providential
destiny of the English race to bring civilization to backward peoples
outside Europe. It was very difficult, however, for most Englishmen at
home to visualize the Empire as a single field of activity opening
a future for the nation as a whole, politically and economically. Pictorial
images of Sydney, Cape Town, Wellington, as the normal mental
equipment of every English child were still unknown. Travel was
expensive and slow, usually in one way only. It was, therefore, natural
that the British Overseas Empire should be associated with strong
emotion rather than with clear pictures in the minds of Englishmen.
Disraeli had no personal experience of colonial life. He had a personal
affection for the words *Empire* and *Imperium*, which repeatedly appeared
in the political manifestos of his literary career and in his political
speeches. They were expressive of his interest in national prestige but
had originally no direct reference to the British Overseas Empire.
Disraeli had no particular affection for or interest in the colonial
Empire. In 1872 he remembered and exploited the intensity of emotion,
which the name Empire had aroused in the preceding years, in order
to advance the interests of the Conservative Party as the leader of the
opposition. He made two elaborate appeals to the country at Conservative dinners—the first in Manchester on 3 April, the second at the
Crystal Palace, London, on 24 June. A special feature of the speeches
was the speaker's new and unexpected concern for the honour and
strength of the British Empire. In solemn declarations Disraeli vowed his
heart publicly to that noble entity.

The Manchester speech, though less celebrated than the Crystal
Palace speech, was more characteristic of the speaker's personality. It

was at the same time a foreboding of a new meaning implied in the word *Imperial*. It was used in connexion with foreign affairs and policy, as Disraeli warned his audience of the need for taking foreign affairs more seriously than Englishmen were inclined to do. He exemplified this admonition by the defeats of the Government in the issue of the Black Sea and the Alabama arbitration. He denied favouring an aggressive policy but pointed to the change the relations of England to Europe had undergone. He attributed the change to the vastness of the overseas countries, dominated by the English Crown. Those and other 'novel elements in the distribution of power' could not but affect the policy of England with respect to Europe, a policy which, Disraeli thought, should be characterized by 'proud reserve'. From those not very substantial explanations he proceeded to a pompous conclusion:

it is not merely our fleets and armies, our powerful artillery, our accumulated capital, and our unlimited credit on which I so much depend, as upon that unbroken spirit of her people, which, I believe, was never prouder of the Imperial country to which they belong. . . . I now deliver to you, as my last words, the cause of the Tory Party, the English Constitution, and of the Tory Empire.[1]

The desire to glory in the name of Empire and to sound it boisterously proves that Disraeli had been influenced by the earlier debates on the colonial Empire. He, however, shifted the ground from colonial to foreign policy, but felt that he and his Party were obliged to show themselves responsive to the Empire interest of those who professed concern for the maintenance and the unity of the colonial Empire. In the Crystal Palace speech he made that subject which he had shunned so far one of the main topics of his peroration.

The closing sentences of the first part of this address, which dealt with 'the maintenance of English institutions', echoed the language of his Manchester speech. He renewed his old maxim of the fundamental harmony existing between the working class and the conservative elements present in the state; but he thought it appropriate to clothe his conviction in the new 'imperial' phraseology. 'The working class of England . . . are for maintaining the greatness of the kingdom and the empire, and they are proud of being subjects of our Sovereign and members of such an Empire.' He then passed on to the 'second great object of the Tory party . . . to uphold the Empire of England'. He launched the heavy indictment against Liberalism that it had deliberately and continuously aimed at the disintegration of that Empire. That had been the endeavour of Liberal statesmen and writers. They had even gone the length of persuading the nation to abandon India, which they depicted as an 'incubus', despite the fact that India had been shown 'with precise, with mathematical demonstration' to be the most costly jewel in the Crown of England. The plausible plea of the need for self-government had been used by those liberal politicians as a device to further the project of Empire dismemberment. At that point Disraeli admitted to have been misled, too, but was not prepared to enlarge on recantation. Self-government, he declared, was a natural form of administration which could not be denied to 'our distant colonies'. The sin of omission of which the Liberals had been guilty was that colonial self-government had been granted without constituting a 'part of a great policy of Imperial consolidation'. Disraeli then listed four points on which such a consolidation ought to have been based—an imperial tariff, imperial trusteeship, imperial defence, and a form of common imperial consultation on a representative basis. Those four essential pillars of imperial strength had been omitted because disintegration and not unity had been the imperial policy of the past. It was a policy which was selfish 'viewing everything in a financial aspect and totally passing by those moral and political considerations which made nations great, and by the influence of which alone men are distinguished from animals'. The destructive attempt of Liberalism, Disraeli said in conclusion, had failed only because of a factor brought from outside. That factor had been the sympathy of the colonies for the mother country. 'They have decided that the Empire shall not be destroyed, and in my opinion no Minister in this country will do his duty who neglects any opportunity of reconstructing as much as possible our colonial Empire, and of responding to those distant sympathies. . . . '[1]

The Crystal Palace speech has often been represented as a really creative and prophetic act of Disraeli, which gave the idea of the British Empire a new standing and direction. This renown is utterly unjustified. The speech was in the main—what most interpreters forget—a criticism in retrospect, not a programme or statement of policy. That the undeserved fame could have arisen at all is to be attributed to the sensational stir which Disraeli's oratory produced on this occasion as on others and to a certain similitude which links his ideas about imperial consolidation to the intentions of Joseph Chamberlain's plans thirty years later. The ideas were in no way original. They had been discussed by the political philosopher of the Age, John Stuart Mill, in the closing chapter of his book on Representative Government. They had become a prominent topic for debate, as we have seen, in the years of the Empire scare, 1869-70. By pretending to an almost visionary conception of what the Empire could be when he simply repeated opinions discussed before on many occasions, Disraeli indulged in demagogic self-advertisement. His denunciation of the Liberal colonial policy and its idea of Responsible Government has as little historical truth in it as his depiction of the Whigs in *Coningsby* or of the intrigues of the Catholic Church in *Lothair*. The inclination of the political novelist to read a plot into the intentions of people he finds obliged to oppose seems to have confused the memory of the party leader and clouded his judgement. There is, indeed, some truth in his assertion, as was in the indictments of Carnarvon and Froude two years before, that spokesmen of Liberalism betrayed a narrow and jejune economy in their attitude towards the colonies but Disraeli's interpretation of the motives which induced the Liberals to grant self-government to the colonies was unwarranted. Liberal papers were entitled to reply, as they did after the Crystal Palace speech, that Liberalism, had, in fact, preserved the Empire.[1]

The historian is naturally and legitimately inclined to ask for continuity in the intentions and ideas of a statesman. But an attempt to antedate the 'imperialism' of Disraeli and to understand his pertinent utterances made from 1872 onwards as the outgrowth of life-long convictions would be futile. The excellency of race was to him—as the perorations of Sidonia in *Tancred* show—manifested above all in the soundness of social life. It is in this connexion, too, that in 1851 he proclaimed the maxim of 'imperium et libertas' when he discussed agricultural distress and praised 'the land of England—the land to which we owe so much of our power and of our freedom'.[2] The only element in Disraeli's advocacy of the British Empire which was really of old standing was his belief in the importance of the Indian Empire. But this conviction was for him no more than for any of his contemporaries in need of an 'imperial ideology'. Indeed, he would have been at a loss, if he had been challenged to explain why he had failed to disclose the alleged Liberal conspiracy against the Empire at an earlier date. Finally, Disraeli was entirely wrong, if he thought that his ideas about Empire consolidation were shared by the colonies as an adequate political translation of 'the sympathies of the colonies for the mother country'. The judgement passed on his views in this respect thirty-five years later by the Prime Minister of Canada at the Imperial Conference 'that any such policy would have had the most unfortunate and, more than that, disastrous results' reflected the real situation.[1]

The speech ended with an exhortation which, forgetting the colonies, concentrated on the emotional aspect of the name Empire. The nation, Disraeli proclaimed, would soon have to decide between national and cosmopolitan principles, between 'a comfortable England' and 'a great country, an imperial country, a country, where your sons, when they rise, rise to paramount positions, and obtain not merely the esteem of their countrymen, but command the respect of the world'. It was that tirade, and not so much the retrospective colonial programme that preceded it, which gave the speech an important place in the emergence of the concept of Imperialism. In its time, however, the whole section of the speech which dealt with the Empire fell flat in its effect on public opinion in England. It met with almost no response in the press. Disraeli drew the consequences and never returned to the subject of the colonial Empire again. He made no use of it in the election campaign of 1874 and had buried the memory of his ineffective recriminations when he took over the Government in 1874. It is quite mistaken to believe that the Crystal Palace speech inaugurated an ideological link between Empire championship and Conservatism. This view would be justified only, if the address had been the starting point for a new consistent policy of the Conservative Party in the colonial field. Such a significance, however, cannot be attributed to it. A distinctive conservative attitude to Empire questions was scarcely in evidence before the second Salisbury administration.

Disraeli did not intend to give colonial matters a prominent place in the work of his Cabinet. He entrusted the care of the colonies to the Earl of Carnarvon, who in 1870 had made a warm-hearted speech in favour of the unity of the Empire and who could be assumed to have his own ideas about imperial policy. The Premier, however, did not choose him, to be sure, with an active colonial policy in mind. The reason for Carnarvon's appointment to the Colonial Office was rather that he was regarded as the Conservative expert on colonial affairs which could be left to him, while the Prime Minister and the Cabinet dealt with more important matters of national policy.

Carnarvon's activities in the Colonial Office displayed his high-minded impulsiveness and the fervour of his belief in the moral excellence of Empire institutions and the maintenance of a strong Imperial tie. Whenever a widening of the Imperial domain could be trusted to serve those ends, he did not wince at the new responsibilities incurred. In the Far East questions of enlargement of British suzerainty had long been ripe for a decision. The annexation of the Fiji Islands had been advocated by the Australasian Colonies and was now eagerly desired by the local chieftains themselves. Gladstone had declined to take any steps; Carnarvon was by nature more inclined towards the request, and on his recommendation the islands were annexed in October 1874. The debates which preceded the formal act of annexation gave rise to solemn Empire sentiment in the Commons and references to Disraeli's Crystal Palace speech. The measure was defended on the grounds that it 'was in harmony with those glorious traditions of the empire which had encircled the globe with free communities of Englishmen', that the slave trade would be crushed and the maintenance and ascendancy of British maritime power in the Pacific made secure. Mr Lowther, Under-Secretary of State for the Colonies, affirmed that the colonizing mission of Great Britain had not yet come to a close. Colonies were a source of strength in war times. A hostile power would not only have to reckon with the thirty-odd millions of the British Isles 'but with many other millions of the Anglo-Saxon race who looked at the mother country with feelings of veneration and regard and were by no means indisposed to accept ... duties ... as members of a great colonial empire'.[1] The Queen's opening speech in February 1875 stressed the prosperity of her Colonial Empire and reported the changed status of the

Fiji Islands.[1] It is, therefore, true to say that, despite Disraeli's lack of interest in the colonial Empire, the echo of his speeches of 1872 lingered in the minds of some of his supporters who believed his Government to be favourable to an expansive interpretation of the cause of Empire. Carnarvon, however, was more hesitant with respect to an extension of British rule in the Malay Peninsula, which the Governor of the Strait Settlements advocated. He gave his assent only after such a step was proved feasible by successful military activities.

The absence of an active policy in Disraeli's mind where the Colonial Empire, apart from India, was concerned could be seen in South Africa. Carnarvon's great objective there was to bring about a federation of the British colonies with the Boer Republics. This plan could not be denounced as being dictated by a desire for imperial supremacy for its own sake. The unending rivalry of small and partly impecunious states and territories was harmful to the whole region. A unified authority was desirable to deal with the dangerous native problem, to pass on more of the financial and military burden of frontier defence to the colonists, and to secure British control of the east coast, which guarded sea routes to India. Already Carnarvon's Whig predecessor, Lord Kimberley, had desired to establish a form of union, and the establishment of responsible government in the Cape Colony in 1872 had been intended as a first step in that direction. Carnarvon chose Froude to be his representative at the conference in Capetown in 1875 where the problem of federation was to be discussed, though Froude had brought home from his first journey to South Africa the year before an unqualified pro-Boer bias. The situation, however, was such as to discourage any hope for a speedy agreement. The Cape Colony demanded pride of place in any union; the Transvaal was averse to any British paramountcy. Its President, Burgers, hoped to escape it by making a deal with the Portuguese neighbour. The two governments agreed on a closer link and tried jointly to float a loan for the purpose of building a railway line connecting the Transvaal with Delagoa Bay. The project failed. Carnarvon realized that South African union would not be reached without outside intervention. Union had become a necessity, and the Transvaal appeared to him to be the most appropriate region to bring about confederation. In September 1876 he wrote to the Prime

Minister: 'The progress of events in South Africa seems to bring a possible annexation of the Transvaal Republic and the consequent confederation of the various colonies and states within sight.'[1] Such a project of annexation as a first step towards confederation could have appealed to a person who had the expansion of the colonial Empire in mind. Would Disraeli—now already Lord Beaconsfield—take the risk? Here he was seriously confronted with the progress of that Colonial Empire for which he had professed such a deep concern in the Crystal Palace speech. What was his answer about South Africa? He had no answer. He postponed a decision until the following spring and then answered: 'I have not any other course to take.' This is hardly the language of one who has worked out a clear plan of colonial policy. It rather sounded like the sigh of one who feels unable to form a clear opinion. How much South Africa had remained *terra incognita* to him was brought out to the full one year later, when he had fallen out with Carnarvon over Russia and Turkey, when at the same time a Kaffir War had brought new troubles to the Cape Colony. Disraeli then expressed his indignation against his former Colonial Secretary in private and pointed out what in his opinion had been Carnarvon's essential blunder. He 'lived mainly in a coterie of editors of Liberal papers, . . . sending Mr. Froude . . . to reform the Cape, which ended naturally in a Kaffir War . . . '.[2] That was what he had understood to be the South African problem.

In those years Disraeli's interest was absorbed by the crisis in the Near East and Europe. He neither cared nor was he free for the problems of the colonial Empire. His eyes were directed to the East. In the 1860's and the beginning 1870's there was a general belief that the rival to British power was the United States in the West. In Disraeli's time the fear that British power might be challenged was nourished by developments in Europe and the Near East. France, Germany, Russia, and Turkey occupied the minds of English statesmen and political thinkers. Empire thought filled with new content, more closely linked with problems of British foreign policy. Disraeli's preference for the Indian possession here gave a certain lead and direction. The Royal Speech of February 1875 mentioned not only the Colonial Empire but also 'the Provinces of my Eastern Empire'. The purchase of the Suez Canal shares in the same year naturally directed more eyes towards that 'Eastern Empire'.

The British move to the Suez Canal was given a dramatic and sensational flavour by the Prime Minister, while it was belittled by Lord Derby, who feared that a noisy celebration of the acquisition might antagonize France and rouse the suspicion of other powers. The Queen's speech in 1876 briefly and soberly referred merely to a transaction in the public interest, while she privately, like many of her subjects, hailed the purchase as a demonstration of British determination and power. There was a general sense of satisfaction, notwithstanding Lord Derby's endeavour to pour cold water on hot national sentiment, that Britain had served notice to the other European nations that she meant to defend her position as a dominant power, despite the fact that the preceding events on the Continent had taken place without her playing any part in their course. The *Edinburgh Review* was dubious about the commercial and financial results of the transaction, which could only be justified, the paper thought, on political grounds and naval strategy, and concontinued: 'It is certain that in directing the policy of a great Empire, mere financial considerations must give way to grand national interests.'[1] This was a reminder that the calculating deprecation of a policy conducted in the defence of the Empire was a thing of the past. Empire defence was, moreover, no longer linked with the defence of a distant Canadian border. Public men together with Disraeli returned to the tradition of Palmerston, Canning, and Pitt when they connected the defence of naval life-lines with British foreign policy. The connexion could already be detected in the Suez Canal Debate in the Commons in February 1876. In reply to the speech from the Throne Mr Ridley referred to the vast group of questions relating to the East with which the House was faced 'and the extreme importance of which to our Imperial interests it is perhaps impossible to over-estimate'. He felt sure that whatever the critics of the Government might say against the purchase of the Suez Canal shares, the final verdict would be favourable 'and that it will be held that Ministers have, by this bold but peaceful stroke of policy, strengthened the position and vindicated the dignity of the Empire'. Another member supporting the same view referred to the successful tour of the Prince of Wales to India at that time, a tour

which had 'by bringing together in the State ceremonials the different
Native Princes, probably given them a common pride in the greatness
of the Empire—a greatness of which, as dignitaries, they themselves to
some extent partake. We, too, when we have read of the assemblage
of those feudatory Princes, have perhaps realized the greatness of that
Eastern Empire as we never realized it before.' That thought naturally
led to the prospect of the assumption of the imperial title by the Queen,
which had been indicated in the Royal Speech, an event, the speaker
commented, which was happily chosen for Her Majesty 'to crown this
great Empire that we have built up in the East, by assuming a title long
foreshadowed by events'. The Eastern Empire, built up by the British
but peopled by alien races, was in the mind of the speaker a separate
entity from the Colonial Empire to which he referred later on as an
Empire held together by bonds of common descent. 'We now justly
estimate the value of our Colonies; commercially and politically they
are pillars of our Empire, and our union with them is secured by ties
stronger and more permanent than those of mere self-interest—the ties
of a common loyalty and a common blood.' The more the Eastern
Empire moved into the foreground, the less easy it became to maintain
the racial concept of Empire which Dilke had so prominently defended.
The only way out was the acceptance of two Empires, the Eastern and
the Colonial. Disraeli made no such distinction. He demanded the vote
of the House for the purchase of the Canal shares in the name of Empire.

Some may take an economical view of the subject, some may take a commercial view, some may take a peaceful view, some may take a warlike view of it;
but of this I feel persuaded—and I speak with confidence—that when I appeal
to the House of Commons for their vote they will agree with the country,
that this was a purchase which was necessary to maintain the Empire, and
which favours in every degree the policy which this country ought to
sustain.[1]

Commenting on the Suez Canal debate in the House of Commons, the
Daily Telegraph defended the purchase, because the Canal was of
peculiar interest to Britain, quite independently of the Eastern Question
and the fate of Turkey. 'In fact, the matter concerns not only Turkey
but something higher—the Empire, in relation to its Eastern
dominions . . .', the *Telegraph* declared. It was also a great assertion of

Britain's Mediterranean interests, the paper stated, reflecting Disraeli's arguments used in the debate. Reverting to the same topic four days later, the *Telegraph* spoke of a British foreign policy of 'security of her rights, imperial and industrial' and again in March stressed the need to consider the interests of 'the Empire at large'.[1] The association of Empire with India and with foreign affairs was strengthened in the following months. The name 'Empress of India' was added to the Royal Title.

Disraeli had not forgotten his enthusiastic Empire speeches of 1872. Such was his kind of statecraft that he only needed another emotional occasion to revert to Empire sentiment. India had always been to him the Empire which really mattered, although he was scarcely more familiar with the details of Indian administration than with those of Colonial affairs. The question of a title suitable to the Sovereign in her capacity as ruler of India appealed to Disraeli's sense of splendour and dignity. The question had waited for a solution since 1858. After the Mutiny the charter of the East India Company was abrogated. At the same time the last of the Moguls, having tried to exchange the role of a pensionary of Britain for that of a conspirator, was punished by formal dethronement. Both acts made the British Crown in name what the British Government had long since been in fact—the ruler of British India and the suzerain of the Indian Princes. The Indian Councils Act of 1861 underlined that connexion. It endeavoured to establish a closer contact between the rulers and the ruled without diminishing in the least the autocratic character of the Government. Neither in India nor in London were the rulers conspicuous for an energetic effort in this direction. The inclination of the Indian Civil Service to keep aloof from the population was even greater after the Mutiny than before. The gap could not be bridged by a Parliament whose greater part was notoriously indifferent to Indian affairs. Small wonder, therefore, that the question of the Royal Title with respect to India had been allowed to remain without an answer all those years. That Disraeli should have become conscious of that omission may be best explained by his love for moving in princely and aristocratic circles. In all probability only a small percentage of the Indians cared very much for a specifically Indian title of the Queen, but the minority who did included some hundreds of

Indian princes. To them it was a source of satisfaction to be able to pay homage to a suzerain who figured as a ruler not of a far-away country but as the crowned head of India.

In England India was usually referred to as 'The Indian Empire'. It would have been difficult, indeed, to find a more adequate name for a domain of the Crown which extended over a sub-continent. The ruler of an Empire was fitly called an emperor, and the title 'Empress of India' to be assumed by the Queen was certainly logical and in keeping with the Indian sense of dignity. To Disraeli these inferences were quite obvious, but he also knew the mentality of his countrymen well enough to realize the psychological obstacles that lay in the way. Though India might be an Empire, the title of Emperor or Empress recalled Roman despots, smacked of the defunct Napoleon III, or reminded Britons of Russian and German forms of government. The War Scare of 1875 had evoked visions of the newly developed German military machine terrorizing Europe. *Punch* had depicted the black Imperial Eagle casting a dark shadow over France. The eagle wore a crown around which was printed in bold letters the word: IMPERIALISM, a sign that the unpopular word which had been associated with the French Empire was applied to the new German Empire.[1] In November 1875 W. E. Forster outlined his concept of the Colonial Empire still in the then accepted sense as federation of self-governing Britons, as a community sharing the same descent, language, values, concepts of government, and capable of maintaining a common patriotism in the hearts of all the Anglo-Saxon fellow-countrymen round the globe. That idea of Empire Forster had contrasted with the German form of government and 'the Latin idea of an emperor, or elected despot'.[2]

Apprehension of rousing such associations in the minds of his countrymen made the Prime Minister use a guarded language when on 17 February 1876 he introduced a bill providing for the addition to the Royal Style and Titles without specifying the exact title the Crown was going to assume. He did not reveal the fact that the Queen desired the title to be 'Empress of India' and was not even averse to 'Empress of Great Britain, Ireland and India'.[3] Disraeli hoped to win over the sympathy of the House by linking the Bill with a reference to the growing Empire sentiment and support of imperial connexion and by transferring that Empire sentiment from its national and racial Anglo-Saxon roots to India, a tactical move which did not quite succeed. A new Royal Title connected with India, he told the House, would be highly satisfactory to the Princes of India but also agreeable to the peoples of the United Kingdom, 'because they must feel that such a step gives a seal, as it were, to that sentiment which has long existed, and the strength of which has been increased by time, and that is the unanimous determination of the people of this country to retain our connection with the Indian Empire', the most precious possession of the Crown that made the Queen feel proud it was part of the British Empire.[1] The debates in Parliament and in the press that followed the announcement, however, showed that all Empire enthusiasm could not obliterate all the evil associations which that noble name evoked in the British mind. It was not the worst that a staunch Whig like Robert Lowe raised an argument about the meaning of the words King, Emperor, and Imperial. Disraeli could hold his own in hair-splitting discussions but Lowe did point to ideas that must have been shared by others. The concept of Emperor was Latin. It was alien to the spirit of the British Constitution, for the king was regarded as subject to the law, whereas the traditional concept of Emperor implied a status above the law. Another line of argument, which was derived from the contemporary concept of Empire as united by bonds of common descent, was bound to find much sympathy. Why should India of all the lands under the British Crown be singled out? Lowe asked. 'It will be putting aside our own flesh and blood, our own descendants, who have so nobly vindicated the character of England in every quarter of the globe, by their industry and success. . . .'[2] W. E. Forster, in keeping with his own views about the nature of the Colonial Empire, declined to accept the title of Empress; it was unsuited to English ideas and displeasing to English feelings. More embarrassing was the motion in the House of Lords by the Conservative Lord Shaftesbury against the proposed new title and the fact that the motion was supported by ninety-one peers. In both Houses of Parliament, it was clear, the majority approved of the Bill mainly out of respect for the Queen.

The reception of the Royal Titles Bill in the country was mixed. The

Bill ran counter to the idea of an Empire of federated Britons. Edward Jenkins, who had been a prominent champion of that idea, now wrote a satirical pamphlet against the Bill. The reaction of *Punch* was unfriendly, too. In Ben Jonson style a Hymn to Victoria was published including the lines:

> Lay the imperial style apart;
> Leave it to the lords of legions:
> Queen in every English heart,
> Be thou Queen in Eastern regions.
> Keep thy style and state serene—
> Who so great as India's Queen?[1]

A week later *Punch* alluded to the bad historical record associated with the title of Emperor in British minds when it wrote:

> And, age by age, that name accurst
> Has still from first to latest,
> Implied of Monarchies the worst,
> But ne'er with us the greatest.[2]

The Queen was shocked at the opposition shown against a title she had evidently set her heart on. She wrote to Theodore Martin, the biographer of the Prince Consort, '... The Queen and her Government will *not* yield to *mere* clamour and intimidation! In the City and Whitechapel on the 7th, she was much struck by *one large inscription* with these words: "Welcome, Queen and Empress", and two or three smaller ones, "Welcome, Empress of India".'[3] The Queen asked Martin to have a small paragraph inserted in some papers to the effect that the Bill would make little difference to the existing position, a mere official addition of 'Empress of India', a name best understood in the East, 'but which Great Britain (which is an Empire) never has acknowledged to be higher than Queen or King'.

The Queen and Disraeli made no longer any effort to give the new title a general meaning. It was localized and confined to India. At the second reading of the Bill on 9 March the exclusive relation of the Imperial title to the India possession of the Crown was stressed by the Prime Minister. The debate showed that a good deal of thought had been given to the meaning of Empire and Emperor in those days. Those who had been too ready to associate the title with the despotic features of an *Imperator* were given to understand by Mr Roebuck that Emperor and Imperial were more closely connected with Empire. 'The general feeling of English-speaking people with regard to the word "Empire" is that of a State which has some dominions subject to it.' In that way and having Ireland in mind the English Parliament first used the term and applied it to England and to the English Crown, 'and, therefore, if we can localize the phrase "Emperor" or "Empress", and keep it applied strictly to India without allowing it to be reflected back upon England we shall . . . accurately describe the position of the Queen of England in India . . .'.[1] Some papers felt that 'in these things everything is in a name' as ancient names gathered sentiments of loyalty and sympathy. The radical and liberal opposition could make political gains out of the fact that the title could not easily be purged of its alien undertones.

One incident of the protest campaign which was launched against the Bill is worthy of special note. The title was denounced by means of the use of the derogatory term of *Imperialism*, a portent of things to come of which not much notice was taken. The cry went up against an attempt to introduce 'a bastard Imperialism' into the English monarchy. *The Times* in its leading articles showed the absence of clear direction on that subject. On 9 February the paper declared the new title would be a compliment to the peoples of India. On 17 March, however, the selfsame title was described as 'threatening the Crown with the degradation of a tawdry Imperialism'. The alternative title of 'Sovereign Lady' was suggested. *Punch* made two direct references to the Prime Minister's newly acquired 'Imperialism'; and a letter to the editor about the change in the name of the Royal Bengal Tiger to Imperial Bengal Tiger was signed 'A WOULD-BE IMPERIALIST'.[2] *Punch*, on the occasion of the Royal Titles Bill, made the name imperialism an expression of criticism not of a foreign government but of the British Prime Minister. The *Spectator*, too, was outspoken in its opposition to the new title and, like *Punch*, chose imperialism as the expression of its hostile attitude.

Already in March the journal commented that the title of Empress was pretentious and artificial. It was disliked by the English people, the

Spectator declared. It sarcastically headed one comment: 'The Empress (Limited)'. On 8 April a lengthy comment on the new title was headed: 'English Imperialism.' The word was still derived from its French matrix and so was its meaning. It was despotism based on the support of the ignorant multitude and ignoring constitutional procedure. Did Disraeli's appeal to the sentiment of the crowd in adding imperial splendour to the throne signify that it had now become Britain's turn to fall for such a policy? The writer did not think so.

It is not easy to realise that such a policy as that of the 'Imperialists', as they are called on the Continent, should have, we will not say any root, but even any possibility of root, in these islands. Yet it is evident that Mr. Disraeli conceived very early in his career the notion that such a policy,—a policy which should magnify the Crown on the one hand, and the wishes of the masses on the other, and should make light of the constitutional limitations on either,—was still possible in Europe, and might even have a chance in England. . . .

In England it was a hopeless policy, because there was no gap between the different orders. A monarchy appealing for the support of the masses against the middle classes and the aristocracy as represented in Parliament would be the loser. The writer feared, however, that the dangerous progress of democracy, i.e. mob rule,

which the present Premier has done more to hasten than any public man of his day, opens the way for any statesman who is so disposed, to alliances with the prejudices and ignorance of the masses, such as constitutes the very essence of the Imperialist policy of France. Despotic decrees, such as are likely to be ratified by plébiscites, are the favourite engines of French Imperialism.

But despotic decrees were hardly likely to gain the loyalty of the people, though Disraeli had made it more tempting for future statesmen to appeal to popular clamour. 'And this, whether it be done by magnifying the power of the Throne directly or not, is really of the essence of the Imperialist policy.' The other characteristic of imperialism, the union of extremes, was hardly possible in English society. The only isolated social class, the writers pointed out, were the agricultural labourers and their union with a royal adventurer was improbable.[1] The critical comment of the *Fortnightly Review*'s April edition included the derogatory term of imperialism as well. The whole thing was a hypocritical mockery, the journal claimed. Everybody knew that the new title was introduced to gratify a personal wish of the Queen and all the reasons of state cited in support of the title were fictitious. At first the public gave its assent and expressed moderate satisfaction. 'This assent was due to carelessness. People had not realised that sycophants would be likely to transform the customary titles into the phrases of imperialism.'[1] Imperialism, as this evidence shows, became more widely used for the first time in spring 1876. It served as an anti-Disraeli slogan of the Opposition and was meant to underline the alien character of the Royal Titles Bill.[2]

The growing awareness of the Indian Empire was reflected in the way periodicals printed more articles on various aspects of India than before. Famine and financial difficulties called for comment. National interest was aroused by the Indian duties on cotton goods. Manchester cotton manufacturers pressed the Government to abolish the 5 per cent duty on Lancashire cotton piece goods. The move was opposed by the Indian mill-owners who feared loss of trade and by the Indian Administration because of the loss of badly needed revenue involved. The issue was of a wider interest as major political principles were at stake. Should Free Trade be imposed on India without mercy and against the interests of a section of the population? Was it fair that the Government should give in to the Lancashire cotton manufacturers because, politically, its fate depended more on Lancashire than on Bombay? Was the Indian Empire to be administered in the interest of the Indians or for the benefit of England? In the end a radical step was avoided and a compromise solution adopted.

Asian sentiments reached the Queen and the Government from foreign sources and through the routine channels of the Indian administration. The Queen was impressed by the report of the Persian Minister on the importance of the imperial title in the outlook of the peoples of Central Asia and their interpretation of European history. Many Asians, she was told, believed that the French Emperor had fought the Russian Emperor and defeated him in the Crimean War in order to become 'King of Kings'. Then the German Emperor overthrew the French Emperor in order to gain the supreme title for himself. To impress such people, the Persian Minister thought, it would be a mistake to confine the imperial title to India.[1] Indian sentiment was reflected in a memorandum submitted to the British Government from Punjâbi sources. The Indian author of the memorandum urged the Government to proclaim the imperial title with all the pomp and dignity throughout India and to accompany the proclamation by some liberal gesture of good will such as a grant of money for an Indian purpose. It was Indian custom, for instance, that on a royal occasion money is granted to widows. 'This idea is purely Oriental and native, but the fusion of ideas of both nations must be the result of mutual concessions', the writer added. That was evidently the meaning of the new title in the writer's view. It was a proclamation to the whole world that 'Her Majesty regards this country not as a conquered appanage to the Crown of Britain, but as an integral parcel of Her dominions, and she has identified the interests of Britain with those of India'. Salisbury referred the problem of an imperial grant to the Chancellor of the Exchequer. The British tax-payer, after all, was called upon to satisfy Indian sentiment and needs. But in 1876 England was in the grip of an economic depression. 'From what I know of the English point of view', Salisbury wrote, 'I cannot say that I write to you in a very sanguine mood. Still I should be glad to know your opinion upon the subject: so far as possible from an "Imperial" point of view.'[2] That imperial view with regard to India became all the more pressing as the Russians were advancing all the time towards the Hindu Kush, a challenge which could not be ignored. Disraeli's pre-occupation with the 'Eastern Empire' was undoubtedly stimulated by that challenge. Sooner or later imperial policy had to be re-stated from an Indian point of view. The 'Great Game' undertook that task.

During those months W. M. Thorburn's book, The 'Great Game', had gone through three editions. Its author was a civil servant of Her Majesty's Madras Service. He presented a view of imperial policy which suited his own position and the intellectual climate of his time. In opposition to Dilke and to the Colonial Reformers Thorburn endeavoured to state the case for an expansive military empire of metropolitan character. The first and second editions contained an introductory chapter deploring the lack of a forceful imperial policy, the deliberate abstentions from territorial acquisitions, the narrow-minded counsel of 'Stay at home and let things take their course'. The third edition omitted that melancholic introduction and reflected the conviction that with Disraeli a new, bolder spirit had at last triumphed and 'a change in the style of public talk about colonies has already become apparent in many public speeches'. Territorial annexations and the audacious use of military force were necessary measures incidental to imperial policy, though not its main objective. The aim of imperial policy ought to be 'the formation of a compact Federal British Kingdom out of the portions of the world now more or less controlled by the Government of the United Kingdom of Great Britain and Ireland'. In pursuance of such a policy the author suggested a large-scale colonization of India by Britons, the establishment of an Imperial Senate in which India and the other British colonies would be represented. The Senate would thus enable all parts of the Empire to have a share in imperial legislation and policy. The existence of such a supreme imperial authority would remove the chief obstacle to an extension of the British Empire. Peaceful intercourse on equal terms was a dubious policy which could not produce the same results as the imposition of a conqueror's stricter order and superior usages. In the international field Thorburn favoured an alliance with Russia and the partitioning of the Ottoman Empire.[1] Disraeli's decision was different. As the crisis in the Near East deepened he went so far as to risk war with Russia in order to defend the integrity of the Ottoman Empire. Otherwise events brought Thorburn's concept of military empire to the fore. In it India and the lines of communication which linked Britain with her eastern possessions played a prominent part. Empire began to be thought of again in terms of imperial power and imperial interests. It began to be thought of as an integral part of British foreign policy. After all it was the British Empire in India which was believed to be threatened by the Russian attempt to gain a dominant influence in the Balkans and the Bosporus. It was impossible to counteract Russian intentions by a European coalition like that which had fought the Crimean War. Neither Germany, nor the Habsburg monarchy, nor France could be counted on as allies against Russia. If Russia's drive to the Near East was to be stopped by the force of arms, it had to be done by the armed might of the British Empire on behalf of its own imperial interests. The Queen was in no doubt that a strong policy to defend the 'true interests of the great Empire' was absolutely necessary, as her letters show. Disraeli agreed with her but he observed great caution in the use of imperial language. The lesson of the Royal Titles Bill had been plain. The nation was suspicious of imperial gestures which recalled the practice of unpopular foreign rulers. Moreover, the country was divided because of the massacre of Bulgarian Christians which the Turks had perpetrated. To the large section of the nation which followed Gladstone, even the phrase 'British interests' sounded suspect after that term had served to shield the 'unspeakable Turk'. The Prime Minister, then, would have had a strong incentive to emphasize that the interests of the British Empire were at stake and that such imperial interests were paramount national interests, but he knew also that the word 'imperial' could all too easily recoil on him: instead of being won over, the nation might be repelled by what it would recognize as a characteristic piece of rhetoric.

On 11 August 1876 the House of Commons debated the Bulgarian atrocities, and Disraeli had to defend his policy of backing the integrity of the Ottoman Empire. He appealed to the Empire sentiment. England was not upholding Turkey from a want of sympathy with the aspirations of humanity. 'What our duty is at this critical moment is to maintain the Empire of England. Nor will we ever agree to any step . . . that hazards the existence of that Empire.'[1] In his Guildhall Speech in November he once more spoke of 'the unexampled empire' for which England would be prepared to go to war.[2] But to judge from the reaction of the British press Disraeli's few imperial utterances, made in 1876, fell flat. Liberal sentiments were on the side of Balkan peoples struggling against Turkish tyranny. The historians sympathized with the Slavs. Freeman assured Madame Novikoff of the wide sympathy the Russians enjoyed in England at that moment. 'Whether we are a majority I cannot tell; but I am sure we are a large enough part of the English people to make even the Jew in his drunken insolence think twice before he goes to war in our teeth.'[3] Yet it is doubtful whether the growing link between the Eastern Question and British imperial interests really depended on the Prime Minister and his views. In 1877

Russia resorted to open war against Turkey. As her army advanced towards Constantinople it became clear that the British Empire would soon face the Russian Empire not only on the Indian border but also in the Mediterranean.

Disraeli's proposal to occupy the Dardanelles in April 1877 found a divided cabinet. The country was ill-prepared for the Russo-Turkish War and for the prospect of a Russian occupation of Constantinople. Moral preparation was necessary to make the public agree to rearmament, but Disraeli himself for the time being could do little to forward this preparation. However, at this juncture he found an important voluntary assistant: the *Daily Telegraph*, which only a year before had displayed nervousness about the introduction of the imperial title. Anyone who looks into the British press of that time will perceive that this newspaper stood out as the champion of a pro-Turkish policy under the watchword of *imperial interests*. For many months in 1877–8 this concept is frequently appealed to in its columns, and it seems clear that the plugging of this theme in connexion with the Eastern Crisis was a piece of editorial policy. Indeed, there is a letter from the editor (Edward Levy-Lawson) addressed to Disraeli's private secretary, Montagu Corry, dated 17 May 1877 and preserved among the Disraeli papers at Hughenden Manor, which expresses deep concern about the military and political situation: 'Russia, say in August, will be able to dictate a peace hostile to England.' To avoid a conclusion so shameful for England and so detrimental to the government the writer suggests that public opinion must be shaken up by lively propaganda: 'The country will defend its interests. But these interests must have champions with courage in their hearts and bold and national utterances on their lips.' This is the concluding sentence of a letter which opened with the words: 'I am in a big fight and I know how to use my guns.'[1] And the columns of the *Daily Telegraph* leave us in no doubt about the bold and national utterances which are to be boomed out by Levy-Lawson's 'guns'. They are 'imperial' utterances; and in this manner Levy-Lawson became one of the more notable promoters of the concept of 'British Imperialism'.

'*British interests*' as well as '*imperial interests*' became popular slogans in that year. The phrases were often interchanged and their emotive character was more in evidence than their precise meaning. *Punch* soon reflected the new pre-occupation with *imperial interests* in varying forms of ridicule, the 'penny patriots' crying 'Hinterests at stake', 'The traiterous chatterers who

> would dare suggestion
> About the rights and wrongs of other States,
> When our Imperial Interests are in question.[1]

A few weeks later *Punch* suggested that instead of boasting about the glittering host it would be 'a true Imperial interest' to relieve the famine in India on a large scale

> to knit my Orient land,
> in closer union with my empire's heart
> Than power can win or policy impart. . . .[2]

Forerunners of jingoism, however, were already in evidence and became associated with Empire consciousness. One night in May Disraeli's private secretary went to a music hall 'to feel the pulse of the holiday-makers'. One song, he noted, was tumultuously cheered for the sake of the refrain which ran:

> We'll give the Russian bear
> A taste of what we are
> And fight to keep our empire of the seas.[3]

Corry reported that the workers of Lancashire were so interested in foreign affairs that the Salford Election had been won by the Conservatives because of the line Disraeli had taken. '. . . The feeling of the working class is neither for Russia, nor for Turkey but thoroughly excited at the prospect of the interests and honour of England being touched.'[4]

The Government had made it known that Britain would maintain a policy of neutrality in the Russo-Turkish War so long as her interests were not impaired. Emotions apart a sober and calculated outline of what constituted British interests was urgently needed. On that point the Government was divided. Englishmen in India warned Disraeli not to permit the Russians into the Mediterranean or else India, together with British naval supremacy, would be lost within ten years. The

British Ambassador in Constantinople urged the Government to occupy Gallipoli, the Queen addressed the Prime Minister in highly emotional and imperial language which Disraeli spoke as well when he assured her that 'the great objects of your Majesty's imperial policy may be secured without going to war'.[1] India had long been an integral part of British policy in the Mediterranean, in Africa, and in the Middle East. Russia and France had been considered the chief dangers to British interests by Disraeli's predecessors, too. In the traditional language of the Government British and imperial interests were hardly distinguishable and had not yet acquired a difference in meaning. The first objective of the Prime Minister and his colleagues had been to prevent an expansion of Russia in close co-operation with other Powers. The outbreak of the Russo-Turkish War in spring 1877 spelt the failure of that attempt. The Government were agreed that it was a British interest to guard the routes to India and to preserve the *status quo* in the Straits and the Persian Gulf. There were some doubts, however, about the extent to which the integrity of the Ottoman Empire was still a British interest. Northcote thought a collapse of the Ottoman Empire and a Russian advance to the Mediterranean a distinct possibility. In May 1877 he suggested to Derby that British interests would best be served by the occupation of Egypt,[2] a view Carnarvon made his own later in the year, and which prompted his resignation in 1878. He was convinced that the Ottoman Empire was doomed anyway and that it was madness to try and defend Constantinople. It was not the British Government which under Disraeli's guidance discovered a new meaning in the 'imperial interests' or was confronted with an entirely new situation. The term assumed a new significance in the relation between the Government and the public. Disraeli had to defend a traditional policy which Liberals and conscientious Christians found repugnant. During the ten years preceding Disraeli's administration many people had grown accustomed to associating the British Empire with the British settlements overseas. India was a different matter. The country was not entirely behind Disraeli in that respect and treated the press-campaign in favour of 'British interests' with suspicion. The notion was challenged in the House of Commons by Gladstone during the Five nights' Debate on the Eastern Question in May.

In Gladstone's eyes the phrase 'British interests' was a pretext for a policy of imperial expansion which knew no bounds. The Liberal leader mustered all his eloquence to impress on the House the fact that Empire expansion meant weakness and warfare. The case of India illustrated his point. First the country had been conquered, next the very possession of such a vast country required additional measures to guard its security and the safety of British rule, so Britain claimed a veto to all political arrangements of all countries and seas on any route to India.[1] Gladstone, in fact, repudiated a concept of Empire which had been growing during the few years of Disraeli's administration, an Empire of massive military might centred in England. The Government was partly evasive in its defence. It stressed Britain's position of strict neutrality in the war, and appealed to Empire sentiment. No fear of ridicule, Viscount Sandon proclaimed, would deter the Government from doing its best 'in our day and generation to hand down to our posterity the great charge we have received of the United British Empire—the most wonderful Republic of nations the world has seen united under the most ancient and most beautiful of Crowns'. Other Government supporters pointed to the importance of maintaining the Empire in the East in the interest of civilization and humanity.[2] Disraeli's voice was not heard. Lord Beaconsfield had taken his seat in the House of Lords a year earlier.

The *Nineteenth Century*, in a comment on the debate, believed both parties desired Britain to remain neutral in the Russo-Turkish dispute but were divided over the nature of British interests.[3] The guns of the *Daily Telegraph* did not arouse the resounding echo Levy-Lawson had hoped for. Public opinion remained divided until far into the new year. As late as 10 January 1878 Queen Victoria in a letter to Disraeli complained of 'the low tone which this country is inclined to hold'. She asked him to 'get something to be written, though the *Daily Telegraph*, *Pall Mall* and *Post* are very strong in the right sense, to instruct the blinded country in this respect'.[4] But Beaconsfield took no such indirect action. He preferred to resort openly to imperial language himself when the hour of drastic action had struck. The Royal Speech closing the parliamentary session in August 1877, however, contained a warning clause which linked the Eastern Question with the fate of the

Empire. 'If, in the course of the contest, the rights of my Empire should be assailed or endangered, I should confidently rely on your help to vindicate and maintain them.'[1] Thus foreign policy in 1877 had blended with imperial outlook. That imperial outlook was directed to the East to such an extent that the annexation of the Transvaal in that year made no impact on the national debate concerning the Empire and its interests. There was hardly any reference to the wider Empire implications involved, apart from the general declaration made in the House that 'financial considerations must be thrown to the winds, when the honour, dignity and interests of the British Empire and the safety of European colonists were as much at stake as they were in this case'.[2]

The Empire advocates of that year in their literary expressions shared a growing militancy and insistence on the aspect of power. In the face of the advancing Russian Empire and the victorious might of the German Empire, it was felt that a United British Empire alone could maintain and muster a comparable strength. The Royal Colonial Institute was a natural home for such thoughts; they were voiced by Labilliere. Never in opposition to but always in rivalry with the American union a great British union, he said, would be strong to carry forward 'that civilisation of the world which Providence seems to have destined the Anglo-Saxon race to accomplish'.[3] Labilliere was sensitive to the derogatory use of the term Imperialism and regretted the fact that it was used in the sense of Caesarism.[4] Julius Vogel in the *Nineteenth Century* noted with satisfaction how much the Empire climate had changed under the administration of Disraeli and his Colonial Secretary, Lord Carnarvon. In 1869 there was still a great deal of anxiety felt in the country on account of the rumoured desire of several members of the Liberal Government to detach the colonies from the Empire. Disraeli's appeal to the masses of the people won the election for him because it included the pledge to respect the integrity of the British Empire. People then felt the Liberals did not care how soon the Empire dissolved. New Zealand, Vogel recalled, was given to understand that the colony was at liberty to leave the Empire. The governors of Canada and the Cape Colony as well as many responsible statesmen in England regarded a separation of those colonies from the Empire as probable, even as desirable. Disraeli had created a different spirit, a firm belief that the colonies were not a source of weakness but of strength. Lord Carnarvon administered colonial affairs in the same spirit contrary to his Liberal predecessor. The annexation of the Fiji Islands and of the Transvaal illustrated the Conservative attitude towards the Empire. Many Liberals sympathized with such a policy and were equally opposed to separation. Vogel listed Forster, Mundella, Torrens, Childers as advocates of colonial interests. Advocating the separation of Hungary from Austria, of Poland from Russia, Alsace from Germany, Ireland from the United Kingdom would be regarded in some countries as treason. The advocates of separation were engaged in an activity which likewise was little short of treasonable. Vogel appealed for the assertion of the authority of the Crown in all the British colonies and the increase of the imperial forces by all the parts of the Empire making their contribution.[1] The newly-arrived Agent General of New Zealand and recognized leading voice speaking for that colony unreservedly backed what he believed to be Disraeli's Empire outlook and policy.

Gladstone, in moving his resolutions on the Eastern Question, had posed an unanswerable question. If Empire meant not a federation of British colonies but military and political power over vast alien peoples, where would be the recognizable bounds to its constant expansion? Could the goal be anything less than a World Empire? Young James Stanley Little began his long career as a writer on Empire by asserting—unlike Dilke—that an Anglo-Saxon world empire in which there was no room for separate English nations was the decree of history. A United Britannic Empire, based on the superiority of race and power, would impose peace on the whole world.[2] Such literary dreams of young men could not have found their way into print so easily but for the change in Empire thinking which had taken place.

Less visionary was Edward Dicey's plea for an occupation of Egypt to counter a possible Russian move into the Mediterranean and to secure the Suez Canal for British shipping. International guarantees, Dicey pointed out, offered no real securities 'on which we can afford to stake our free communication with India, or, in other words, the security of our Empire'. England had no choice. She must follow her manifest destiny and carry the burden of Empire. Like Rome England had acquired an Empire because she was strong. She held it in defiance of half the world and in consolidating it she must not shrink from extending its area. Dicey attacked Gladstone and his school of thought for upholding what he termed 'the anti-imperialist theory of English statecraft'. The British Empire had been established, he maintained, not to benefit anybody but the British. India was ruled by Britain 'because we deem the possession of India conducive to our interests and our reputation, because we have got it and intend to keep it'. The Empire added materially to British power, greatness, and fame. Thus Dicey, the by then well-established editor of the *Observer*, made himself the literary spokesman of an Empire spirit which was illiberal and militant, a spirit which the political crisis in the Near East had helped to hatch.[1]

Disraeli came to power without having any clear theory of Empire in mind and without a clear plan of Empire policy. For long periods in his administration he gave little thought to the Colonial Empire and knew nothing of its problems. Yet the legend which linked his name with imperialism had its legitimate foundation after all. During the years of his administration a concept of Empire developed which gave the word a new ring of power and confident assertion among the public. It stressed the possession and defence of a considerable portion of Asia. Disraeli's imperial language alone—from which he desisted when political reasons required it—or his personal romantic preference for the glamour of the Indian possession would hardly have sufficed to bring about a change in Empire thinking, if it had not been assisted by the rise of the great Empires on the Continent; by the realization that in the face of those new empires the British Empire required a greater centralizing authority to muster and command a balancing power. In the face of the Russian expansion it was difficult to entertain a liquidation of the Empire by agreement, 'parting as friends'. The notion of Empire as a voluntary association of self-governing British settlements contained demonstrable points of weakness, when self-governing colonies encroached upon common defence, trade, and foreign policy in the face of the mighty military machines of Europe. The notion of an Empire as a compact entity, ready for combat, commanded from one centre, and relying on its collective military force—as in the Napoleonic Wars—became more acceptable again, although Disraeli did not create it. He occasionally emphasized it. His language popularized it, perhaps. It is the semantic factor which must be added when the legendary link between Disraeli and Imperialism is examined. It is the term Imperialism itself which played an important part in promoting the legend, for it was during the years of Disraeli's administration that Imperialism was first used in British party politics and started on its long career as a political word of international fame. It first became a popular word in the English language as an anti-Disraeli slogan.

VI

THE ESTABLISHMENT OF IMPERIALISM AS
A SLOGAN IN BRITISH PARTY STRIFE

The Turks successfully stopped the Russian advance at Plevna and through autumn 1877 kept the invader at bay. In December, however, Plevna fell and a Turkish defeat now appeared probable. In January 1878 the Russians occupied Adrianople and the Porte sued for peace. Thus during the first weeks of 1878 the Russian advance and victory brought about a crisis in the direction of British policy. Should Britain intervene? Disraeli ordered military preparations and moved the fleet into the Sea of Marmara through the Dardanelles. The nation remained deeply divided over the issues of foreign policy and the division split Disraeli's own cabinet. Carnarvon and Derby refused to support a policy of defending Turkey at the risk of war with Russia. 'I cannot therefore knowingly be a party to the idea of war with Russia and a Turkish alliance which finds so much favour in many quarters', Carnarvon wrote after a cabinet meeting in December 1877, which had brought out the wide difference of opinion existing between him and the Prime Minister.[1] The Liberals were jubilant over the embarrassing situation Disraeli faced, which offered only two equally damaging results—retreat from the loudly proclaimed defence of imperial interests and acquiescence in the new control Russia stood to gain in the Balkans, in Armenia, possibly in the Straits and in the Aegean Sea, or waging, single-handed, a war against Russia with one half of the nation in angry opposition. 'Surely we have "got" Beaconsfield at last!' the editor of the Northern Echo, W. T. Stead, wrote to Gladstone in January, 'I heard one man mutter tonight. "Ten millions! Two pennyworth of lead would settle the whole thing!" and I fear that was possible, should Beaconsfield really try to drag us into war, he may be the first victim'; and a few days later he again wrote: 'If Lord B means war he will have to face such sedition as England has not seen for generations.'[2] The strong emotions stirred by the crisis led to clashes in Hyde Park between pro-Turkish demonstrators passing resolutions in support of Lord Beaconsfield's 'patriotic determination to support the interests and the honour of the British Empire' and their anti-Turkish opponents.[1] The Russian reply to Disraeli's strategy was a further advance as far as the outskirts of Constantinople. 'Jingo' became the popular word in February and March as music hall patriotism reflected the growing war-fever. The Treaty of San Stefano, signed on 3 March, recognized the Russian advance in the Balkans and Armenia. Through the control of Albania and Bulgaria Russia had become a Mediterranean Power. Disraeli told the Cabinet that an emergency had arisen, the balance of power in the Mediterranean had been destroyed, and the interests of the Empire were at stake. He proposed to send an expeditionary force from India to occupy Cyprus in order to counter-balance the Russian conquests in Armenia and guard British interests in the Persian Gulf.[2] The Foreign Secretary, Lord Derby, thereupon resigned. In the cabinet Disraeli had campaigned for his point of view under the headings of the maintenance of the Empire and the maintenance of peace.[3] A Royal Message calling up reserve forces referred to the necessity of 'taking steps for the maintenance of peace and for the protection of the interests of the Empire'.[4] Having demonstrated the seriousness of the situation to the country and to Russia by calling up the reserves and ordering Indian troops to Malta, Disraeli himself for the first time after two years resorted to eloquent imperial language. On 8 April 1878, in the speech in which he announced the military moves and decisions in the House of Lords, he raised the standard of 'the British Empire'. In a confession of faith he said: 'I have ever considered that Her Majesty's Government, of whatever party formed, are the trustees of that Empire. That Empire was formed by the enterprise and energy of your ancestors, my lords; and it is one of a very peculiar character. I know no example of it, either in ancient or modern history. No Caesar or Charlemagne ever presided over a dominion so peculiar. Its flag floats on many waters; it has provinces in every zone, they are inhabited by persons of different races, different religion, different laws, manners, customs. Some of these are bound to us by the ties of liberty, fully conscious that without their connection with the metropolis they have no security for public freedom and self-government; others are bound to us by flesh and blood and by material as well as moral considerations. There are millions who are bound to us by our military sway, and they bow to that sway because they know that they are indebted to it for order and justice. All these communities agree in recognizing the commanding spirit of these islands that has formed and fashioned in such a manner so great a portion of the globe.'[1] Those lines contain the nearest approach of Disraeli to an imperial theory. He characterized that Empire as maritime and far-flung, multi-racial and multi-religious, showing a wide diversity in manners and customs. In that Disraeli differed from the racialist outlook of earlier Empire characterizations in which the element of racial and religious diversity had not been stressed but where, on the contrary, the identity of kinship and outlook had been emphasized. Disraeli accepted that school of thought as applicable to one part of the Empire, the part tied to Britain 'by flesh and blood', but then there were self-governing parts of the Empire—he must have been thinking of the French in Canada—bound to Britain by free institutions and security only. Lastly, Disraeli added the tie of military power, which gave millions justice and order. Its commanding centre was in the British Isles where all the power was centralized. It made the British Government the Government of the Empire and, therefore, its foreign policy could not but be imperial policy. How far the centralized, military Empire was consistent with the decentralized self-government of the British settlements was not a question Disraeli could have been expected to dwell on in that hour of crisis. It is doubtful whether he realized the contradictory elements contained in his Empire concept. The Empire passage in Disraeli's speech evoked little comment and interested the press least of all.

The cause of the United Empire was pleaded in the same month by its staunch advocate, Julius Vogel. He undertook to refute the thesis that all the external possessions of Great Britain were a burden to the country, a view which in those days was most prominently defended by Robert Lowe. Lowe even avoided the hated name of Empire and merely referred to 'the foreign dominions of the Crown'. He became the Liberal politician who most emphatically took exception to the imperial language of his contemporaries. The days when, as an Australian politician, he had warmly welcomed the value of the imperial connexion lay far behind him. He and Lord Blachford, who publicly agreed with much Lowe wrote, gave ground for the assumption that a section of the Liberal Party still preferred the Lesser Britain to the Greater Britain. Blachford did not believe that a permanent association between self-governing states not arising out of geographical neighbourhood was practicable. In an article bearing the title *The British Empire* Vogel defended imperial unity on political and economic grounds. Britain, he maintained, has been and is known to the world not merely as an island but rather as a nation 'whose foreign interests are mainly if not entirely connected directly or indirectly with her exterior possessions'. The crisis in the Near East had demonstrated that fact. Without India and her colonies England would be a fat, limbless, bloated body, racked with internal disease. The utter refutation of the arguments which purported to show that Britain could regard the loss of her colonies with equanimity, however, lay in the economic field. Britain possessed an immense surplus in capital and men and had at her disposal large territories to absorb either. As long as the other nations had not adopted free trade—and many had not—the best approach to free trade was to be made through the Empire. British investors were offered the unique advantage that their investments within the far-flung British possessions were protected by British laws. 'In this short sentence lies the utter refutation of all the arguments' of the Empire opponents in Vogel's eyes.[1] Meanwhile events did not stand still. The new military and Eastern aspect of Disraeli's Empire was demonstrated by the move of 7000 Indian troops to Malta in May. Those were not volunteers. They were despatched to their new stations solely in virtue of what the Prime Minister had called 'our military sway' and because they bowed to that sway, as Disraeli had so proudly declared. Britain, however, did not. Although opposition was immediately voiced on emotional and con-stitutional grounds, the real issue was the future character of the British Empire.

Punch had consistently ridiculed shallow patriotism and had never taken Disraeli's imperial language seriously. In fact, throughout those years *Punch* built up a vivid image of the Prime Minister as a clever trickster, a slightly fraudulent mountebank who performed on the platform in front of an audience that could not be expected to take him too seriously. The move of the Indian troops to Malta was too good a subject for *Punch* to be missed. Under the title OUR 'IMPERIAL' GUARD a cartoon placed Disraeli between India and Britannia. India had come to help Britannia who had so often helped India, as the Prime Minister assured her. Britannia, however, looked very doubtful and in the words of *Punch* 'doesn't exactly know how she likes it'.[1] In the same issue the Prime Minister was depicted musing about the figure 7000, adding some more zeros to it. '. . . Seven hundred thousand! A few strokes more or less with a little pen, and we can wake this Empire up in all its Titan strength, with remoulded shape and swarthier limb bid it astound the wondering world.' A week later Mr Bull was shown consulting Dr Gladstone and Dr Beaconsfield. Dr Beaconsfield referring to his colleague said: 'He is jealous of the fame already acquired for my Indian Tonic, which, even should the fever attack you— and that is always possible—would safely pull you through it. Mr Bull (doubtfully) But how, in the long run, would it affect my Constitution? Dr Gladstone (triumphantly) Ah! *That's* the question!'[2] Again a week later the Prime Minister appeared on a cartoon in the guise of a trainer leading a horse—it was Derby week—to the race course. The horse was dark and was called *Sepoy*. The cartoon had the title THE 'DARK HORSE'. In the background a light horse, called *Congress*, is seen surrounded by European statesmen. On being questioned about the high cost of the 'dark horse' and its chances to win the race, the trainer replied: 'He can force the running for "Congress".' A poem bearing the same name, 'The Dark Horse', included the lines:

> There never was a Dark 'Un more discussed
> Than this same *Sepoy*, out of *India*, by *Imperial Policy*.[3]

The discussion referred to was sparked off by the many awkward moral and constitutional issues which the despatch of the Indian troops had aroused.

Right from the start the *Spectator* called attention to the serious character of the move. Subject races were invited to fight for Britain. Did that not smack of the Roman Empire in its decadence? Asia was called in to repress Europe. It meant, according to *Spectator*, a civilization without a future was armed against a civilization of progress, it was armed to repress Christians on behalf of Moslems. So much for the moral issues involved. The constitutional issues were no less serious. Parliament did not control or pay Indian forces. Contrary to the spirit of the Bill of Rights the Crown could maintain an army in India without the authority of Parliament. If the Government moved that Indian Army about as if it were part of the British Army, there was no bar to Indian troops garrisoning London in the future, and Englishmen would begin to live in a military Empire. The *Spectator* felt the nation was not prepared to tolerate such an imperial attitude.[1] A few weeks later the journal commented on the Parliamentary debate on the employment of Indian troops that there was a danger of Lord Beaconsfield desiring in all foreign and imperial affairs to bypass Parliament.

The Commons debated the whole issue on three nights, 20, 21 and 23 May. It was a debate which must rank among the finest of the period for eloquence, depth of historical and constitutional knowledge, and analysis of the issues involved. The debate was formally opened by a motion of the Opposition which in so many words declared the Government's despatch of Indian troops a violation of the Bill of Rights. In the words of Hartington, who moved the resolution, it was a measure 'which raises totally new questions concerning the relations between this country and our Indian Empire'.[2] Sir Michael Hicks-Beach, who had become Colonial Secretary when Carnarvon resigned in protest against Disraeli's policy, defended the Government's measure as necessary 'to show quickly and decisively to the world that we were able, if need be, to wield the Forces of an united Empire'.[3] Opposition against the military concept of Empire was voiced in the House by supporters of an Empire based on Liberalism and free co-operation. Those wanted the Government to consult Indian feelings and interests. If India was called upon to help Britain carry out British foreign policy, India was entitled to the status and consideration of an ally rather than a dependency.[4] The motion of the opposition was defeated; but the suspicion remained that constitutional vigilance was called for with a government in power, which had proved in the case of the Royal Titles Bill and through the despatch of Indian troops to Malta that it was often inclined to ignore Parliament. The Congress of Berlin gave new nourishment to that suspicion.

The Government, in fact, had intended to impress not only the world outside but also the separationists by its surprise move of Indian troops to Malta, as Northcote revealed in a letter to Sir John A. Macdonald, the Solicitor General for Scotland, written a few days after the debate.

I hope, and believe [he wrote] that we shall maintain peace; and if we do, it will be not a little on account of our having done something to show that we can use, and mean to use, our Imperial strength in defence of Imperial Interests—But there is more to be done in this direction. We ought to be able to show that our Colonies are supports to the Mother Country,—not, as some would have it, causes of embarrassment and weakness to her.

He thought it would be a good thing if some of the colonies declared their readiness to help protect shipping. 'The ocean is the common highway for all British vessels, and those of us who are interested in any portion of our Commercial Marine have as true an interest in assisting to defend that highway as to defend their own soil.'[1]

Beaconsfield's triumphant return from the successful Congress of Berlin, which had preserved peace and the 'Imperial interests', was crowned by his speech in the House of Lords. In laying before the House an account of the achievements of the many and complicated negotiations and the new territorial adjustments agreed to, he also made mention of the new military alliance concluded with Turkey and the taking over of Cyprus, a responsibility, he maintained, not entered into recklessly or unnecessarily. There was only one responsibility 'from which we certainly shrink; we shrink from the responsibility of handing to our successors a weakened or diminished Empire', he affirmed with imperial pathos. The occupation of Cyprus had become necessary in the interest of peace and the maintenance of the Empire. It was a measure designed to preserve peace, though Britain did not fear war. This was the conclusion of Disraeli's speech:

Her Majesty has fleets and armies which are second to none. England must have seen with pride the Mediterranean covered with her ships; she must have seen with pride the discipline and devotion which have been shown to her and her Government by all her troops, drawn from every part of her Empire. I leave it to the illustrious duke in whose presence I speak, to bear witness to the spirit of imperial patriotism which has been exhibited by the troops from

India, which he recently reviewed at Malta. But it is not on our fleets and armies, however necessary they may be for the maintenance of imperial strength, that I alone or mainly depend in that enterprise on which this country is about to enter. It is on what I most highly value—the consciousness that in the Eastern nations there is confidence in this country, and that, while they know we can enforce our policy, at the same time they know that our Empire is an Empire of liberty, of truth, and of justice.[1]

The Prime Minister thus proclaimed at the climax of his career the concept of Empire that had re-emerged during his term of office, and to which he now gave his official recognition and blessing, a military unity, controlled by the British Prime Minister and embodying an imperial idea of internal liberty, justice of administration, and intellectual endeavour based on truth. When speaking of justice the author of Sybil had in mind not only justice in the legal sense but also in the social sense. That his idea of Empire was at the moment of delivering his speech India-orientated is shown not only by his arguments justifying the occupation of Cyprus—'In taking Cyprus the movement is not Mediterranean, it is Indian'—but also by his surprising statement that Her Majesty's troops had come from 'all the parts of the Empire', when, in fact, they had come from all the parts of India only. There were no Australian or Canadian troops involved, but the beginning of conceiving the imperial forces as one army had been made. Lord Salisbury, like the Prime Minister, emphasized the new spirit of Empire unity. It was that imperial unity which defeated France in the eighteenth century and Napoleon in the nineteenth. The Government's policy was, therefore, no innovation, he explained at a banquet given in his honour by the Conservative members at Knightsbridge on 27 July. '... We were striving to pick up the thread—the broken thread—of England's old Imperial traditions.' Turning against the separationists Salisbury argued against their views on their own ground, commercial prosperity, saying:

For a short time there have been men, eminent in public affairs, who have tried to persuade you that all the past history of England was a mistake—that the duty of England, the interests of England, was to confine herself solely to her own insular forces, to cultivate commerce, to accumulate riches, and not, as it was said, to entangle herself in foreign policies. They were men who disdained empire, who objected to colonies, and who grumbled even at the possession of India. Even for their own low purpose the policy of these men was a mistake. The commerce of a great commercial country like this will only flourish—history attests it again and again—under the shadow of empire, and those who give up empire in order to make commerce prosper will end by losing both.[1]

The *Daily Telegraph* was jubilant. This newspaper on 14 August declared that official lips had adopted almost the exact expressions of the *Telegraph* and made them the basis of the policy of the Cabinet.

This self-praise was not unjustified. But it was as fateful as ever self-praise was. The Liberals, already disquieted by the prospects of foreign entanglements resulting from the new policy, now took alarm at the concept under the sign of which this policy was propagandized. The *Daily News* wrote on 23 July: 'We may remark that the absurd misuse of the word "Imperial" is becoming of late an intolerable nuisance.' The annoyance expressed here was voiced repeatedly during the following weeks, among others by Gladstone. Opponents of the Government complained the word 'Imperial' was sounded whenever a doubtful political step was taken. They were alarmed by the popular acclaim which greeted the Prime Minister after his return from Berlin and by the fact that the main provisions of the Treaty of Berlin were agreed to and ratified without the knowledge of Parliament. Was not the whole character of the Empire changed without Parliament by the new alliance with Islam? It would be the new British mission, opponents pointed out, 'in this new Semitic dispensation' to send out Englishmen to organize bands of Sepoys and Redifs.[2] The critics were not only unfair in their judgement but also ignorant about Disraeli, who was less responsible for the acquisition of Cyprus than Lord Salisbury. The latter had a greater share in the shaping of policy than the opposition was prepared to attribute to him. The *Spectator* felt the country was drifting towards a personal government and was using *Tancred*, Disraeli's oriental fiction, as its textbook in its foreign policy. Meanwhile the Constitution was set aside. The journal thought that the recent methods of concluding foreign treaties had been no less outrageous than it would be to summon Parliament to meet at Delhi.[3] The effect of repeated emphasis put on imperial unity could not be otherwise. There was a revulsion of sentiment in the country due to the impression that an alien form of government was being imposed and that foreign affairs had assumed an adventurous character. The sentiment found different expressions. As early as January Goldwin Smith had written Disraeli's life had been one vast conspiracy to gratify his own vanity and to subvert parliamentary government.[1] In the Commons Robert Lowe warned the country it was heading for militarism and calamity and asked:

Have we a right to adventure on such a scale? We are told it is Imperial policy. Well, when anything very foolish is to be done we are always told it is an Imperial matter. . . . The power of Imperial Rome was broken in conquering the world; it dwindled away, century after century, because commerce would not flourish. It was so imperial that its people were robbed to sustain the Imperial policy.

He then referred to Louis XIV of France and to Napoleon who left France weaker and unhappier after their rule than she was before. Britain, Lowe explained, colonized but did not conquer. Conquest was not the vocation of England.[2] The two hostile schools of thought were surveyed by the *Nineteenth Century* in an article, *Foreign Policy of Great Britain, Imperial or Economic?* W. R. Greg, the author, believed the country had reached a point where a choice between two rival policies had become necessary. There had been in the past an imperial policy, in particular during the years 1790–1815. The following period had been a reaction to a time of glorious victories and venture. Peace, retrenchment, and reform were the watchwords of the new period lasting until 1875. Since then the imperial spirit had been revived. Prestige, power, the ownership of a vast Empire and its usefulness were acclaimed by a section of the British nation which the author termed 'the imperialists'. In the opposite camp, the author found what he termed 'the economists'. Those claimed that doctrines of empire were liable to passionate, indiscriminate application and policies which served the upper ten thousand but starved the poor. They maintained that imperialists had adopted a policy of dishonesty as recent events had proved. In the name of the integrity of the Ottoman Empire Britain was summoned to defend her imperial interests and found that a few months later two reluctant

Turkish provinces were handed over to Austria, some to Russia, while Britain helped herself to Cyprus.[1] In the same issue Gladstone stated his reflexion on the open national split over the issue of the future character to be given to the British Empire. He called his article *England's Mission*. Gladstone took Disraeli's claim to have brought from Berlin 'Peace with Honour' as his starting-point and put a big question mark behind the alleged honour gained. European law, he protested, had been broken in a flagrant manner by the British occupation of Cyprus and British alliance with servitude and barbarism. It had no value to England but was merely the symbol of the expanding imperial appetite under Disraeli's administration, which had led from the annexation of the Fiji Islands and of the Transvaal to that of Cyprus. Salisbury's claim that commerce flourished only with and through territorial dominion was really an appeal to cupidity. The Government's policy was characterized by 'territorial aggrandisement, backed by military display'. The country was subjected to false imperial ideas of which Gladstone gave a few selections. 'Empire is greatness; leagues of land are empire; your safety is measured by the fear you strike into other nations; trade follows the flag: he that doubts is an enemy of the country.' Britain, Gladstone insisted, had lost morally and materially from the policy pursued by the Government by claiming more than equality of rights and by over-looking the right proportion between resources available and obligations undertaken. If the dominant passion of the English was the extension of empire, it had to be kept in check by the integrity and prudence of their statesmen. Unfortunately, ambition and cupidity were no longer restrained by the Government which, neglecting home affairs, was bent on fictitious interests abroad. Against this Gladstone held up a Liberal view of Empire of free, growing communities remaining in political connexion not by force but out of their own free choice and knowing that Britain was ready to defend them in times of danger. Such relations he saw develop in Canada, Australia, and New Zealand. Again those colonies were looked upon from two different angles by the two imperial schools.

It is the administrative connection, and the shadow of political subordination, which chiefly give them value in the sight of the party, who at home as well as abroad are striving to cajole or drive us into Imperialism. With their opponents, it is the welfare of these communities which forms the great object of interest and desire.

If their welfare ultimately required their severence from the mother country, 'we prefer their amicable independence to their constrained subordination', Gladstone quoted, alluding to the disaster that overtook Britain in North America in the eighteenth century when a policy of imperial force was attempted. 'The substance of the relationship lies, not in dispatches from Downing Street, but in the mutual affection, and the moral and social sympathies, which can only flourish between adult communities when they are on both sides free.' Gladstone condemned the ostentatious boast to the world, made by Disraeli, of the military aid received from India. Colonies were something better than 'food for powder'. 'To give birth and existence to these States, which are to form so large a portion of the New World, is a noble feature in the work and mission of this nation, as it was of old in the mission of Greece. Nor are the economical results of this splendid parentage to be despised.' It was mistaken, however, to treat the portions of the Empire, separated by thousands of miles of ocean, as if they were like continuous territories. Gladstone pleaded not only for a liberal, free, co-operative, and decentralized Empire but also for a truly British Empire. He had no liking for British rule over alien races held in submission.

We do not want Bosnian submissions. Especially is it inexpedient to acquire possessions which, like Cyprus, never can become truly British, because they have acquired indelibly an ethnical character of their own. In them we remain as masters and as foreigners, and the connection at its best has not the ennobling features which, in cases like America and Australasia, give a high moral purpose to the subsisting relation, and compensate for the serious responsibilities which in given contingencies it may entail.

Under the present administration Britain had been over-committed, neglected her own affairs at home 'to amuse herself everywhere else in stalking phantoms'. The things by which England could make true gains were modesty in thought and language and equal rights granted to all states and nations.[1]

The Liberal leader's attack against the administration's foreign policy had reached a new stage. In 1876 his invectives were directed against the callous pro-Turkish policy of Disraeli notwithstanding the Turkish suppression and massacre of Christians. That stage ended in the Five Nights' Debate in May 1877 and almost resulted in a moral set-back. In his polemics with Dicey the controversy was extended not only to include Egypt but already the issue of the fundamental character of the Empire; and Gladstone was depicted as an anti-Imperialist by Dicey. The campaign waged by the Liberals against the so-called 'British interests' in the Eastern Question was increased to become an anti-Jingo and anti-war campaign in 1878 before the Congress of Berlin. The Congress over, the Opposition directed its attacks against the aura of triumph emanating from the Prime Minister and against the Cyprus Convention. Gladstone's article, *England's Mission*, constituted another shift in the attack. The Eastern Question no longer figured as a main subject. The main issue was the principles guiding British foreign and imperial policy. As Disraeli and Dicey had always counter-attacked him in the name of Empire, Gladstone this time accepted the challenge and fought the enemy on his own ground of Empire, demonstrating thereby that the Liberals were by no means opposed to the British Empire as such but possessed the purer and nobler view of an Empire, more truly British than the current, alien idea of Empire based on ostentatious splendour and militarist rule of force, an idea that appealed to the masses perhaps but corroded the true British spirit and undermined the Constitution. One word expressed that false idea best because it contained all the condemned elements. It was Imperialism, a word Gladstone now hurled against his political enemies as an abuse which meant to characterize their erroneous concept of Empire. Gladstone's definition of the two opposed views of Empire became the starting-point of an ideological battle, which was intensified and widened in the Midlothian Campaign.

In the first chapter of this study we showed how the term Imperialism became associated in the British mind with the despised regime of Napoleon III and we pointed out in subsequent chapters how the term occasionally recurred to denounce an alien form of a government that made use of direct appeals to the multitude, false military splendour, adventures abroad, Empire expansion, and practised arbitrary despotic rule; it all fitted so perfectly with what the Liberals felt Disraeli represented, the fraud, the charlatan, as *Punch* called him, when in its own way it presented to its readers the two hostile schools of thought. There was Betsy Prig representing the Government supporter in the street, exclaiming:

> ... ain't it lovely to see 'ow Britannia improved 'er position,
> Since Benjy picked up the dropt threads of Old England's
>   imperial tradition?

To this the Muse of History replied:

> Fine phrases and flatulent figures (sez she), are the
>   charlatan's tools;
> But the wise are not duped by sham watchwords which
>   rally the legions of the fools.
> Imperial? Many sensed word that makes music in many
>   long ears!
> The Muse is not fired by its *sound*. Better wait till its
>   *meaning* appears![1]

Once the Liberal leader had given the cue, *Imperialism* became an anti-Disraeli slogan. The modern career of the word in its relation to Great Britain, which had begun in spring 1876, was taken a step further along. The slogan began to sink in. Mundella, addressing an audience at Sheffield, warned his hearers against being led captive by a 'sham Imperialism' and asked them to take France as a warning in that respect.[2] The *Daily Telegraph* soon tried to give the name *imperialist* an assertive and laudatory ring when referring to Irish politics and the split in the Home Rule Party. Its Imperial section was led by O'Donnell, whom the paper called 'an enthusiastic imperialist'.[3] The derogatory use of the word, however, became more dominant. To the October issue of the *Fortnightly Review* Robert Lowe contributed a long philippic. Its title was: *Imperialism*. The slogan at the outset of its British career, it must be noted, had nothing at all to do with the Colonial Empire and only in passing with Indian problems. The article focused on the foreign policy of the Government. And however much one may appreciate his high moral seriousness, the author of the article on *Imperialism* cannot be absolved from having bestowed on the term two fateful misrepresentations. Lowe asserts that *Imperialism* was a word brought into circulation by the present Tory Government itself. He asks rhetorically whether good traditional English policy should now be replaced by 'what in the language of our Secretaries of State is called Imperialism'.[1] In fact, though the Foreign Secretary had spoken of imperial traditions, neither he nor his colleagues, nor any other Tory personality had used the word *Imperialism* so far. Actually Lowe was the first to give political prominence to it. And it was only because the word was not as yet encumbered by any positive and laudatory interpretations that Lowe could make it the symbol of a policy which was alleged to have abandoned any compatibility with moral principles.

What does *Imperialism* mean? It means the assertion of absolute force over others. . . . If we can, by abating somewhat of our extreme right, or even by larger concessions, avert the calamities of war, that is utterly repugnant to Imperialism. But if by the menace of overbearing force we can coerce a weaker state to bow before our will, or if, better still, we can by a demonstration of actual force attain the same object, or, best of all, if we can conquer our adversary in open fight, and impose our own conditions at the bayonet's point, then, as Dryden sings, 'these are imperial arts and worthy thee'. It does not follow that the strongest party is always in the wrong, but the triumph of Imperialism is most complete when power is most clearly manifested; and of course the victory is doubled when the victory is not only over weakness but over right.[2]

Supporters of the Government, Lowe goes on to say, tell us 'that the question is between a great and a little England. Whether there may not also be a choice sometimes between a happy and a great, between an imperial and a just England, we are never desired to consider.' Imperialism to Lowe was the apotheosis of violence. It was a notion fraught with a dangerous delusion of power.

These are only samples of the outbreaks of indignation which accompany the word as it sets out on the critical period of its history. This indignation could not have intruded so easily and so violently, had it not been from the outset attached to the notion of 'the Imperial', which was already in the author's mind. Lowe unconsciously discloses the source of his revulsion against imperial notions when, in an aside, he refers to 'two samples of Imperialism', which according to him carry useful warnings. One of them is Prussia; but the other, on which he lays more emphasis, is 'the Emperor of the French' who 'having no just title to fall back upon, determined to be ultra-imperial, i.e. to maintain by glory what he had gained by fraud and murder'. Again it is the shadow of Napoleon III that set the concept 'imperial' upon its modern track. And this is confirmed when Lowe, passing from foreign policy to constitutional behaviour, detects there also an 'imperialistic' manner: the high-handed policy of the Government which has incurred heavy responsibilities without consulting Parliament. The House was deceived as to the movements of the fleet, kept in the dark about the movement of Indian troops, and committed without knowing it to a new and hazardous policy in Asia Minor.

The people should be put on their guard against the flimsy but dangerous delusions to which they are exposed. . . . They should be guarded against those odious sophisms which, under the vulgar mask of Imperialism, conceal the substitution of might for right, and seek to establish the dominion of one set of human beings on the degradation and misery of another. And above all, the public ought to be warned against that abuse of the prerogative of making treaties, by which, in defiance of constitutional practice and theory, we have been entangled in the most tremendous liabilities without the previous consent of the Parliament that should have sanctioned, or the people who must bear them

Lowe wrote in conclusion of his article. It opened a press campaign which formed an essential element of the party feuds that filled the last years of Beaconsfield's administration and represented the first stage in the career of the term Imperialism as a powerful weapon in political warfare. The values associated with the word did not remain exclusively negative. It became possible soon after the attack to profess belief in Imperialism.

So little did the Empire mean anything to Robert Lowe at the time when he wrote the article that he could denounce the Imperialism of the Government without coming to grips with the issue of the future of the Empire. Lowe was not really interested in any imperial future. Other Liberals, however, were. A few days later the *Spectator* summarized the article and agreed with Lowe's sentiment but thought that there was no getting away from the fact that for good or ill Britain ruled a chain of innumerable dependencies which, like India, were by no means the fruit of an ambitious government policy. Those territories had all their own needs and dangers. The problem arose when the interests of the dependencies and those of the mother country had to be balanced. Imperialism arose out of the failure to achieve the balance 'from a disproportionate regard to the interests of the dependencies, as compared with those of the country whose dependencies they are'.[1] An unbalanced, imperialist policy meant a double standard of political behaviour and morality. What a local government would not dare to do in a county, an imperialist government was permitted to do in a distant dependency. A British minister became a Minister of the Empire, who, so long as he needed no British funds, could act in an irresponsible and arbitrary manner. As a result Imperialism was bound to become 'a perpetual conspiracy against the English Constitution' and to lead to a state of affairs where an Englishman's honour was no longer in his own keeping. A policy advocated for the dependencies which was fatal to the mother country was a clear absurdity, as the colonies had a vital interest in the welfare of the mother country. The interests of Britain could not be merged in the interests of the British Empire. Should a colony find that it could not stand the test of interest priorities, it had better separate. Cyprus would be an instance in point according to the *Spectator*.

In October 1878 the issue of priority of interests was underlined by the growing economic depression in Britain, the plight of Irish farmers, which produced a rising animosity against the English and Protestant landlords, and the development of yet another crisis in connexion with Britain's imperial commitments. The centre of that crisis was Afghanistan where the Amir had welcomed a Russian mission in summer but had turned back a British mission despatched by the Indian Viceroy in September. Lord Lytton felt that British prestige would greatly suffer unless some strong action was taken at once. Afghanistan must not be allowed to come under exclusive Russian influence. Should Afghanistan go by default, the Indian border would be exposed to Russian military pressure. The *Daily Telegraph* defended the forward policy of the Viceroy and hoped that such protests as had been raised by Mr Lowe against what he termed Imperialism might remain without response as the security of the Empire was at stake.[2] Joseph Chamberlain, on the other hand, in a private letter to the editor of the *Fortnightly*

Review told him to oppose that infamous policy in the strongest terms. 'What is especially desirable to make clear is that this infernal Afghan business is the natural consequence of Jingoism, Imperialism, "British interests", and all the other phrasing of this mountebank Government.'[1] He, too, had accepted Lowe's contention that Imperialism was a Tory phrase. What infuriated him was the self-perpetuating effect of imperial commitments. Once undertaken new obligations grew out of the old. When the *Nineteenth Century* reviewed Indian finance in October under the heading *The Bankruptcy of India*, the author of the article pointed out that the impoverishment and decay of India was a question that concerned not only the Indians but also the English, as an empire might be lost by economic blundering. There was no retreat possible from the imperial position taken up by Britain. 'We have entered finally upon a wide-reaching Imperialism, but its success or its hopeless failure depends wholly on ourselves', the author stated.[2] This was an early instance of the use of Imperialism in a form expressing emotional neutrality. Such examples are very rare. The term in this context carried none of the overtones derived from its foreign origin. It plainly meant an imperial policy, a national engagement on behalf of the Empire as a whole, in the words of the author 'a constant endeavour on the part of the whole nation to secure liberality, welfare, and contentment in every part of the British dominions, to knit together the various communities under our flag . . .'.

The Government recognized Imperialism as a hostile slogan of party warfare when in the middle of October Sir Stafford Northcote, the Chancellor of the Exchequer, made a number of speeches in the Midlands in which he tried to rebut the attack of Robert Lowe. Northcote stressed the Government's duty to defend national and imperial interests and was cheered when he said the nation would reject the idea that the cares of England could be confined to the British Isles. Britain had assumed the responsibility for a widespread empire. That was a fact which could not be argued out of existence. 'I am not one of those who at all desire to use fine language about a great Imperial position and the extension of the Empire. All that we desire is to do our duty to the Empire with which we are charged.'[3] Northcote desired to remove the impression that the Government was carried away by delusions and hollow phrases or that those by then well-known phrases were covering up a disreputable policy. The Liberal press noted his studious abstention from the use of imperial flourishes and called him 'the tame elephant of the Imperialists'. The *Daily News* followed a purpose in applying the abuse also to the Chancellor of the Exchequer. He had shown his Imperialism by revealing how much he subordinated Britain to the Empire. As North Uist was to the United Kingdom, the United Kingdom was to the whole British Empire in Sir Stafford's eyes, an instructive illustration of imperialist thinking.[1] The *Daily Telegraph*, on the other hand, thought that the Chancellor had overthrown the hideous monster set up by Mr Lowe and labelled by him 'Imperialism'.[2] By the end of October the feet of that monster were firmly planted in British political warfare and the vitality of the creature was not impaired by the attack of a 'tame elephant'. Early in November *Punch* commented on Northcote's Midland speeches: '. . . by the light of such brilliant flashes, the thought of the Berlin Convention, the Afghan difficulty, the expanding expenditure—even fever in Cyprus—become, not only tolerable, but delightful. Here's to "Imperialism"!'[3]

In November it was realized that Imperialism had become established in the political language of the time, though its emotive intention was often clearer than its precise connotation. It was used in a derogatory sense in most cases but, as we saw, occasionally the term was still used in an assertive and constructive sense. In an address on Imperial Administration at Edinburgh the Earl of Carnarvon attempted to tackle the meaning of the new word in his own way. In the concluding portion of his address he spoke of the perplexing, new term. 'I have heard of Imperial policy, and Imperial interests, but Imperialism, as such, is a newly coined word to me.' There was special applause when he continued to say: 'In one sense the English Constitution knows nothing of Imperialism.' He admitted, however, that there was an imperial element embodied in the Constitution and had been there since Tudor times. He disliked the name *Imperial* 'for the obvious reason that it suggests uncomfortable Continental associations'. Carnarvon, who had parted company with Disraeli in January 1878, was free to speak and to criticize. He obviously opposed Disraeli's imperial style, yet he refused to make common cause with the Liberals and their use of the new word. He, therefore, tried both to accept the word and to reject it by distinguishing between a false Imperialism and a genuine one. False Imperialism was Caesarism, personal rule, a second-hand copy of Continental despotism. Its benefits were short-lived, its teachings false. It was the belief in mere bulk of territory and in the multiplication of subjects. Nations were not measured by size or number. False Imperialism was militarism and vast standing armies, a spectacle presented by the Continent whose great empires cast their colossal shadow over the smaller states; it was restless intrigue and reckless expenditure, it held out mere prospects of doom. England and her Empire still possessed the brighter and more peaceful outlook in her Empire which represented the true Imperialism. Its strength lay in the self-governing Anglo-Saxon Colonies. Those followed in the track of English traditions and belief. 'These are Imperial Arts, and worthy Thee', he stressed affirming Dryden's words which Lowe had quoted in derision. Genuine Imperialism was a service, was keeping the peace between tribes or settlements that would otherwise fight endless bloody wars; it meant developing in a country like Ceylon productive works of great value, it meant relieving famine and educating peoples towards self-government. It gave negroes their freedom, regulated coolie labour, put down usurious extortions, and raised the standard of savages. It was serving mankind, in fact, by its humanizing effort. Thus it gained the acquiescence, if not the gratitude, of hundreds of millions of natives who regarded Western civilization as either a necessary evil or a dubious good. It gained the loyalty of millions of British settlers, bound to the Empire by common origin, faith, language, laws, and allegiance to the Crown, and it prepared the way for the realization of that noble dream 'which may yet in the fulness of time be realized, of a great English-speaking community, united together in a peaceful confederation, too powerful to be molested by any nation, and too powerful and too generous, I hope, to molest any weaker state'.[1] In the discussion the Earl of Rosebery stressed that the fate of the British race as an imperial race would not be decided by flaunting words of eminence and imperialism about; and Lord Houghton underlined the democratic nature of British Imperialism, resting as it did not on authority but on consent. The words of Lord Carnarvon were widely reported and found approval in the press. *The*

Times in a leading article agreed with the attempt to give the new word a more attractive look. '. . . The term has been adopted, for good or for bad, into our political vocabulary, and, that being the case, it is just as well that it should be divested at once and by common consent of certain misleading and not very attractive associations.'[1] It is interesting how quickly the growth and diffusion of the new slogan was noticed and its meaning discussed in public and says much for the critical vigilance and political alertness of the press and public men, impressive evidence of the high standard of British political life at that time. The tide of political emotions surged high, but there was little chance for romantic or aggressive emotionalism to sweep away all sober judgement and critical evaluation.

Carnarvon's branding of false Imperialism had focused on the domestic scene rather than on the British Empire. He denounced Caesarism and personal rule. This was, of course, the older meaning of the word of which he was not aware when he confessed the word was new to him. The charge of personal rule became a prominent Liberal weapon in the campaign against Disraeli. The accusation was substantiated in an article written by a leading Manchester journalist, Henry Dunckley, editor of the *Manchester Examiner and Times*. He had made a reputation for himself as a Liberal writer on the British Constitution by opposing the view that the royal prerogative should be strengthened. In November 1878 he rejected that opinion again and combined his opposition to Sir Theodore Martin's and Baron Stockmar's constitutional doctrines with an attack against Disraeli in an article, called *The Progress of Personal Rule*. The evil progress had started in 1874, according to Dunckley, when Disraeli became Prime Minister and the first volume of Sir Theodore Martin's *Life of the Prince Consort* was published. Theory and practice of personal rule were revived. As a result, after four years,

we can now understand more clearly how the Parliamentarians of France must have felt when M. Rouher used to register his master's decrees in the Legislative Body, or when, at a later moment, a few rash words which France did not hear plunged the country into the lowest depths of humiliation and hurried the dynasty to Sedan. Our experience of Imperialism has not yet gone so far, but what we have already tasted may be only the beginning of sorrows.[2]

Disraeli was on his best way, the author declared, to 'imperialize' the British Constitution. The Suez Canal coup was brought off without the knowledge of Parliament, which was treated with disrespect when the new Royal Title was introduced and a name given to the British Crown which Napoleon had made odious. Disraeli had refused to include in the Bill the provision that the title of Empress should not be used in the United Kingdom. He had pointed out that Parliament existed by the prerogative of the Crown, a statement which could only justify the suspicion already roused by the nature of his administration. By the logic of his Imperialism the English 'would find their proper place as a fractional part of an empire which included the two hundred millions of Hindostan'. The insults to Parliament were multiplied in the course of the Eastern Question, the movement of Indian troops to Malta, the Treaty of Berlin, and the secret conclusion of the Anglo-Turkish Convention. Having put the nation into an imperial mood, the new 'Grand Vizier' could take advantage of the passions he had excited; but neither peace nor honour were gained thereby. Henry Dunckley thought the key to an understanding of Disraeli's Imperialism was his books and his Jewish descent. Being of Jewish descent he had no sympathy with English political life and mocked all parties. His mind being Asiatic, it was natural that Disraeli should prefer a type of government which was 'an absolute monarchy tempered by sacerdotalism'.[1]

As Imperialism had assumed a domestic as well as an imperial meaning, a derogatory as well as a laudatory tone, it is understandable that by the end of November people were conscious of the existence of the new word but a little confused about its meaning, as *Punch* put it:

> Imperialism! Hang the word! It buzzes in my noddle
> Like bumble-bees in clover time. The talk on't's
>   mostly twaddle;
> Yet one would like to fix the thing, as farmer nail
>   up vermin;
> Lots o' big words collapse, like blobs, if their sense you
>   once determine.[2]

Dunckley's ideas were echoed in Parliament in December. Anglo-Afghan relations had worsened in November. With the Indians watching how Britain would react to the humiliating treatment of her mission, retreat was difficult without loss of face. Lytton never contemplated retreat. His ultimatum sent to the Amir remained unanswered and in December Britain found herself at war with Afghanistan. A motion introduced into the House of Commons that the House disapproved of the Afghan policy led to a debate in the course of which the Liberals were not slow to point out that the new Empire conception was to blame. It carried the nation away by its own momentum. The evil war spirit was no longer the slave but the master of the Government and was driving the country relentlessly towards its Sedan. In this way Sir William Harcourt expressed his criticism of the Government: 'The policy of the Government was an Imperial policy! Yes, it was an Imperial policy—it was a servile imitation of the Imperialism of the Second Empire.' That Empire, however, ran its fatal course through little wars, foreign expeditions, the exaltation of its own race, and the gratification of French pride to the final disaster, Harcourt warned the House.[1] A day later Mr Gladstone, speaking out against the forward policy of the Government, referred to the Tories as having drunk deeply 'of the intoxicating beverage of the new Imperialism'.[2] The new slogan even penetrated into the *Annual Register* and gave its pages an anti-Disraeli slant. Its editor eventually lost his position. There we find it chronicled that the Governor-General of India 'and then our representative in South Africa, caught the infection of "Imperialism"'.[3] It was clear, therefore, that the slogan of Imperialism had struck root in the field of party politics by the end of the year 1878 and was adopted by the Liberal Opposition in their political struggle against the Conservative Government.

The economic depression lasted through the winter of 1878/9 and was linked with Imperialism, for Liberal critics argued that imperial wars and adventure impoverished the nation. Occasionally 'Jingoism' takes the place of Imperialism in Liberal propaganda. At other times Imperialism was made responsible for the impoverishment of India; so when Lord Lytton's Afghan policy was criticized in the *Contemporary Review* by Lt.-Col. R. Osborn, the author maintained the Imperialists gloried in war but shrank from paying the costs of such transactions which in the case of the Afghan campaign was borne by the Indian tax-payer. The repeal of the cotton duties in India also had an imperialist function in the eyes of the writer. They were meant to restore the prestige of Imperialism in Manchester after it had suffered a set-back in Afghanistan, again at the expense of the Indian tax-payer.[1] In Bradford Forster told his audience the real meaning of Imperialism was the setting up of absolute government by the Premier; once the Premier had been chosen, it meant minding the business of every country but England. In the pages of the *Nineteenth Century* Wilson defended the Government and even the slogan which, he wrote, Mr Forster held up to execration

as the cast-off raiment of Bonapartism. But the Imperialism which in truth disquiets those whose ideal of policy is England's minding her own business is an old, not a new habit of mind with Englishmen—a native, not a borrowed principle of government. . . . To guard the multiform and complex interests of our Indian dominions, our colonies, and our dependencies all over the world, seems to the majority of the English people a duty that they owe to those who went before them, and to those who will come after them.[2]

For the first time since the Napoleonic Wars, Wilson pointed out, all the empires of the earth were on trial again. If England was unable to maintain her Empire, its ruin would be calamitous and unmeasurable. *Punch* in the first months of the new year reflected the fixation of the slogan as anti-Tory in character and as a frequent equivalent to 'High Jingo'. With complications and open hostilities in South Africa and in Afghanistan John Bull, as represented by *Punch*, remained baffled, befogged,

> half-blinded by Imperialism's craze
> He knows not, hour from hour, what hated part
> May be prepared for him by statecraft's art,
> But loses hold on all his high traditions,
> Prey to a policy of false positions.[3]

Liberal pamphlets and political satire that year made a good deal of use of the new slogan.[4] A satirical biography in verse by James George Ashworth was called:

> *Imperial Ben. A Jew d'Esprit.*

It included the following lines:

> Imperialism will never do
> Where Hampden, Cromwell, had a birth;
> Our fathers' spirit doth imbue
> Their children all the wide world through,
> And now they know its worth!
> Imperialism! what is it, save
> Presumptuous arrogance and pride?—
> A monstrous self love that would crave
> All for its own of good and brave—
> Self-crowned, self-deified!
> A huge monstrosity of lies,
> And juggling and double-dealing,
> And lofty-handed tyrannies,
> And barbarous, brutal cruelties,
> Inhuman and unfeeling.[1]

The events of 1879 kept the new slogan fully alive. The new High Commissioner for South Africa, Sir Bartle Frere, had provoked a war against the Zulus and suffered an alarming set-back in January. Costly reinforcements became necessary, and in addition to the Afghan troubles the nation found itself plagued by yet another unwanted war. In the Commons Joseph Chamberlain observed that the spirit of Imperialism had infected the minds and judgements of many in positions of authority.[2] That impression was correct as far as Frere was concerned, who was a staunch supporter of the idea of a strongly centralized, unified, military Empire. His forward action in Africa caused a good deal of embarrassment to the Government and to Disraeli personally, who was really not in control of South African affairs, but it all helped to strengthen in the minds of the people an image of Disraeli as a bellicose, vainglorious adventurer and arch-imperialist. Throughout the year some writers still kept on wondering what the new, noisy word was all about. The Duke of Argyll defended the imperial spirit of the Englishman who was not content with counting up merchandise but was conscious of his imperial duties and rights, though his imperial energies might sometimes be employed in the wrong direction and produce the noisy nonsense 'now so rampant on the subject of what is called "Imperialism" . . .'.[3] Some people still thought the word emanated from the Government. One Liberal writer wondered whether the ministers knew how to define 'Imperialism' which, he alleged, they so lately and loudly preached. 'If it merely means the protection of the best interests of the English, every Englishman is an Imperialist. But if it means the spread of annexation and the growth of absolutism, a loss of liberty and a gain to power, every Englishman who loves his country will be earnest in his protest against it.'[1] The author's definition of Imperialism in the derogatory sense came as close to its current meaning as was possible for a contemporary observer who had some partisan views of his own. It exhibited the double meaning of domestic menace and high-handed policy in foreign affairs.

British political life served as a model even where it was not intended to play that part, and often the model was misunderstood by foreigners. In the eighteenth century French and German public men and statesmen read and adopted slogans and ideas broadcast by the Opposition in Britain without understanding the political context of either the issue involved or the role of the Opposition in British politics. A similar process began to take shape in 1879. Indian writers took note of the arguments of the Liberal Opposition and echoed their ideas and the new slogan of Imperialism. Some of the Indian grievances were, however, quite genuine and their outcry against Imperialism reflected a true continuation of the imperial issue that had split views in Britain. In that respect the case was similar to the link between the British Opposition and the American colonists in the eighteenth century.[2]

In September 1879 the British Mission to Afghanistan, installed there only a few months earlier after a successful military campaign, were murdered. The war against that country was thereupon renewed. No end to imperial troubles and complications seemed in sight. While the Liberals could proclaim in triumph: We told you so! the Government, led by an ailing Premier, was losing ground as the parties were getting ready for the election campaign.

The nature of the British Empire and its future development was made an issue in the election campaign. The Premier had raised the banner of 'Empire and Liberty' in his Guildhall Speech in November 1879, which drew Gladstone's retort that it meant 'Liberty for ourselves, Empire over the rest of mankind'.[3] Separation was no longer a real issue despite the fact the Conservatives used 'Dismemberment of the Empire' as the anti-Liberal slogan when the election campaign reached its height in spring 1880. The slogan was directed not so much against the Liberal tendency to dispose of the Colonies as against their support of home rule for Ireland. The Liberals with Gladstone at their head fought the campaign as self-confessed Empire supporters. They maintained that the quarrel with Disraeli was not the existence of the Empire but its character. In his Midlothian speeches Gladstone outlined an Empire based on co-operation, on the consent of the dependencies and colonies expressed in colonial parliaments. Such parliaments, in Gladstone's conception, should have sovereign authority over the military forces raised on their own territory. Gladstone developed that point in contrast to Disraeli's Indian policy and the use of Indian troops. He denounced the doctrine that the Crown was entitled to wage wars and raise troops anywhere in the British Empire without Parliamentary consent or control, so long as Parliament was not asked to foot the bill.[1] As for British rule over alien races Gladstone established two principles. He agreed to British rule over backward races as far as that rule had already been set up as a 'moral trusteeship'. He opposed the extension of that trusteeship and upheld the second principle of equal right for all nations.

Modern times have established a sisterhood of nations, equal, independent; each of them built up under that legitimate defence which public law affords to every nation, living within its own borders, and seeking to perform its own affairs; but if one thing more than another has been detestable to Europe, it has been the appearance upon the stage from time to time of men who, even in the times of the Christian civilisation, have been thought to aim at universal dominion.[2]

Gladstone thought of Louis XIV and Napoleon. Such a quest for universal Empire was to him un-Christian and un-European. His quarrel with the Tory Government was inspired by Canning in that respect: a British Government should always retain sympathy with national independence and with the spirit of liberty. Disraeli was stifling both. He built up an Empire kept together by force and weakened by growing over-extension. The strength of the Empire was maintained at home—in good government and a sound economy. The Government had neglected both while it had inflamed the public with high-sounding phrases. Gladstone took pains not to imitate the Government in that respect. In his election campaign he studiously abstained from employing the Liberal phrases of the street, jingoism and imperialism. They had become too cheap in his eyes.

There is, in fact, evidence that by spring 1880 party slogans such as were in popular use at that time had lost a little of their freshness. Thinking men had wearied of them. Gladstone was not alone in avoiding them. An article on Home Rule, published in the *Nineteenth Century*, reflected the feeling of slogan-weariness, so natural when an election campaign has reached its height, in the words: 'For a practical people the English are strangely governed by words and phrases. . . . With certain minds a phrase settles a whole question.'[1] Those words were evoked by the overworking of the slogan of 'Dismemberment of the Empire'. Election pamphlets and articles, on the other hand, could not do without the established slogans of their time. The *Contemporary Review* offered its readers studies of Disraeli and Gladstone, each presented from a Liberal and a Conservative point of view. Those studies show that at that time the name of 'imperialists' was accepted by both sides as an apt term denoting Disraeli's followers.[2] The Liberals in their pamphlets accused Disraeli of personal rule and disregard of Parliament. The ghost of Napoleon III still hovered over the election campaign. Some pamphleteers spoke of 'Napoleonic Imperialism', which Disraeli was alleged to impose on the British people. A moderate Liberal writer expressed his belief that all the hubbub against Imperialism was staged by radical and revolutionary elements in order to deprive the Crown of all power and to strengthen republicanism.[3]

On the eve of the election the banker and historian Frederic Seebohm published an article, called *Imperialism and Socialism*, proving that the boot was on the other foot. Imperialism itself, he maintained, was the flag of the radicals and revolutionaries and menaced the social order. His thesis revealed deep thought and insight which were inspired by his sincere Christian faith. Seebohm explained that the imperial crisis which Britain faced in 1880 was part of a greater European crisis of Empire. The Continent had witnessed the rise of new, great, imperial states, armed to the teeth, living in constant dread of one another and in equal dread of their own people, whom the new Empires had to arm in order to maintain themselves as powerful military machines. The welfare of the people and good government were subordinated to the dictates of military policy and the needs of foreign affairs. The result of the subordination of domestic life to military requirements was the rise of socialism. French Imperialism had led to the Commune. It claimed to rule by virtue of popular will but when popular will was asked to act it was merely in order to surrender the reins of control to the people in power. The effect was an alliance between the rulers and the mob. Imperial policy relentlessly drove countries into foreign adventures and left popular wrongs and requirements at home unredressed. Britain, being a nation ruled by a free Parliament, whose government was not a union between the mob and the monarch, could have remained outside the fatal development of Imperialism to be followed by Socialism.

And yet this moment, when Continental Imperialism is everywhere confronted by Socialism, is chosen by the ruling party of the English nation—the party calling itself conservative—to let itself be drawn by its leader into a policy which he himself has cynically and theatrically recommended to the nation under the ill-fated name of 'Imperialism'! The new-fangled policy of Lord Beaconsfield may be only a mock Imperialism, and be intended to stop far short of a real one; but it has succeeded in ostentatiously displaying the distinctive marks and notes of its Continental prototype.[1]

The first results of that British brand of Imperialism could be already observed in Britain itself, Seebohm pointed out. Home affairs were neglected for the sake of a spirited foreign policy. He asked: 'Are we to neglect our part in the problem of the internal development of this vast people for the sake of some Imperial phantom of ascendancy in Asia? With this tremendous stake in the problem of the guidance of our own democracy, are we to ape the methods, the style, and the false glitter of Continental Imperialism?'[2] The true roots of democracy were derived not from Rome but from Christianity. Imperialism failed to understand the meaning of democracy. A Christian and democratic England could make herself the Athens—not the Rome—of the English-speaking world as the classical land and home of the highest English culture. Seebohm did not oppose colonies. He opposed colonies administered along imperial lines such as he observed in Indian administration, which spent too much money on military enterprise and too little on popular welfare. The danger lay not in the colonial Empire as such but in the imperial spirit that pervaded parts of it. That spirit constituted the real moral threat. Seebohm believed that a major issue in the election campaign was the liberal and moral character of the Empire and its future development. He wrongly attributed the term Imperialism to Conservative pronouncements, as did Lowe and others before him. The imperial language of the Conservatives had shown a remarkable restraint, as it happened. Disraeli did not choose to answer the many accusations that were hurled against him. He hardly read them. His last word on imperial policy and foreign affairs was uttered in November 1879. If the wealthiest Empire in the world kept aloof from Continental affairs and neglected its own strength, Disraeli said in his Guildhall Speech, it would soon become an object of general plunder. In the light of Continental developments during the following decades Disraeli's words revealed a sense of political realism which was hard to refute. His goal of 'Imperium et Libertas' was the crux of the problem. How could imperial strength be combined with a liberal spirit? Unfortunately, the British public was given the impression that a choice would have to be made between Liberalism and Imperialism and that the latter contradicted the former.

Imperialism thus became entrenched in the public mind as a watchword of political controversy, invented to brand Disraeli's policy as alien and undemocratic. '"Imperialism" was a word invented to stamp Lord Beaconsfield's supposed designs with popular reprobation. But the weapon wounded the hand that wielded it, and a suspicion was engendered, which seriously injured the Liberal cause, that Liberalism was in some sort an antithesis to Imperialism.' In these sentences, whose semantic evidence has been overlooked by lexicographers as well as by political scientists, *The Times*, on 11 March 1880, commented on the issues of the election campaign.[1] The word had become symbolic of alleged tendencies which under the auspices of Disraeli had jointly insinuated themselves into the national mind—subversion of parliamentary authority, aggressiveness, connivance at reckless expenditure for purposes of vain ambition and military adventures, boisterousness, vain over-commitments, and centralization of imperial control. The defenders of sound Liberal principles had been warned to be on the alert.

At this juncture the great theme becomes apparent which first infused life into the concept of Imperialism and its meaning in English political language and which has never ceased to lay claim to it, much though the word became burdened with accessory meanings. This theme concerned the attitude which the nation was to take towards its most conspicuous achievements abroad. National energies of different character had concurred in establishing the unique structure of the British Empire. The very existence of this widespread political edifice required constant maintenance and repairs, constant watchfulness. It led to political engagements whose long-time effects could not be clearly predicted. Those engagements were, moreover, bound up with the application of military force. Should all this be countenanced as a responsibility which national honour bade not only to shoulder but even to welcome? Was the material risk incurred not also a moral risk? Would energies displayed on behalf of the Empire not be necessarily at variance with the virtues practised or at any rate preached at home? Could the interest in acquisition and influence abroad be made a primary national cause without conflicting with such ideals of justice and liberty as were supposed to go with the English name? Could it be allowed to compete in importance with internal affairs? These questions bordered on the interpretation of British history as a whole. Confronted with them the national conscience was drawn into two opposite directions—one pointing to the growth of Empire and bearing its name, the other recoiling from both. These two contrasting attitudes are a constitutive element in the modern political life of Great Britain. They cast their shadow across many affairs connected with the existence and development of the British Empire. In the handling of those imperial affairs the concept of Imperialism repeatedly displayed the function with which it was invested in the days of Disraeli. It has often been understood as the shibboleth by the use of which one section of the nation expressed its low opinion of the political morality allegedly possessed by another section.

VII

IMPERIALISM—THE NATIONAL DESIRE
FOR ANGLO-SAXON UNION

The political defeat of Disraeli and the formation of a Liberal Government which was committed to a policy of thrift and retrenchment in imperial matters removed the motive for the use of Imperialism as a party slogan. The word disappeared from the political scene, though it was not forgotten. The study of political slogans shows not only astonishing changes in the meaning of political words and emotive expressions but also demonstrates their surprising longevity. Slogans may hibernate, as it were, through periods of unfavourable political conditions only to appear again with new vigour in another political spring.

The first years that followed Disraeli's downfall and death were unfavourable to imperial sentiment and language. In June 1881 it was noticed that to assert imperial interests and plead Empire duty carried little popularity. Even Disraeli's death could not appease the Radicals' animosity against Imperialism.[1] The Government was determined to cut down commitments in South Africa and Afghanistan. Eager supporters of that policy of retreat became impatient when they thought the Government lacked promptness in that respect. The notorious imperial activist, Sir Bartle Frere, was not recalled from South Africa at once as anti-imperialists had hoped, and Liberal writers feared that 'emotions of puerile vanity' might have gripped the public and the Government. Were they afraid of implementing the policy of cool calculation which had been promised? 'Six years of tawdry imperialism can scarcely have so demoralized' the public as to render it incapable of mature reflexion,[2] the Fortnightly Review commented on Gladstone's slow change of front in colonial matters. But the obnoxious word became rare.

As the incompetence of the Government in dealing with colonial affairs became apparent and its set-backs grew, Disraeli's name acquired a new glitter. A legend of his imperial vision began to grow and his name was often associated with the awakening of the imperial spirit. Froude in 1890 wrote that the imperial spirit Disraeli imagined he had aroused slept in indifference.[1] Neither part of the statement was quite true. Outside Britain Disraeli was a legendary figure even in his life-time and associated with the restoration of Britain's position and status as an imperial Power.[2] The events of the 1890's and the first two decades of the twentieth century gave the Disraeli legend a growing momentum. In 1921 his reputation as Britain's master imperialist had already grown to such an extent that a reviewer of his biography by Monypenny and Buckle could state that it was Disraeli who had raised the credit of Great Britain among the nations and 'formulated the theory of Empire, which, rejected for a time by Gladstone, gradually became the accepted ideal not only of Great Britain herself, but of the British Dominions and the Empire as a whole'.[3] Such a sentence is entirely based on legend, whose existence forty years after Disraeli's death should not surprise us, as we saw how many public men even in his own time believed him and his government to have coined the word Imperialism and to have been captivated by the idea the term was believed to express. Opposi-tion to it was also seen in a legendary light and expressed in the terms of a later period. Such a retrospective projection is evident in the thoughts of W. Stead on the agitation in 1876 concerning the Bulgarian atrocities. His paper had been the centre of agitation in North England, and nobody could be expected to have been a more competent witness and authority on the character of the movement; yet about thirty years later he wrote of the agitation that it was the first in the annals of England 'in which the Democracy sprang to its feet by an instantaneous impulse, without waiting for the guidance of its leaders, in order to compel a reluctant and hostile administration to repudiate the traditional policy of the Empire'.[4] Every part in that statement is unhistorical. The writer sees the beginning of the period in the terminology and the concepts of its end. Yet there is some truth behind those words which is not directly stated. The concept of Empire and its peculiar association with Disraeli took its post-Disraeli course of political myth from the days of the Eastern Question onwards. As the Gladstone administration was rocking under the blows of ill-fortune in colonial affairs and was showered with accusations of being 'disruptionist', the name of Empire was again purged of the evil smell that had clung to it in the mud-slinging of the years 1876–80. That tendency was increased by the issue of Home Rule, which concerned not a distant colony but the island on the other side of the St George's Channel.

A link between the Irish Question and Empire sentiment existed already in the election campaign of 1880. Supporters of the Home Rule Movement were branded as enemies of the Empire, and such phrases as 'breaking up the Empire', 'dismemberment of the Empire', 'disruption', 'separation' were frequently used. Disraeli himself blended the Irish and imperial issues in his last election manifesto when he accused his political opponents of the desire to break up the Empire and the United Kingdom. 'There are some', he proclaimed, 'who challenge the expediency of the Imperial character of this realm. Having attempted, and failed, to enfeeble our Colonies by their policy of decomposition, they may perhaps now recognize in the disintegration of the United Kingdom a mode which will not only accomplish, but precipitate their purpose.'[1] The 'Unity of the Empire' became the rallying cry of all who fought against the plan of setting up a parliament in Dublin. After Disraeli's death Lord Salisbury wrote and spoke against Home Rule in the name of imperial unity.[2] Yet imperial unity was never the real issue. Gladstone, as all the evidence shows, in the years 1885–6 when the Home Rule issue reached its first climax, desired to maintain the unity of the Empire just as much as his opponents. The real issue since the days of Disraeli had been the character of the Empire, not its existence of which the whole nation was at long last aware. What should the attitude of the country be towards its great achievement of the century? Disraeli's administration had given that question prominence for the first time. Gladstone inherited from Disraeli among all the other imperial problems also that problem of the nation's own appraisal of the Empire and its plans for the future. He and his political friends believed in a decentralized and autonomous system which allowed each community to govern its own affairs. 'What I say on Ireland is simply an expansion and adaptation of what I have already said often, namely, that Ireland may have all that is compatible with the unity of the Empire', Gladstone wrote to Hartington in November 1885.[3]

Violence and restlessness had been smouldering in Ireland and occasionally breaking out into serious conflagrations during Gladstone's administration, but the Irish troubles were not confined to the Green Island. The Irish members of Parliament brought instability of government, uncertainty, and disorder to Westminster where in 1885 they were in the position of making and unmaking governments. When Gladstone formed his third administration in February 1886 he made Home Rule his major legislative venture and for a few months this became the outstanding political issue. Its imperial implications were numerous. Why should Ireland be denied what had been conceded to Canada and to Australia? What powers should be reserved to London and what powers should be surrendered to Dublin? How much centralized authority was good for the British Empire?

There was a strong Home Rule sentiment in Canada and Australia.[1] Unionists formed 'loyal and patriotic' associations. Their Toronto chairman was Goldwin Smith. Like John Bright, Smith belonged to those Liberals who admired Gladstone's belief in the force of liberal institutions but feared its practical application. With a peculiar logic of his own Goldwin Smith was an ardent supporter of Canadian autonomy but an equally fierce opponent of Irish home rule. His pamphlet, *Dismemberment no Remedy*, bears a demagogic title and contains emotional appeals to the effect that the disruption of the United Kingdom could never lead to a wider and mightier imperial federation. An existing solid unity was given up for the sake of a wider one which was but a dream. 'I have never been an Imperialist or a Jingo', Smith assured his readers. 'I have always held that England ought to move among nations, not like a Roman citizen in a conquered world (which was too much Lord Palmerston's ideal), but like an English gentleman among his equals, respecting their rights and honours while he quietly maintains his own.' Here 'Imperialism' appears in the mind of Goldwin Smith closely associated with Jingoism and denoting offensive manner of an assertive, boisterous, imperial bragging.[2]

Among fundamental questions raised during those months of Home Rule debate was the dubious nature of the name 'British'. Was the Empire British? Would that epithet not exclude the non-British members, Ireland among them? One writer thought the term 'imperial patriotism', which he hoped to see develop in Ireland, was a better name than 'British patriotism'.[1] Another writer believed the use of that adjective reduced the status of Irishmen 'by giving legal effect to our constant assertion that our foreign and colonial policy, and in fact all our Imperial policy, is "British" . . .'.[2] While a heated debate was in progress as to whether a federal or a centralized character would serve the Empire better, Empire unity was accepted by both home rulers and unionists as their avowed goal. Nobody came forward with a plan for peaceful separation. Those days were gone. Gladstone argued that the Canadian example had proved the soundness of autonomy and had demonstrated that it was in no way 'detrimental to the Unity of the Empire', a cry that was also heard when home rule was first introduced in Canada, 'a cry which has slept for a long time, and which has acquired vigour from sleeping—it was the cry with which we are now becoming familiar—the cry of the unity of the Empire . . . but it was the remedy for the mischief and not the mischief itself which was regarded as dangerous to the unity of the Empire. Here I contend that the cases are precisely parallel.'[3] Gladstone's long political experience had taught him the lesson that political slogans may occasionally lie dormant for a time only to rise again to new life when the force of political magic calls them afresh. The unity of the Empire was an appeal strong enough to split the Liberal Party and to reject Home Rule for Ireland.

What had been rejected, however, was not only autonomy for Ireland. The federal character of the Empire was at stake. Dicey had argued that Home Rule challenged the supremacy of the Imperial Parliament and the unity of the Empire. There was a good deal of confusion in the public mind about the actual meaning of words. Imperial as well as Empire, we remember, had been applied to the United Kingdom only as recently as the early Victorian period; and so it could happen that during the Home Rule debate the defence of the Imperial Parliament meant the legislative authority of the United Kingdom, while the defenders of imperial unity also thought of the British Empire in its wider and more recent connotation. Imperial Parliament, in fact, was not used in the modern sense; but when people spoke of the unity of the Empire, they invariably meant the relation between Britain and all her colonies and dependencies. The older meaning had been forgotten.

Edward A. Freeman, provoked by the emotional appeal to the unity of the Empire by 'imperial patriots', attempted to remind his contemporaries as an historian of what he believed the historical meaning of Empire to have been. 'Disruption of the Empire', Freeman declared, was a meaningless phrase. The 'Empire' did not disintegrate when Canada and New Zealand were granted home rule. It was not likely to break up, if Ireland received self-government. The whole expression of Empire was a myth. Freeman—mistakenly—believed it to be of recent origin, stating, '. . . it is plain that the word "Empire" cannot be used in the sense in which it has of late become the favourite name for the Queen's dominions as a whole'.[1] In that assertion Freeman is in the wrong and ignores the meaning of the British Empire in the eighteenth century. He is right to declare that in the days of King Henry VIII the name of Empire asserted British rule over Ireland. In that sense, he went on, political agitators were more correct than they knew when they referred to home rule for Ireland as threatening the Empire. 'It was, therefore, with perfect truth, with far greater truth than can be found in the commonly received babble about "Empire", that orators in the late election called on the ruling, the Imperial, nation, not to give up the Empire. . . .' The Empire was the fact, the United Kingdom the fiction. Freeman made it quite clear that he was convinced that imperial rule was bound up with human nature. The strong would always be reluctant to give up their possessions. English rule was imperial in Ireland and in India. Practical dependence of nations on stronger states had always existed. Without going into the question of moral evaluation, so much a historian could find out in his own studies. More Freeman did not desire to give. It amounted to a recognition that the foundation of imperial rule was conquest and to a justification of the *status quo*.

Not everybody had such an elastic mind as Goldwin Smith and could be Empire unionist in Britain and home ruler in Canada. A liberal and trained legal mind could not but regard the rejection of the Home Rule Bill with dismay, because it spelt the defeat of the federal principle on which the Colonial Reformers had hoped to erect the edifice of a progressive political association of colonies and dependencies. The defeat of self-government was a blow to the idea of a liberal Empire. The man, who behind the scenes had been working for that idea and had helped Molesworth and Gladstone frame their bills in his capacity as parliamentary draughtsman, now stepped down with Gladstone in 1886 and stated the legal implication of the set-back. Henry Thring was a home ruler by legal and liberal conviction. Already in 1851 he had published an essay in which he defended the principle of self-government. In March 1887 he once again stated his ideas about the imperial implication of Home Rule in an article, called *Home Rule and Imperial Unity*. Anglo-Saxon constitutional law, Thring explained, had developed a dual system of authority and a composite form of nationhood in contradistinction to the centralized and uniform structure of other nations. The United States had a federal authority and the British Empire an imperial authority, vested in the President and the Crown, respectively. The authority to maintain good order, internal peace, and good government was found in the North American state and should be found in a British colony or in the administration of the mother country. Those were the legal principles of double authority on which were built up 'the two great Anglo-Saxon composite nations—namely, the American Union and the British Empire—'.[1] The example of the United States proved that the division into state power and imperial power did not weaken a nation in any way. The parts that made up the British Empire were not contiguous but were in fact all linked by the 'right of the British Crown to exercise Imperial powers' such as making war, concluding foreign treaties, and making peace. Imperial unity was not the result of central control. An Anglo-Saxon colony or territory gradually rose to maturity assuming the right to Home Rule. Canada, New Zealand, Australia, and many American states had set the pattern. If Ireland had followed them, she would have been contented and Imperial unity would have been preserved—an opinion which looked to the authority of Edmund Burke for its support.

Home Rule for Ireland had an imperial implication as it concerned the principle of federation. It so happened that the champion of a federated Empire and chairman of the Imperial Federation League, W. E. Forster, passed away a short time before Parliament rejected Home Rule. His death in spring 1886 gave rise to further comment on the link between the Irish Question and the future character of the Empire.[2] Federation suffered a set-back in Ireland, but the Irish Question promoted the cause of the League all the same. It helped to purge the name of Empire and Imperialism of their negative and derogatory associations which had accompanied them from the days of Disraeli. The newly enfranchised voters came out in favour of Empire unity. As Liberals they followed Chamberlain, who had declared he would sacrifice the unity of the Liberal Party rather than the unity of the Empire.[1] In the course of the three preceding years the British public overcame its imperial weariness, which had followed the Midlothian Campaign and Disraeli's downfall. Apart from the work of the Imperial Federation League, with which we shall deal later in this chapter, the most influential factor in the development of Empire awareness was the publication of John Robert Seeley's Cambridge lectures on the *Expansion of England* in 1883.

The lectures met with a great public response. The author desired to demonstrate a fruitful way of historical interpretation and prediction. He chose the expansion of the English race over the earth as an illustration. It was a topic which had a future as well as a past, and Seeley tried to treat his subject both ways. Still under the impact of the Disraeli era—the lectures were delivered in 1881–2—Seeley confessed that the word Empire 'seems too military and despotic to suit the relation of a mother-country to colonies'.[2] The Colonial Empire was settled by Englishmen and was thus really an enlargement of the English state. The expression Empire was misleading. Unlike the Empires of the Romans and Persians, it was not founded on conquest and not on the rule over alien races. Seeley called that Empire by the name Dilke had made popular, Greater Britain. Its rise formed a main historical theme during the last two centuries. Greater Holland, Greater Spain, and Greater France had vanished, but Greater Britain was still there, sole survivor of a family of Empires, but actually no Empire at all, 'only a nation so widely dispersed that before the age of steam and electricity its strong natural bonds of race and religion seemed practically dissolved by distance'.[3] The United States and Russia had proved that political union over vast areas was possible. Greater Britain would do the same and thereby form the third world power.

How closely Seeley was still linked with the political climate of the Disraeli Ministry can be observed in his use of the word Imperialism.

It appears twice and means despotic rule when the author referred to Cromwell, and another time when he contrasted the democratic policy pursued by Britain in Australia with the despotic form of government practised in India where 'the foremost champion of free thought' stood out as 'a great military Imperialism to resist the march of Russia in Central Asia at the same time that it fills Queensland and Manitoba with free settlers'.[1] And Seeley is also close to the Disraeli era in the way he regarded India as the part to which the name Empire was truly applicable, though he firmly rejected the literal interpretation of India as a British possession and property of the Crown. 'In ordinary language the two notions of property and government are mixed up in a way that produces infinite confusion.'[2] England derived little profit out of her Indian rule, but if she were to give up India at once, the harm would be done not so much to Britain but to the larger and poorer India. The sudden withdrawal even of an oppressive government was a dangerous experiment. Anarchy might follow, such as followed the dissolution of the Mogul Empire, and misery. Withdrawal from India would be a most inexcusable crime and cause a stupendous calamity. Seeley, therefore, supported British rule in India on the basis of the responsibility which Britain had undertaken and which she could not now throw off. He reached the conclusion that the two schools of imperial thought which had acquired a great popularity in the past, the one 'lost in wonder and ecstasy' at the immense dimensions of the Empire, the other regarding it 'as founded in aggression and rapacity, as useless and burdensome',[3] were both impractical extremes. Extent by itself meant little and sentiment could become too burdensome and expensive. Political unions existed for the good of their members. 'It would seem to us insane that if the connection with the colonies or with India hampered both parties, if it did harm rather than good, England should resolve to maintain it to her own detriment and to that of her dependencies.' So far the author sided with the Empire 'pessimists' against 'the bombastic school'. He saw nothing intrinsically glorious in an Empire 'upon which the sun never sets', in the phrase of Empire enthusiasts. On the other hand, there was nothing base or unnatural about the Empire and Greater Britain. The latter served as a natural outlet for Britain's surplus population. As the ties with the British settlements grew stronger, emigrants would not be thought of as lost to England. '... The result might be, first that emigration on a vast scale might become our remedy for pauperism, and, secondly, that some organisation might gradually be arrived at which might make the whole force of the Empire available in time of war. In taking this view I have borne in mind the example of the United States.'[1] They had steadily expanded over a vast area and firmly refused to allow their Union to be broken up. They were indicative of a new historical phase in state building. 'The federal system has been added to the representative system.' The British Empire, far from being an obsolete oriental type of political union, was precisely the type which modern conditions of industry and political thinking required. Russia was another country which, once federated and industrialized, would press heavily on the nation states of Europe, Seeley predicted. 'Russia and the United States will surpass in power the states now called great as much as the great country-states of the sixteenth century surpassed Florence.'[2] Britain, therefore, was faced with the choice either to be Florence or a country-state, to be a European nation-state with her greatness passed, like Spain, or to strive for future greatness on a level with the federated unions to come, the U.S.A. and Russia.

The success of Seeley's historical view and imperial vision has been fully attested. It became a directive force. 'The *Expansion of England* has become a household book and a household phrase', H. A. L. Fisher wrote in 1896,[3] and the *Westminster Gazette* a year earlier confirmed the decisive impulse the work had given 'to what may be called, in the slang of the day, "the new Imperialism"'.[4] In Canada, however, Goldwin Smith expressed his doubt about the success of the federal principle when applied to the British Empire. Canada, he pointed out as an observer on the spot, had her own aims and outlook. She had her own problems of corruption, intrigue, debt. Her 'Imperialism' had embarked upon a vast undertaking to knit together 'the scattered and disconnected provinces into an Empire of British North America, which shall balance the power of the United States'.[5]

Goldwin Smith's argument that the British colonies were developing their own ambitions and policies, thereby making imperial federation a remote ideal, was borne out by events in Australia, when Queensland in spring 1883 proclaimed the annexation of East New Guinea without authority from the Colonial Office, which promptly nullified that step. At the suggestion of Lord Derby an inter-colonial conference was convened at Sydney in December 1883. It issued something like a Monroe Doctrine for the South Pacific declaring any further acquisition of territory in the South Pacific by another Power as injurious to Australasia and the Empire. The Conference hoped the Imperial Government would give effect to the resolution. It did not; and North East New Guinea became a German colony as the Australians had feared. Finally, in October 1884 the British Government gave a belated approval of the establishment of a protectorate over South East New Guinea. Nor were Canada and Australia the only regions where self-governing colonies became expansionist on their own account. No sooner had Gladstone restored self-government to the Transvaal than the Boers began expanding towards the Kalahari Desert in the West and the Indian Ocean in the East, with resulting hostilities in Bechuanaland and Zululand. The Basutos placed their country under the Imperial Crown. Thus the action of the self-governing 'South African Republic', as the Boers called their country after the Pretoria Convention of 1881, heaped new, unwanted responsibilities on Gladstone's administration. Things went particularly badly in Zululand. The policy of non-intervention and inactivity adopted by Lord Derby in Gladstone's administration turned out to be neither cheaper nor safer. Crowds of refugees poured into Natal from the anarchical region of the Zulus, and troops had to be brought up from the Cape Colony at great cost. People in Britain began to wonder whether it was not cheaper after all to annex and pacify a territory such as Zululand. Above all, the question was asked whether the concept of self-government was at all clear. Did anybody have a precise idea how much expansionist initiative was at the discretion of a self-governing colony or to what extent a colony had to rely on local resources? Where should imperial control be and how should it be exercised? The urgency of such questions is reflected in articles commenting on African and Australasian affairs, as the fabric of Empire was annually becoming more complicated and the need for new answers pressing.[1]

The suspicion expressed by public men that the country lacked clear thought on imperial matters and that the Government's colonial policy was composed of hesitance and make-shift was well founded. The Government had come to power pledged not to increase imperial obligations. As the case of Egypt had shown, they left it to events to do so and to carry a reluctant administration along. The prevailing anarchy in Zululand left the Colonial Secretary at a loss. 'What are we to do with that country?' he asked Gladstone in a letter in December 1883.

Can we leave the whole matter alone? That is the simplest course: but it will lead to civil war and to a general disturbance among the natives. . . . I am afraid we cannot wash our hands of the affair, much as I should wish it. Lastly, should we as a provisional expedient occupy the country temporarily up to Usibebe's boundary, to keep order till something permanent can be settled? You will not like this notion nor do I: but we cannot go on long as we are and as at present advised. I really do not see what else is possible. . . . There seems no known means of getting the Zulus to say what they like best —they have not been used to being consulted. If you don't approve of my suggestion, can you offer one? I don't see my way.[1]

The letter is typical for the lack of imperial direction and planning which characterized Gladstone's ministry and proved Seeley's dictum with which he introduced his lectures, that the British seemed to have conquered and peopled half the world 'in a fit of absence of mind'. The more patent the governmental 'fit of absence of mind' became, the more impatient grew those men who believed with Seeley in the need for definite measures towards the development of the United States of Greater Britain.

With the approval of Seeley and the active support of W. E. Forster, Lord Rosebery, and public men belonging to both parties, the constitutive committee of the projected Imperial Federation League met in London in July 1884. Their objective was to secure a permanent unity of the Empire by publicizing the idea of federal union and formulating new legislative and constitutional measures in furtherance of imperial union. It was the intention of the first conference to record a protest against the belief, which still existed at home and in the colonies, that there was still a party in Britain or a political section which disregarded the connexion of Britain with her colonies and advocated separation. It was significant for the sponsors and their concept of Empire that non-British dependencies were not considered; and it required a special motion to include, at any rate, the West Indies in the list of addresses to which copies of the committee's resolutions should be sent.[1] No mention was made of Africa, Asian imperial outposts, or India. Another main problem, what economic advantage federal union would bring to England, was left out of the discussion, although its importance as an anti-separatist argument was obvious. A third group of constitutional problems was not discussed either. There was a tendency not to arouse opposition at that early stage by being too specific about the possible share colonies should have in controlling foreign policy, defence, and in sustaining other imperial responsibilities. Forster vaguely stated the need for common counsel. Gisborne, representing New Zealand, valued a federation from the point of view of common defence and the right of the colonies to be heard in the 'organization of war', whereas British representatives, such as Rosebery and W. H. Smith, stressed problems created by the growing population in the British Isles and the need for emigration. Rosebery pointed to the unique historical position which pressed for action. A high tide of emigration had come. There was a chance to direct the emigrants to loyal and attached communities in Canada and in Australia, 'two great countries—empires, if you will, stretching forth their hands to you in passionate loyalty and devotion to the country from which they spring. If you will not avail yourselves of that sentiment now, the time will come when you will bitterly repent it.'[2] Racialist sentiment and hopes for world domination were also expressed by men who had absorbed Dilke's ideas. Lord Bury praised the superior colonizing qualities of the Anglo-Saxon race which were such 'that that race will eventually become the dominant race of the world, and we only require to be welded together in one homogeneous whole to hasten that very desirable event'.[3] The first meeting thus demonstrated imperial sentiment rather than legal and constitutional thought. Its language, however, linked imperial sentiment of the 1880's with that of the 1890's in such phrases as appeared for the first time in the perorations of the imperial federalists, and which implied a belief in the global mission of the Anglo-Saxon race to establish 'a material guarantee for the peace, order, and good government of the world'.

The meeting was welcomed by the British press. *The Times* stressed the rise of a new empire sentiment and the decline of Cobdenism. The *Standard* and the *Pall Mall* observed the change in the intellectual climate as well. The latter in a leading article referred to the change which the word and idea of 'imperialism' were undergoing. Seven years earlier, the paper pointed out, there was a danger that the reaction against 'the bombastic Imperialism of Lord Beaconsfield'—an echo of Seeley—might lead to the revival of the school of extreme non-intervention. 'For some time after our advent to office the reaction from Jingoism rendered it almost impossible for advocates of a reasonable Imperialism to gain a hearing. Time, however, and experience have done their work. Imperialism is no longer tainted with the foul association of a swashbuckler Jingoism.'[1]

The language of the conference quickly spread to the colonies. Its resolutions were repeated verbatim a year later in New Zealand when the House of Representatives approved of the Imperial Federation, while Sir Julius Vogel suggested that the British colonies should send elected members to the British House of Commons for a trial period of three parliaments.[2] Forster had preferred a consultative body composed of the Agents General in London. The *Fortnightly Review*, in two critical articles on Empire Federation, doubted whether the presence of Canadian, Australian, and South African members of parliament would fit into the traditional pattern of British politics. The arguments of Adam Smith against political ties and the history of Anglo-American relations spoke against federation. Between friendly countries no federation was necessary; between hostile countries no federation could serve a useful purpose. Imperial Federation could not add any advantage that did not exist already, the journal concluded.[3] The *Spectator*, too, had second thoughts. At a Cambridge meeting, presided over by Seeley, Forster had dramatically called for an alliance between England and all the English-speaking dependencies. 'Let us turn Great Britain into Greater Britain', he declared. Seeley made it clear that Imperial Federation had no militant character and that nothing in his book suggested plans favouring a policy of expansionism. The *Spectator* did not doubt the peaceful intentions and sincerity of the League and the absence of militant feeling at home. In the colonies, however, sentiments were different. There, the journal observed, expansionism was popular, as the

Boer Republics, India, and Australia had shown. Disraeli had stimulated jingoism in the colonies. It had acquired its own momentum and was threatening to carry Britain along with it.¹ The strong impression that Britain was being carried along in an imperial current much against her will came into the open in spring 1885 and must be responsible for the new chill that damped imperial enthusiasm. The disaster of Khartoum had occurred in January. Political observers were puzzled. An irony of fate followed the administration. The Government had taken office committed to a policy of retrenchment of expenditure and imperial responsibilities. Nobody doubted Gladstone's own sincerity. Yet within a short time imperial expansion had taken place in South Africa, the Niger Valley, in Egypt, the Sudan, North Borneo, and New Guinea as a result of circumstances over which the Government had no control. Other powers, such as France and Germany, had begun to force the pace. Should Britain keep step and take over additional vast territories in Africa? 'It looks as if an epidemic of mingled acquisitiveness and adventure has set in which will soon leave no eligible slice of the globe's surface without the sovereignty of a civilising power.' That was the new element in the situation as surveyed by Joseph Cowen, member of Parliament for Newcastle and editor of the *Newcastle Chronicle*, in a speech made in February 1885. He spoke of the 'irresistible drift in human affairs' which left ministers perplexed. Between an insular outlook and an imperial view Great Britain was still confused. 'What ought to be England's relation to her dependencies and what her attitude to the States with which they may draw her into collision, are questions which recent events have forced into delicate prominence.'² Cowen saw England committed to an imperial course. She could not draw back, even if she wished to do so. If the pessimists after the new troubles and disasters in Africa said the Empire had become too big and its organization too loose, their dream of becoming a prosperous maritime Switzerland or Florence was against 'the decrees of fate', which had made England a colonizing power. Cowen opposed the new doubts which the sad end of General Gordon's activities in the Sudan had raised. 'Englishmen may not have mastered the philosophy of Imperial expansion, but their instincts and impulses will prompt them to oppose a spiritless surrender of lands that have been watered by the blood of their best and bravest . . . .' Cowen obviously did not believe that the lesson of the Sudanese set-back was retrenchment. In the Commons he supported Northcote's vote of censure on the Government for their conduct in the Sudan. Later in the year the language of that Northumbrian radical became more and more defiantly imperial and here, too, we find as in the case of the Empire Federalists, with whom he sympathized, phrases which foreshadowed the imperial style of the 1890's, as in his prediction: 'The African continent will, in time, be occupied by a mighty nation of English descent and covered with populous cities, flourishing farms, with railways, telegraphs, and all the other devices of civilisation . . . there is a promise of almost illimitable usefulness and grandeur lying before our colonists, and ourselves in unison with them . . . .'[1] Another voice, which before had been raised in support of social reform and radical causes, was heard speaking out for imperial unity and concerted action in Africa and Australia. Joseph Chamberlain, heading the Board of Trade in Gladstone's ministry, referred to the German occupation of North East New Guinea with regret, because it took place against the wish of the Australian colonies. Britain, he explained, could not stop foreign powers in their colonial ventures, but the rights and interests of British colonists 'are as dear to us as our own; and if ever they are seriously menaced, the whole power of the country will be exerted for their defence, and the English democracy will stand shoulder to shoulder throughout the world to maintain the honour and the integrity of the Empire'.[2] In linking democracy—in the nineteenth-century radical meaning—with the Empire, Chamberlain demonstrated that the imperial sentiment and language could be imbued with the democratic spirit. Those who had gone out to Australia were after all nearer in outlook to the working classes of the Midlands and the North than to the captains of commerce and the City of London bankers, whose Liberalism had a more international character and whose sense of balance, budget, and banking made them wince when they counted the cost of the futile battle for Khartoum in which the Government became involved against its own conviction. They were more inclined to agree with Bright, who condemned the idea of a federated Empire, organized as one country, as ludicrous and as opposed to the lessons of history. Not so, Forster replied in an article written in March

1885. The lesson of history, taught by Gordon's death, was the ready offer of help in money and men that came from Canada, New South Wales, Victoria, Queensland, and South Australia, which thereby proved their declared belief that 'the United Kingdom, with all its colonies, do form one country for the purposes of defence'.[1]

Opinions differed, however, how that imperial unity should be given formal expression, if any at all. Seeley had ignored the development of an Australian, Canadian, and New Zealand spirit of nationhood and believed these colonies could remain as British in outlook as Virginia, New York, and Massachusetts remained American. Rosebery was more realistic and perceived the development of peculiar national traits in a country like South Australia. But unlike Seeley, he did not think that a new colonial nationality was incompatible with the Empire and would lead to separation. He conceived the Empire of the future as a league of nations or, as he put it at Adelaide in 1884, as 'a common-wealth of nations',[2] a phrase which meant a community of free and equal members bound together by the same basic laws, though maintaining local traditions. The word had been used by Burke when he described the position of Europe as one of basic unity underlying local diversity. Commonwealth, however, had a democratic ring and was well chosen in an address to such a democratic community as South Australia and in a year which saw the extension of the franchise in Britain to nearly double the figure of what it was before. The word Commonwealth also suggested the days of Cromwell when Britain's maritime power was powerfully asserted and Sir James Harrington sketched the expansion of Oceana, the perfect British 'commonwealth' of the future.

It was that name Oceana, rather than Empire, which James Froude chose as the title of his book, written in 1885. It was a travel account of the English-speaking world and comparable to Dilke's first venture in that field, though lacking Dilke's originality of approach and freshness of observation. As he travelled via South Africa to Australia, New Zealand, and the United States, Imperial Federation was very much in his mind. His book was intended to show how strong the sentimental attachment to Britain was among the colonists and of how little use a paper constitution of federation would be. Froude had no faith in

'Empire' as an inspiring name denoting the future bond of the lands settled by the English race. He proposed 'Commonwealth' as a better name to express the common pride and strength of the British.[1] He had no faith either in the wisdom of politicians. Nor did he trust Parliament, which, he thought, had mishandled Irish affairs and was about to create a second Ireland in South Africa. Imbued with the spirit of Carlyle, he hoped to see in the British colonies a better England, free from sordid industrialism and the worship of mammon. The idea of an Imperial Parliament like that of Imperial Federation was considered and rejected by the acting Premier of New South Wales with whose views Froude sympathized.[2] Froude, however, toyed with the idea of creating colonial life-peers, but his Australian friends, more democratic in outlook and tradition, ridiculed the prospect of Australian lords. So Froude saw no future in formal federation. The unity of the Empire would ultimately rest on free consent.[3] Trade, too, Froude maintained, would not need politicians to foster greater unity within 'Oceana', the British Commonwealth. The book was popular despite its many inaccuracies. Its arguments constituted a counterpoise to Seeley and Forster and to the notion of a United States of Greater Britain.

The pros and cons of Imperial Federation were debated throughout 1886. After the challenge thrown out by Froude, the death of Forster, and the rejection of the federal principle in the case of Ireland, Imperial Federation sailed into fairer weather again, when in summer 1886 the Colonies and India Exhibition in London demonstrated the reality of the Empire to the people of England. The Exhibition received a permanent home in South Kensington in 1888. Visitors could find there some information about the colony to which friends and relatives had emigrated. More sophisticated observers linked this illustration of colonial opportunity with the social problems at home. Here emigration provided a possible solution. Empire awareness in summer 1886, stirred up by the Exhibition, made it possible to speak of 'Imperialists' without an undertone of derision, simply as of people who were very keen on advancing the interests of the Empire such as the Imperial Federalists. There was no party animosity in that word any more. 'The topics of Emigration and Imperial Federation and Imperial Defence have attracted most attention, these three topics being supremely interesting questions of the hour to Imperialists.' This remark was made in August 1886 by the *Fortnightly Review*.[1]

In that summer one of the most successful Irish-born British colonial governors, Sir George Ferguson Bowen, read a paper on *The Federation of the British Empire* at the Royal Colonial Institute. In its way the paper backed Seeley and his plan for a union based on the model of the United States. Imperial Federation would keep the British Empire as one state in relation to other states through the organization of common defence and through a joint foreign policy. Morally, the common loyalty to the throne, language, literature, and common hopes for the future would provide additional imperial bonds. Without a common organization of imperial government, however, Bowen argued in full agreement with Forster, self-government of the colonies would eventually lead to separation.[2] In 1986 more Britons would be living in the colonies than in Britain, Bowen predicted, and they would be unwilling to share the expenses and the hazards of imperial existence with Britain, unless they were given a voice in an Imperial Council or a Federal Assembly, in the same way as the states of the United States were represented in Congress. French, Spanish, and Portuguese colonies, too, sent representatives to the national legislatures of Paris, Madrid, and Lisbon, Bowen argued. England alone excluded her colonists from her national council. A future imperial council, like the Reichstag in Berlin or Congress in Washington, would be dealing only with imperial matters such as the armed services, foreign affairs, war and peace. Local parliaments in England, Scotland, Ireland, and in the colonies would deal with similar matters with which American and German states were concerned. A division of labour would prevent the House of Commons from becoming bogged down in detail of local legislation and would give Ireland those institutional concessions which sooner or later would inevitably have to be made anyway. Both Ireland and England required a genuine Home Rule. Bowen then interpreted Disraeli's motto of 'Imperium et Libertas' in a federal sense of imperial control and local self-government. His economic argument in favour of federation was again summed up in the phrase which in 1886 had already won a wide recognition: trade follows the flag. There was also the other imperial argument which at that time had come into use and which justified the British Empire as a guarantee of world peace and progress. The vision of Pax Britannica loomed higher as Empire commitments widened and made Empire designs more and more global in character. As for India, neither Froude nor Bowen considered it as involved in the issue of federation. It was not a British colony in the sense Imperial Federalists and non-Federalists discussed the problem. Bowen wanted India to be treated as a Crown colony 'in statu pupillari'. Its natives should with growing political maturity acquire the rights of British citizens, just as aliens could become Roman citizens in the Roman Empire. The imperial language and spirit generated by the political atmosphere which prevailed in summer 1886 pervades Bowen's solemn conclusion of his paper on Federation.

Finally, thousands of those who recently witnessed the opening by the Queen-Empress of the Imperial Exhibition (as it may justly be called), which owes so much to the Prince of Wales, the President of the Institute, hoped and prayed that this grand national spectacle may prove a foreshadowing of permanent union and of future Imperial Federation. Thus we should be brought nearer to the prophetic vision of Burke, when 'the Spirit of the English Constitution, infused through the mighty mass, shall pervade, verify, unite, and invigorate every part of the Empire.' In the words of the stirring appeal of our national poet:

> Britain's myriad voices call,
> Sons, be welded, one and all,
> Into one Imperial whole....[1]

The Prince of Wales had requested the Poet Laureate, Lord Tennyson, to write an ode for the opening of the Exhibition, and Arthur Sullivan composed the music. The imperial mood was given royal expression in the Queen's Speech at the end of the parliamentary session in September when the cause of Imperial Federation found new encouragement in the royal words: '... There is on all sides a growing desire to draw closer in every practical way the bonds which unite the various portions of the Empire.'[2] There was no longer anything shameful in being referred to as an 'imperialist'. The term had shed its alien association and changed its meaning. It meant those who desired to 'draw closer the bonds which unite the various portions of the Empire'. They had received the royal blessing now. To be called an 'imperialist' in 1886 was a praise rather than an abuse. At the worst it was a factual denotation. Political abuses of that year branded alleged opposition to Empire unity. Their supporters—mostly fictitious now—were called 'parochialists', 'disruptionists', and similar names indicating lack of imperial patriotism and outlook.[1]

The Colonial Conference of 1887 was the only institutional success of the Imperial Federation League. It became the prototype for many more such conferences. Its first meeting was suggested by the League when on the occasion of Queen Victoria's first jubilee the colonial premiers had come to London in an atmosphere of great imperial enthusiasm. The specific results of the Conference were disappointing to federalists, but there can be no doubt that the actual experience of the meeting stirred the imperial sentiments of many and heightened imperial consciousness. An ex-premier of Victoria who took part in the Conference described his impressions in the following words: 'I tell you frankly that, meeting for the first time with representative colonists from the Cape, Newfoundland, and Canada . . . I had a high appreciation of my position as a citizen of the British Empire and I felt that nothing could harm the British Empire so long as men of that sort were to be found defending its interests. . . .'[2] The pride felt in the British Empire in that case was a pride in the world-wide association of British settlers. The Indian aspect of Empire, which was so prominent in Disraeli's days, had faded by that time. The partnership, which it was hoped to achieve one day, was composed of white Anglo-Saxons. It is clear from the expression of the main speakers of the Conference and writers on colonial affairs that the Irish, French, Dutch, or West Indian elements—not to speak of the Indian—were often left out of the mental picture of Empire which was presented to the public. The Empire was then regarded as the supreme political organization of the British living in the United Kingdom and in the colonial settlements. The demand to conceive Anglo-Saxon federation in a way so as to include also the United States was, therefore, not unnatural when so much of the notion of the British Empire was still based on the Anglo-Saxon race. Dilke's original interpretation of Greater Britain was revived by Joseph Chamberlain and by Dilke himself.

One grievance which the colonial premiers of Australia and Canada brought to London in 1887 was the indifference of London towards their local conflicts with other Powers. They demanded that colonial policy should be incorporated much more into imperial policy, that Anglo-French and Anglo-German relations should reflect more than hitherto the complaints of the Australians about the German and French seizure of islands and territories in front of their doorstep. Newfoundland was engaged in fishing disputes with France and with the United States and desired to be more consulted in the settlement of those long-drawn-out quarrels. Lord Salisbury in 1887 decided to send Joseph Chamberlain to North America to negotiate a settlement. Chamberlain's work was a turning point in Anglo-American relations and also in his own imperial approach. At Toronto he declared that the federation of Canada 'may be the lamp lighting our path to the federation of the British Empire' and took his stand on the Greater Britain idea of Dilke as a notion embracing 'the young and vigorous nations carrying everywhere a knowledge of the English tongue and English love of liberty and law. With these feelings, I refuse to speak or to think of the United States as a foreign nation. . . .'[1] Dilke in his review of European politics in 1887 opposed Seeley's use of the term 'Greater Britain' as too narrow, because it did not include the United States. The latter was just as much part of the proud growth of Anglo-Saxon democratic government as were Canada and Australia, a point Dilke stressed all the more as the European Continent seemed to him to fall more and more into the grip of the rule of force and militarism.[2] Formal federation, however, could not be brought about in a hurry. Dilke did not think the British Government could make a move in that direction before the colonies were ready for it.[3]

At the end of 1887 there were, therefore, three schools of thought concerning the future organization of the Anglo-Saxon world. Some federalists followed Seeley and desired to establish a federal Empire as one state taking the United States as their model. Other federalists, the chairman of the League, Rosebery, among them, hoped to develop a league of free British nations. Both parties of federalists excluded the United States from their plan. A third view was presented by Dilke. It laid less emphasis on political constitution and stressed the moral and racial bonds. It refused to take the political division between the United

States and the British Empire too seriously, regarding it as a temporary aberration. It had no sympathy with federalist schemes which treated the Anglo-Saxons of the United States as political foreigners. When Joseph Chamberlain made his first imperial speeches in England after his return from America in 1888 he showed he had become converted to the first school of thought.

For Chamberlain the ultimate union of all the branches of the Anglo-Saxon race, including the United States, was less pressing than the union of the British Empire. The desire for that union was rooted in sentiment. In April 1888 he said: 'I am willing to submit to the charge of being a sentimentalist when I say that I will never willingly admit of any policy that will tend to weaken the ties between the different branches of the Anglo-Saxon race which form the British Empire and the vast dominion of the Queen.'[1] Sentiment was, in Chamberlain's eyes, a powerful cohesive factor even in commerce. Trade followed the flag as it followed sentiment. On the other hand commerce, too, had a binding force. A growing part of the British population became dependent for their livelihood on the interchange of commodities with the colonies. Imperial federation, therefore, had a specific function in the field of commerce and defence. Without mentioning by name John Bright, who in March had described imperial federation as a dream and an absurdity, Chamberlain pointed in reply to the readiness of the Colonies to come to the aid of Britain in Egypt, motivated by no other than purely sentimental interest. He then argued in favour of a common system of imperial defence by appealing to the lessons of history as Seeley had taught them.

I suppose the colonists read history; and if they do, they will know that every great war in which this country has been engaged since the great French war at the beginning of the century, and that every dispute which has seriously threatened our peace, has arisen out of the concerns and interests of one or other of the colonies or of the great dependency of India. Under these circumstances it appears to me that it may be at least as much to the interests of the colonies, as to those of the mother-country, that we should seek and find a concerted system of defence.[2]

The prospects for a commercial union, Chamberlain at once foresaw, were not encouraging. He knew that protectionism was popular in the colonies and tariffs were an important source of revenue to colonial governments.

Dilke's pessimism about developments on the European Continent was shared by others. Germany increased her military preparations; there was new tension in the Balkans and a sharp conflict between Austria and Russia about their zones of influence there. In maritime warfare inventions became more rapid and forced Britain to build a new class of warships. It was felt that in a crisis the Empire depended on the British navy. Next to Lord Rosebery, Lord Carnarvon became a champion of imperial federation and in 1888 said in Australia that the European situation had become very grave. Naval defence was being modernized and the latest Naval Defence Bill had greatly added 'to your security, both in the material force which it will ensure . . . and also quite as much in that it has exhibited to Europe the absolute union of these colonies with the Mother Country for the joint protection of Imperial interests. By Imperial I mean, of course, Australian and British combined.'

Imperial federation found an indefatigable champion in George Parkin, who visited Australia in 1889 in order to campaign for the federalist idea. His vision of imperial defence and trade encompassed the Suez Canal, the China Seas, and the trans-continental links of his own native Canada. Britain was a natural market for Australian produce, he explained. Australia and other colonies were natural outlets for British emigrants, whom a federal policy ought to divert from the United States to the dominions of the British Empire. Those would be developed much more rapidly in that way, and with a stronger Empire to support her, Britain would become less dependent on Continental quarrels and less vulnerable. Imperial federation was, Parkin believed, the best guarantee for the continued existence of British civilization. The almost perfect freedom in the control of local affairs, however, accentuated the anomaly of the colonies having no voice in the shaping of imperial policy. That anomaly was as inconsistent with Anglo-Saxon ideas of government as leaving one part of the nation to bear a disproportionate share of the imperial burden.[1] In the debates which followed Parkin's addresses Australian opposition to federation was voiced and appeared to have been formidable. Doubt was expressed that an Imperial Parliament or Authority could enforce its mandates against the will of a colony without breaking up the federation. Speakers expressed the belief that definite written stipulations in black and white would only lead to quarrel, that England's interests were different from Australia's. Others expressed their dissent in a harsher language. Federation, they said, was 'a Tory dodge to enslave the world', a 'step towards German despotism'; federalists wanted an Empire for war not for progress, they wanted 'to boss the world'. It was better to belong to a poor nation than to one whose object was self-aggrandize-ment. Irish Coercion Bills were mentioned as an argument against close federation with the British, who had so far not yet evinced a sympathy for Colonial interests. The *Sydney Morning Herald's* comment on the opposition shown against Parkin's campaign was that a more sensitive regard in England for Colonial interests was needed, 'more spontaneous indications of sympathy with Colonial feeling, and more of practical proof that the Imperial connection is a source of safety, not of danger, of gain and not of loss to the Colonies'.[1] When it came to practical, specific measures Empire federalists could make little headway. Opposition was encountered not only in the Colonies but also at home. The Government in 1889 proved unco-operative. Salisbury declined to receive a deputation of Empire federalists who desired to persuade the Government to invite representatives of the self-governing colonies to another conference. The sponsors of the new conference hoped for the establishment of closer and more substantial connexions between the mother country and those colonies. For that very reason Salisbury thought it inadvisable for the Government to take the initiative in a matter where their assistance was not required and might only lead to misapprehensions. It would imply that the Government was about to lay before the self-governing colonies a plan for closer imperial relations.[2]

By 1890 Empire patriotism was a fairly widespread and recognized sentiment, yet the cause of federalism itself was declining. The public in Britain had come to take a pride in their kinsmen overseas, but there was no agreement as to the formal and constitutional expression of such sentiment. In 1890 Dilke published a new book on Empire problems, which was more balanced and mature than the first he had written in

1868. He noted with pride the expansive force of the Anglo-Saxon race, he stressed the novelty of the British Empire, which was the result of a colonizing effort undertaken mainly in the nineteenth century, and expressed his doubts about imperial federation. Australia was not favourably disposed towards that idea, he declared, and the creation of an imperial parliament to which colonies would send representatives would of itself destroy the Empire. If federation, on the other hand, was to come about as a union of all colonies on equal terms, the power of the Crown would be increased more than the present democratic trend in Britain and the colonies would tolerate.[1] The Imperial Federation League had only one practical suggestion to offer. They wanted a series of colonial conferences to discuss federation. Dilke did not think that even such a moderate programme was likely to meet with success. Conferences could not be frequent, if important members of colonial government were to take part in them, and some colonies would not even want to attend a colonial conference whose major subject for debate was federation.[2] The most useful and pressing subjects for colonial conferences were defence and communication. The least harmony existed in the system of tariffs, the very crux of Imperial Federation. Britain was unlikely to agree to protectionism, whereas the colonies favoured tariffs. There was no chance of setting up an imperial customs union or of levying a defence duty on all foreign goods. The issue of Home Rule for Ireland had weakened the prestige of the League in Australia, because Lord Rosebery was in favour of Home Rule. In Australia the prevailing sentiments of the federalists had been unionist and the growth of anti-federalist Australian sentiment was shown in the meetings of Mr Parkin in New South Wales. Finally, there was the plan of setting up a Council of Agents-General. Dilke did not think that plan would work either. It would merely demonstrate the fact that the colonies had little interest in one another's business. On the other hand the status of the Agents-General, Dilke suggested, should be improved and they should occasionally be invited to attend cabinets.[3] In conclusion Dilke stressed the benefit which the existence of the Empire bestowed on Britain and on her colonies. The future of the world, he predicted, would be largely shaped by the Anglo-Saxons, the Russians, and the Chinese. The military situation of the Empire gave rise to some anxiety but the lack of homogeneity, Dilke felt, was not only a weakness of Greater Britain. It was also her abiding strength, making her the most intelligent and the most cosmopolitan of states.

The Imperial Federation League foundered, as Dilke had already suspected it would, on the rock of tariffs and economic policy. It had, however, effectively worked for public acceptance of the Empire. The Primrose League, whose members were pledged to devote themselves to the maintenance of religion, the estates of the realm, and 'the imperial ascendancy of the British Empire', had about one thousand members in 1884. In 1891 membership had grown to one million. In the early 1890's no Empire patriot would object to being referred to as an 'imperialist'. Dilke in his description of Cape politics described the leader of the Dutch party as an 'imperialist who has even gone so far as to draw up a scheme of his own for a customs union of the British Empire'. He spoke of Rhodes and his friends as imperialists and denoted the supporters of imperial federation by the same name with no ill intent.[1] Imperial federation, though not practical as yet, was a popular catchword. At the general election in 1892, Baden-Powell observed, every candidate promised to uphold the unity of the Empire. The Imperial Institute, he demanded, should be the symbol of the imperial idea 'seeking to provide full knowledge in support of the zealous pride in their Empire now so widely instilled into the nation; affording convincing reason to all Imperialists for the faith that is in them. . . . We believe our great Empire to be, in Lord Rosebery's eloquent words, "the greatest secular agency for good the world has yet seen".'[2]

In the ten years that followed the death of Disraeli the wide rift that had divided the British in their attitude towards the Empire disappeared. The Empire was welcomed as a source of wealth and sentimental pride, and as an association of kinsmen. It was British rather than Empire. One study of federation, published in 1892, dropped the name Empire for that reason and called the association of future British union '*Britannic Confederation*' for want of a better name with which to characterize a relationship that was still in the making.[3] Gladstone in that year told Stead about his feeling of pride in the civilizing mission of the English and his belief in the great future that was in store for Britain.[4] Lord Rosebery, a year later, reminded the members of the Royal Colonial

Institute that it was 'part of our responsibility and heritage to take care that the world, as far as it can be moulded by us, shall receive the Anglo-Saxon and not another character'. The evolution and expansion of Anglo-Saxondom was also the light in which Sir George Grey viewed the Empire. The ex-Governor of South Australia, New Zealand, the Cape Colony, and former Prime Minister of New Zealand had come to London in 1894. In an interview he said he was impressed by the change in the public attitude towards the Empire. Twenty-five years had turned the majority from the cry: Cut the Colonies off! to the resolution: Let us do our best to get closer together![1] Grey had helped to give New Zealand universal manhood suffrage. He believed the future belonged to democracy, which had found its greatest support among the Anglo-Saxon race. Anglo-Saxons and democrats were destined, he believed, to lead humanity in the future. Grey gave his whole-hearted backing to the idea of imperial federation, a 'United States of Great Britain', whose parts, he suggested, should all enjoy home rule as the states do in the United States of America. He hoped that the two United States of Britain and American would eventually join hands. Their union would bar all wars, safeguard the ascendancy of the Anglo-Saxons in the world and with them that of Christian morals, English literature, language, liberty, and tolerance.

The growth of the imperial spirit among the Liberals and the Conservatives is evidenced in the election campaign of 1895 and in observations made by competent judges of political life in England at that time. Edward Dicey found it difficult to detect a difference in principle or even in tone between the foreign policy as directed by Lord Salisbury or by Lord Rosebery. 'Conservatives and Liberal Unionists are absolutely at one in their desire to maintain peace abroad, to consolidate and develop the British Empire. . . .',[2] even to extend British dominion by direct annexation in order to open up fresh markets. A retrospective view taken in 1893 at African politics ten years earlier marvelled at the apparent slowness of the British Ministry to counter German colonial activities in that region. The writer then explained: 'But the new Imperial spirit had hardly then been born, and there still lurked in the minds of a certain school of politicians an aversion to increase "England's responsibilities".'[3] A few noisy Radicals, Dicey wrote, tried to revive the 'Little England' theory, but there is no evidence that they were successful in those years. Harcourt and Morley, whose lack of Empire enthusiasm was well known, both lost their seats in the election.

The new enthusiasm for the British Empire, which was then named Imperialism, a term to which no blemish was attached any more, was racial and national in character. It regarded the Empire as an association of white Anglo-Saxons. It hoped to perpetuate in it and through it a close connexion between the mother country and the self-governing dominions, 'New Britains over sea', as Lewis Morris sang in honour of the new Imperial Institute in May 1893. The Reviews declared Imperialism as an established popular sentiment.[1] No man was more responsible for the growth of that sentiment than Lord Rosebery. His work in imperialist education was assessed by an unfriendly critic of his alleged lack of political conviction. As an imperialist Lord Rosebery did not belong to any party. 'Lord Rosebery has, however, done such good educational work in making the English-speaking race, both here and over-sea, realise their unity, that no word of disparagement should be said of him under this head.'[2] In Disraeli's time Rosebery had been opposed to the way the Government then used the word Empire, a word about which he felt 'a gloomy foreboding'. It then lacked liberty and smacked of oriental despotism. It was too closely associated with India. In 1884 Rosebery gave Empire an interpretation that made it already more acceptable as a word. It was, he said, 'held together by ... the union of races'. When in 1888 he declared Imperial Federation to have become the passion of his life, he asked for patience with 'your giant offspring abroad' and in 1893 declared, as we saw, that it was Britain's responsibility to take care 'that the world, as far as it can be moulded by us, shall receive the Anglo-Saxon and not another character'. Finally, in his election campaign of July 1895 he proclaimed himself a 'liberal Imperialist' and explained the meaning of that term in the following words: 'Liberal Imperialism implies, first, the maintenance of the Empire; secondly, the opening of new areas for our surplus population; thirdly, the suppression of the slave trade; fourthly, the development of missionary enterprise; and fifthly, the development of our commerce, which so often needs it.'[3]

The impact of the international situation and colonial rivalry apart, the racial and nationalist element which manifested itself in the new Imperialism of the 1880's and early 1890's must be regarded as one reason why that expression had become acceptable, and even popular, only ten years after Imperialism and Empire had been so low in popular esteem. In Disraeli's time those two terms had been closely associated with foreign and alien concepts. In the days of Rosebery and Chamberlain, however, Imperialism and Empire were given a meaning that had a wide appeal, because it was both liberal and national, democratic and traditional. Yet during that period another Empire was in the making which was not Anglo-Saxon nor was it liberal or democratic. Public utterances referring to that other, dark Empire under the tropical sun were as yet less frequent or clear.

VIII

THE INCORPORATION OF AFRICA INTO THE IMPERIAL IDEA AND THE CLIMAX OF POPULAR IMPERIALISM

Imperialism, in its earlier derogatory connotation and in its later expression of national sentiment, reflected not only a national attitude towards the Empire but also the nation's awareness and interpretation of its own place in history. From time to time some writers attempted to step back and survey an historical development from a distance. Thus the expanding Empire of Anglo-Saxon colonists was 'discovered'. Such a discovery summed up not only a process of the past. It pointed the way to the future. Not all history was the result of political decisions made at Whitehall. Gladstone's second administration had been manifestly powerless in the face of what many Englishmen of that time preferred to call 'Providence' and 'Britain's destiny'. Imperialism as understood in the early 1890's was the expression of an historical interpretation given to political reality. History seemed to have decreed the double expansion of Anglo-Saxondom and democracy. It had taken two generations to become aware of and welcome that twin growth. By that time, however, yet another expansion was well under way, which made a purely Anglo-Saxon view of Empire look somewhat obsolete. Since 1884 Britain had assumed responsibility for the Niger Coast, Somali, for portions of Malaya and New Guinea, for Bechuanaland, Zululand, for regions in East Africa and beyond the Limpopo River, for Upper Burma and Zanzibar.

The acquisition of the tropical Empire was a result as well as a steady cause of friction with European powers. Episodes of diplomatic uneasiness, which arose from international disputes over spheres of influence or dominance in overseas countries, followed one another, from the wrangling with Bismarck over South West Africa to Fashoda and its aggravating influence on British-French estrangement. The new expansion, moreover, entailed the likelihood of financial liabilities the future amount of which might well far surpass its present modest demands on the national purse. Shouldered in the beginning by private enterprise this expansion could in the course of time lead to conspicuous increases in the budget. This apprehension became evident in the affairs of Uganda in 1893. Indeed, public men who saw the interconnexion between colonial development and broader political interests, arrived at the conclusion that the nation must be taught to understand colonial matters as national affairs. Such an interpretation, as we have noticed, could scarcely look back to a tradition in the annals of public opinion. It had to be impressed on the public mind with uncommon emphasis. Champions had to arise for the cause comparable to those for whom the editor of the *Daily Telegraph* had wished in 1877—writers who had 'bold and national utterances on their lips'. Such advocates did arise, and, to carry their point, the appropriate language in the 'nineties was that which had offered itself in the Eastern Crisis: the concept of imperial causes. The demonstrative use of the concept was justified by circumstances somewhat analogous to those which had promoted its emergence. Interests of the Oversea Empire had become linked up with questions concerning the position of Great Britain in relation to other Powers. They were seen to involve the vital interests of the nation, and the inference was that the nation had to become conscious of being an 'imperial' nation also in regions which were not settled by Anglo-Saxons. We saw that such an attempt failed in Disraeli's time when no lasting popular sympathy could be created for 'imperial interests' in Asia. Could popular support be gained for 'imperial interests' in Africa?

There was certainly no popular will to act as the driving force, when imperial responsibilities were enlarged step by step by a hesitant government in the 1880's. That the occupation of Egypt should not be maintained for long was not only a dogma for Gladstone and his cabinet but also a leading maxim for Salisbury until 1887, and at that time it was accepted opinion in England generally. Allegations that secret intentions inside the Gladstone cabinet were at variance with public declarations concerning the temporary character of the occupation of Egypt are easily disposed of by Dilke's diary entries and the Granville Papers. With regard to public opinion at that time it was worth noting that Chamberlain hoped Egypt would become a second neutral Belgium.[1] *The Times*, indeed, spurred by its Cairo correspondent, demanded an Egyptian protectorate while Gordon's mission to London still looked hopeful.[2] But after the catastrophe a publicist like Dicey, who maintained that the establishment of a British Protectorate over Egypt was a course demanded by 'the vital interests of our Empire', found himself in mournful isolation.[3] The builders of the new African Empire, Goldie, MacKinnon, Johnston, and Rhodes, did their work without encouragement from home and did not ask for it. Rhodes, eager to have Afrikander support for going north, was for a time even anxious not to attract English popular acclamation, which might conjure up the portent of the 'imperial factor'. In this device he was rather too successful. He was suspected to prepare for a great South African republic with himself as President.[4] The 'Mercantile Company', by dint of which Rhodes wished to make his way, was a danger signal to W. A. Henley, one of the few men at home who in 1889 believed in a British mission in these regions.[5] When New Guinea and Zululand were discussed in 1883-4, Derby's remark that 'England has already black subjects enough' became again a winged word. That 'the Cabinet do not want more niggers', was Kimberley's comment on the meeting of 22 March 1884 which decided against an increase of the Zululand Protectorate.[6]

Public attitudes towards the affairs of Zululand are especially characteristic. It was clearly a British responsibility to care for a stable regime in this native community, whose strength and cohesion had been broken by British arms. An extension of the Protectorate was the only promising way for giving effect to this responsibility. Gladstone and most of his colleagues were not ready for such a step. But they were allowed, too, by public opinion, to cling to an irresolute attitude for two years. In July 1884 the matter was suddenly brought up for discussion in the House of Commons by Conservative members, who branded this default 'of a power which boasted that on its dominions the sun never set' as a shameful betrayal. But when in the debate speakers on the Government benches referred to the Conservative appeal as an 'imperial spread-eagle policy', this was thought to be an insult. Press comments on the whole betrayed only embarrassment and did not urge more resolute action. Of prominent London papers only the *Standard* fell in with the opposition. Stead, in the *Pall Mall Gazette*, somewhat timidly offered the opinion that British responsibilities towards the natives went further than the Prime Minister assumed.[1] Impending enlargements of the colonial area were not chosen as a topic of propaganda, when the Prince of Wales and his assistants cared to bring home to the English public the value of the Empire by the foundation of the Imperial Institute. Dilke's enthusiasm for Greater Britain did not extend to Black Africa. The only excuse he could find for the annexation of African regions was the principle of free trade. In the hands of other countries such as France those territories would be closed to outside commerce, he believed. But he viewed the progress of British rule in Africa with regret. 'The only excuse that we can make is that, if we had not laid hands upon their territory, France or Germany would have done so.'[2]

Now, if the great territorial acquisitions of the 1880's were so clearly not the outcome of strong national passions, were they forced upon the Government and nation by economic interests? Until very late in the century, little happened to justify the belief that powerful economic considerations were taking shape. In England the prospects of the African market were glowingly depicted to the Manchester Chamber of Commerce by H. M. Stanley. But he did not then advocate British colonization in the Congo basin. He spoke in favour of King Leopold's 'association'; he wanted it to be protected against Portuguese encroachments on the lower reaches of the River. The merchants of Manchester gave a ready response; they published a report of the meeting and fervently endorsed Stanley's entreaties on behalf of 'the earnest efforts of His Majesty the King of the Belgians to establish civilization and free trade on the Upper Congo'.[3] The year after they—and the London Chamber of Commerce with them—gave also a support to Taubman Goldie's endeavours to secure a Charter for his National African Company. But this time, when existence of a nascent British colony was at stake, the businessmen did not emphasize national trade interests. They only demanded 'the establishment of an adequate police force to overawe predatory tribes as well as to enforce the decisions of judicial officers'.[4]

Of the Chartered Companies the eldest, that of North Borneo (1881), was perhaps the most optimistic about the prospect of attracting capital from Great Britain. Their managers inspired an English journalist to write a colourful propaganda book in which the foundation was called the 'New Ceylon'. He compared the firm with the old East India Company and prophesied that its work would initiate 'a new era in the history of the colonizing aspirations of the Anglo-Saxon'.[1] His book has since been forgotten and the colony has not become one of the most renowned parts of the British Empire. Goldie's Royal Niger Company kept to practices and earned successes which, on first sight, have some similarity with what was represented later as 'economic imperialism'. The commercial monopoly which had been planned by Goldie in his treaties with the native chieftains, but was decidedly rejected by Salisbury, was carried into effect by his managers. Salisbury took offence and authorized the inquiry of 1889. Sir Claude Macdonald reported that the manner in which the Company directed the channels of local commerce was to the unqualified detriment of native traders and that it robbed of their markets those of the Western Niger delta, direct subjects of the Crown. Nevertheless, the Government did not take action. It swallowed also the injunction of the Company on its servants not to make public any facts concerning the administration and business of the Company. That was certainly capitalist high-handedness, from which the shareholders benefited. Nevertheless, it would have been difficult to make the case appear a major instance for the dependence of colonial regime on the ascendancy of 'monopolist capitalism'. For the financial interests, which were stimulated by Goldie's creation, were not large and widespread enough. The manifest reason why the Government, in the end, withheld interference was that it accepted the reasons which had made Goldie insist on monopoly rights. Restoring unhampered competition in the oil trade on the River might have resulted in such a decline of the Company's returns that its whole activities—including new government work—would have been paralysed.[2] MacKinnon of East Africa could less than any other man be suspect of capitalist ambitions. When after his and H. H. Johnston's protracted struggles with the Germans he finally founded the 'Imperial British East African Company', he had, like Goldie before him, to enlist subscribers in order to make certain that the Company would be equal to its administrative undertaking. In the list the names of Sir John Kirk and of military men are prominent; it is certainly not a galaxy of big capital interests.[1] Rhode's South African Company was more closely connected with speculative capitalism. Of its original stock one-fifth represented the investment of the profits of De Beers. The exclusive claim to the exploitation of mineral resources, which was granted to this company as to the others, was in its case bound up with fresh speculative expectations. But in the opinion of Rhodes, as well as in that of the wary Charles W. Dilke,[2] the likelihood of the country being opened rested on its being specially suitable to agricultural development, and it was expected to attract numerous British settlers. Finally, the fact that British capital was at all available for colonial enterprise was not yet known as a cause for complaint. The enthusiastic Henley mentioned it, by the way, as one of the advantages which the imperial country could offer as no other could.[3]

Salisbury's treaties of 1890 with Germany, France, and Portugal coincided with signs of growing sympathy with and belief in the work of the African companies. Rhodes on his visits to England won the confidence and even the admiration of important men. The 'studied plainness' of his appearance made his success in South African business and Cape politics appear to promise the greatest accomplishments in the service of the race. Henley, who brought out this impression in an inimitable character sketch, was now ready to drop his misgivings about the 'mercantile company'; he became convinced that the 'financier, filibuster, statesman' was 'a typical hero for a commercial age'. W. T. Stead discovered in him the man destined by Providence for making Englishmen understand their own providential mission in 'the upward trend of human progress'.[4] Chamberlain, who not long before had thought the Boers to be indispensable instruments of civilization in South Africa, forgot his anxiety lest injustice should be done to them by English expansion.[5] Rosebery made this expansion the main object of his enthusiasm for the imperial mission of the race. Gladstone, who could not share such belief without reserve, admitted in private that he had 'fallen behind the age in point of colonial information'.[6] Harcourt, indeed, was known to have remained immovably inimical to colonies;

but poured out in letters only his anger at liberal apostates to 'Jingoism'.[1] The very fact that in 1892 Gladstone had to entrust Rosebery with the Foreign Office indicated that the African policy to which Salisbury had become converted would be continued by the Liberal cabinet. The new Foreign Secretary felt entitled to proclaim that the nation was 'engaged ... in pegging out claims for the future'.[2] The phrase was understood to refer to a topic of the day, which was Uganda.

There the East African Company faced great difficulties; the financial responsibilities which it had to face surpassed its means even if railway building was postponed. Its enterprise would be jeopardized, unless Parliament agreed to expenses on its behalf. The discussion of the Uganda problem extended quite naturally to the whole African policy which was under way. It is interesting to see how the economic aspects were handled on this occasion. The irreconcilable Radicals exposed, of course, the dangers of financial waste, of which the small expenditure demanded at first would be only the prelude. One of them declared himself to be bound in honour and as a Christian to protest against a government which might be prepared to expend millions of sterling in Central Africa, while in their own country 'millions of people were living under shameful and insanitary conditions'. But such social objections were not yet accentuated by the charge that the expense was to serve class interests. The sin which Labouchere felt bound to stigmatize was simply lust for aggrandizement: 'Jingoism'. 'These Jingoes were most remarkable men; they did not seem to care whether the land they required was valuable or valueless. They were like magpies, they loved stealing for the pleasure of stealing.'[3] Dilke, on the occasion of the Uganda problem, restated his confidence in Rhode's enterprise, but disapproved of the inclination of the Liberal party to enter into 'a rivalry with the Conservative in the race for the heart of Africa'. In his opinion nothing 'likely to prove profitable' to the nation could be gained there. His dislike of chartered companies, which dated from the North Borneo affair, acquired substance now that a company was about to commit the imperial parliament 'to the costly occupation of unhealthy districts, exposed to war, and out of reach'. But he, too, had no scruples as yet about the gains which a company might earn while committing the nation.[4] On the other hand, the Government and the

Conservative and Unionist supporters of the Uganda grant had little to say about economic prospects. They laid stress on the obligation to civilize Africa, to fight slavery, to come up to expectations and, besides this, mentioned strategical needs concerning the Nile Valley. 'We must think not merely of our own day, but of the future, and of the destinies of our Empire', the member for Cambridge University said and stressed the existence of social problems at home as one of the strongest reasons for retaining Uganda.[1] Lugard, in his *Rise of our East African Empire*, which was written as an appeal to the national interest, mentioned only by the way the 'commercial necessity of finding new markets'.[2] Chamberlain in the Commons debate enlarged on this point only a little more. In answer to the member who postulated priority for social misery at home, he called attention to the 'great proportion' of the people which 'earned its livelihood by the trade brought to this country in consequence of the action of our ancestors, who were not ashamed . . . to peg out claims for posterity'. He went on to glorify 'the spirit of travel and adventure and enterprise distinguishing the Anglo-Saxon race' and proclaimed expansionism as his creed in the words: 'I and those who agree with me believe in the expansion of the Empire, and we are not ashamed to confess that we have that feeling, and we are not at all troubled by accusations of Jingoism.'[3] He did not choose Imperialism as the term likely to be used by his accusers, because the derogatory connotation was no longer generally associated with Imperialism as it was with Jingoism. His words inaugurated the style in which he was to co-ordinate economic and patriotic arguments when conducting colonial and a good deal of the foreign policy of his country. Anti-expansionists spoke a different language. Despite their missionary activities in Africa, conscientious Christians hesitated to identify themselves with the work of the chartered companies and the agitation for extending British rule in Africa. The Chairman of the Congregational Union of England and Wales, a friend of Gladstone and a recognized nonconformist leader, James G. Rogers, spoke out against Uganda, the 'damnosa haereditas' of the Conservative Government.

Rogers was particularly annoyed at the use of pious words and arguments in support of imperial claims. He did not think British intervention in an African country could or should be justified on the grounds that Christian missionaries would have to be protected. The Church Missionary Society, he explained, claimed no responsibility for intervention in Uganda and never upheld the 'civis Romanus' theory, even when missionaries came to grief. Worse even was the appeal to Providence and the claim that God had made Uganda for the British. The philanthropic argument of making an end to the slave trade in that area was suspect and a little embarrassing when it appeared mixed up with trade. Captain Lugard, who extracted treaties from unwilling savages, was hardly a typical example of a Christian philanthropist. Could it be maintained, Rogers asked, 'that because an African chief has been cajoled or coerced into a surrender of his rights, by the agent of an English trading company, the nation is bound, without regard to any question of justice or expediency, of its own interests, or the rights of the other party, to hold fast by these acquisitions?' As a critic of expansionism Rogers uses the word Imperialism without pride and foreshadows a later stage when Imperialism was used by many more critics of imperial policy in Africa towards the end of the century. He speaks of 'aggressive Imperialism', of 'Imperialist passion . . . strong to the verge of fanaticism' sighing for new regions to conquer. Occasionally he speaks of the 'Jingo policy' in the same sense as 'aggressive imperialism' and thereby reflects the earlier identification of the two notions of the Disraeli period. At the time of writing the article Rogers was over seventy years old and could, therefore, vividly reflect his anti-Palmerston bias and opposition to Palmerston's imperial policy as well. 'Personally, I was never in sympathy with the views of the extreme Manchester school,' he writes in conclusion, 'but the longer I live, the more strongly do I feel the peril of that Imperialist policy which lowers instead of exalting the nation whose name it associates with deeds of high-handed aggression.'[1] It was the protest of the old generation of nonconformists. They could never see in Imperialism a friendly force or a congenial spirit, for their associations with the word were formed in the days of the Eastern Question. Their views were no longer typical for the age. A new enthusiasm for Africa was already in the air and attested by publicists.[2]

When in 1893 people asked themselves for the reason why public interest in Africa had grown they were still capable of overlooking economic motives or even the rivalry of European Powers but would quote the old spirit of adventure, the desire to support the good work of civilizing the natives, and the hope of stamping out for ever the slave trade. These reasons were listed in the *Edinburgh Review*. The reviewer of the increasing flow of books on Africa still took a cautious view of the prospects held out by the Dark Continent. In Uganda the difficulties were enormous and the benefits uncertain. In other parts of Africa reality was harsher than the many dreams and visions people had had in England.

Interest in Africa in 1893 did not yet mean that people regarded African possessions in the tropics as vital to the Empire, or the progress and failure of chartered companies as the progress and failure of national policy. Gladstone's fourth administration concentrated its efforts on Home Rule for Ireland and on local government. Harcourt as Chancellor of the Exchequer was the last person to encourage a mood of imperial expansionism. Complaints were heard, therefore, that the 'ruling spirit' was declining again, that while the Queen was opening the Imperial Institute in South Kensington with a solemn benediction and royal wish to see 'the lands peopled and held by the English' knit closer together, at the other end of town Parliament was busy destroying the web of Empire by cutting the Irish thread; that newspapers 'lost their heads completely at the mention of the word Empire', but that there was a marked hesitation to accept responsibilities in Africa.[1] When Stanley presented himself in 1892 as a Liberal-Unionist candidate to the people of North Lambeth, his popularity was closely linked with Africa. In his election campaign he spoke of Uganda as a possible new British settlement. He depicted its future in promising terms and explained how the Uganda railway would open up the country to British enterprise. 'Gentlemen,' he said, 'my one mastering desire is for the maintenance, the spread, the dignity, the usefulness of the British Empire. I believe that we Englishmen are working out the greatest destiny which any race has ever fulfilled, but we must go on,—or we shall go back.'[2] He lost the election. Empire expansion in Africa in the early 1890's was not a topic likely to rouse wide enthusiasm in England. Even those who advocated the permanent control of Egypt in the interest of the Suez Canal and the way to India met with a lukewarm response.

In March 1890 Chamberlain wrote to Hartington that he had come to the conclusion that Britain must stay in Egypt 'for an indefinite time' and said so in public.[1] Alfred Milner put before his countrymen for the first time the complicated nature of the British task in Egypt, when in 1892 his book on *England in Egypt* was published. He had written it while he was engaged in the work of restoring the country to financial health. It was more than a clear account of the complicated legal and financial issues involved. He attempted to show that Britain had saved Egypt from anarchy and the European nations from great financial losses. He described the devoted work of many British officials in the Egyptian service and the immense task Britain had undertaken in Egypt without realizing it. Milner did not directly propose an indefinite occupation of the country, but he made it plain that there could not be any thought of withdrawal in the near future, that a reconquest of the Sudan was a necessity which was required by the welfare and security of Egypt as well as by honour and humanity.[2] He also hinted that the control of Uganda was highly desirable as was the control of the headwaters of the Nile, a country rich in first-class warriors. Milner made it clear that he hoped to see self-government restored to Egypt but at the same time he plainly advocated, if not British occupation, at any rate the establishment of a predominance of British influence along the whole Nile Valley. It is interesting to note that the reviewer of the book in the *Spectator* chose not to make any mention of that aspect of Milner's account and merely commented on the success of British administration in Egypt despite the lack of a clear policy.[3] Dicey on that occasion reverted to his favourite plea for making the occupation of Egypt permanent, for otherwise, he pointed out, the work of reform would be a waste and sheer folly. Unlike Milner he had no faith in the Egyptian capability for self-government but believed Egypt was essential to the vital interests of England.[4] There was little echo in support of such a radical view in 1893. After Chamberlain came into office in June 1895, the whole aspect of colonial policy and of oversea engagements changed within a very short time. Economic arguments were, by advocates as well as by adversaries of such engagements, discussed far more specifically. The political climate and public mood became more expansionist. In 1896 it seemed more obvious that the control of Egypt was 'a matter of the first moment to the Power which is the possessor of India and owns three fourths of the tonnage passing through the Suez Canal,' that, in fact, the average Englishman would welcome the annexation of Egypt to the dominions of the Crown.[1]

The election of 1895 gave Salisbury and Chamberlain a majority which could be interpreted by contemporaries as a large vote for Empire expansionism and a defeat of the 'Little Englanders'. The renewed Empire enthusiasm of autumn 1895 was different from the preceding Empire boom of the late 1880's. Its emphasis was not so much on race but on markets, and it no longer overlooked Africa as a field of promising colonial activities. It had a part to play in solving the problem of England's growing population. It was then calculated and predicted with a high measure of accuracy that England and Wales would come close to forty million inhabitants by the middle of the twentieth century and it was generally believed that the addition of nine million Englishmen would create more social and industrial problems. One remedy suggested was organized emigration to Canada and to South Africa on a large scale. But a new menace had arisen which threatened the livelihood of many Englishmen at home. Hostile tariffs set up by Germany, the United States, and France were narrowing old markets, and it was felt that Britain would in future be able to support so many people on her small island only if new markets were opened up. In September 1895 the *Spectator*, commenting on the situation, explained that tropical Africa could make an important contribution towards solving the economic problem of Britain.

in respect of the opening-up of new sources of demand for British manufacturers, Mr Chamberlain's large schemes for the development on business lines of the Crown Colonies in the tropics are full of promise of employment, not only for the present industrial population of Great Britain, but for much of that great increase which in any case we must anticipate.[2]

The champion of British control in Uganda, Captain Lugard, in the same month presented the case for tropical Africa as a new British market in persuasive detail. Expansionism, Lugard wrote, was forced on the nation by the increasing wants of a rising population. It could no longer be regarded as 'jingoism'. It is interesting to see that Lugard rested his case on economic arguments, on the hostile tariffs imposed on British goods by other nations, on commercial rivalry, on the change of British customers and former consumers into producers and rivals, and on the rise of Japan as an economic force in the Far East. The 'Little Englander', Lugard affirmed, was the man who was blind to the signs of the times and to the necessities of the future because of his limited horizon. New markets in Africa would stimulate British trade and prosperity.

Let us admit that commercial enterprise in Africa is undertaken for our own benefit, as much as and more than for the benefit of the African. We have spoken already of the vital necessity of new markets for the old world. It is, therefore, to our very obvious advantage to teach the millions of Africa the wants of civilisation, so that whilst supplying them we may receive in return the products of their country and the labour of their hands.[1]

The tropical Empire was to be expanded, Lugard explained, in the name of trade and future history. He realized that commercial rivalry would make the opening-up of tropical Africa inevitable and hoped to secure a predominant share in that process for Britain. His historical outlook was reinforced by his Darwinian philosophy. Nature, he believed, decreed that vitality and virility were inseparable from expansion. Joseph Chamberlain during the same period made speeches which agreed with the substance of Lugard's views. Trade was declining and unemployment was rising. Both were the result of an overpopulation in Britain and of hostile competition abroad. The remedy, Chamberlain was convinced, was colonial expansion.[2] In 1890 it was still possible to speak of Africa and the 'Negroland' as being just good enough to be bartered away to satisfy Australia and Canada by wringing concessions from France and Germany in their favour.[3] Such arguments were no longer seriously put forward in 1895. Thus in 1896 George Goldie, in his struggle for British control in the Niger Valley, could feel confident he would have the public on his side, if and when his ventures succeeded.[4]

The Jameson Raid and the subsequent Kruger Telegram of the German Emperor moved colonial and national policy closer together.

International jealousies and British isolation produced a sentiment of apprehension. The anti-British mood of other countries was commented on, and imperial defence became a favourite topic. Public men began to speak about the Imperial and also the Imperialist idea. It was a vague notion but it was no longer confined to the colonies settled by Britons. It also included tropical Africa as a national interest, a field for commercial expansion and, as a national obligation, the establishment of British rule and Pax Britannica. In May 1896 Edward Dicey undertook to explain to those persons, who, he wrote, would be indignant at being called Little Englanders and whose sympathies are enlisted 'on the side of the British Imperial idea' but who advocated greater patience in South Africa, why South Africa could not wait. British South Africa was in Dicey's definition the area lying between Capetown and the 15th parallel. He did not include much of the area to the north of the Zambezi, contrary to the views of ardent expansionists. 'I am aware that ardent advocates of the Imperialist idea would repudiate the notion of confining British expansion in South Africa within such narrow limits', he wrote, but thought such a restricted view of political aims to be more realistic for the present generation. The real issue, as he saw it in 1896, was whether South Africa was to become an independent republic, an African United States, or whether it was to become another dominion like Canada. He felt convinced all imperialists would regard the latter course as desirable and the former alternative as a fatal blow to the British Empire. But he warned 'that inaction on our part at the present crisis may imperil the realisation of the Imperialist idea'.[1]

Chamberlain went beyond mere imperial unity and control when he attempted to describe the 'Imperial idea'. It reflected, according to him, a change in historical outlook and in the political reality with which Britain was confronted in the 1890's. The idea of empire had incorporated two different schools of thought and political organizations. There were the self-governing British dominions. 'We think and speak of them as part of ourselves, as part of the British Empire, united to us, although they may be dispersed throughout the world, by ties of kindred, of religion, of history, and of language, and joined to us by the seas that formerly seemed to divide us.' They were part of the Empire but not all of it. There was the much more numerous population in tropical climates where the native population must always outnumber the whites.

and in these cases also the same change has come over the Imperial idea. Here also the sense of possession has given place to a different sentiment—the sense of obligation. We feel now that our rule over these territories can only be justified if we can show that it adds to the happiness and prosperity of the people, and I maintain that our rule does, and has, brought security and peace and comparative prosperity to countries that never knew their blessings before. In carrying out this work of civilisation we are fulfilling what I believe to be our national mission . . . in almost every instance in which the rule of the Queen has been established and the great *Pax Britannica* has been enforced, there has come with it greater security to life and property, and a material improvement in the condition of the bulk of the population.[1]

Imperialism, therefore, reflected this new expansionism which was economic and full of civilizing zeal as it incorporated Africa into the imperial idea. In fact, it was the reality of Africa and the long and patient work of private British enterprise which gradually brought the public round to a slow recognition of its achievement in Africa as part of the national effort worth incorporating into the imperial idea and to be regarded as part of the Empire. The realities in West Africa were such that it was by no means certain that a basketful of human hands had been collected from the dead, that the sickly smell emerging from a village was not from a human sacrifice, and that the meat offered in the market place was the meat of an animal. If the riches of a country were a strong incentive for British expansion, the savage customs of African tribes could not leave Victorian Englishmen indifferent. The expedition against the Ashanti and their cruel King Prempeh in 1896 was justified by Chamberlain on those two grounds, mineral riches and evil government.

I think the duty of this country in regard to all these savage countries over which we are called upon to exercise some sort of dominion is to establish, at the earliest possible date, Pax Britannica, and force these people to keep the peace amongst themselves (cheers), and by so doing, whatever may be the destruction of life in an expedition which brings about this result, it will be nothing if weighed in the balance against the annual loss of life which goes on so long as we keep away.[2]

Popular response to the Jameson Raid gave grounds for the expectation that public opinion would concur with more spirited interpretations of Empire causes in official demonstrations and politics. The Poet Laureate of the day was by no means disgraced by the eulogy of the conspirators. 'The country's love' was pledged to them by the *Evening News*, whose editors after a few months proclaimed the pledge, to make their new paper, the *Daily Mail*, 'the embodiment and mouthpiece of the imperial idea'.[1]

The Government rose to the situation in two ways. To the surprise of Lord Cromer in Egypt, it initiated the conquest of the Sudan. Chamberlain chose to make the Queen's Diamond Jubilee the occasion not only for disclosing his views on Empire reform to the conference of colonial prime ministers, but also for arranging the pageant of 22 June 1897, which made the man in the street visualize his Empire more tellingly than the Imperial Institute had done. 'Imperialism in the air—all classes drunk with sightseeing and hysterical loyalty'; so Beatrice Webb noted in her diary. For once her feelings were shared by Rudyard Kipling, who saw his countrymen 'drunk with sight of power' and invoked the merciful castigation of the Lord. But the self-satisfaction which had been sanctioned by the Jubilee celebrations did not die away after they were over. When in the following month the Report on the Jameson Raid had been discussed in Parliament and Rhodes's honour declared by Chamberlain to be unblemished, *The Times* wrote that the raid had 'taken its place in the perspective of empire building'.[2] For John Morley, the old sceptical Radical, this view was, naturally, a proof that the whole perspective was wrong. He ventured to direct the attention of his constituents in Cornwall to the ominous implications of the case;

All this empire building—why, the whole thing is tainted with the spirit of the hunt for gold . . . I do not say of Mr Rhodes himself that his imperialism is a mere veil for stock operations and company operations; but this I do say that he is surrounded with men with whom imperialism is, and cannot be anything else, but a name for operations of that ignoble kind.

The effect of this censure was lost at that time just because of its wording. The *Spectator*, who professed to think of Rhodes no less severely, regretted that Morley had not realized, 'that the way to fight the dangerous and sordid Rhodesian imperialism is not by condemning the Empire altogether but by contrasting Rhodesian imperialism with the truer, nobler, and saner imperialism which, whether sound or not in policy, is at any rate clear and honest'.[1]

The paper saw 'the true English imperialism . . . working on well-tried Indian lines', expounded by Sir Harry Johnston. Yet to the popular mind this imperialism was, a year later, exemplified not by acts of colonial administration but by Omdurman and Fashoda. The cause of the Empire was again a matter of excitement, even military excitement.

The new imperialist spirit in Britain caused a great deal of satisfaction to the British colonists. Australians who had believed Britain to be declining and decadent were delighted at the encouraging signs of British vitality. They felt a new pride in their association with Britain. 'Grasp this fact, and you realise something of the significance from the colonial side of the new Imperialism with which these Jubilee celebrations have stamped the closing years of the Victorian era', an observer of the colonial scene wrote. He felt that the new imperialism was not the monopoly of one political party. It was no longer the monopoly of the mother country either. Canada, South Africa and other colonies made their contribution to imperialism. The *Toronto Globe* was quoted with approval for the view that it was of little value to set down imperialism in legal phrases and constitutional language. The Empire was constantly expanding and its bond was a strong sentiment of mutual goodwill.[2]

Twenty years after the proclamation of the imperial title in India, Disraeli's move was regarded by historians in the light of their new imperialist vision. Disraeli's intentions were construed in a way which would have been scarcely possible twenty years earlier. His imperial foresight was discovered, 'his prescience as to the broader issues of imperialism', as Holland Rose put it in 1897. 'However much the imperialism of Lord Beaconsfield may be criticised in regard to details, there can be little doubt now that he laid down the general lines of policy which must be followed by the British race, if it is to hold a foremost place in the world.'[3]

The year 1898 was the climax in popular enthusiasm for imperialism. It had fully incorporated Africa into the sphere of imperial and national policy. In April 1898 the *Contemporary Review* criticized the Government for underrating the hostility of France and Russia and the determination of a combination of European Powers 'to hinder the foundation of an Africo-British Empire'. The choice was, as the critic put it, 'between the maintenance of the Government and the maintenance of the Empire'.[1] The *Nineteenth Century* commented favourably on the rise of imperialism and wrote: 'International struggles and dangers, the thunder of war abroad, the revival of the Imperialist spirit, the urgent necessity of converting England once more into a great naval and military Power, taught us the old lesson that nations do not live by bread alone: not even if the bread is buttered.'[2] Omdurman and Fashoda put Britain into a defiant mood, a readiness for battle which imperialism now expressed, and which did not escape the attention of foreign observers. The mood spread to the other great English-speaking nation. It, too, had become involved in a colonial dispute.

There was much talk that year on both sides of the Atlantic about the superiority and the destinies of the Anglo-Saxon race.[3] Hopes were held out for realizing those destinies by co-operation in world affairs. Chamberlain himself hinted at that prospect. He did so just at the time when Admiral Dewey's fleet attacked Manila and the acquisition of the Philippines became the foremost topic in American discussion on war-aims. This moment opened a new chapter not only in American politics but also in the development of 'imperial' ideas. Americans had heeded the rise of these ideas in England. Now many of them were eager either to adopt them or to show that their implications were at variance with the hallowed traditions of the republic. For some weeks the former of these attitudes prevailed. 'We see the beginning of an "Imperial" party here', wrote W. H. Page to James Bryce on 9 May 1898. And a few weeks later the *Washington Post* asserted that empire had become the cry of American democracy. 'A new consciousness seems to have come upon us.... We are face to face with strange destiny.... The taste of empire is in the mouth of the people even as the taste of blood in the jungle.' 'It means an imperial policy....' The *Washington Post* enjoyed the fame of being a level-headed paper and had been respected just because of its caution; its acceptance of imperial feelings as an irreversible current was therefore particularly noticed.[4]

Congressmen and publicists were, indeed, quick to denounce the 'spectre of imperialism'—and the advocates of annexation themselves came to think unfavourably of imperial phraseology.[1] But, in fact, it was the attitude implied in this phraseology which prevailed. In the context of American politics imperialism in summer 1898 meant 'the absorption by the U.S.A. of several existing European colonies',[2] the change from a policy of isolation and non-intervention to a system of expansions. 'I understand by imperialism, in the best sense in which the term is used, a theory of national policy in accordance with which the U.S. is to add to its territorial possessions, for the purpose of extending American trade and American political influence. We are to change our traditional policy of independence and non-participation in the general politics of the world, and to adopt a policy of territorial expansion, of wide contact and control.'[3] The same source also testifies to the comparatively sudden appearance of the word Imperialism in American political usage as a result of the war with Spain. A wave of militancy and assertive spiritedness engulfed the English-speaking world in 1898.

At the end of the year it was said to have affected also the minds of many Englishmen.

At the moment when I write these lines there is noticeable through the British Empire a very strange alertness of concentrated attention . . . my own memories go back faintly, so far as to the Crimean War; never in all those variegated years have I seen anything approaching the attentive silence of to-day. The lion has straightened his front paws, and rises, and listens.

In such terms were Englishmen represented to Americans by Edmund Gosse at New Year 1899.[4]

Observers who were less given to rhetorical images found the temper of the nation by no means 'silent'. The *Spectator* stated that current 'talk about "empire" was at once eternal and exaggerated'.[5] Foreign writers who then stayed in London were startled by the fervour of the 'imperial' ideas which were current everywhere. They became aware of the passions symbolized and the problems implied in these topics as something relatively new. The German anglicist W. Wetz noted that the press spoke no longer of the Kaiser and the Czar as of 'emperors'. Words relating to 'imperial' causes had by the British become reserved for their empire, Greater Britain. This was, he thought, the result of 'the imperialist movement in England', which expressed itself in newspaper discussions, associations, and books. The movement, he confessed, had made him reverse his views on the spirit of the nation.[1] Olindo Malagodi, who visited London clubs, found their members since 1898 constantly involved in 'quella capitale questione che è scoppiata improvvisamente, col folgore di un gigantesco fuoco artificiale sulla frontiera oscura di due secoli: la questione dell' imperialismo'.[2] And Françoise de Pressensé asked Englishmen to consider the 'curious thing, but a fact beyond dispute, that when the masses are on the verge of rising in their majesty and asking for their rights, the classes have only to throw into their eyes the powder of "imperialism", and to raise the cry of the fatherland is in danger'.[3]

These observations are strikingly unanimous and strikingly simultaneous. They go far to show that, though prepared by manifold antecedents, the surge of imperial sentiment in 1898 was, like the corresponding excitement in America, remarkably sudden. Attempts to interpret it in terms of sociology and to trace it back to literary influences have been made by the same contemporary writers who directed attention to it. But no explanation can be adequate which does not take full account of the one fact that the waves of 'imperialism' between 1897 and 1899 were not only in the nature of a social phenomenon, but also in the nature of historical events. The nation had come to accept African and Asian possessions as part of the Empire. Doubts had been dispelled by economic and moral arguments. Imperialism had become the expression of a sentiment which many Britons could share for different reasons. It expressed Anglo-Saxon kinship and solidarity with the self-governing dominions, it gave expression to a feeling of racial superiority, to imperial pride, to a determination not to be ousted by foreign rivals, to grow and expand economically. Thus the nation regarded the exploits of the Royal Niger Company, the advance of Kitchener into the Sudan, the defeat of the Khalifa, and the clash with French interests at Fashoda as matters of Empire and national policy. When religious doubters pointed to the selfishness of British motives in Africa they were countered by theology. If history was the manifestation of divine will, the concentration of power in the hands of the British could only mean an act of Providence. Britain was meant to take a leading part in the educational and civilizing process of the black races. That was her mission. It was, therefore, easier for a conscientious Christian to embrace Imperialism in 1898 than it had been in 1878 when Disraeli backed the Turks, the persecutors of Christians, in the Near East. When the Armenian massacres caused a new wave of anti-Turkish indignation in Britain, there were no longer any 'imperial interests' that could prevent the British Government from identifying itself with that popular indignation. Imperial policy in Africa and in Asia could be represented not only as good British policy but also as responsible Christian Policy. The Englishman of 1898 liked to think of the British Empire not only as the most secure and extensive but also as the most beneficent the world had ever seen. Conquest in Africa for the first time in African history was undertaken for the betterment of the Africans themselves. The conqueror was asked to donate money for the schooling of the conquered by Kitchener, the victorious general.

> Knowing that ye are forfeit by battle and have no
>   right to live,
> He begs for money to bring you learning—
>   and all the English give . . .
> Behold, they clap the slave on the back,
>   and behold, he ariseth a man!

Kipling's verse in 1898 captured the mood of that year, the romantic pride in the virility and vastness of the Empire and the belief that it was an Empire with a difference. Its might and authority was wielded for the good of the backward races.

> They terribly carpet the earth with dead,
>   and before their cannons cool,
> They walk unarmed by twos and threes,
>   to call the living to school.

Kipling's advice to the Sudanese to accept British tutelage and belief in the sincerity of the British educational effort was undoubtedly in keeping with the views of many other Englishmen who abhorred cruel abuse of power and looked for its use in the service of a noble, humanitarian cause.

> Go, and carry your shoes in your hand and
>   bow your head on your breast,
> For he who did not slay you in sport,
>   he will not teach you in jest.[1]

A noteworthy attempt was made by J. L. Walton, Member of Parliament for Leeds, to state the elements that were contained in the word Imperialism, now on everybody's lips. Writing as a Liberal and self-confessed imperialist, Walton regarded imperialism as a principle of statesmanship which guided the Government in relation to the Empire. Beyond that it was an expression of pride in the magnificent heritage won by the courage and energy of past generations and a sacred trust bequeathed to the present generation. So much for sentiment. Imperialism also expressed a conviction that British rule was beneficent and just, and that the Anglo-Saxon race was equal to the tremendous task it had undertaken by accepting the responsibility for the government of a portion of mankind. Imperialism was a protest against weary insularity. It was alive to the social needs of Britain's teeming millions. The imperialist was convinced that he was merely marching along the only way history had opened for him. His father's eyes had been opened to the breathtaking expansion of the British around the globe. His own eyes had been opened to the gigantic task posed by the tropical Empire and its numerous races. 'We are Imperialists in response to the compelling influences of our destiny', was a rather pale summing up by the author of the historical self-awareness of his own generation, for Imperialism expressed the position which most Englishmen then believed they had to take up in the relentless advance of history. In Walton's mind—and this we have seen, was no exception—the notion of Empire combined two separate parts. One part was white and British; the other part, coloured and backward. Race was the one fundamental basis of imperialism. Moral obligation was the other. Certain historical processes were inevitable and could be clearly seen in the offing. In 1899 Walton foresaw that nothing could stop the invading force of civilization in Africa. The only question was whether those forces would come to the Africans and savage races in other parts of the world in a British form or in a French, German, Belgian, or Portuguese form, or a Russian form as in parts of Asia. The British imperialists believed with Walton that in their struggle with the new invading civilization subject races could be offered no greater boon 'than the strong and humane authority of British rule'.[1] Africa was becoming 'Our Black Empire'. It looked as if a territory larger than India with seventy million inhabitants, 'half-devil and half-child' as Kipling had it, would become Britain's responsibility for a long time, throwing up new problems every year and requiring vast resources in wealth and manpower. The imperialist was the person who accepted that challenge of history with enthusiasm as guardian, educator, and vocational trainer of the black races. He hoped Pax Britannica would be imposed and welcomed by the subject races, because they would derive from it safety, personal freedom, and new economic and intellectual opportunity.

At the beginning of 1899 Kipling published his famous poem *The White Man's Burden*. It expressed in verse the latent thought of those years:

> Take up the White Man's burden—
> Send forth the best ye breed—
> Go bind your sons to exile
> To serve your captives' need
> To wait in heavy harness,
> On fluttered folk and wild—
> Your new-caught, sullen peoples,
> Half-devil and half-child.

It sang of the frustrating struggle against ignorance, disease, famine, and it heightened in the reader the sense of the historical moment. Africa was waiting at the front door. Its animals were still a novelty in the white man's zoos. Its savages were hardly known, and most Europeans believed they were animals in human form. Kipling brought home, in the words of the *Spectator*, 'the duty of the white man to conquer and control, probably for a couple of centuries, all the dark peoples of the world, not for his own good, but for theirs'.[2] Failure to civilize the Africans would spell untold misery to the civilizers. With their new powers supplied by science the 'sullen peoples' could extirpate the white man with glee, the journal pointed out, unless they were given 'our character and our creed'. For thousands of years a third of humanity had lived in the great river valleys of the Nile, Niger, Congo, and Yangtse without making progress. The only justification for the white man to interfere there was 'to take up the burden'. One day, the *Spectator* felt, the white man's work in Africa and Asia would be judged and assessed by those he had educated. That was why the last verses of Kipling's poem seemed to contain the wisdom without which Imperialism could not carry out its task properly:

> Take up the White Man's burden—
> Ye dare not stoop to less—
> Nor call too loud on Freedom
> To cloak your weariness.
> By all ye will or whisper,
> By all ye leave or do,
> The silent sullen peoples
>   Shall weigh your God and you.
> Take up the White Man's burden!
>   Have done with childish days—
> The lightly proffered laurel,
>   The easy ungrudged praise:
> Comes now, to search your manhood
>   Through all the thankless years,
> Cold, edged with dear-bought wisdom,
>   The judgement of your peers.

Imperialism, no doubt, became so widely acceptable in Britain because the impact of Africa had given it a strong sense of moral obligation. It was no longer an assertion of collective selfishness either in a racial or an economic garb alone. There had always been many people in Britain who were not prepared to accept a policy of pure selfishness, and who desired to see British power employed in the service of a moral purpose. The betterment of the subject races and the education of black savages seemed to be such a cause, which had raised the moral appeal of imperialism in the last years of the nineteenth century. To the idea of Anglo-Saxon kinship and imperial bond of brotherhood had been added the moral duty of trusteeship in the tropics.

As 1898 was drawing to a close, imperialism had reached its zenith of respectability and popular acclaim. It mirrored the political and moral sentiment of the late Victorians and their philosophy of history. Its shining glory was shattered by the Boer War, which shook the nation's confidence in the moral character of imperialism and once again split the British in their attitude towards their Empire and their role in history. But as imperialism again became associated with an evil, it remained no longer within the domain of one party as in 1878–9. It spread beyond Britain and began to play a part in international life. This was possible because of further changes which occurred in the meaning and function of the term in the new century.

IX

THE REVULSION AGAINST IMPERIALISM

When Imperialism became a party slogan in 1878 the shadow of Napoleon III and the echo of his fallen empire were still detectable in the connotation of the partisan concept. Alien despotism and military adventure were associated with the last French Empire, which was held up as a warning to the British public by the Liberals. By 1898, however, the derogatory meaning of the word had paled. Many Liberals were proud 'imperialists', and the word had changed from a partisan abuse to become a national gospel. Its reversion to the status of a partisan abuse was mainly the result of the Boer War. It is important to note, however, that imperialism came in for sharp criticism before the outbreak of the Boer War and that the points made by the critics formed a basis for the interpretation of the War and for further criticism. Hobson and Morley stood out as early and influential critics of the methods and the spirit of Imperialism.

In 1898 John Atkinson Hobson attacked the notion, so dear to Chamberlain and other expansionists, that British trade profited from the extension of British control. Hobson showed that trade figures furnished no proof for the assertion that trade followed the flag. Trade followed the price list. It did not follow the flag into the regions of the Niger, Somali, Bechuanaland, Zanzibar, Burma, and Uganda. Others like Farrer confirmed the fact that trade figures showed the biggest increase in the exchange of goods between Britain and her industrial rivals rather than her own colonies. So why insist on colonies? The old Cobdenite tradition was revived. In 1889 Hobson had formulated his 'Theory of Underconsumption' according to which periodical crises were caused by the maldistribution of wealth. The theory itself was a clear product of Marxist thought. Too much capital was accumulating in the hands of too few, who automatically oversaved and thereby reduced demand for consumer goods. Hobson's remedy differed from Marx in degree and method but not in principle. He demanded a more equal distribution of wealth. This theory he applied to his criticism of imperialist policy in 1898. The surplus capital, he claimed, which accumulated in the hands of the well-to-do required new investments. It desired to force open new markets as old ones began to close because of protective tariffs. To break into new markets the public purse was employed for the purpose of private profit, the military machine was expanded to force on the 'lower races' in the colonies goods the British working class—impoverished by unproductive armament and maldistribution of wealth—was too poor to buy.[1] Militancy and expansionism were thus shown by Hobson to be the direct result of the existence of a social evil at home. Imperialism was incompatible with social progress and reform. A few months earlier another critic reviewed the record of British administration in India and came to the equally shattering conclusion that Britain became more and more entangled in the economic and political misfortunes of the Indian Empire and would one day have to choose between that Empire and her own political liberty and economic health.[2] What such investigations called for was a more careful examination of the forces and interests which guided the hands of statesmen and evoked the emotions of the multitude in affairs called 'imperial'.

On 17 January 1899 John Morley informed his constituents of his resolve 'no longer to take any active and responsible part in the formal counsels of the heads of the Liberal party'. He summarized the dividing issue in two words which had, he insisted, recently become nearly synonymous: 'you may call it Jingoism, you may call it Imperialism.' Remembering the censures he had incurred sixteen months earlier, he recognized this time that 'imperialism' could be interpreted in a favourable sense to mean 'national duty, not national vainglory . . . the guardianship and the guidance of a great state'. But that was not 'what "Imperialism" is in the sense in which it is now used'. The current significance of the word was exhibited in the Sudan expedition with its cruel incidents of posthumous decapitation, in the Fashoda crisis, the only palpable result of that expedition, and in the prospect of militarism, which meant gigantic expenditure and inevitably led to war. Imperialism was the state of mind which acquiesced in all that, as the Liberal leaders were doing.[3] The tenor of the speech was not very different from that of the essay in which twenty years earlier Robert Lowe had launched the indictment of 'imperialism' against Disraeli's Oriental policy. But the

situation was different. Consequences far more momentous than those
which had immediately resulted from Lowe's invective ensued now
from Morley's solemn confession of faith. It gave the cue to a lively
discussion which focused on the concept of Imperialism and was protracted for months in party speeches and dignified addresses, in newspaper articles and pamphlets, until late in the year it was merged in the
altercations aroused by the outbreak and conduct of the Boer War.[1]

In this discussion champions of imperialism were the first to raise the
question of economic interests. Chamberlain was not the only one who
emphasized the interconnexion of Empire and commerce. George
Wyndham at the War Ministry defined an imperialist as 'a man who
realizes . . . that those places which were recondite, visited at great
intervals by travellers, are now the markets, the open ports, the ex-
changes of the world to which every energetic Briton should tend his
footsteps and where a great part of the capital of Great Britain is
invested'. *The Times* railed at Morley who still clung to the ideals
which had been valid in the year of the Great Exhibition, 'while the
world has not stood still . . . and nations . . . have learned that wealth
and progress, like all other good things, have to be guarded by strong
hands and stout hearts'. This assertion was somewhat more militant than
the similar remark of J. Holland Rose a year earlier; and so was that of
the Liberal J. L. Walton that 'the motive for the Manchester School has
outlived the pacific philanthropy . . . . Now that markets are in danger
of closing, the industrial spirit is imperialist and even warlike and demands
that they be kept open.'

Such opinions were certainly voiced among the businessmen themselves.[2] But, in the course of the year, they encountered answers.
Demonstrations of protest and distrust followed three different lines.
One was that indicated by Morley: disgust with the bravado and the
reckless desire for further expansion. This sentiment was expressed
most forcefully by Leonard Courtney and John L. Hammond[3]; it was
countenanced by Campbell-Bannerman, who thought abjuring 'the
vulgar and bastard Imperialism of irritation, and provocation, and
aggression' a hopeful device for avoiding an incurable rift within the
Liberal party. Other critics like Hobson warned against the dangers of
'the capitalist era which is now slowly superseding the industrial era'.

Capital flowing abroad into the spheres of 'imperial interest' would soon stimulate the productive forces of other nations instead of those of the mother country. From colonial countries in particular it would in fact not come back, and only shareholders would benefit from this investment. This was the economic reality into which 'pegging out for posterity' was about to be transformed, as long as 'a sham imperialism turns our heads'. The economist who uttered this warning[1] directed attention to an aspect of the case which a special group of critics thought to be no less morally revolting than were the militant emotions and, indeed, suspiciously allied to these. Material greed seemed to lurk behind all the noble talk. F. Greenwood in April 1899 stated that 'the lords and princes of British commerce are not in all things and in all ways the patriots they probably believe themselves to be' and were comparable to farmers who looked out for new virgin soil before they could properly till the land they already possessed. In the two-hundred-odd pages in which John M. Robertson expatiated upon the mutual relations between 'patriotism and empire', this alliance between 'the temper of national pride' and the interests of investment which cried for new markets was reserved for the concluding chapter. The 'commercial aristocracy and rich middle class' was about to occupy the place which feudalism and the landlord system had held before. Among them 'the sinister interest of those industrial sections which thrive on the production of war material' was notable. Alongside the 'mere pride and passion of nation and race which had been characteristic of Disraelian Imperialism', there was now 'the concept of commercial interest' emerging more and more distinctly. It was more dangerous because it could hold its own better against criticism. And it was all directed only 'to the end of heaping up more capital for investment', while 'our own toilers are not to do more consuming'. Finally, besides the commercial and capitalist interest there was another stigmatized, though only occasionally, by the author: the service interest, which, since Gladstone abolished purchase in the army, had also become a middle-class interest.[2]

These short indictments were to become headlines in later anti-imperialist literature. Upon contemporaries their impression was lost because they were ejaculated only in passing, and because Robertson repelled readers by his disparagement of patriotism. Another radical, however, made a great impression by attacks in a similar vein. Robert Wallace exposed what he called 'the seamy side of Imperialism'. He wanted to back Morley, but surpassed him in that he charged the Liberal party with having become dependent on 'a thousand firms, financiers, adventurers and company promoters who seize on every new market'. More important still, he extended the charge to the business-men who traded and made money in the colonies, and thereby he extended it to the dependent Empire at large. The native was to those people merely an object of manifold exploitation, now by dispossessing him of his land, now by selling him gin; 'and then expansionists boast that trade is following the flag'. And Wallace saw no difference between these modern ways and 'the mode in which the Empire generally had been acquired'. There was no great difference, in the eyes of the author, between so-called bastard and legitimate imperialism. It meant a low standard of living for those on the Clyde and the Thames, because civilizing energy was being diverted to the Nile, Ganges, and Yangtse with highly dubious results, economic and moral. To the Liberal imperialist who justified expansion by pointing to the civilizing mission Wallace answered: 'You are not making a civilised man of the Hindoo—often a much cleverer man than yourself—nor will you do any better with the Egyptian, the Arab, or the Soudani. You are not making men of them. You are training them to be permanent babies in leading-strings.' To the over self-confident, irresponsible and insatiable expansionist Wallace could only say that he was suffering from a mental delusion and a false idea of greatness, which was not identical with bulk. There was more greatness found within the two miles radius of the British Museum than in the whole of Asia. 'Expansionist Imperialism means more Despotism abroad and more Aristocratic recrudescence at home', Wallace concluded.[1]

The stirring effect of these strictures is best measured by the fact that Mary Kingsley singled them out for special refutation when in autumn 1899 she went on a lecture tour in order to make the manufacturing towns of the North share her interest in West Africa. She was appalled by 'the spectacle of a distinct outbreak of anti-imperialism up here in England'. In a way she thought men like Morley, Courtney, and

Wallace deserving the gratitude of the nation 'for their honest endeavours to keep England's honour clean and to preserve her imperialism from sinking into being in our times a stockbroker's nigger business'. But she felt, of course, compelled to emphasize the national merit of the 'buccaneers, privateers, pirates' of yore without whom 'we should not be Imperial England', and to defend the honour of the colonial merchants of the present day to whose expert understanding she would have chosen to confide the Empire in Africa.[1] The *Spectator* held, like Mary Kingsley, 'that it is the business of England... to take over and rule the inferior races of mankind'. But in October the paper saw reason to speak of people who nowadays practised this 'taking over' in terms not very different from those of Wallace. 'New jingoism' was afoot, which was 'tainted by the desire for great and rapid gain.... From China, from Central Africa, from West Africa, from South Africa and from the Pacific we receive the same messages which mean: use force, coerce the dark men, defy the white men in battle, and then Englishmen will have new trades, new concessions, new mines, new pecuniary prosperity.' The writer was satisfied that the wrongdoers had 'little hold on Parliament and none on the Administration'; probably by censuring the new jingoes he wished also to parry the detractions of anti-imperialists.[2]

War at the Transvaal border was imminent when the article appeared; but the author made no sign of being disquieted by the fact that the British Government had espoused the Uitlanders' demands, which were prompted by 'the desire for great and rapid gain'. An economist to whom the relation of capital accumulation to social welfare had been for years the crucial problem of modern economics held other views. Hobson went out to South Africa for the *Manchester Guardian* in 1899 in order to inspect and report on the conditions underlying the crisis. He was horrified by the mentality which pervaded the society of Johannesburg, and gave vent to his impressions and conclusions in his reports, which were republished in his book *The War in South Africa* in 1900. It was an indictment of Chamberlain's policy and of 'the application of the new Imperialism to the affairs of South Africa' in the service of ruthless capitalists who were not even British. They were German and Russian Jews. Hobson introduced a strong note of anti-Semitism into his attempt to compromise imperialism in the eyes of his British readers. We saw that already the first revulsions against imperialism in the days of Disraeli carried mild anti-Jewish overtones. Since those days anti-Semitism had become a prominent feature of European life, most often employed as a political weapon against Liberalism and the advance of capitalism. Hobson himself had an uneasy conscience about his contention that the British were called upon to fight for Jewish capitalists. He claimed to have stated the truth and dissociated himself from an 'appeal to the ignominious passion of Judenhetze'. Yet his statements were passionate rather than sober and calm judgements where the Jewish factor came in. Jewish strength was underestimated, he stated. Jews did not take part in the Uitlander agitation. 'They let others do that sort of work.' They outwitted and outcompeted the Briton and a little ring of Jewish financiers controlled the most valuable resources of the Transvaal. They required the help of the state and, therefore, entered into the fight as 'Imperialists', adopting a most loyal, British tone and language in their official announcements and in the press they controlled. Many organs of British African opinion were already 'in devoted sympathy with the Jew-Imperialist design that is in course of execution'.[1] Imperialism was 'unmasked' by Hobson as a capitalist and Jewish conspiracy to draw Britain into a fight for the benefit of Jewish financiers and their ruthless British capitalist allies like Rhodes. The British people were being led into a crime by capitalists for the sake of capitalist interests.

Thus, when the South African War broke out, thoughtful Englishmen were just in the mood to inquire severely into the prospects as well as into the roots of all that was now called imperialism. In this inquiry economic acquisitiveness was the object of special suspicion. The manner in which England was drawn into the war could not but make such reflexions highly unpopular. President Kruger, determined to maintain the independence of the Transvaal and the political supremacy of the Boers, had sent an ultimatum on 9 October, demanding the immediate withdrawal of all British troops that had been brought to South Africa since 1 June 1899 and opened the attack two days later. To all appearance he was the aggressor. To say, even to suggest that the war was the responsibility of the men in charge of imperial policies, or, still worse, of pecuniary interests countenanced by such men, was to lower the national morale. And the maintenance of this morale was urgently necessary in view of the initial reverses and of the light which they threw on the national preparations. But it was just this situation that aroused searchings of the heart which could not be satisfied by overcoming the danger, still less by conquering the Boer countries. The depth of the shame with which conscientious hearts watched the next months is impressively brought out in reflexions which high-minded women confided to their diaries.[1]

Protests against the war were loudly voiced in the House of Commons by Irish and Welsh members, the young Lloyd George being among the latter. They endeavoured to agitate against the war by a prominent use of anti-capitalist and anti-Jewish arguments. It was a war, they maintained, waged for a handful of Jewish millionaires, a monstrous outrage against a small nation. One Irish speaker told the House:

Here are the names of some of the 'fine old English gentlemen' for whom the British Empire is going to war. They are nearly all millionaires and leading Uitlanders—Beit, Wernher, Eckstein, Rouilot, Barnato, Adler, Lowe, Wolff, Goldmann, Neumann, and Goertz. I wonder how many of these millionaire masters of Her Majesty's Government are now at the front with your soldiers to face the music?

Rhodes alone was fighting, he admitted, but then added pointedly, 'his name is Rhodes, and not Rhodes-stein'. His fellow-countrymen also tried to make the most of anti-Semitic agitation in order to compromise the war, and Lloyd George took a similar line of attack.[2] Anti-Jewish feeling was roused by the war also in the Labour camp, as the diary entry of John Burns showed.[3] The Liberals were split into three groups one of which, led by Courtney and Stead, upheld the Boers and denounced the war as unjust. W. T. Stead's influential *Review of Reviews* refused to give support to the war and said in October that 'the more unlovely side of our Imperialism' was now visible to all, and a few months later in an even more bitter vein claimed 'there is not a millionaire in the crowd who believes as much in peace and Liberalism as Mr Rhodes believes in Imperialism and conquest'.[4] Such a condemnation from the pen of Stead was a stirring event, because Stead as editor of the *Pall Mall Gazette* and the *Review of Reviews* had been a leading supporter of imperialism. Rhodes and Milner were at a loss to understand the change of heart that had taken place. 'We all learned our lessons from you, and now you go and oppose us', they protested. Stead owed his former followers and political friends an explanation. He tried to offer one in May 1900 in an article, called 'The true Imperialism', an imperialism which grew naturally in the open air without forcing the pace, an imperialism which was allied with commonsense and the Ten Commandments. Stead insisted on the moral basis. He rejected the War as the outcome of a false Imperialism of grab and proud arrogance. True imperialism did not keep its Christianity and its liberty for home consumption. 'The Empire must be based upon the consent of the governed', he wrote and protested, 'All our money is wanted for bloodshed and devastation. It is only another instance of the difference between Jingo and anti-Jingo Imperialism.'[1] Privately Stead admitted his feeling of guilt, having idealized and glorified Rhodes before and having helped to move Milner into his position in South Africa. He felt morally responsible for the conflict and his nonconformist conscience prompted him to mobilize Liberal opinion against the War.[2] He felt like Leonard Courtney that the new arrogant, materialist imperialism would ruin the country.

We observe how the decline in the status of the word is evidenced by the use of face-saving adjectives. Having been committed to a strong advocacy of imperialism, its champions now felt the need for qualification and reservation. Robert Buchanan, too, tried to save a nobler vision of Imperialism from the effect of the deplorable drift of English society away from the humanitarian traditions of Wordsworth, Shelley, and Wilberforce. Writing in December 1899 in a dejected mood and surveying the English scene a short time before his disablement and death, he felt the great English statesmen, the men with a conscience left, had vanished from the political scene with Gladstone.

There is an universal scramble for plunder, for excitement, for amusement, for speculation, and above it all the flag of a Hooligan Imperialism is raised, with the proclamation that it is the sole mission of Anglo-Saxon England, forgetful of the task of keeping its own drains in order, to expand and extend its boundaries indefinitely, and, again in the name of Christianity it has practically abandoned, to conquer and inherit the Earth.[3]

What does the nobler imperialism stand for ? According to Buchanan it stood for the federation of Great Britain with her colonies for the purpose of spreading what was best in English civilization, the application of justice, and the message of freedom.

There were a number of other attempts to preserve a better and purer idea of imperialism than the one more and more critics began to reject as vulgar, materialist, and bellicose. Middle-of-the-road Liberalism desired to uphold the idea of a defensive 'true' imperialism against the aggressive policy of Mr Chamberlain, which they deplored. They desired to vindicate 'an Imperialism which cares only for the safety and does not desire the extension of the Empire, to which the policy of land-grabbing is intensely offensive'.[1] The eminent Liberal lawyer, R. T. Reid, condemned the new imperialism, for it was an Imperialism which meant the annihilation of small nations and growing militarism at home.

If Imperialism means sober pride in the great Empire we control, a most earnest desire to knit together in the bonds of friendship the various populations that belong to it, a firm determination to preserve the integrity of our Empire at all costs, and the using of the means of advancing civilisation among all kinds and conditions of men—then there is no one more of an imperialist than I am. But if it means departing from the old and honoured tradition of this country to respect the freedom of other nations, even if they be small nations, and to advance rather than to retard liberty . . . then it is the duty of every honest citizen of this country to destroy that spirit, because otherwise that spirit is certain to destroy us.[2]

Imperialism can be compatible with the freedom of the small nations, Reid claimed. Many other agonized Liberals clung to imperialism as a respectable idea and attacked an evil form of imperialism for which they would have preferred a different term. More examples of that nature would not add much to the general picture which shows how the word imperialism had been split into two opposite interpretations and evaluations. They merely reflected the major split which rent the national conscience on account of the Boer War. Each side adopted the word for its own political use. Lord Rosebery commented upon this phenomenon in his rectorial address in Glasgow in November 1900, when the subject chosen was 'Questions of Empire'. That word, too, had become abhorrent to some in the course of the preceding months, while it stood for a deeply felt faith in the mind of others.[1]

In December 1899 a special meeting of the Fabian Society was convened at which a resolution was submitted, which read: 'That the Society should dissociate itself from the imperialism of Capitalism and vainglorious nationalism and condemn the War.'[2] The resolution was not passed by the Fabians, but more resolutions were forthcoming from Socialists and Radicals to the same effect. Organized British workmen were reported by F. Maddison, Labour leader and Member of Parliament for Sheffield, to be opposed to the War, because they regarded it as the outcome of 'a capitalist conspiracy', set on foot by 'a small clique of capitalists, in which the German Jew is conspicuous, to grow rich at the expense of the wretched Kafirs. . . . To the representatives of labor the trail of these Shylocks of a gambling commercialism is apparent right through the devious tracks which led to the war . . . this inflated Imperialism does not pay.'[3] In the Commons John Burns spoke out against 'wild Imperialism' succeeded by militarism and a war to enfranchise a lot of uitlanders, 'mostly Jews, who if they got their vote would sell it'. The War was, in the words of Burns, 'a war for gold and capitalist domination inspired and directed by the financial Jews'.[4] In May 1900 the Independent Labour Party in London issued a pamphlet which bore the title *Imperialism*. It defined the word as 'a world policy, and not merely a Colonial policy. It implies that in our relations with other States we are to be guided not so much by the ideals of co-operation as by the assumption of superiority; it inevitably leads to territorial expansion and to an increasing burden of political responsibility over native races.' The pamphlet denied the superiority of British civilization and favoured the blending of cultures. Pax Britannica did not permit the nations under British control to develop their own life. 'The result is not an extension of the area of civilization, but an increase in the number of dead nations.' Imperialism led to constant extension of territory and to the continued subjection of other peoples. It also destroyed liberty and social progress in the home country. With reference to recent studies such as Lord Farrer's it was stated that trade did not follow the flag but business enterprise. There was very little Socialist theory in all that, and in some aspects the pamphlet was in disagreement with Marxist views when it stated that Socialist conditions did not require an earlier capitalist period, and that 'the Capitalism of Imperialism is established under conditions which make further evolution impossible.[1] The pamphlet was drawn up with a view to the forthcoming elections which, Bernard Shaw wrote in *Fabianism and the Empire*, 'will turn, we are told, mainly on the popularity of Imperialism'.[2] Shaw and many of his Fabian friends were at that time convinced that Britain had to embrace imperialism in order to serve the interests of the working class and to maintain Britain's ability of governing in the interests of civilization as a whole.

Thoughtful political writers at that time became concerned about the growing confusion over the meaning and the use of imperialism. The *Monthly Review* observed that two distinct political ideas had unhappily come to be called by the same name, 'that hated word Imperialism'. One interpretation of the word comprised the idea of a commonwealth of autonomous states. The other interpretation—derived from Emperor rather than from Empire—smacked of militant, centralized despotism. The former idea underlay British imperialism, the latter was Continental in character. George III had tried and failed to establish the objectionable type of imperialism in Britain, because Liberalism was too deeply rooted in the country. The mark of Liberalism was indelibly sealed on the British Empire. Liberalism 'has established, and must uphold, a democratic autonomous commonwealth'.[3] In the following years, however, it became wellnigh impossible to preserve the association of the concept of a free commonwealth with the word imperialism. In the passions aroused by the Boer War imperialism lost its respectability more and more. Was it a patriotic attitude? The man in the street was still inclined to equate patriotism with imperialism, and the daily press in their majority branded all as unpatriotic who 'will not utter the Shibboleth of Imperialism', W. H. Kent wrote in the *Westminster Review* in February 1902. Patriotism and imperialism were, however, mutually destructive, the writer claimed, the one being the love of our own country, the other 'a lust for the lands of others'. Justice and liberty called for the support of the little nations 'in their resistance to the onward course of Imperialism'. How the spirit of a nation like the British could become corrupted by 'the noisy carnival of triumphant

Imperialism' had been illustrated by the Boer War. But, the writer prophesied, sooner or later the sordid material interests behind Imperialism would come to light and the English people 'will at last weary of worshipping the brazen idols of Imperialism'.[1] Agitators against imperialism were apt to idealize the Boers, but they were less concerned with the nature of the Boers than with the future character of the Empire and of Britain. In the eyes of some the civilizing of the East of London was a more urgent task than that of Africa; imperialism was condemned because it offered the wrong choice.

As the name Commonwealth was free from the disagreeable associations which were evoked in many people by the words Empire and Imperialism, it came to be preferred as a term expressive of a liberal and socially progressive relationship between Britain and the dominions. In a pamphlet Commonwealth was put in opposition to imperialism. 'What is Imperialism? Subjugation by force of other nationalities. What is a Commonwealth? Communities joined together by consent to promote the common interest of each and all.'[2] The burning of Boer farms and the establishment of concentration camps in which Boer women and children were badly supplied provoked Liberal opinion again. In the wave of protests the *Daily News* wrote on 1 January 1901 that imperialism destroyed the variety and the beauty of the world. How could some Liberals still lift up their heads in the name of imperialism? The Party was hopelessly split over the issue of Boer policy. One comment on Lord Rosebery's speech at Chesterfield in December 1901 was that he was obviously in agreement with the Government Boer policy, but so many other Liberals raising the war cry of Imperialism were not. Imperialism, in fact, had become 'a war-cry better calculated to rally one-half of the Liberal party against the other than to carry dismay amongst the followers of Lord Salisbury and Mr Chamberlain'.[3] By 1902, therefore, Imperialism was a recognized symbol of a strong moral revulsion on the part of a minority with Liberal, Radical, and Labour leanings, or with strong religious scruples.

Three groups of argument stood out in the anti-imperialist agitation. The arguments correspond, broadly speaking, to the themes which had turned up in the discussions of 1899. The first group fastened on the international situation. Anglophobia had increased in France as well as

in Germany and might be welcome to statesmen of both Continental
power-groups. To contemplate this danger was the more painful
because it was now difficult for a scrupulous mind to draw a distinctive
line between British imperialism on the one hand and German militarism
or French chauvinism on the other. This trend of thought had historical
implications. It was no longer of first importance that in the overseas
expansion of the last two decades French and German politicians had
shown more initiative and lust for prestige than those of Great Britain.
There was, in fact, one imperialism which pervaded all the great nations,
including America and Russia. But—and that was a second line of
thought—England had a responsibility of her own rooted in a past
which was wholly her own. England had grown into the British
Empire, which had become the model for the other nations. Was not
imperial greatness a doubtful boon, fraught not only with political and
financial risks but no less necessarily with moral evils? The young
joint-authors of *Liberalism and the Empire*, who were 'blind neither to the
glories nor yet to the responsibilities of the British Empire', expressed
regret that the 'ambiguous and unfortunate' word 'empire' had blurred
the great distinction to be made between the relations of England to free
Canada and free Australia on the one hand, and her rule over 'all those
tropical provinces which she has won as a conqueror and holds as
a foreign despot'.

The third group of arguments dealt with the connexion between
politics and economics. It was attached to two main issues. One was
the danger threatening the great national principle of free trade. Was
not 'every imperialist' at heart an 'emporialist'?[1] The second dominating
issue was the particular connexion which to all appearances existed
between imperial expansion and capital accumulated at home. It was
the animating influence of overseas enterprise on the Stock Exchange,
which made thousands of agents busy for a considerable section of
society. And it was the reciprocal influence which these interests might
bring to bear on an obliging press which made them indiscernible from
the national cause.[2] Both these dangerous elements of capitalist society,
abettors of protection and speculators in exotic investments, had been
already shown up before the war. But the second species appeared an
ominously commanding power now that it might be identified with

those capitalists who had handled transactions in, and earned big gains from, Transvaal mines and the Chartered Company. The 'average citizen' was to be informed that his Empire, so 'magnificent and once so magnanimous', was liable to be overruled by the 'black magic of Imperialism' which made sordid motives direct the actions of 'little minds' in government and parliament, Hirst wrote. He, too, made occasional ironical allusions to the Jewish element in South African finance.[1]

All these indictments were inspired by spontaneous disgust and sincere moral apprehension. Nevertheless, one cannot fail to discover in them the influence of two master-minds—one of them long dead and often declared to be completely out of date, the other to many people still the 'Grand Old Man'—Cobden and Gladstone. The ethics were Gladstone's; the teachings were Cobden's. Fabians, indeed, wished to part with Gladstonian liberalism which 'thinks in individuals'[2]; but at that time there were other things than that to be learned from liberalism, and from Cobden in particular. Cobden had spoken with disrespect of the intellects working in Foreign and Colonial Offices. Cobden had preached to his people that economic wisdom and peace would prevail in the world, if only England would take the lead. Cobden had been convinced that the Empire connexions of Britain were obstructing this prospect. He, finally, had denounced particular class interests as being the ultimate mischief-makers, whose unearned privileges barred the path to material and moral progress. These interests, indeed, had been different from those which had to be faced now. They had been those of the feudal landlord class, whereas now the economic antagonists of peace, humanity, and public welfare were detected in the capitalist class, whose enlightened self-interest was according to him a steady element of progress. This made it difficult for a Liberal to weld all the indictments against imperialist statecraft and imperialist society into a coherent system of interpretation.

The interpretation of the Boer War as a direct result of capitalist expansion is as old as the Boer War itself. The development of an Uitlander problem in the Transvaal was undoubtedly an outcome of the advance of industry and capitalism into the mining areas of South Africa. Without huge investments and without the interest in gold speculation

Johannesburg would not have grown into a large industrial and commercial centre. The actual conflict of 1899, however, would have been avoided, if the capitalists of the Rand alone had had a say in the matter. The Milner Papers and the life-histories of such men as Beit make it clear that the conflict in South Africa was not the outcome of greedy capitalists but arose out of a clash between two groups living in the same country, one a group of urban, dynamic immigrants, the other a nation of rural, traditional, pastoral folk. It was a conflict similar to that between Jews and Arabs in Palestine. The pressure of Jewish migrants from East Europe was a factor in the situation, too. Milner and Kruger personified rather than caused the struggle. If the question is asked where the misinterpretation of the conflict as a conflict of 'economic imperialism' occurred first, the answer can only be: in England. In the United States the revulsion against imperialism started at the same time as in England, towards the end of 1898, and reached a climax in 1900 as well. The word itself, however, did not mean the same and was denounced for a different reason.

Imperialism in America did not contain as in England two incompatible sets of ideas. To those who approved of it and to those who rejected it alike the word meant oversea expansion of United States political control; it meant aspirations for colonies and for the status of a world Power; more specifically in the years 1898–1900, it meant the annexation of the Philippine Islands. National emotion had reached a climax in 1898, when many Americans believed expansion in the Pacific Ocean to be the 'Manifest Destiny' of American history, the pre-ordained course of the natural law of growth, the will of the Almighty. Some saw expansionism in the light of a civilizing duty just as in England, others as an economic necessity. As late as September 1898 the theory that expansion was an economic necessity was propounded in great detail in the *North American Review* by C. A. Conan. Excessive savings and the accumulation of goods, he maintained, were apt to cause economic crises. There were three solutions possible. The first was the socialist solution of increased consumption and the abandonment of saving and investments by private savers. The second solution to economic crises was the creation of new demands at home. The third solution was the productive employment of capital in other countries and the procurement of new markets for surplus commodities. The third solution was the one the writer recommended. The United States being unable to afford any longer a policy of isolation, imperialism was an economic necessity. 'The writer is not an advocate of imperialism from sentiment but does not fear the name if it means only that the United States shall assert their right to free markets in all the old countries which are being opened to the surplus resources of the capitalistic countries and thereby given the benefits of modern civilization.'[1] Voices warning against the danger of imperialism, however, began to be heard from autumn 1898 with increasing intensity and frequency.

One of the earliest warners was Goldwin Smith, who denounced Socialism and Imperialism alike as diseases of European origin. Imperialism constituted a grave domestic racial hazard and constitutional threat. 'No man of British race,' Goldwin Smith explained, 'though he were desirous of union with the American Commonwealth, would desire union with a scattered empire embracing an indefinite number of people of inferior races, Negroes, Hawaiians, Chinese, and Malays.... Imperialism, in short, is likely to be the death of Continental Union.' Imperialism would introduce into the United States not only militarism but also aristocracy and autocratic power. It would mean the end of democracy.[2] The argument that Imperialism would surrender the United States to a form of Caesarism and centralized power had survived in the memory of Goldwin Smith from the days of the first anti-imperialist campaign twenty years earlier; but nobody was aware, of course, of that curious echo of the Disraeli period. The attention of the public was focused on the peace negotiations with Spain in October 1898. There was no clear indication as to what the administration planned to do with the Philippines. The decision to annex them became known at the end of the month, and President McKinley in a trans-continental trip made expansionism a prominent theme in his public utterances. Anti-expansionism then became an organized movement and 'anti-imperialist' societies and leagues sprang up in the last weeks of 1898.

At Boston the anti-imperialist league was reported to have been formed for the purpose of resisting 'what is commonly called imperialism, or the annexation of territory not contiguous to the United States',[1] a definition which remained in the American mind. It was thus possible for an American to maintain a favourable view of the expansionism of past generations across the American continent towards the West Coast. The epithet 'contiguous' served to distinguish between legitimate American expansion and an undesirable colonial oversea expansion which was imperialism. The anti-imperialist movement enjoyed the support of the dollars and the pen of Andrew Carnegie, then still the steel-king of America, whose literary output commanded all the greater attention because of the leading position of the author in American industry. Carnegie's connexion with his native Britain had remained close during all those years, and he had formed ties of friendship not only with Gladstone but also with the undaunted British opponent of Imperialism, John Morley. Another prominent leader of the anti-imperialist movement was Carl Schurz, the veteran statesman, ex-soldier and ex-senator of Missouri. Both Carnegie and Schurz were not native-born Americans and both believed that, having become Americans by choice and not by the accident of birth, they had a purer concept of American ideals than many of their fellow countrymen. Americanism, as they understood it, could never become reconciled with imperialism.

In January 1899 Carnegie contributed an article to the *North American Review* which branded imperialism as un-American. Americanism stood for government by consent and equality of rights. Imperialism denied both. It denied liberty and the great heritage of Lincoln. There were those who believed in the humanitarian and christianizing mission of imperialism. To those moral imperialists Carnegie replied that the reluctant Philippines would have to be kept under the control of the United States not by missionaries but by soldiers. Soldiers in foreign countries, however, were anything but a civilizing element and would require missionaries and civilizers themselves. He hoped the American people would not discard their own lofty ideals of liberty and equality for 'the narrow liberty-denying, race-subjecting, Imperialism of President McKinley'.[2] Carnegie's reference to the President foreshadowed the election campaign of 1900. In January 1899 other Democratic leaders issued pronouncements which indicated their intention to make imperialism the main issue of the election. The President's Democratic rival, Colonel Bryan, himself adopted the anti-imperialist plank.[1] All through January the Philippines formed a topic for political debate in the United States as President McKinley had submitted the peace treaty with Spain to the Senate. There such outspoken opponents as Senator Hoar of Massachusetts warned against the danger of the republic, based on the principles of the Declaration of Independence, being transformed into 'a vulgar, commonplace empire, founded upon physical force'.

The public addresses of Carl Schurz contained similar arguments in his attack against imperialism. He was more specific and academic in his Chicago Convocation Address, delivered on the occasion of the 27th convocation of the University on January 4, 1899. It bore the title *American Imperialism*. Schurz attempted to prove that the annexation of the Philippines could not be regarded in the same light as the incorporation of Louisiana, Florida, Texas, or even Alaska into the United States. Those were all situated on the American Continent, in the temperate zone. Those territories had been thinly populated and were suitable for white settlement so as to become self-governing states later. Their development did not require a material increase of the U.S. army or navy. All those factors did not apply to the Philippines, and it would be a dangerous delusion to think the islands could be Americanized in the same way. The islands were out in the Pacific, were tropical, unsuitable for white settlement, and unlikely to be governed by consent. It would mean a departure from American tradition, if they were to be held by force. The Americans would, like the Spaniards before them, turn into conquerors and would be carried by the force of events

as Napoleon was when started on his career of limitless conquest. *This is imperialism* as now advocated. . . . If we take those new regions, we shall be well entangled in that contest for territorial aggrandizement, which distracts other nations and drives them far beyond their original design. . . . We shall want new conquests to protect that which we already possess. The greed of speculators working upon another government, will push us from one point to another.[2]

The revolt of the Filipinos in February confirmed the anti-imperialist argument that it would be impossible to achieve American government by consent on those islands. More and more troops were required in preparation for a regular campaign against the rebels in autumn. A protracted guerilla warfare began, which did not end before 1902. A good many arguments voiced by British anti-imperialists like John Morley in connexion with the Boer War were immediately echoed in America and applied to the war against the Filipinos. Liberals on both sides of the Atlantic and many observers on the European Continent were alarmed by the spectacle of Britain and America fighting two small nations and by the emergence of an Anglo-Saxon Imperialism. Like the Boers the Filipinos appealed to the European Powers for sympathy and help. American liberals complained that the nation had relapsed into the British tradition. The Hessians were turning in their graves or just grinning with bitter irony. The cost of imperialism was mounting. 'Whatever else is true of Imperialism, British or American, it is an expensive luxury', the *Nation* commented in June.[1] Self-government in the Philippines seemed remote. The only prospect in sight was government by martial law. Schurz mounted the platform of the American Anti-Imperialist League and proclaimed its anti-imperialist faith in the style of the Declaration of Independence when he said:

We hold that the policy known as imperialism is hostile to liberty and tends towards militarism, an evil from which it has been our glory to be free. We regret that it has become necessary in the land of Washington and Lincoln to reaffirm that all men of whatever race or color, are entitled to life, liberty, and the pursuit of happiness.[2]

Another meeting held in Philadelphia in February 1900 was addressed by Schurz in a similar vein.

In summer 1900, as the parties were getting ready for their conventions, events occurred in China which brought about a military intervention of the European Powers, Japan, and the United States. The Empire of China seemed on the point of insurrection and disintegration. Voices were heard in America favouring the acquisition of a portion of China by the United States. A Republican Congressman, Mr Bromwell, foresaw a possible partitioning of China among the Powers. In such an event, he maintained, the United States, too, must guard her own interest in that country by obtaining control over part of the dismembered Empire. Such a demand added more fuel to the anti-imperialist fire. It was angrily refuted and branded as 'rank imperialism'.[1] On the threshold of the new century horrified Liberals in America looked around and found everywhere the Liberal spirit in decline and international politics degenerating into a general territorial plunder and a lawless jungle. The word imperialism became in their eyes the symbol of that ominous development. What made matters worse, the United States by her own imperialist policy had lost her voice of moral leadership in international affairs and could no longer express her sympathy with any oppressed people without being checked by the unanswerable question: How about the Filipinos? That was the intellectual and political climate when the Democratic Party met in convention in Kansas City in July 1900 and decided to make imperialism the main issue of the presidential campaign. Bryan, the Democratic candidate in the campaign, wrote on the subject of the issue of the election:

One of the great objections to imperialism is that it destroys our proud pre-eminence among the nations. When the doctrine of self-government is abandoned, the United States will cease to be a moral factor in the world's progress. We cannot preach the doctrine that governments come up from the people, and, at the same time, practise the doctrine that governments rest upon brute force.[2]

Between July and November when the election took place, Imperialism, 'a new word in American politics' as A. E. Stevenson observed, remained the foremost slogan. Stevenson, nominated for vice-president by the Democrats, declared the lust of empire to be the great plague that had come over America in the closing hours of the century. The new policy of imperialism was inspired by corporate greed.[3] The fact that imperialism was identified with a policy of holding alien races in permanent and military subjection, without a share in their own government, prevented the Republicans from accepting the Democratic challenge and officially proclaiming themselves as proud imperialists. They avoided the word and did not wish to be identified with the attitude it implied. An attempt to prove to the Americans that imperialism represented an honourable policy and was perfectly compatible with Christianity stemmed from the pen of the Dean of

Canterbury.[1] There is no evidence that the argument of the British church leader made any impact on the American public. The Republicans and President McKinley never made support for imperialism a platform in their campaign, because the negative aspect of the slogan was too obvious a handicap.

As in England, the anti-imperialist platform failed to carry their American supporters into power. The word and the attitude it represented, however, remained an important factor in political life. It contributed to the American view of European and world politics in both world wars and beyond. President Wilson, addressing Congress on war aims and issuing the famous fourteen points, added: 'In regard to these essential rectifications of wrong and assertions of right we feel ourselves to be intimate partners of all the governments and peoples associated together against the imperialists.'[2] When Wilson represented the First World War as a war against imperialism, a war for the liberation of small nations, subjected by militarism and without a share in their own government, he reflected a Democratic attitude and used a language that echoed the election campaign of 1900. He also wished to make it plain to doubting Americans that the country was not in the war to defend what many of his countrymen suspected to be British and French Colonial imperialism. In the Second World War that tradition had by no means weakened, and Attlee recorded his own impression that President Roosevelt, having been brought up to regard imperialism as a danger to world peace and to the freedom of small nations in the American tradition of the word, was never free from eyeing British policy with suspicion.[3] In the present post-war scene of American politics imperialism as a partisan slogan has been most frequently employed against the Soviet Union by speakers and writers of both parties. The meaning of the word has changed less in America than in Britain or France.

To the north imperialism, in the American as well as in the British sense, came to mean something French and English Canadians began to dislike. English-speaking Canadians feared that the militant Imperialism, symbolized by Chamberlain and the Boer War, might threaten their self-government and increase the burden of imperial armaments, that their nationhood might not be fully recognized and respected by the British, and that their trading relations with the United States and with other countries might be interfered with. They did not, on the whole, object to the existing connexion with Britain but were determined not 'to permit the new Imperialists to degrade us, to take away any portion of our self-government—not even the right to do wrong to ourselves'. By their schemes, English-speaking Canadians felt, Imperialists had weakened rather than strengthened the British connexion.[1] French Canadians felt a strong sympathy for the Boers. The wave of pro-Boer feeling in France was not the only factor. The French of Quebec felt the Boers were fighting for them, too, in a way; they defended the right of little nationalities like their own against the sinister plan of the Imperialists, as they understood it, 'to turn us all into uncompromising Englishmen'.[2] The pro-Boer sentiment of French-speaking Canadians was understandable. The intensity of pro-Boer sentiment in France, however, and indeed in the whole of Europe was far more complicated in its nature.

The strong and almost universal condemnation of Britain by Europeans during the Boer War started the word imperialism on a new Continental career. The word was adopted by Europeans at first as a word signifying an inflated and arrogant form of English nationalism. In the United States imperialism meant a policy. In the Europe of 1900 it meant a sentiment peculiar to Britain and dangerous to other Europeans. The violent protest against imperialism was caused not only by the fate of the Boers alone. It was an expression of resentment directed against British power and against capitalism. Continental nationalism and socialism were roused against the British for different reasons. The anger of the French reflected the frustration colonial expansionists had suffered at the hands of the British in earlier years. The situation in Germany was similar. German resentment was heightened by a feeling of racial kinship with the Boers and the inadequate naval power commanded by Germany to help them, a bitter disappointment to those who wanted to see Germany taking her place as a world Power. In both France and Germany anti-British feeling was accompanied by anti-Jewish sentiment and agitation.

The serious French papers and journals such as *Le Temps* and the *Revue des Deux Mondes*, as well as anti-Semitic rabble rousers like *Libre Parole*, adopted imperialism as a convenient term to brand British policy and the persecution of the brave Boers by the fierce, greedy English. Serious-minded French Liberals, too, felt alarmed. What was going to happen to the world, if that war-fever which had affected even the United States and Britain was to spread? In America the warning voice of a Frenchman was heard who, at that time more than any other person, represented the living conscience of mankind because of his brave stand in the Dreyfus case. In April 1900 Émile Zola warned against the growing desire of fostering the military spirit. With reference to England he wrote:

There is in England much of what we call *imperialism*; that is to say, a sort of national impulse which may lead her to extremes, a desire to extend her colonies, to make herself mistress of the most important posts in the world, or to acquire what the word imperialism denotes, dominion over the world. Such is England's dream, and her symptoms in this regard are indeed alarming.[1]

The *Revue des Deux Mondes* referred to imperialism as a dangerous germ. 'Cet impérialisme se glisse, inaperçu comme un streptocoque, dans le sang de la foule, l'empoisonne, et fait fléchir sa conscience.' The nation that falls victim to that epidemic gradually loses its moral judgement. The germ affects capitalists, aristocrats, the electoral machine, the press, and the government in its progress. The example of Britain was all the more distressing as the disease of imperialism had struck a people of moral and political excellence. However, all was not yet lost, and the names of Morley, Harcourt, Courtney, Stead, and Labouchère gave rise to the hope that Britain might yet recover and 'revienne à elle-même et renonce à son rêve d'Impérialisme; sinon, l'Impérialisme finira par la perdre, comme il perdit la Rome de l'antiquité'.[2] The Roman Empire perished because of luxury and lack of respect for the rights of the other peoples, readers of the journal were told, two major defects which appeared again in the British Empire of modern times. The Dutch writer compared Rome with Britain, Crassus and Lucullus with De Beer and Rhodes, the loss of the Roman legions in the German forests with the loss of British regiments in South Africa. 'Eh bien! cet impérialisme est une obsession', the author exclaimed. It is apt to corrupt the British as it corrupted the Romans.[3] The *Revue de Paris*, commenting on what it called 'l'Empirisme Anglais', regarded that phenomenon as the symptom of growing British backwardness in science and industry, British contempt for learning, and British insularity. British commerce was peer-ridden and an organized lottery for the lazy; limited companies were fair game for speculation. The whole country, in fact, presented a picture of decadence. Imperialism was a means of misleading the workers about the real state of affairs. Those were deceived 'par les grosses caisses patriotiques et les musiques militaires de l'impérialisme'. Imperialism was, in fact, an attempt by British lords and bourgeois monopolists to exploit mankind. It was parasitism of the worst kind and was hostile to the working classes, because it desired to break up the unions and forbid strikes, as events in Wales had recently proved. Imperialism was the successor of Napoleonic rule and conquest. A little nation of peasants had stopped Imperialism in South Africa. The author of that article who made that optimistic statement was a scholar of Greek of some eminence. His reflexions showed that the socialist interpretation of the conflict was not confined to working-class leaders or the ranks of the proletariat following them. It also proves that in the minds of some French thinkers the association of imperialism with Napoleon was still possible, although it was not frequently expressed. The conclusion of the scholar pointed towards close spiritual attachment to the German spirit, the spirit of Kant, Bismarck, and Wagner as the true guides of philosophy and progress.[1] It was, perhaps, less the tradition of Madame de Staël than the common strong sentiment of Anglophobia which in 1900 linked the minds of many Frenchmen with the Germans. There is strong evidence that this French attitude was reciprocated in Germany, where anti-British passion resulted in vehement verbal aggressiveness and popular doggerel rhymes calling on German men and women to give the British a good hiding.

A report published in the *Contemporary Review*[2] on the intensity of German Anglophobia in 1900, alarming as it was, still failed to convey to British readers the extent of hatred and the dangerous state of mind which the Boer War had created in Germany. German liberals were restrained in their expression of dismay, but political agitators of the Right at once sensed the popularity of Anglophobia and were quick to seize the opportunity for making political capital of what had become

Germany's most beloved hatred. Pan-Germanic meetings, societies of so-called German and Christian Socialism, and naval leagues demonstrated against the British. Some of those demonstrations became anticapitalist and anti-Semitic in character. The French pun of 'la guerre de la Bourse contre les Boers' was echoed even among those who had been hostile to the use of any foreign words in German intercourse. Imperialism assumed the role not only of a bogey of marked British features. It assumed also the mask of the hated Jew. Mob fury was whipped up against what was called 'the robbery committed by international Jewry' by some or 'British piracy' by others. It was plausible for those Germans to see in Disraeli the symbol of that wicked combination of evil forces.[1] The social-democratic leader, Kautsky, reprimanded the British workers in sorrow rather than in anger as he deplored the rise of imperialism as the most prominent obstacle to the progress of mankind. 'Zu unserer schmerzlichen Überraschung zeigt uns die jetzige Stimmung in England, wie sehr der Imperialismus sich auch der Arbeiter bemächtigt hat.'[2] Kautsky foresaw a decline of democracy as a result of the progress of imperialism. A disappointed German liberal resigned his post at the University of Glasgow and gave an account of his impressions of Britain in her 'adolescence'. He had hoped to find in Britain solutions to the great social problems. He found none. 'Ich hatte erwartet das Wunder eines im tiefsten Kerne demokratischen Staates zu finden, und musste das offene Bekenntnis Englands zum kriegerischen Imperialismus erleben.' Imperialism, he was convinced, had arisen out of the naked selfishness of the British people. When liberalism could no longer satisfy their needs, the English cast it away and showed their true nature. Liberalism and democracy had been a mere blind.[3] Another German observer remarked that imperialism was the name which the Americans and the British gave to a general phenomenon of the new century, the aspiration of the great Powers for world dominion and expansionist militarism.[4]

Swiss opinion was not as vehement as German opinion in public but a deep note of alarm and dismay was sounded and occasionally utter incomprehension and lack of sympathy were stressed. Forms of British nationalism appeared to Swiss observers to be bordering the grotesque. Nationalism in Britain looked like a new religion. It was proselytizing in nature and maintained a queer link with the Bible in a way Europeans could never grasp. One such paradoxical form of English nationalism was the movement of the Anglo-Israelites and the belief in the British as the chosen people, a belief that went together with the belief in the British mission to conquer the world. A Swiss observer was only too ready to generalize, and it appeared to him that imperialism was the expression of that strange notion. '... Der Glaube an den Beruf Englands, die Welt nicht nur wirtschaftlich zinsbar, sondern geradezu englisch zu machen, lebt stärker oder schwächer in der Seele jedes guten Angelsachsen. Der Imperialismus ist der Ausdruck solcher Gedankenentwickelungen.'[1] From Zurich the voice of the Christian philosopher and pacifist, F. W. Förster, warned that the world was entering a new era of wars; the new conflicts were radically different from the old type of war. They arose in the midst of industrial power and science. Their political doctrine was imperialism, the doctrine of the military conquest and economic exploitation of weaker races. The American war against Spain and the British war against the Boers were mere preludes of the new imperialist era and its devastating conflicts.

Diese neue Kriegsbewegung ist der Imperialismus, d.h. die politische Lehre, welche durch die kriegerische Eroberung neuer Länderstriche und Vergewaltigung schwächerer Racen neue Ausbeutungsgebiete für die angesammelten wirtschaftlichen und technischen Kräfte der grossen Industrie sichern will und darum die Nationen zur äussersten Anspannung ihrer militärischen Machtmittel treibt, damit sie bei der Verteilung der Erdkugel nicht zu kurz kommen.[2]

Imperialism had its origin in England. England had been an imperialist country since Queen Elizabeth. In England, Förster believed, imperialism was practised a long time before it became a doctrine of politics and economics. He followed the imperialist awakening in England since Disraeli and described how imperialism was employed by Chamberlain to solve the social problems of Britain. Förster was convinced such a way of force was futile and immoral. It must lead to unrestricted brutality. '... Der Imperialismus wird hier zum Sammelwort gemacht für die Entfesselung aller ungebändigten Menschenkraft.'[3] It was criminal to declare in public—even in verse—imperialism to be identical with the progress of civilization, as Kipling had done. The British doctrine of force, Förster noted with satisfaction, had called forth an equally sweeping emotion of the social and humanitarian conscience in every civilized country in protest against it. No new man could ever be shaped by imperialism, as the fate of India and China had proved, and Christianity, officially defamed by imperialism, could not earn anything but utter contempt.

Förster's observations made in summer 1901 prove more than the universal indignation directed against Britain and the revulsion against imperialism as a form of British nationalism. They show how widespread the impression was that a new era of dangerous conflict lay ahead. We saw how such an interpretation of events was offered by other opponents of militarism and by thinking political observers of the time. One cannot but be impressed by the accurate assessment many writers made of the dangerous state of mind found in so many countries at the end of the nineteenth century and of the growing militancy; by the correctness of their prediction that the world was entering a period of wars of new and unprecedented dimensions. There was also then a clear recognition of the fact that politics had become more global in character than it had ever been before and that imperialism was a fit name for what appeared to be a developing struggle for world dominion. Many viewed with alarm the waning of a liberal and humane epoch and the advance of socialism and imperialism, tantamount in their eyes to revolution and conquest.

Förster's observations are also interesting from another point of view. His philosophical mind registered imperialism no longer as the expression of a nationalist sentiment, nor even as the name for a particular policy, but as a political and economic doctrine. In 1901 there was as yet no elaborate general theory of imperialism in existence. Imperialism and anti-imperialism were still sentiments and beliefs of vague and varying content in the British Isles. There and in America a minority of alert minds had set into motion an anti-imperialist campaign and created a pattern of ideas and a terminology which formed the fertile soil for such a theory to emerge. The Boer War was, indeed, more than a local clash of two nations and opposing political and economic interests. It was more than a chapter in the history of the industrialization of Africa. In the career of imperialism it was an essential turning point.

It made the word an international slogan in Europe, just as the Spanish War had made it a slogan in America. It also gave rise to the world-wide misinterpretation of the Boer War as a capitalist plot. That misinterpretation became the basis of all subsequent theories of imperialism. Imperialism as a political and economic theory first emerged during and immediately after the Boer War. It originated in England.

X

FROM SENTIMENT TO THEORY

Sharp political conflicts, particularly wars, always arouse strong passions. It is an observable phenomenon that such passions are quickly transmitted to others even without factual information or clear connotative meaning of language. It is also possible to prove that political sentiments are easily absorbed by young persons through words and symbols whose full meaning they are as yet unable to grasp. Sentiment precedes theory, and the latter is often the result of the former. The history of political thought illustrates the fact that this rule is not confined to young people but also applies to political thinkers and writers and to many historical scholars. The revulsion against imperialism began in 1898 and reached its climax in the Boer War. The world, it seemed, was turning away from the forms of peaceful, civilized existence to dangerous doctrines and practices of military expansion. Those who revolted against that new trend towards armed conflict desired to understand more fully the true nature of the evil in order to oppose it with greater effect. J. A. Hobson was among them. In the last chapter we already pointed to his theory of under-consumption and his earlier attempt to explain the growing use of force in international conflicts with the help of that theory. We also noticed Hobson's personal experience of life in South Africa. The Boer War deeply stirred his anti-imperialist sentiments and led him to expand his theory of imperialism.

The literary output of Hobson during the years 1900–1 is an indication of the fierce pressure with which he drove on his pen. He violently condemned Jingoism, its brutality, vainglory, religious hypocrisy, its abuse of the press and the pulpit. He wrote a book against Jingoism, and almost the whole book was exemplified by incidents and features of the Boer War.[1] He wrote an article in reply to Garrett's pro-Milner contribution to the *Contemporary Review*. Hobson's pen depicted Milner as the incarnation of aggressive Imperialism. Milner had received

his training in Egypt and applied his newly acquired skill to South
Africa. 'History seldom repeats itself with more exactitude than in these
two exploits of aggressive Imperialism applied to South Africa.'[1] Like
Froude, Hobson judged, Milner was a 'temperamental Imperialist of the
sentimental academic school'. That failing and his lack of ability to
judge character were to blame for the fact that he allowed himself to
become the instrument of wreckers and their powerful financial backers.
To expose those financial forces Hobson called his first theoretical
analysis of events, *Capitalism and Imperialism in South Africa*. It was
a simple and plausible hypothesis stated as a fact. The Boer War was the
most dramatic result of the same forces as had been at work in Egypt,
China, and South America. They were a combination of aggressive
imperialism controlled by a small number of capitalists. The latter had
developed a diamond monopoly to exact a maximum profit, with
Rhodes, Beit, Barnato and Rothschild as the leading figures.

This same group of men, with a small number of confederates, chiefly
foreign Jews, representing the most highly organized form of international
finance yet attained, controls the entire gold industry of the Transvaal. . . .
This little group of capitalists are the real 'economic men', about whom text-
books of Political Economy used to prate, but who have been generally
relegated to mythology. Most of them are Jews, for the Jews are par excellence
the international financiers, and, though English-speaking, most of them are
of continental origin. Their interest in the Transvaal has been purely economic;
they went there for money, and those who came early and made most have
commonly withdrawn their persons, leaving their economic fangs in the
carcass of their prey.[2]

Those predatory Jewish capitalists, Hobson explained, stood to gain by
upsetting the Government and thus became the prime movers in the
Transvaal conflict. Neither they nor Rhodes were genuine Imperialists
by sentiment. In his earlier career, Rhodes, in fact, had been very much
opposed to imperial control, but—and this was Hobson's main thesis—
capitalism required aggressive Imperialism and knew how to mould it
for its own purpose. So the Rand capitalists engineered

the medley of aims and feelings to which the term Imperialism is commonly
applied. Though no exact definition of the nature and objects of Imperialism
is possible, it contains certain clearly distinguishable threads of thought and

feeling. Among these certain genuinely social and humane motives stand prominent,—the desire to promote the causes of civilization and Christianity to improve the economic and spiritual condition of lower races, to crush slavery, and to bring all parts of the habitable world into closer material and moral union.

Those motives were, in the eyes of the author, genuine and praiseworthy but were not the main directing forces of Imperialism. Under the pseudo-patriotic cloak the financier remained the power behind the throne. Imperialism had an economic nucleus to which other economic interests such as iron and shipbuilding, armament industries, military services, and the professions were attached.

These strong definite economic interests are the principal propellers of aggressive Imperialism, consciously or instructively using, in order to conceal their selfish dominance, the generous but often mistaken impulses of humanitarian sentiment, and relying in the last resort upon one powerful secret ally which ever lurks in the recesses of the national character. This ally is that race-lust of dominance, that false or inverted patriotism which measures the glory of its country by another's shame, and whose essential immorality is summed up in the doctrine that British paramountcy is a 'right'.

To that brutal lust the financiers made their appeal, which is driven home all the more effectively by means of a controlled press. All those observations were made in connexion with the Boer War, but Hobson gave them a generalized theoretical character.

Hobson's indictment contained exactly the same elements which we found on the Continent of Europe at the same time. The blame was found to rest with capitalism, Jewish finance, and British racial pride. Hobson moved from the idea that capitalism *used* Imperialism to a more extreme position, that imperialism—not Imperialism as an endeavour related to the British Empire but military expansionism in the American sense—*was* a form of capitalist expansionism. The American election of 1900 and its political background with its specific use of imperialism as political slogan were incorporated into Hobson's theory in 1902 when he wrote another article on *The Economic Taproot of Imperialism*. The Boer Republics had been defeated and annexed. Hobson agitated against tropical annexations on the grounds that those tropical acquisitions had proved to be poor markets and that Britain's most profitable trade was with her industrial rivals. Surveying the American scene he found his economic theory confirmed. Capitalism created an accumulation of wealth in the hands of the few, and capitalist production outstripped home demand. Surplus capital and goods, therefore, looked for new investment and markets in other countries and adopted imperialist methods to enforce their advance. Rockefeller, Morgan, Hanna, Schwab and their associates 'need imperialism because they desire to use the public resources of their country to find profitable employment for their capital, which otherwise would be superfluous'.[1] On that basis Hobson attempted a new general definition of imperialism as an economic phenomenon and wrote: '... imperialism is the endeavour of the great controllers of industry to broaden the channel for the flow of their surplus wealth by seeking foreign markets and foreign investments to take off the goods and capital they cannot sell or use at home.'[2] Imperialism was thus found to be the fruit of a false economy in the same way as poverty and unemployment were; the basic evil was capitalism, the remedy, socialism. Under socialism wealth would be more evenly distributed. As a result all classes could convert their wants into effective demands. There would be no over-production, no need to conquer new markets. Hence trade unionism and socialism were the natural enemies of imperialism 'for they take away from the "imperialist" classes the surplus incomes which form the economic stimulus of imperialism'. Having uncovered the capitalist nature of imperialism Hobson set out to prove that all other doctrines of imperialism, racist, biological, or belief in national excellence, were really fictitious and that imperialism was the result of class government, which only a system of popular democratic government and international federation could effectively remove.[3]

Hobson finally published his theory of imperialism in a book in 1902. It bore as its title one word only—IMPERIALISM. The book expanded some of his articles and added statistical material illustrating trade figures and armament expenditure. It begins with the words: 'This study of modern Imperialism is designed to give more precision to a term which is on everybody's lips and which is used to denote the most powerful movement in the current politics of the Western world. Though Imperialism has been adopted as a more or less conscious policy by several European States and threatens to break down the political isolation of the United States, Great Britain has travelled so much faster and farther along this road as to furnish in her recent career the most profitable guidance or warning.' And as Britain had been selected as the best illustration of imperialism Hobson tabulated chronological data which showed the overseas areas acquired during the previous twenty years. Thus he made clear that he desired to bring the whole colonial development of that period under the head of 'imperialism'. He then proceeded to show that those imperialist acquisitions had been valuable neither as 'outlets for population' nor as markets for the commerce of the metropolitan country such as former colonial foundations had been. He thought relatively little of the imperialist driving force domiciled in mercantile counting houses. These exclusions appropriately lead to the inference that only 'certain sectional interests that usurp control of the national resources' could have made for imperialist expansion. The 'economic parasites' were on the one hand the industries and professions which profited immediately from annexation and war; more fundamentally significant were, however, the financial parasites: investors, dealers in investments or 'financiers', and certain industrial magnates who looked out for big establishments in undeveloped countries because the home market was bound to yield diminishing returns. And here Hobson connected imperialism with the great defect which earlier meditation had led him to discover in the capitalist system, under-consumption, over-saving, maldistribution.

Parasites are discovered who are sheltered by the prevailing economic system. They make this system act against the true interest of society. They make it pervert politics. They find the way to foster passions, romantic as well as savage. In this edifice of ideas a Cobdenite ground-plan is unmistakable. But the original motive has been transferred, so to speak, to another historical level. The pernicious parasites are no longer identified with the privileged remnants of feudal society; they are the outgrowth of capitalist society. The process of capitalist profit-making has developed so far that it sees no prospects of further expansion other than those opening in colonial and other exotic investments. This discovery entails an historical conclusion. Colonial enterprise, and other political operations overseas which made investment necessary, are to be understood solely on the basis of the urge of accumulated capital to be turned to profit in undeveloped countries. This urge, at the same time, can work only because capital is not put to healthier social use at home. It follows that the whole recent colonial development, which clearly coincided with large capitalist gains, can be understood only as a consequence of the unhealthy organization of society. The driving force issuing from these conditions necessarily forced the hands of the men who had been active in these enterprises. It is this interpretation that gives unity to the whole process. It explains, in very fact, the dimensions of modern colonial exploit, the 'measure of imperialism'. The 'age of imperialism' assumes a shape under this one aspect. 'Imperialism' is conceived as being one and the same as 'economic imperialism'.

It would not be impossible to weigh against each other the modicum of historical facts to which this deduction can be supposed to refer, and the volume of other facts which make its full implications appear a distortion of historical evidence. Hobson's theory has not stood the test of critical examination. The examples given by him for the fateful influence of capital investments overseas—South African mines and Chinese concessions—proved of ephemeral significance. The assertion that modern capitalism tends to prefer colonial investment to home investment is a most uncertain generalization. The whole question of the role played by Western capital in exotic countries has won new aspects by the fact that it is not only a question of capital profits but also one of the elementary needs of the underdeveloped countries as well as those of the capitalist regions. The significance of the colonial investment nexus for international politics was certainly overrated by Hobson. The political world to which he addressed his warnings was steering towards the First World War. Whatever the reasons of this catastrophe, the attempt to lay it at the door of colonial investments is certainly the most unreal interpretation. Hobson's reply to the critical judgement of the historians concerning the origin of the First World War was contained in his introduction to a revised edition of his book in 1938. He admitted that it was possible to argue that the First World War was brought about by power politics rather than by profit politics, but he maintained that the peace treaty of Versailles was concluded on the false assumptions that territorial annexation was profitable to the annexing country, that the extortion of huge reparation payments was possible and advantageous to the recipients, that national economic self-sufficiency was gainful, economically and strategically. Hobson claimed that the peace treaty was another instance of imperialism and that the subsequent depression and imperialist demands of Germany, Italy, and Japan confirmed his general theory that imperialism was opposed to true democracy. Economic nationalism combined with politics of external imperialism as a result of economic maldistribution.

In the career of imperialism as a political word Hobson's theory of imperialism constituted an important turning point. In public speech and political writing the term became imbued with suggestive connotations which could combine with the most different issues of the day. The passionate abusiveness which radiated from it was not mitigated by the attempt to provide the word with the scientific dignity of denoting a historical reality. On the contrary: the assumption of theoretic validity had made the term more apt to excite irrational attitudes. This rise to a pseudo-scientific status went together with another far-reaching change in its career—a vast enlargement of the scene on which it was used. In this respect, too, Hobson's book signifies the point of transition. His doctrine was applied to the contemporary politics of the great Powers in general. But the bulk of his argument was confessedly taken from English politics. Economic experience was only a part, though an indispensable one, of the reality which gave rise to the concept of 'economic imperialism' and, as we shall see later, to that of the 'age of imperialism'. The most powerful motives had been generated by political morality, above all in England, where these motives were deeply rooted in the English tradition, as indeed was the Empire with which they found fault. On the Continent, especially in Germany, Anglophobia deepened the derogatory interpretation of imperialism in relation to the country of its origin. Imperialism became a by-word for all that was suspect or blameworthy in British foreign policy and in the growth of the British Empire. The term was adopted from English under circumstances unfavourable to Great Britain. French misgivings about British politics were bound to become subdued after the conclusion of the Entente Cordiale in 1904. In Germany, on the other hand, looking askance at British power assumed the character of a habit in which national feeling found moral satisfaction. There was, in German eyes, something ignoble in a Power which relied so much on commercial wealth and did not parade military virtues. Nevertheless, some admiration for British sea-power and colonial expansion was always present in the German attitude towards Britain at the turn of the century. British expansion had been held out as a model for German 'Weltpolitik'. Such an ambiguous attitude could, however, not be sustained for a long time. The more the persuasion gained ground that Britain was possessed of undue advantages in relation to Germany and that this discrimination must be eliminated, the less the assumption could be tolerated that the claims of both nations to leadership in the world were of equal validity. For the solution of this mental problem of opposing British expansionism, yet advocating German oversea acquisitions, the word imperialism, coloured by the conditions and emotional connotations of the Boer War, came as a godsend. It could be used so as to form, implicitly at least, a contrast to German 'Weltpolitik'. The existence of a German Empire could not hinder the derogatory use of imperialism. Emperor and Empire were called 'Kaiser' and 'Reich' so that moral indignation over imperialism could be easily dissociated from the German Empire.

Since the Boer War imperialism was considered by many observers to be a world phenomenon, and numerous theories were advanced which tried to explain it. Like Hobson other authors kept the Boer War in mind when describing the new phenomenon and occasionally embalmed in their theoretical work the passions which that war had aroused. Other Empire issues of the years following the Boer War, such as the use of Chinese labour in South Africa and Imperial Preference, furnished additional arguments and illustrations to the new interpreters of imperialism. Britain's position in the markets of the world was apparently deteriorating. Foreign observers noted the rising competitive power of German and American trade and industry and saw in imperialism a desperate attempt to counterbalance the loss in economic resources by the British having recourse to political safeguards in defence of national monopolies. A new application given by an English statesman to 'imperial' terminology gave colour to this conception. Joseph Chamberlain fought his tariff campaign under the motto 'think imperially'. The numerous and varying interpretations of imperialism offered in the first decade of this century suggest that the exclusive association of imperialism with capitalist acquisitiveness had so far failed to establish itself. The vogue attained by the word contributed only to still more meanings being read into it. Old meanings were not forgotten. In England an 'imperialist' could still simply mean a person who took an interest in the Empire.[1] Imperialism could also be applied to the history of empires generally. 'In a sense it may be said that imperialism is as old as the world'; so Lord Cromer justified his thoughtful comparison between 'Ancient and Modern Imperialism', the first of many disquisitions to which the concept meant neither more nor less than the phenomenon of empire-building throughout history.[2] As a branch of moral philosophy derived from Gobineau, Darwin, and Nietzsche, imperialism found another interpretation in France,[3] while in Germany the circumstantial scholarship of Schulze-Gaevernitz tried to present British imperialism as the joint result of diverse historical factors: Puritan education of will-power, new national restlessness, and economic apprehension. Hobson's presentation had been the fruit of speculative journalism. Schulze-Gaevernitz and others made events in Britain the object of speculative scholarship. Imperialism was found by theorists of the Continent to constitute a new form of combination between economic and political power which could best be studied in Britain. A large number of investigators agreed on that point with Schulze-Gaevernitz.

In 1905 Max Weber attempted to demonstrate the link between capitalism and the Reformation. Schulze-Gaevernitz a year later applied that theory to his study of political power. The new capitalist spirit, bred in Puritan Britain, created a powerful political and economic force. The ideas of Hume, Adam Smith, Ricardo, and Bentham were examined in that light. England created the spiritual basis of the modern 'money man'. Supported by Newtonian philosophy of causality and his Puritan faith in his own destiny, the English capitalist, Schulze-Gaevernitz concluded, became the effective agent of British power, and the 'chosen British people' conducted their imperial policy as a Protestant enterprise. Cromwell was the prototype of the Imperialist.[4] The economist, G. Schmoller, noted the weakening of support for free trade in Britain and the growing use of political power for economic purposes. More and more those systematizing German scholars projected the conflicts of their own time into the past and were inclined to regard British history as the outcome of design. From that point of view the imperial debates assumed the character of calculated fraud to deceive the other nations. Those were assured by British statesmen, Schmoller contended, that Britain was not interested in new territorial acquisitions; yet British imperialism expanded the Empire step by step.[1] Ruthless expansionism promoted by usurious, greedy capitalists also characterized the new imperialism of the United States. Schmoller foresaw that imperialism, thus described, would lead to wars for the dominion of the world between France, Britain, Russia, the United States, and Japan, unless it was checked. Imperialism as a world-wide idea equal to that of socialism and liberalism was the theme of another German scholar's reflexion. Erich Marcks explained the new idea as a political system of increasing the power of the state by combining it with economic forces. Capital as a means of expanding political power was a growing occurrence, which spelt the end of the era of liberalism and a return to the methods of mercantilism on a larger scale. The new means of power infiltration, used by Britain, Russia, America, France, and Japan as well as Germany, were capital, railways, steam lines, commercial agencies, and missionaries. Colonial rivalry was increasing as the competition for markets increased. Behind all that economic activity there was the planning, guiding hand of the state.[2] Such interpretations in Germany could constitute a subtle form of political agitation. They were pleas for the adoption of similar methods by the German government. Erich Marcks himself, in fact, wrote in glowing terms of the wonderful combination of economic and political power he believed to have found in the British variety of imperialism in order that Germans might be able to 'learn from England against England'.[3] No person embodied that new connexion between economic power and militant expansionism better than Joseph Chamberlain. His struggle for an imperial fiscal policy vividly illustrated the growing union between political, military, and commercial forces. 'Protection contre libre-échange', a French student of politics observed in 1905, 'c'est ainsi que l'on résume le plus souvent la lutte engagée par M. Chamberlain. La formule est inexacte, à le moins incomplète. C'est "impérialisme et protection" qui est la vraie formule. . . .'¹ A Belgian scholar attempted to analyse what he called with the Italian Amadore-Virgili the 'imperialist sentiment' by drawing attention to the features Chamberlain, Theodore Roosevelt, and the Emperor William II had in common. It was an ardent belief in the superiority of their own nation, a desire to appeal to national pride, and a message of abundant wealth to be found beyond the national confines. Sports activities assisted in fomenting and promoting that imperialist sentiment. Imperialism was the new creed of the semi-intelligent. 'Le sentiment impérialiste est une croyance. Il vise au prestige mystérieux qui cristallise les espérances populaires. C'est une mystique.' The English had gone farthest in developing that imperialist mysticism. They had imbued the whole population with it to such an extent that it was no longer possible to say whether the merchants were preachers or the missionaries traders. Imperialist sentiment, the author stressed, was only the surface of the phenomenon. Underneath lay hidden the real motives, which were economic in England as well as in Germany and America. Commercial interests and the Stock Exchange were the inseparable ingredients of imperialism; shares, profit rates, machines, industrialism, transport, and communication wove a vast network of commercial and industrial interests whose centre was London, as already Disraeli had pointed out when he said that London was the key to India. 'Londres, c'est-à-dire la Bourse.'²

French foes of the Entente Cordiale like Emile Flourens, anti-British agitators of the Right, found it natural to depict British expansionist power in league with international finance. Flourens desired to persuade his French readers to believe in an Anglo-masonic plot, the purpose of which was to seize power in France in the interest of the City of London and its Jewish bankers.³ In Austria the Balkan crisis gave rise to a similar theory of British power. It was the nature of British power to be clever and hidden at the same time. In a book, which saw seven editions before the outbreak of the world war, and which some German political leaders were prepared to take seriously, the Austrian author, Alexander von Peez, developed his theory of Britain as the consistent enemy not only of Austria but also of Europe. In order to continue her policy of colonial conquest, Britain successfully kept Europe divided. The crafty islanders had contrived to divert Napoleon from his intended invasion of Britain to a campaign against Austria, they had again fabricated a set-back for the Austrians in the Balkans and were about to have Russians and Austrians fight each other for the profit of British merchants and Jewish bankers, who lived by wars.[1] Whether directly influenced by Hobson's interpretation of imperialism or not, Continental men of letters showed a common tendency of viewing imperialism as a calculated system. It was described either as the expansion of political power with the aid of commerce and industry or vice versa; politics and economics seemed to them welded together in a new age of expansionism and of the return to mercantilist methods.

In Britain imperialism retained its older meanings and also its sentimental nature. With the Liberals in power since 1905 and John Morley a cabinet member, social reform began to occupy a prominent place in political life, and there was no political reason for imperialism to have a strong partisan appeal. German naval armament made Britain and her dominions look to the Royal Navy as symbol of Imperial unity and strength. The desire for unity grew and could again proudly call itself imperialism. Doctrinal tensions aroused by that word during the Boer War lessened. Milner and Curzon could uphold their imperialist faith in public and call on the rest of the nation to share their creed. Both described accusations made against Imperialists as caricatures, which had no foundations either in the past or in the present. Imperialists were neither aggressive militarists nor greedy materialists. Speaking at Birmingham in December 1907, Curzon explicitly refuted the identification of imperialism with commercial activities. Trade, he emphasized, did not follow the flag. It usually preceded the flag, as it did in America, India, and Africa. Essentially imperialism was a faith. It could not be defended on material grounds alone.

there is a certain risk lest the Empire be defended too exclusively as a commercial speculation, as a splendid investment for the population of these islands. Both of these it can be shown to be. But unless it is much more, it will no more survive than did the trading Empires of the Portuguese or the Dutch, both of which perished because they rested exclusively upon the extraction of commercial profit from their subjects or victims.[2]

In plain contrast to Chamberlain's brand of imperialism, Curzon's ideal was supported by the deeply felt conviction that the Empire was one of the human agencies through which God spoke, and the service of which ennobled and inspired man. He did not want his listeners to think of Cromwell, Chatham, Pitt, Beaconsfield, Cromer, or even Chamberlain as having served the Empire for the purpose of material gain. He did not want them to believe either that Socialist ideals and Empire ideals were incompatible. Imperialism could still be the hope and faith of the whole nation. Milner felt that the tide of imperialism was rising, and meant that, as he was writing in 1913, more people than ever believed in and worked for imperial unity.[1] Moral and material defence of the Empire came to the fore with the growth of the German navy. The Duke of Westminster, making his appeal on behalf of the Imperial Fund, could with justification speak of the imperial feeling in most Englishmen in his plea to substitute constructive for sentimental imperialism[2]; and Sidney Low could call imperialism 'one of the political fashions of the moment' and point to the new Imperial Union for Maritime Defence as a landmark on the way to practical imperialism, a way which Australia, New Zealand, and Canada had chosen with enthusiasm.[3]

The impact of Hobson on the thinking of British Fabians and Socialists is not evident in the first decade of the century. If it existed, it failed at any rate to give imperialism an important place in their political vocabulary. Protests against bellicose and alarmist views were made. They were directed against militarism or jingoism, never against imperialism. In May 1913 the *New Statesman* could still praise Milner's 'high ideal of Imperialism'. Continental theories on the capitalist basis of imperialism were translated into English and published by the Socialist press, but there is little evidence to show that they became an important part of the intellectual and theoretical equipment of the Labour Party. When in 1911 the struggle for power in North Africa between France and Germany reached a new climax and Italy annexed Tripoli, the *Socialist Review* printed a comment purporting to prove that the same economic forces that were behind the dealings of Roman capitalists with Phoenician settlers 'are working to-day in the new imperialism and cosmopolitan finance'. It was, the writer thought, mainly a juggle of rival bankers using the contending peoples as their pawns.[4] Such an interpretation of the struggle for North Africa in the tradition of the Boer War opponents was not typical of the British Labour Movement, whose leaders, on the contrary, warned their followers against the use of cant and facile cliché. They rejected as modern superstition the thesis that wars were caused solely by plotting bankers, although such a view was popular at Continental Socialist meetings. So when a Socialist anti-war conference was about to be convoked at Basle, an editorial article of the *Socialist Review* warned against the belief in phrases 'in which war is solely ascribed to predatory ambitions of Capitalism. It is truly amazing', the editor wrote in December 1912, 'that a Socialist Congress or, indeed, that any Socialist with an elementary knowledge of history or anthropology, should fall into the soap-box banality of that kind.'[1] A Socialist essay on white capital and coloured labour, published in 1910, shows how remote its author was from uncritical jargon when he wrote: 'No colony can be made by a theory of Imperialism: it can only be made by people who want to colonize and are capable of maintaining themselves as colonists.' Neither Imperialist sentiment nor anti-Imperialist prejudice, he claimed, coloured his impression that European imperialism was supported by a public opinion which was philanthropically disposed and derived a good deal of justified satisfaction from administrative success achieved. Moral or philosophical criticism, however, was quite secondary in importance. So was the readiness to carry 'the white man's burden'. The will of the colonists to seek commercial and industrial profit came first. But if all altruistic interpretation of Imperialism was a sham, so was the view that all European administrators and officials serving in the colonies were parasites.[2] We see that Hobson's way of looking for a causal connexion between capitalism and militant expansion had not found many followers among British Socialists at the end of the first decade of this century. The Labour Party had not retained Imperialism either as partisan slogan or as theory. The word was no longer an issue that divided the nation. It was still a sentiment which, many Englishmen believed, was capable of uniting the country and linking it with a wider Empire patriotism that could embrace all British possessions.

H. N. Brailsford's *The War of Steel and Gold* was published in 1914 and described the armed peace. It was the first serious attempt to lead

Socialist thinking in Britain back to Hobson. Once again it focused attention on Hobson's interpretation of imperialism as a form of capitalist manipulation. Imperialism was state power in the service of Hebrew bankers and European industrialists, who desired to exploit cheap native labour. That was the reason why manufacturers and mine-owners more and more looked to Africa. In the interest of capitalists seeking higher profits and industrialists seeking cheap labour, concessions were wrung from weak colonial regions with the help of the British fleet and the diplomatic service. Brailsford maintained that the whole struggle for a balance of power was in fact a struggle to map out exclusive areas of financial penetration. The export of capital became more important to the ruling class than the export of goods, and so the Liberals turned into Imperialists. Imperialism in Brailsford's definition meant 'the acquisition of economic opportunity by political pressure'.[1] In that sense the term was still rarely used in England before 1914 and Imperialism remained more of a sentiment than a specific social theory. Semmel's book on *Imperialism and Social Reform* does not distinguish between what it calls a theory of imperialism and ideas which its author himself originally denoted as such. It describes Mackinder as theorist of Imperialism, but Mackinder himself does not. He hardly mentions the word in his books *Money-Power and Man-Power*, *Democratic Ideals and Reality*, or *The Nations of the Modern World*. Confusion is created when scholars fail to make it clear whether the term imperialism is their own description or the original description, and in which sense the term is used. Hobson's theory of imperialism was followed up mainly by Socialist authors in Germany and Austria, who incorporated it into the framework of Marxism.

Hobson's theory had a close affinity to Marxism. It upheld determinism, stressed class-government, and believed in the accumulation of capital in the hands of the few. Like Marx he endeavoured to detect beneath the ideological superstructure the potent force of economic class interest. It was Hobson who was destined to become the most influential interpreter of capitalism after Marx, as the century entered into its third decade, although he was never recognized as their teacher by the millions who accepted his theory in the way Marx was. But at first Hobson's recognition even among Continental Marxists was slow.

From Sentiment to Theory

At the beginning of the century Kautsky and Rosa Luxemburg observed the approaching end of laissez-faire economics and the rising tendency of nations to secure new markets by force. America and Britain were uppermost in their minds as well as the militant mood of Germany, where colonial conquest, military and naval expansion, pan-Germanism, suppression of Poles, protective tariffs, and measures against organized labour were either widely advertised or more quietly practised. In 1902 Kautsky believed Germany, not England with its greater liberal tradition, was showing the future trend of capitalism towards militarism. Luxemburg, too, believed in world politics and militarism as an inevitable phase of capitalism.[1] Imperialism was not yet their word for it but the basic theory was already clear. A few years later Otto Bauer and R. Hilferding, two leading Austrian Socialists, elaborated that theory in greater detail. Bauer in 1907 predicted that Austrian capitalists, allied with the army, would try and win new markets in the Balkans by force. He was convinced that militant expansionism would be required by capitalists everywhere sooner or later and adopted the name imperialism for that phase of militant capitalism just as Hobson had done. Hobson had studied imperialism as a general theory in Britain. Bauer studied it in Austria. Unlike Hobson, Bauer endeavoured to give imperialism its place in the Marxist concept of class struggle. Austrian capitalists and the allied military might of the double monarchy would use nationalist ideologies, such as the self-determination of the nations, in order to advance their imperialist designs and create tension among the nations, especially in the Balkans. In that way it would become easier for the imperialist country to impose its exploiting rule on the warring small nationalities. The conflicts created by imperialism abroad and the conflicts created by capitalism at home were seen as one and the same class struggle. Otto Bauer wanted Socialists to understand that message so as to be able to fight imperialists with a true Marxist faith. 'Wir müssen zeigen, wie grade die kapitalistische Expansionspolitik innere Gegensätze innerhalb der Nation schafft, wie der Kampf um den Imperialismus zum Klassenkampfe wird.'[2] Hilferding's economic essay on the nature and flow of investments conveyed the same message to its more intellectual readers. *Das Finanzkapital* was originally written in 1905. It stressed the new forms of capitalist competition such as tariffs, cartels, monopolies, and colonial expansion. South Africa's mine-owners and their use of coolie labour and military power served as convenient illustration of the significance of imperialism. Capital required the intervention of the state to 'pacify' those whose work and land were exploited. In its relentless drive for monopoly capital desired to portion out the world. It wanted domination not liberation. So in its advanced monopolistic stage capitalism needed power politics. In Marxist terms: capitalism needed a new ideology. Liberalism and pacifism began to pale. The new ideology was imperialism. Capitalism, Hilferding concluded, could follow no other but an imperialist policy in the future and must needs lead towards a violent collision. In order to be prepared for that military phase the capitalist would, Hilferding predicted, increase taxes and tariffs as the armament race grew in pace. Life would then become more expensive, poverty would increase, and the dictatorship of the big capitalists would reach its climax. Finally, the imperialists would join battle and the proletariat would know that the time had arrived to establish their own rule.[1] In the language of German-speaking Socialists that theory of the impending imperialist Armageddon became known as the theory of catastrophe.

In the following years as the Dreadnoughts were building in British and German shipyards, as the Austro-Russian truce in the Balkans was shattered and Franco-German animosity flared up again, the theory of catastrophe was gaining more adherents, who became converted by events as much as by Hilferding's arguments. Rosa Luxemburg regarded imperialism in the same light. She defined it as the political expression of capitalism in its final stage, a phase which inevitably led to catastrophe and the elimination of the system. 'Der Imperialismus ist der politische Ausdruck des Prozesses der Kapitalakkumulation in ihrem Konkurrenzkampf um die Reste des noch nicht mit Beschlag belegten nichtkapitalistischen Weltmilieus.'[2] Loans and industrial undertakings were opening up large parts of Asia and Africa, whose peasants and fellahs were exploited for the higher profits of the capitalists. Rosa Luxemburg believed that such a development would lead Asian and African countries into a greater dependence on European states and cause the disappearance of pre-capitalist native cultures. She tried to extend the Marxist view beyond the history of Europe to Asia and Africa, so as to explain why capitalism had not effaced itself as early as Marx had expected. China, Turkey, and Russia, Luxemburg explained, had given capitalism a new lease of life. There new markets had been opened up. The inevitable doom of capitalism would follow all the same as soon as no further expansion was possible, when all the world markets had been opened up and developed. With such a mental picture of economic development in mind she wrote: 'Der Imperialismus ist ebensosehr eine geschichtliche Methode der Existenzverlängerung des Kapitals, wie das sicherste Mittel, dessen Existenz auf kürzestem Wege objektiv ein Ziel zu setzen.'[1]

At the beginning of the second decade of this century the rank and file of the German and Austrian socialists began to absorb those theories in a diluted form and imperialism in the sense of those theories became more and more the war-cry of social democratic agitators.[2] Pamphlets were published in German under such headings as 'Hie Imperialismus —Hie Sozialismus'. Not all German Socialists were convinced that either the meaning of imperialism was correctly interpreted or the trend of history predicted in the right way. Some questions were asked, no doubt, in the local meetings about a proper Socialist attitude towards the export of German goods to Africa. Was that imperialism? Did it not bring in work and money to German workers and benefit Africans as well? Would it not be right to stop Africans from putting some Germans into their village pots? One answer given was that imperialism was military and political annexation, not exports or the legitimate protection of citizens.[3] How far was a patriotic feeling legitimate?—other German Socialists wanted to know. Bebel defended national sentiment at the International Socialist Congress at Stuttgart in 1907. At that Congress an anti-war resolution was adopted against 'militarism and imperialism' and confirmed by the Congress of Basle in 1912. The Austrian Government tried to prevent the anti-war resolution from becoming known in Austria-Hungary. Socialists became alarmed. Perhaps the prophets of doom were right after all. Kautsky in the midst of Balkan troubles thereupon pointed to Vienna as the centre of European war-mongering.[4] 1913 found German Socialists bewildered and divided. One section still hoped for a control of

Austrian expansionist designs by a German policy of restraint and agitated for an amicable arrangement with Britain about naval armament and trade. The London Conference on Balkan affairs seemed to them to be an encouraging sign that all was not lost by any means. Others were less optimistic. All indications were, they argued, that German middle-class opinion, backed by the Army and Navy, were in favour of developing Germany as a world Power. That being the case, the only way Germany and Britain could come to an agreement would be by carving out spheres of influences, i.e. on an imperialist basis. No Socialist could under-write that kind of 'peace'. Some clearly became enamoured of Armageddon and final doom, as their language showed. 'Out of the bloody chaos of world war there will arise the proletarian world revolution like a fiery nemesis.'[1] Others began to speak of the 'imperialist era' as the last phase of capitalism out of which world revolution would be born 'mit innerer Notwendigkeit'. In a way some social revolutionaries would welcome world war, if it came, as the beginning of the end of capitalism. The more critical minds found that constant harping on the coming imperialist battle irritating and mis-leading. Too many people, they felt, became entangled in abstraction of their own making. Capital, Bourgeoisie, Imperialism were no persons of one mind or one plan, they pointed out. 'Vor allem aber sind unsere Parteigenossen, bei denen neuerdings das Schlagwort *Imperialismus* eine beängstigende Rolle spielt, immer wieder davor zu warnen die imperialistische Bewegung der Gegenwart als eine einheit-liche anzusehen. Sie birgt in sich Gegensätze, die grösser sind als die irgendeiner andern sozialen Bewegung. . . .'[2] In all that discussion mention was made of the Balkans and North Africa, of China and Russia, but the classical example of capitalism in its imperialist stage remained South Africa and the Boer War, the classical country of Imperialism, Britain. While Socialists were still arguing about the significance of imperialism, the guns of Europe drowned their arguments. Armageddon did arrive as had been predicted, and Vienna, again as predicted, turned out to be one centre that sent out the military host to conquest. Two things could not be forgotten: The prophets of doom had been right about imperialism; international Socialism however, although it had been aware of the rising tide of war, had been unable to stop it.

Socialist revolutionaries thought they could offer both an explanation and a policy. The explanation of the failure of the organized proletariat to stop the war was sought in the betrayal of its reformist leaders. The policy suggested was the transformation by the proletariat of the imperialist war into a civil war. Such a policy could not be advocated in public in the belligerent countries where the revolutionary socialists were soon in jail anyhow. In Zürich on neutral ground, however, the exile Vladimir Ulyanov Lenin made those points a central message of his unceasing writings and political agitation.

At first Ulyanov Lenin was a pretty isolated figure. A small group of Russian socialists met in Berne and passed a resolution which he had drafted. It began with the words: 'The European and World War bears the sharp marks of a bourgeois-imperialist and dynastic war. A struggle for markets, for freedom to loot foreign countries, a tendency to put an end to the revolutionary movement of the proletariat and democracy within the separate countries.'[1] A month later, in October 1914, lecturing at Lausanne on the proletariat and the war, he emphasized that the conflict was of an entirely new character. 'It is imperialism that lends the present war an entirely different imprint; it is imperialism that distinguishes it from all the past wars ... Imperialism is a state of capitalism, when, having fulfilled all that is possible for it, capitalism makes a turn towards decay.'[2] Lenin's language was studied agitation and was rendered in a laboured simplicity. The only policy he could suggest was that of revolution by emulating the Paris Commune. The final test must come behind the street barricades. In 1915 Lenin prepared a pamphlet, called *Socialism and War*, which was translated into German, French, and Norwegian for illegal distribution inside Europe. Its final paragraph read: 'Imperialism is the period of an increasing oppression of the nations of the whole world by a handful of 'great' nations; the struggle for a Socialist international revolution against imperialism is therefore impossible without the recognition of the right of nations to self-determination.'[3] Lenin, therefore, gave imperialism *two* functions in his agitation. It became the symbol of the exploitation of the proletariat by the capitalists. It also became the symbol of the oppression of small nations by big Powers.

Lenin decided to devote a more theoretical study to the subject of imperialism and in looking for material selected Hobson as the author best suited to his purpose. He also incorporated material taken from the books of Hilferding, Sombart, and Schulze-Gaevernitz, which were mentioned above. It was natural, therefore, that in his pamphlet *Imperialism, the Highest Stage of Capitalism* the impact of the Boer War —seen through the eyes of Stead and Hobson—was still heavy. Lenin equated imperialism with capitalism as the latter had passed on from the stage of free competition to monopoly through cartels, syndicates, trusts, and the manipulation of bank capital by a small number of monopolist banks. 'If it were necessary to give the briefest possible definition of imperialism we should have to say that imperialism is the monopoly stage of capitalism.'[1] The world was being divided among a few capitalist oligarchies. The characteristic feature of its economy was the export of finance capital, which caused the great Powers to adopt an annexationist colonial policy. That appetite for land, however, was by no means confined to colonies, Lenin stressed. It affected European territory as well. Germany wanted Belgium and France, Lorraine. Rivalry and conquest were the marks of the imperialist era, as already Hobson, whom Lenin extensively quoted, had pointed out in 1902. We find in Lenin's pamphlet echoes of the American war against Spain and of the American protests against imperialism.[2] Finally, Lenin in agreement with Hilferding dwelt on the connexion between imperialism and national oppression. Again, American policy in the Philippines was taken as an illustration; Lenin had hoped to obtain the approval of the Russian censor and had, therefore, carefully avoided taking his illustrations from Russian policy. It had not been his original objective to pick out Britain and America as the major imperialist culprits in the dock. What was a secondary matter of convenience and tactics, however, became of prime importance later when the association of imperialism with 'Anglo-Saxon plutocracy' was the object of political agitation after the world war. Lenin's main purpose at first was to make it clear to his countrymen that fighting the war against Germany was nothing but bleeding for international capitalism. The world-wide influence of his pamphlet dates, however, from 1920 when it was translated into German and French. It helped to enhance the reputation of the earlier books of Hobson, Hilferding, and Luxemburg. But by that time doctrines of economic imperialism directly derived from Hobson had found favour with socialists, who did not profess Marxism.

Leonard Woolf, by his *Empire and Commerce in Africa* and his more popular pamphlet *Economic Imperialism*, started the campaign of the English Labour Research Department for winding up colonial empires. In 1921 'economic imperialism' was the subject of a series of lectures delivered by the French Professor A. Viallate at the Institute of Politics, William's College, Mass. These lectures were published in English and French in 1923. The author, who twenty years earlier had interpreted the protectionist imperialism of Chamberlain as a contribution to British self-sufficiency,[1] now enlarged on the subject of imperialist expansion. It was, according to him, dictated by the desire of the 'great industrial nations' to find 'outlets both for the utilization of their available capital and for the surplus of their production'. This economic imperialism, he said, had worsened international relations before the war; people ought to be warned against the portent of its being intensified now.[2] Soon afterwards economic imperialism in this meaning became a topic of a vast American literature which was by no means intended to further the cause of socialism. W. S. Culbertson emphasized the influence of surplus capital on the scramble for raw materials and the ensuing international frictions. Carlton Hayes and Parker T. Moon set out to see recent European history in the light of 'substitution of the more peaceful and subtle methods of economic imperialism, of investment and trade for the aggressive military imperialism of the old regime'. A flood of publications written in the same vein followed. Economic imperialism was made more or less responsible for the world war. 'Dollar diplomacy', the name once chosen for the politics of Presidents Th. Roosevelt and W. Taft, was now taken to represent the American brand of a world-embracing movement. J. Viner stated in 1929 that the term imperialism had become 'a downright nuisance'; but in the meantime the economic views expressed by it had been adopted in general historical literature.[3]

The three post-war groups of thought and propaganda, which we may call the Marxist, the Fabian, and the American, by no means represent an identical attitude towards contemporary society and politics. But their mutual independence gives only greater importance to the fact that they all at the same time have seen reason to elaborate J. A. Hobson's ideas and that they have arrived at views on history much akin to each other. They have joined in achieving a victory for the concept of economic imperialism. This success has indeed been frequently and convincingly contested by historians and sociologists. But scholarly criticism was unable to prevent the forming of an international *communis opinio* for which economic imperialism has become an accepted fact. This acceptance has had enormous consequences. The historical view expressed in the term has gone far to stereotype popular attitudes towards Western civilization and Western states, Britain and America in particular. For communists, all the world round, it has given shape to the background against which their new world is to emerge. But it has had an impact no less vehement on minds not converted to communism. It may have greatly contributed to mutual distrust between America, Europe, and the British Empire. In England it has been a moral solvent. It has made people averse to colonial activity of any kind and apathetic towards imperial misfortunes; these could be easily construed as retributions for the economic imperialism of former days. The concept has finally become widely known among the peoples who had reasons to regard themselves as objects of 'imperialist' expansion. It has inspired and embittered national movements in Asiatic nations, in colonies, and in mandated countries; it has widened the gulf between their intellectuals and the Western nations, Great Britain in particular.

In all these directions the impact is still felt. To ask how modern political and economic developments came to be understood by the terms of economic imperialism, and how this interpretation was able to carry conviction, is to put questions capable of historical investigation. This study, it is hoped, has provided some of the answers.

Matters would have been clearer if the advocates of the concept of economic imperialism had succeeded in making good its postulates. For this purpose they would have had to clear the concept of its ambiguities and show it to embody an adequate interpretation of a certain category of political and administrative actions. This brought out, it should be shown, that in these actions groups of capitalists have taken a leading part. The activities of these capitalists ought finally to be demonstrated as consequences of the economic structure of capitalist society. If all this were a matter of convincing proof, there would be no need to ask why the concept has proved convincing.

Some advocates of the historical view implied in the concept have indeed been very active in explaining it and in collecting evidence in its proof. But the criticism with which they have met has been based on arguments more conclusive than the thesis itself. The criticism is equally convincing when it dissects the Neo-Marxist tenets (as J. A. Schumpeter has done[1]), as when (in the writings of J. Viner and E. M. Winslow) it exposes the exaggerations and misconstructions which have marred American scholarship. It has been demonstrated again and again that statistical data do not in fact, as has been asserted, bring out the tendency of surplus capital to flow into colonial and other 'imperial' enterprise rather than into other investments.[2] It has been shown (by W. K. Hancock and H. S. Frankel) that the practical problems of colonial economics are by far too serious to be disposed of by the indictment of imperialist greed.[3] Research on diplomatic history, even if prepared to accept economic influences in general terms, has seen no occasion to trace them individually. What carried conviction were not the statistical data marshalled for or against the theory of economic imperialism but its plausible simplicity which satisfied the needs of political propaganda and a deep human desire to understand the past and read the future. It purported to provide collective crime with a motive. Soon the historians of imperialism emerged who attempted to give an account of the plot.

The readers and writers of the history of the First World War took it for granted that government of a country meant possession of a country, and that possession of a country yielded power and wealth to the nation that governed it. They unhesitatingly accepted the assumption that the policy of the great Powers had been a calculated design to increase their own dominion and to fool other rivals in the field. That interpretation of events was particularly widespread in those countries that had suffered defeat. Their inhabitants preferred to regard themselves as the victims of a hidden conspiracy, all the more so as the outside world insisted on putting the blame for that great catastrophe on German and Austrian statesmen. The peace treaty of Paris was concluded on that assumption, yet it laid itself open to the censure of imperialism. More evidence came to light in the following years concerning secret agreements made among the victorious nations, on the basis of which regions of Asia were allotted to France, Britain, and Italy without the slightest consideration shown for the views of the inhabitants. A heavy burden of reparations was imposed on Germany without a clear idea of how Germany was to pay them, if her goods and services were not wanted. The German Mark collapsed, and the ensuing inflation benefited traders and foreigners, while it impoverished many sections of the German people. In that atmosphere of bewilderment and despair the fallen German war leaders came out with their story of the war. It was told in terms highly reminiscent of the Boer War revulsion and its subsequent political agitation. Essentially, it was the story of a British plot.

General Ludendorff, Admiral Tirpitz, and the German Kaiser seemed to agree that Germany had been systematically encircled by the cunning British, who wanted to rid themselves of a dangerous economic rival. A clever propaganda tricked the world into believing in the lofty humanitarian aims of the Anglo-Saxons. The purpose of that propaganda was to mislead the Germans and to undermine their morale. It made the work of the Anglo-Saxon capitalists of enslaving the Germans much easier, particularly so, the war leaders alleged, as they were assisted by allies within Germany, the Jews and the Freemasons. With their help Wall Street and the City hoped to destroy Germany and Austria, the two main obstacles to Anglo-Saxon world domination.[1] The historians readily took up that theme. They projected British Imperialism into the past and looked for its beginnings in More's *Utopia*,[2] in Puritanism. If Weber had found capitalism to be the outcome of British Protestantism, the same origin might be proved for imperialism. English literature was studied from that point of view. It was found by speculative scholars that Elizabethan literature, indeed, already showed the roots of imperialism and its intimate connexion with the Jewish spirit of the Old Testament. A series of lectures on English literature delivered by F. Brie had the purpose to demonstrate 'wie der englische Imperialismus eine Folgeerscheinung des Protestantismus calvinistischer Richtung ist, dessen Gedanke der Auserwähltheit sich verknüpft mit dem Anspruch des Inselvolkes, das Meer und die überseeischen Gebiete als seine Domäne zu betrachten, und mit den freiheitlichen Ideen der englischen Revolution'.[1] German scholars as well as German statesmen in those years often pointed out what they, no doubt, genuinely believed, that British imperialism had been systematic and conscious of its aim, 'zielbewusst', from the start. Eduard Meyer and Friedrich Meinecke, two leading historians, were so convinced of the existence of an Anglo-American scheme to attain and secure world domination that they gloomily prophesied a lasting Anglo-Saxon 'dyarchy', more dangerous than the Roman Empire, for those Anglo-Saxons controlled trade and raw material.[2] In the eyes of Wilhelm Dibelius, America represented a more inflated form of British imperialism on the other side of the Atlantic, striving, like Britain, for the government of the world.[3] With the advent of Anglo-Saxon world domination the dream of Rhodes had been realized. Schmoller, the economist, spoke of Britain's policy as 'planmässig', as having been in accordance with a plan since Disraeli. At first British imperialism tried to gain its objectives without war. When that proved impossible, the English did not hesitate to achieve their aims in a world war.[4] Britain, Schmoller taught, adopted an imperialism of brutality and conquest in order to remove the undesirable German competition by force. Sooner or later such a policy could only result in war.[5] Oswald Spengler wrote about Anglo-Saxon imperialism—like Dibelius—in order to teach his readers the realities of historical existence as he saw them. The struggle for the planet had begun. The British, their unerring Viking blood in their veins, had known how to forge new weapons out of trade, organized robbery, and piracy. Daring plunder characterized new English imperialists like Rhodes.[6] Those reflexions were in part political agitation. They meant to repudiate the idea that Germany was to blame for the war. But they were often intended to go beyond a mere refutation of war guilt. They wanted the Germans to look at England not with the admiring eyes of an earlier generation of Liberals but with the eyes of a people that was ready to learn from the ruthlessness of the victors, who were depicted as cunning, unscrupulous enemies of Germany and of the Continent. On that point there was hardly any difference between the German Right or Left. A Socialist was just as ready to declare British imperialism as the enemy of Europe.[1] The idea had been as old as the French Revolution and had been the mainstay of Napoleonic propaganda. Part of that propaganda had been incorporated in a German history book, written by Schlosser, which could still be found on many German shelves. The need was felt to bring that famous nineteenth-century *Universal History* up to date. The Austrian historian H. Friedjung undertook to accomplish this task and called his book *The Age of Imperialism*.

Friedrich Schlosser had been a radical at a time when German radicalism was hostile to Britain. In the opinion of Schlosser Britain represented a detestable alliance of aristocracy and plutocracy, privilege and greed. Being hostile to the advance of capitalism and industrialism alike, Schlosser believed that machine-labour and capital would ruin Britain in the long run. As an historiographer Schlosser had been a moralist. His philosophy was that of Kant. Kant had condemned British rule and methods of trade. So did Schlosser. Friedjung's work reflected a good deal of Schlosser's moral judgement. The Age of Imperialism, he wrote, had succeeded the Age of Liberalism and the Age of Nationalism. It was characterized by the desire of the peoples and their rulers for a growing share in the domination of the world.[2] The beginnings of that new age could be found in the Seven Years War. The new dogma of power, as Friedjung called it, subordinating religion, trade, and industry, conquered the world. It produced deep hatreds and was responsible for the world war. Britain, Russia, and France realized the rapid progress and superiority of German trade and industry, so they joined an alliance of hatred and envy. Hunger for power and economic advantage were the motives, and the defeat of Germany was the aim. American imperialism was not different from British imperialism. Friedjung like Schlosser regarded the Anglo-Saxons as political hypocrites and as the enemies of the Continent. The Boer War illustrated on a small scale what the world war proved on a continental scale: greedy imperialists and small nations cannot exist side by side. The Boers were put under the yoke of imperialist rule with brutal violence.[3] Alexander v. Peez was referred to as authority on the danger of Britain to the Continent, and Rudolf Hilferding was the source which supplied the arguments supporting the effect of the savage expansionism wrought by surplus capital,[4] while the theory of encirclement gave British imperialism a sinister, scheming look. The main theme of the work was the collision between British and German imperialism, the British brand being fierce, exclusive, unscrupulous, while the German variety was depicted as peaceful, commercial rivalry. Friedjung died before he could finish his work. Otto Hoetzsch, in the completing part, asked whether the Age of Imperialism had come to an end. He answered that question in the negative. The treaty of Versailles was proof of the continued imperialist age. The lesson was plain. In such an age it was not the humanitarian phrase that counted but the military and economic power. Many Germans had made the mistake of taking English and American liberalism and humanitarianism seriously. They were a mere blind which Anglo-Saxon imperialism traditionally adopted. Other German writers and thinkers, like F. Salomon, F. Wichtl, and Rudolf Steiner, expressed their views in similar ways. Steiner wrote that Wilson was the embodiment of the godless phrase, that British economic imperialism was devoid of spiritual values, and that the principle of self-determination was a fraud.[1]

Thus during the first years following the collapse of 1918 Germans began to view imperialism as a calculated political system of Anglo-Saxon world rule. That system was not confined to capitalist exploitation, often regarded as an Anglo-American invention. It incorporated the activities of many other institutions such as the church, sports, lodges, and seemingly humanitarian associations. It made every Englishman an agent of imperialism. Anglo-Saxon imperialism, German writers contended, had reduced Europe to the state of India. It had succeeded in conquering the world because it was the most ruthless, cunning, and all-embracing political system. Europe had been enslaved by Anglo-Saxon imperialism and by Russian communism. The Continent, many German writers believed, could be freed only by mastering the new ways of political life, by adopting imperialism as its own way to power. Germans were, therefore, called upon to learn how to be equally ruthless in politics and equally unscrupulous in their moral judgements, to develop the same unity of political purpose and social uniformity as appeared to be the characteristics of the Anglo-Saxons. In that new Age of Imperialism, international law, the League of Nations, and treaties between states were mere tools of imperialist rulers. Political writers and agitators in Germany thus sought to open the eyes of what they regarded as the misguided, trusting German public with its ideals and dream-world about British humanity and Western democracy. That political interpretation of events had its eschatological message of hope. Both Marxists and nationalists in the first years of the Weimar Republic were looking forward to a new and better era to dawn after the evil age of imperialism had passed. That hope was soon to be shared by many colonial peoples in Asia and Africa. For all of them, communists, European nationalists, and colonial intellectuals, the historical concept of an Age of Imperialism assumed an eschatological aspect and encouraged political agitation for a new world order.

The seemingly impossible came to pass. Of the widely differing meanings and applications of the word imperialism a definite selection emerged on whose condemnatory use writers and orators of all the political world came to agree, however much the interests for which they stood might clash in other fields. In the shape of a few simple speculative theories imperialism became a global word after the First World War, a symbol of world struggle. That development was, in fact, the result of the First World War. Communism emerged as an intellectual force of global dimensions. It lent authority and the whole might of government propaganda to one of the economic interpretations of imperialism. How this version could take more than one leaf from German detraction of British imperial policy had become apparent already before 1914. German moral rearmament began as soon as the war was over. It reached its climax in the 1930's. At times it dwelt on the 'plutocratic' character of Anglo-Saxon imperialism in terms almost identical with those used by the communists. At other times German writers stressed the alleged anti-European or the Jewish character of Anglo-Saxon imperialism. Both interpretations coalesced in a branch of world opinion which had scarcely been in existence before 1914. Spokesmen of the nations which had been the objects of the policies denounced by the term—intellectuals of India, of the Arab countries, Africa, and the Far East—became increasingly aware of the outstanding opportunity offered to them by a term in whose abusive sound the white nations seemed to condemn themselves. By appropriating this term they could proclaim that their agitation conformed to a historical mission which affected the whole world. And in the United States public opinion, bent on disowning the entanglements of European politics found the word highly suitable for branding the unregenerate characters of the Powers of the old Continent. British radicals, now becoming Socialists, had new scruples about the Empire. Latin-American writers feared their continent might be turned into North America's India. So it came about that in the period following the First World War, imperialism rose to global eminence as the leading slogan of three world struggles, the struggle against capitalism, against Anglo-Saxon domination, and the struggle against white colonial power.

XI

HATE-WORD OF WORLD STRUGGLE AGAINST ANGLO-SAXON DOMINATION

The aim of propaganda is to make converts by creating a state of mind and of emotions favourable to and in sympathy with the propagandist, who is an agitator but not necessarily a liar. His own faith may be sincere. In many cases the propagandists themselves are deceived by their own sentiments and political philosophy, by the many half-truths which they take for the whole truth. In most cases the political agitator is not aware of the origin of his ideas and slogans. Propaganda does not invent a faith. It uses inherited thoughts and clichés for its own purpose. The peoples of Europe—unlike the inhabitants of the English-speaking world—have inherited more from the traditions of Roman Catholicism, absolutism, the French Revolution, Napoleonic rule, and German philosophy. Words like state, power, culture, and government carry associations and meanings on the European Continent which are different from the associations of the Britons or the Americans. European intellectuals long refused to make peace with the industrial and commercial revolution, let alone ever tried to understand the intricacies of banking, marketing, or the stock-exchange. There has been a wide discrepancy between Europeans and Anglo-Saxons in the use and administration of political power. In Europe individual liberty, material comfort, and wealth were less highly prized than political power centralized in a state, which often assumed authoritarian and paternal features. State worship and power worship made many Europeans believe such social attitudes to be universal. When they surveyed the world of the early 1920's and found Britain and the United States in the position of unrivalled world Powers, they were easily convinced that this state of affairs had been the overriding desire and the long-term objective of every citizen and every government in those two countries. They could, therefore, be persuaded to believe that every Englishman was a secret agent of the Foreign Office, if not in fact, at any rate in his behaviour and mental attitude. Europeans, too, could be led to believe that all British history was a single plot whose end was world domination, because Continental historians who studied the British past were inspired in their enterprise by the same belief. No European society was quite as empirical as the people of Australia, North America, or Britain. Continental Europeans were more used to being directed by centralized authority and were inclined to imagine political life to unfold in accordance with a wise plan in a way Louis XIV of France, Frederick II of Prussia, and Tsar Peter the Great had planned and guided political action. As a result history was experienced and policy interpreted in a highly personalized form. England was viewed as if she was a person of one mind, one memory, an acting human being, in fact. That was, however, not the only distortion of reality. Many more false assumptions were made in Europe at that time.

Since the early days of recorded history man has been reluctant to attribute events to accidents either in his personal life or in his collective existence. He was often convinced that what happened was intended to happen. As long as that interpretation was part of a theology man bowed to the superior wisdom of divine providence. Without that faith, however, he was in adverse political circumstances driven to the conclusion that he had become the victim of a conspiracy. Another result of the desire to find simple answers was the more recent belief in history as the logical and necessary effect of one major cause. The key to an understanding of the past as well as to a knowledge of the future would be revealed, as soon as the major cause could be exposed. Events were shown to be controlled by impersonal logic; their course fixed and inevitable. In the chaos of the early 1920's many a European wanted to know who was to blame for the world war and its shattering consequences. The popular answer was contained in the word imperialism, which contained both the notion of conspiracy and the idea of an inevitable process. Marxists preferred the latter as the more 'scientific' answer. German nationalists, on the other hand, were often satisfied that they had become the victims of an imperialist conspiracy whose author, they believed, was King Edward VII.

The Marxist thesis that the world war was the logical and inevitable result of imperialism, i.e. of militant, monopolist capitalism in its last stage, was more impressive than the German assertion that it was the result of a fiendish plot of encirclement. The scientific character of the Marxist thesis seemed vindicated by the fact that many Marxists had predicted the war. After the fulfilment of their prophecy they went on predicting new imperialist wars. The leading imperialist Powers, the United States, Britain, France, and Japan, would sooner or later fight one another again, if Lenin's interpretation was correct, although some German nationalists sadly remarked that one could not 'hope' for such a war in the near future, which would give Germany the chance to rise again to new glory, while her enemies fought over the loot of the last war. Yet even the correct prediction of an event proves no superior wisdom. A child can predict the chiming of a clock without any understanding of the clockwork. 'I can predict; therefore, I know'—an ancient fallacy. Knowledge is, indeed, capable of correct prediction, but correct prediction is not always a sign of knowledge.

Lenin's theory of imperialism was suitable for propaganda among the half-educated whose power of criticism was not fully developed. It was still too complicated for the more primitive minds who experienced all history as a battle between the good and the bad. For them communist propaganda simplified matters still further and devilized imperialism. The ancient oriental vision of history as the manifestation of the struggle between light and darkness, a good and an evil spirit, the wisdom of the magi, was revived. Once again the message was clear and simple: here Ormazd—there Ahriman! The world was divided into the camp of the devil and the camp of the Lord in medieval dogma, into progressives and reactionaries in the rationalist belief of the nineteenth century. Communism adopted the same vision of a polarized world. In February 1919 Stalin wrote: 'The world has split into two irreconcilable camps: the camp of imperialism and the camp of socialism.'[1] That world view was accepted by the eighth Congress of the Russian Communist Party a month later. From that moment the continuous world struggle between imperialism and socialism became communist dogma, and until 1934 imperialism was the most prominent communist hate-word signifying all the hostile forces communists encountered in their struggle. It became the basis of historical interpretation and tactical decisions. Under the banner of the fight against Western imperialism

Lenin and Stalin called on all the social and political malcontents of the world, on the oppressed nationalities and workers, on the colonial peoples, on the 'toiling Moslems of Russia and the East,' to rally to their side.[1] The peoples of the Middle East and Central Asia were told that the Western imperialists had been the 'age-long oppressors and exploiters of the nationalities of the world' and that the Russian October Revolution had inaugurated a new era of socialist progress and struggle 'against imperialism in general', against all oppression; an era of religious freedom and national self-determination.[2] As Commissioner for the nationalities Stalin issued the watchword: 'All power to the labouring masses of the oppressed nationalities.' Together with Lenin he gave the Marxist idea of class struggle a new interpretation, which incorporated the struggle of the colonial peoples. The class struggle was two-fold in character. It was a struggle against oppression at home and a fight against foreign oppressors. In the colonies the foreign oppressor and the native oppressor were often identical, the foreign oppressor residing in the West, the subjugated peoples living in the East. The polarized world of the two camps of socialists and imperialists received its geographical orientation as the camp of the oppressed East and the camp of the imperialist West. 'Thus from the particular question of combating national oppression', Stalin wrote, 'the national question is evolving into the general question of emancipating the nations, colonies, and semi-colonies from imperialism.'[3] In that struggle Russia, in Stalin's mind, was to form the bridge of revolution between the socialist proletarian West and the enslaved East, 'having created a new front of revolutions against world imperialism, extending from the proletarians of the West, through the Russian revolution, to the oppressed peoples of the East'.[4]

Wilson's enthusiasm for the principle of self-determination and his declared opposition to imperialism was a little disturbing to the communists. The two-camp world would have looked more convincing, had the Americans annexed some territory or at any rate taken over some country as a mandate if not as a colony. It was difficult to describe Wilson as an imperialist. The communists, however, tried to defend their picture of the world situation and declared Western enthusiasm for national self-determination as false and as imperialist deception. In

1919 Stalin said the imperialist camp was organizing itself—a desperate measure of imperialism in its death throes—into a league of robbers, the so-called League of Nations. Here, again, America was not fitting into that picture at all. The United States remained outside the League. Indeed, from the point of view of the defunct imperial societies of Russia, Germany, Austria, and Turkey, not only Russia's socialists but also America's democrats represented truly revolutionary societies. The defeated aristocrats, officers, and other dignitaries of imperial Austria-Hungary or Germany or Russia were quite right in the feeling that their 'old Europe' had been overthrown by an enemy in the East and an enemy in the West, a sentiment which was destined to linger on for many years and to play a part when Germany appealed for co-operation in the name of European salvation during the Second World War. America never questioned the political wisdom of the principle of self-determination or its natural limits. What acts of folly was a nation allowed to commit in the name of the hallowed principle? How were small states to come by political security and economic prosperity? Hamilton had made it clear why each of the United States could be given only a limited sovereignty, and Lincoln refused to negotiate a treaty of separation with the Confederate States. In the thick of the civil war Stalin was confronted with the problem of secession, too. Should the principle of national self-determination be interpreted to mean the right of secession? The problem which Lenin, Stalin, and their friends faced was complicated. They had to meet a military emergency which required a maximum concentration of forces in their hands. But they also desired to win over the peoples of the East as allies in their struggle against capitalism and imperialism. The situation required them to be tsarist and non-tsarist at the same time.

Stalin formulated a solution in 1920 in an article on *Marxism and the National Question*. It was based on his concept of the polarized world. If the whole world was divided into two fighting camps, there could not be room for a third grouping of forces. A demand for secession from the socialist camp, therefore, was tantamount to a demand for the right to join the imperialists. Countries of the border region like Georgia and Armenia in this life-and-death struggle between proletarian Russia and the imperialist Entente were confronted with only two alternatives: '*Either* they join forces with Russia, and then the toiling masses of the border regions will be emancipated from imperialist oppression; *or* they join forces with the Entente, and then the yoke of imperialism is inevitable.' Trotsky agreed with Stalin on that point. The principle of self-determination did not exist in the abstract non-political vacuum. Its application always led to important political consequences. Hence the principle deserved the full support of the communists 'wherever it is directed against feudal, capitalist, and imperialist states. But wherever the fiction of self-determination, in the hands of the bourgeoisie, becomes a weapon directed against the proletarian revolution, we have no occasion to treat this fiction differently from the other "principles" of democracy perverted by capitalism.'[1] Imperialism, Trotsky believed, was the attempt made by predatory capitalism to capture the control of the world economy. That belief had no factual meaning; but it carried a good deal of imaginative meaning in the mind of Trotsky and other members of the Central Committee. With world revolution as an objective of Soviet policy, imperialism was a better hate-word than capitalism, for in the highlands of Iran and in the valleys of China or India there were as yet few commercial banks and even fewer belching chimneys, but many landlords, fighting warlords, and foreign troops. These were more important to an illiterate peasantry than Marxist ideas, which were more suitable for an urban proletariat. Communists, therefore, fought British influence in Persia to save 'the Orient from the clutches of English imperialism' and attacked the Persian Government as puppets of that imperialism.[2] In China they attributed the civil war to an imperialist plot which, it was alleged, had been instigated for the purpose of retarding the progress of China's industry. Consequently, at its third national congress in 1923 the Communist Party of China decided upon two central slogans, 'down with the warlords' and 'down with international imperialism'.[3] Even after the Russians had abandoned their drive for world revolution with the rise of Stalin to supreme power in 1925, Moscow persisted in its anti-Western policy, for Stalin was convinced that sooner or later his country would be attacked by the West. The policy of maintaining good relations with the Kuomintang was continued. Russia had given up all her extra-territorial rights in China, sent military officers to train Chinese nationalist forces, and undertook to restore Mongolia to the suzerainty of the Chinese Republic. Collaboration with colonial nationalism on the part of the communists was a sign that it was generally recognized that the class struggle in West Europe and in America had failed to yield the expected results and that the Asian anti-imperialist front looked more promising. In their interpretation of the world situation the communists in 1925 found a disappointing stabilization of the political situation in France, Britain, and the United States but saw encouraging developments in the European colonies, in India, Egypt, Syria, and Morocco. In December 1925 at the Fourteenth Congress of the Communist Party of the Soviet Union, Stalin could not report the decline of capitalism, but he could paint a picture of colonial unrest and tottering imperialism.[1]

The exploitation of political sentiment engendered by frustrated nationalism was characteristic of communist strategy not only in Asia but also in Europe. Imperialism was made the key to an understanding of the war and the subsequent peace. The Treaty of Rapallo, signed in April 1922, had brought Russia and Germany closer together in an anti-Western alignment and a joint opposition to the post-war international order. German communists agitated against the 'imperialist peace' of Versailles in a language similar to that of the Right-wing parties. 'Down with the robbery of Versailles! War against imperialist wars!' were the communist slogans of 1923, when France occupied the Ruhr.[2] Together with the German nationalists the communists took part in the resistance against the French forces. In the following years the German communists agitated against every political step which might regulate or improve the relations between Germany and the West. They fought the Dawes Plan of reparations as an imperialist trap designed, they asserted, by American imperialists to enslave the German workers. They fought Stresemann's proposed Locarno agreement as an imperialist pact, which, they claimed, had the purpose of aiding British imperialism to keep the Soviets and the French in check. The communist paper, *Die Rote Fahne*, on that occasion carried a front page with a drawing. A fist was seen tearing up a geographical map around which generals were seated engaged in discussion. The text in capital letters simply read: GEGEN DEN IMPERIALISMUS![3] When Germany entered the League of

Nations in 1926, the communists endeavoured to interpret that event as a bellicose step directed against the Soviet Union. Stresemann, the *Rote Fahne* wrote, had made it certain through his agreements with the British imperialists that Germany would become involved in any future war against the Soviet Union.[1] This agitation of German communists had a counterpart in Russia and was often reflected in the pages of *Pravda*. It undoubtedly expressed a constant and real fear of the Soviet leaders that one objective of international Western diplomacy was another invasion of Russia. When in 1928 the world looked more stable and prosperous than ever since the beginning of the First World War, the vision of scheming imperialism was harder to maintain. Germany had joined the Kellog Pact for the renunciation of war. Reparations were being reviewed in terms more favourable to the Germans, and the complete evacuation of the Rhine region was envisaged. Communism had manifestly failed to make progress in West Europe. Its co-operation with the Chinese nationalists had come to a dismal end in 1927. The Sixth Congress of the Comintern, meeting in Moscow in 1928 together with the Chinese communists, had to take stock of the political situation. Did the slogan of imperialism still represent political reality? The communists decided that it did.

In a political resolution the Congress of the Chinese Communist Party stated that world revolution in West Europe had failed because the Social Democrats had betrayed it. In its first stage world revolution had succeeded only in Russia, but in the present second stage imperialist conflicts would grow and thus enable the toiling masses of India, China, Morocco, and other colonial territories to carry on their struggle for liberation. In the future third stage, the Chinese communists predicted, new and old conflicts brought about by imperialism would grow in intensity. Imperialist powers would wage war against one another and against the Soviet Union. The Congress approved of ten party slogans, of which the first was the overthrow of the rule of imperialism, because it had caused the failure of the Chinese revolution.

The imperialists, the arch-enemy of the Chinese revolution, were very strong and are the organizers and controllers of all reactionary forces. By means of their political and economic power and some puny concessions to the national bourgeoisie, they *split* the national united front through coercion and bribery

—using the traditional methods of bribing the warlords, of suppressing the revolution by forceful gun-boat 'diplomacy' and economic blockade.

The strength of the imperialists was manifold. It lay in banks, corporations, warships, and troops.[1] The Sixth Congress of the Comintern, too, regarded the colonial anti-imperialist struggle as the most promising aspect of the world situation and recorded that the 'toiling masses of the colonies struggling against imperialist slavery represent a most powerful auxiliary force of the socialist world revolution'.[2] It was then argued that the colonial policy of the imperialist powers contained two aspects favourable to the advance of communism. It aroused the antagonism of the colonial peoples—witness Egypt, India, Palestine, Morocco, Syria—and it heightened the conflicts between the colonial powers themselves, which would inevitably lead to new imperialist wars. Those wars would offer new opportunities to the proletariat of the imperialist powers and their dependencies. As the contradiction between the imperialist world and the Soviet Union was sharpening, the danger of an imperialist war against the Soviet Union, it was contended, became more acute; and so the leaders of the Sixth Congress of the Comintern warned the delegates of the impending struggle between the world proletarian revolution and world imperialism. In that struggle temporary agreements with nationalist movements in the colonies were envisaged. It was also realized that— in Marxist terms—colonial peasants were often struggling against feudalism rather than against capitalism; occasionally tribes like the Riff or the Druse rose only against foreign oppression. Imperialism, therefore, was still the best word to signify the enemy in *all* his forms and masks, capitalist, foreign oppressor, local feudal lord, general, high commissioner, and anti-communist. In June 1930 the political weather bureau of the Party warned that 'the danger of an imperialist war has become still more imminent'.[3] The prediction was correct, but the fulfilment of the prophecy came about in a way which the prophets of imperialist wars had not expected. In the wake of an economic crisis parliamentary democracy in Central Europe collapsed, yet communism was more ruthlessly suppressed than before and was soon wiped out as a political force. Japan invaded China and Italy conquered Ethiopia. That was expected. But the imperialist powers of the West, rather than go to the expected war against their new imperialist rivals, Germany, Italy, and Japan, made one concession after another and even sacrificed some of their European allies. Hitler's policy appeared to favour an agreement with the West and expansion towards the East. Stalin, therefore, looked to the West as an ally against the German threat. In 1933 diplomatic relations between the Soviet Union and Great Britain improved, and diplomatic contacts with the United States were developed, which eventually led to the recognition of the Soviet Union by the United States. In 1934 the Soviet Union entered the League of Nations and in 1935 signed a pact of alliance with France. Step by step with that development agitation against Western imperialism disappeared. Imperialism, in the language of the communists, changed its epithet from Western to 'Hitlerite', 'fascist', or 'Japanese'. As the Russian need for non-communist allies grew, imperialism lost a good deal of its emotional power and was replaced by slogans which appealed to communist as well as to nationalist sentiments, until, finally, in June 1941 the 'imperialist' war turned into a 'patriotic' war in one night, when for the second time in one generation Russia was invaded by a German army. In July 1941 the Russian and the British became allies in a war which was then fought by the Russians for sheer physical survival. The idea that the world was divided into two warring camps with all the communists fighting on the one side and all the imperialists on the other, made no sense any more in 1941. All factual content had been manifestly drained out of the concept of the divided world. The division had occurred in a different way, and it by no means divided the whole world. In the world of 1941 the 'imperialist' Londoners, like the inhabitants of Leningrad and Moscow, faced the same fate which the Germans had meted out to the inhabitants of Warsaw and Rotterdam. In the battles of 1941 a rise of the peoples of Egypt, Iraq, or India against British imperialism was the last thing any communist wanted. And so reality knocked the hate-word of imperialism out of its communist shape. It had to be demoted and for six years it remained in obscurity. In Central Europe, on the other hand, imperialism retained its position as hate-word and served the Germans better than the communists.

We saw earlier that imperialism had never been an exclusively communist term of propaganda and that, in fact, it was frequently used in Britain and in America in the 1920's. We pointed out how Hobson's theory of imperialism affected German historical thought in the first years after the war. The legend that Germany had been trapped by cunning Anglo-American imperialists in 1918 enabled nationalist pride to keep another legend intact, the myth of the invincible German army.

The view that Germany was encircled by a world-wide conspiracy could be maintained in the first years of peace on the basis of the allied blockade, the occupation of the Ruhr, the imposition of war reparations, the inflation, communist risings inside Germany, and the establishment of the Soviet Union. In each national misfortune a Jewish element was seen operating as a common factor. Bolshevism and Western capitalism, in the eyes of German nationalists, were two masks of the same devil, who had decreed the destruction of Germany. The devil was world-Jewry which, it was maintained, controlled Anglo-American capitalism and Russian bolshevism as well. The anti-Western aspect of that paranoic outlook had much in common with the communist attitude. It opposed capitalism, the Weimar Republic, the post-war settlement, and international order. It nursed its war-time hatred of Britain and America. It was less intellectual and more sentimental than communism and had no interest in any theory of capitalism. It was satisfied that capitalism was the instrument of Jewish world power, which had its headquarters in London and New York. Imperialism was not so conspicuous as a slogan with German nationalists as it was with the communists, but it remained part of their propaganda campaigns and political agitation until the second collapse of the German army in 1945.

In the days of the Weimar Republic most educated Germans were inclined to agree that all great Powers had been imperialistic before the war, in the sense that they pursued a policy of militant expansion, but, they would argue, while Germany was merely striving for a place in the sun, Britain's political objective had been world domination. Imperialism was most often used in that sense. It was occasionally translated into a German term like 'Weltmachtstreben' or also 'Weltherrschaftsanspruch'. Imperialism was thus rendered in the Germanic shape to signify the striving after or the claim to world domination. It implied a consistent and planned policy and was at times regarded as the expression of the rule of the rich, of plutocracy. The latter became a favourite slogan of German political leaders and writers after 1933. In the polarized world as the Germans saw it after the rise of Hitler to power, the evil part of the world was found grouped around Central Europe. It was composed of Western plutocrats, Jewish Bolshevists, of inferior coloured and southern races. The evil part of the world stood for material ends and threatened the 'Kultur' and the genuine communal socialism, the idealism of the heart of Europe which the Germans meant to defend. But German nationalists like Spengler, Moeller van den Bruck, and Dibelius favoured a policy of expansion. They believed it would have been better, if Germany had adopted imperialism as ruthlessly and steadfastly as Britain. They shared with many other Europeans the credo in political power as the sole virtue of the state and they believed British Imperialism expressed that virtue in its best form, much though they hated to see it triumph in Britain and not in Germany. Spengler exhibited the curious ambivalent hate-love of British power which characterized many Germans. He could be enthusiastic about the strong 'Viking instinct', which he believed to see operating in American and British millionaires, in the 'proud British robbers'. On another occasion he would see the world facing the momentous choice between Anglo-Saxon capitalism and Prussian socialism.[1] Moeller van den Bruck in his book, *The Third Reich*, spoke with approval of British imperialism in terms reminiscent of Joseph Chamberlain. He was convinced those Englishmen were right who said that trade followed the flag, or as he put it: 'In England namentlich fühlte man im Volke: Macht geht vor Wirtschaft her.'[2] He wanted the Germans to learn from English imperialism and to assert the white man's rule over the dark races in co-operation with Britain. Hitler agreed with that outlook of German publicists and historians. He was convinced that economic conquests were established by military power and defended by the sword and he believed the British example showed best how brutality and ruthlessness built up economic power. The distinguishing feature of British states-manship, in Hitler's eyes, had been its ability to draw economic acquisitions from political strength and at once to recast every gain in economic strength into political power.[3] It would be futile, however, to look for logical consistency in Nazi interpretations of British power. The Hobsonian tradition that much of that power was guided by

Jewish capitalists had received a new lease of life in the writings of Ludendorff and Tirpitz, as we saw in the last chapter. It fitted into the Nazi propaganda as soon as Hitler realized that his plan for Anglo-German co-existence—a free hand for Britain overseas and a free hand for Germany on the Continent—was unacceptable in London. Hitler like so many other Europeans failed to understand the difference between British rule and British ownership. He believed that the British Government could dispose of the British Empire and Commonwealth in the way a general could dispose of his troops. When he decided to fight the Empire, he thought it would be possible, once victory was secured for Germany, to redistribute British colonies and dominions as if they were the scattered possessions of a person overcome by highwaymen. As the war drew on, he liked to see himself as the defender of Europe against both Jewish Bolshevists in the East and Jewish capitalists in the West. His account rendered on the point of defeat was the same as Ludendorff had given as an explanation for his defeat. Once again, Germany, he alleged, had fallen victim to the conspiracy of international finance and world-Jewry.[1] Imperialism, therefore, became prominent as a slogan of German agitation after Munich and was directed against Britain and America.

Sombart was still a leading German writer on economic subjects in the 1930's. The line between political agitation and scholarship was never easy to define in his work, most of which was, indeed, agitation. In his book *Deutscher Sozialismus* he described Western capitalism as a system based on fraud. It enslaved other nations and was controlled by a few banking houses. In the language of Hobson and Hilferding Sombart quoted the following words: 'Es entstand jener "unheilvolle und fluchwürdige finanzkapitalistische Internationalismus oder Imperialismus des internationalen Finanzkapitals, der sich überall da zu Hause fühlt, wo sich ein Beutefeld auftut".'[2] The words which Sombart quoted were not taken from the writings of Hobson or Hilferding, however, but from the papal encyclic 'Quadragesimo anno'. The dogma of Hobson had meanwhile received the blessings of the Pope. Sombart gave modern imperialism his own interpretation. Its purpose was economic exploitation, its form capitalism, its spirit was Jewish. Germany, therefore, had to be freed from all the aspects of modern imperialism. C. Brinkmann revised his work on Britain and the Empire in 1938, giving greater prominence to the Boer War as a war against Anglo-Jewish capitalism[1] and its alleged tendency to rule the world. On 3 September 1939 the German Government in reply to the British ultimatum sent a memorandum to the British Government in which alleged British intention to rule the world was publicly branded.[2] Robbery and lies paved the way of British imperialism, Ribbentrop declared in his speech on foreign affairs, delivered in Danzig on 24 October 1939. The Führer was striving for peace. Britain wanted world domination. 'Es gibt kein Gebiet der Erde, wo nicht die britische Flagge gegen den Willen der betreffenden Völker weht, wo nicht Gewalttat, Raub, und Lüge die Wege des britischen Imperialismus kennzeichnen.'[3] Anglo-American imperialism as the enemy of Europe became a favourite topic of German publications during the Second World War.

Official propaganda applied the traditional German anti-British clichés to America, too. The spirit of America was declared to be imperialistic and Jewish. Europe's struggle against America under German leadership was, in the pages of S.S.-pamphlets, the struggle of European 'Kultur' against technological barbarism. A good many sentiments hostile to the advance of industrialism and capitalism were incorporated in German war-time propaganda directed against the West.[4] A book, written in Austria in 1939, spoke of the 'anti-Western revolution' of Europe in a style which endeavoured to coin new slogans such as 'the West *is* Imperialism'[5] or 'Die Parole lautet: Ethos gegen Imperialismus'.[6] The author maintained that the West was defending imperialism, whereas Germany fought for a new moral world order, for European greatness, which the British always tried to prevent. Another author coined the word 'Europafremdheit' of the Anglo-Saxons. Europe, saved by the efforts of Adolf Hitler, was pushing back the Bolshevists into Asia and the Anglo-Saxons into the sea. Imperialism, for ever greedy, for ever swallowing up continents, and ready to betray Europe, was at last breaking up, E. Fleischer assured his readers in a book called *Europe and the New World Consciousness*.[7] Eager to find a common image of evil between bolshevism and the Western Powers, German writers of the war-time period usually stressed their alleged anti-European character and Jewish leadership. One author claimed to have found bolshevism and plutocracy as the expression of a nomadic way of life, derived from the Jews and inimical to the peasant culture of Europe. Against the Anglo-American imperialism he proclaimed his slogan of 'Europe for the Europeans'.[1] Dr Goebbels in many of his speeches made use of the same ideas but did not give prominence to imperialism as hate-word. He used the Germanic forms such as 'Weltmachtstreben'. Plutocracy as a slogan was more favoured by official Nazi propaganda than imperialism. It is difficult to establish whether that was a conscious choice made in deference to Mussolini's Empire. But, then, Mussolini himself used imperialism as a term of anti-British propaganda.[2] When academic teachers dealt with the plutocracy of the West—slogans often precede academic treatment—they had little to add to the traditional theory of imperialism except that they changed the name to plutocracy. Thus a Leipsic university teacher in a book on the concept and essence of plutocracy presented Britain as the example of 'totalitarian plutocracy' in the last stage of its existence, when further colonial expansion was no longer possible. K. H. Pfeffer's book was a curious version of Lenin's work on imperialism, presented in academic form and in Nazi terminology, an illustration of the many points of ideological contact between German and Russian writers in their attitude towards the West. In the German propaganda of the Second World War imperialism meant the alleged determination of the Anglo-Saxons to reduce Europe to the status of a colony, without political rights and subjected to capitalist exploitation. A good many historical books and essays endeavoured to provide historical evidence for the official view of imperialism as the enemy of Europe.[3] Pfeffer argued that British imperialism was only possible in a capitalist world. Germany had taken up the fight to rid the world of both, capitalism and imperialism, a fight for a 'post-capitalist' Europe.[4]

It was natural that the men who fought with and for Hitler were asking themselves what the war was really about. Hitler himself became so occupied with the military operations that he found little time to ponder the wider issues involved. German writers, however, tried to find a moral justification for the German occupation of the Continent. They genuinely yearned for a new Europe free from the

Anglo-Saxon West and its capitalism and secure against the communism of the Russian East. Bolshevism and imperialism expressed the negative emotions of political hatred. To many Germans, undoubtedly, Europe was the emotional word which best expressed the positive meaning of their struggle, if ever they could discover one. There was still much of the nostalgia for the Europe of Ranke and Burckhardt, a Europe led by the Germanic and Romance peoples, a Europe of small, trim cities, of neat farms, a Europe peopled with thrifty and honest merchants, skilled, hard-working craftsmen, and god-fearing peasants, where life was interrupted by local fairs and folk festivals. It was an idyllic picture of life before the industrial revolution at the beginning of the nineteenth century. In those days of struggle many Germans reflected a good deal on their past, on the wars fought by Frederick of Prussia, and on the time when in the first decade of the nineteenth century Europe was blockaded by British sea-power, because another leader of armed Europe was convinced that Britain was the enemy of the Continent and that the 'modern Carthage' was perfidious. He, too, had led a great European army into the wintry vastness of Russia. Was not there something in the European fate that transcended Napoleon and Hitler? The Germans could not hope to find allies for their European cause among the Anglo-Saxons or the Russians and did little to win the sympathy of the Ukrainians or the Poles but made a considerable effort to secure allies in the Middle East and in Latin America, one the victim of British imperialism, as they saw it, the other the victim of North American imperialism. In the German edition of S. Nearing's book on *Dollar Diplomacy* one German editor added a chapter on *The USA Imperialism of today*. Professor F. Schönemann of the University of Heidelberg believed to have found in President Roosevelt the typical symbol of American imperialism, a man who represented the solidarity of foreign policy with mammon, whose policy was leading towards war, because Jewish finance found it profitable. Schönemann wrote the chapter for 'the thinking European and Ibero-American'.[1] An earlier editor, K. Haushofer, had believed Europe's best hope lay in a conflict between the United States and the Soviet Union. It would ban the double menace which otherwise the Continent would be constantly facing.[2] During the war that hope was for a while overshadowed by a hope for a German victory. In the latter case the Germans promised Latin America and the Arab world the end of Anglo-Saxon imperialism and Jewish power.

Branches of the Nazi Party were founded abroad before Hitler came to power. They were directed by the 'Aussenamt' at Hamburg, which was the Nazi propaganda centre for foreign countries. Political propaganda was spread first through individual agents and later through branches of the Nazi Party abroad and the political use of the German diaspora. Books, lectures, films, and meetings were organized along specially designed patterns of distribution. In the Middle East the Nazi Party recruited its first members in 1932. It rapidly increased its membership after the establishment of Hitler with Cairo, Haifa, Beirut, Baghdad, and Teheran as regional centres. Those centres took their direction from Stuttgart in later years.[1] Active anti-British propaganda was intensified from 1939 and was similar to communist propaganda with the addition of the anti-Jewish aspect. In 1938 the director of the German short-wave programmes—a powerful propaganda weapon in the Middle East—toured the area and collected the data, which enabled him to plan his propaganda efforts in the following years. The Arabs were informed by German broadcasts that the British Empire was held captive by world Jewry. Since King Edward VII the Jews controlled the City and dominated British and French oil interests. Those interests were closely connected with the political interests of Zionism. British imperialism and Zionism aimed at suppressing the Arabs and taking away their lands. In fighting the British and the Jews, Germany, broadcasts declared, was also fighting for Arab interests. The Mufti of Jerusalem was won over by the Germans. Arab governments were impressed not only by Nazi propaganda but even more so by the Axis victories in the early years of the war. A climax of anti-British sentiment in the Middle East was reached when in April 1941 the Army of Iraq attempted to drive the British out of Habaniya, a move which then had the sympathy of the communists as a move against British imperialism.[2]

The Mufti of Jerusalem made regular anti-British broadcasts from Baghdad early in May so long as fighting was in progress, while German broadcasts made the most of the German military success in Greece. A book by I. Kirchner on the Near East best captured the tone and the ideas of German short-wave broadcasts to the Arabs. It interpreted events in the Near East as a plot of British imperialists and Zionists.[1] The Soviet Union recognized the short-lived Rashid Ali government in Iraq. The communist parties of the Middle East agitated against the 'imperialist war' and against the 'Zionist criminals' and thus established the appearance of a common front with Italian and German propaganda in the context of which imperialism invariably stood for British rule.[2] That situation lasted between the years 1939–41 and made many a nationalist Arab look either to Stalin or to Hitler as his future liberator. In spring 1941 it looked as if the latter would arrive in the Middle East first. A few weeks later the anti-imperialist propaganda of the communists in the Middle East was given up when Hitler invaded Russia, and the field was left entirely to the anti-imperialist German propaganda, a good many elements of which survived the downfall of Hitler.

Nazi-inspired propaganda against Anglo-American power was not confined to Germans. Some writing—as A. Nikuradse's book on the struggle for Europe showed—simply reflected German clichés without adding anything new. For Nikuradse—who chose the pen-name of A. Sanders—a new struggle for global control had begun. The issue was whether the world was to be dominated by world capitalism, communism, by Anglo-American imperialism, by Russian Bolshevism, by freemasonry, and international Jewry, or whether Europe was to retain her independence with her spiritual and political identity intact. The year 1918 had spelt the spiritual and economic subjugation of Europe by the West. Its economic domination brought to the peoples of Europe misery and exploitation. A new Struggle for Europe had begun in 1938, when world capitalism and bolshevism used Czechoslovakia as their anti-European bulwark.[3] French anti-British sentiment had remained particularly strong among Right-wing organizations. It was not difficult for German propaganda in its anti-British or anti-communist notes to find a genuine resonance in Vichy France. There were many more people besides Admiral Darlan who had never made their peace with the Third Republic, and who had disliked strong ties with Britain. French anti-Semitism had been particularly strong among Right-wing Frenchmen, and so it was possible for some Frenchmen to view the struggle for Europe in a similar light as Nikuradse had seen it. The pro-German press of France contained allegations that the Jews were responsible for the war, and that the world was to be partitioned into three Empires, if the anti-European forces were to win it. The three allegedly projected empires would be Russian, British, and American. All three empires, however, would be controlled by the Jews.[1] Continental Europeans, therefore, who believed in the justice of their cause in the Second World War against the West and the East—by no means Germans alone—hoped to guard Europe against communism and against imperialism, to preserve the Continent against the intrusion of Russian and Anglo-Saxon political power. Imperialism in their minds meant the Anglo-Saxon hegemony with which they associated the period between the two wars.

Similar thoughts could be found among their Japanese friends and allies in the Far East. Japan had had genuine grievances against the attitude of the Anglo-Saxon governments, which had shown little sympathy for her pressing population problem after the First World War and enacted discriminating immigration laws. Together with the Germans and the Italians the Japanese regarded themselves as a people who had been excluded from the wealth of the earth by Britain and America. Japanese militarists, such as the members of the influential Black Dragon Society, prepared the nation for a war against the United States, which they regarded as inevitable. Despite the fact that Japan was an empire and that the adjective 'imperial' had a patriotic Japanese connotation, imperialism was employed as a term of abuse. It was directed against Britain and America. Thus Kinoaki Matsuo's book, *The Three Power Alliance*, which militated in favour of a war against the United States, could speak of 'the noble Imperial Spirit of Japan' and contrast it with the 'imperialism' of her enemies.[2] Shigetomo Sayegusa in March 1941 explained how in the inter-war period the imperialist democracies had used economic and ideological weapons so as to ensure their own rule. The renewed world-wide struggle was, therefore, a rise of the starving nations against the satiated states, a rise against the injustice of an economic system based on imperialism. 'In short, the movement for a new order in Europe and Asia is only a reaction against super-capitalistic imperialism and thus only a natural outcome', he wrote.[3] There was no doubt what imperialism meant to him. It was the word which denoted the hated 'Anglo-Saxon hegemony', the 'guardian for economic injustice'. The history of the preceding years was viewed and interpreted in that light. World War I had completed the Anglo-Saxon hegemony over the world. 'The Second World War, therefore, is a revolution against the imperialism of Anglo-Saxon hegemony and the world economic system based on plunder.[1]

Anglo-Saxon hegemony was resented not only in Europe and Asia but also in Latin America. Its peoples were often inclined to blame the North Americans for their own political instability and economic backwardness. They associated the term imperialism with the policy of the United States. Resentment against the 'imperialismo norteamericano' had grown since the American-Spanish War in 1898. In the post-war period the United States, having replaced the European countries as the major creditor, occupied a dominant position in the economic life of Latin America. Internal tension was heightened by the growing inequality of wealth, which was a result of the rapid process of industrialization. Discontent was fed by the dependence of many South American enterprises on a fluctuating world market, by world depression, and by the direct or indirect exertion of political power on the part of the United States. Her policy of 'dollar diplomacy' was decried in the 1920's and her policy of 'the good neighbour' distrusted in the 1930's. Protests against alleged American interference were strongly voiced at the fifth Pan-American Conference at Santiago in 1923. Latin Americans charged their northern neighbour with imperialism when the U.S.A. directly intervened in the Dominican Republic or in Haiti. North American imperialism was also seen at work in Colombia. Latin American writers would, therefore, agitate for a common front against North America and call for 'una resistencia uniforme en Iberoamérica contra ese imperialismo'.[2] American capital had the odium of being economically harmful, politically treacherous, and morally wrong. That odium was increased by influential pronouncements of the Catholic Church. Pope Leo XIII in May 1931 declared against the danger of economic imperialism. In May 1932 his successor, Pope Pius XI, in the encyclic 'Caritate Christi compulsi' turned against imperialism as a nationalist sentiment and policy. Communist pamphlets, too, battled against American imperialism. They claimed to have exposed 'yankee imperialism' in mining and railway building. Communist agitators adapted Lenin's theory of imperialism to Latin American conditions. They attacked the 'penetración imperialista' of South America by the United States.[1] Even the liberal press of South America shared the general suspicion of the North. The Bogotá paper *La Razón*, for instance, warned its readers against Roosevelt's policy and maintained that the Republic of the North still dreamt of pursuing imperialistic policies.[2] French observers of Latin America noticed the phenomenon of the widespread South American hatred directed against the United States. Occasionally those French observers sympathized with the anti-American sentiments of their angry fellow-Latins in South America.

For Frenchmen like A. Tardieu and L. Guilaine there was in the Latin opposition against the Anglo-Saxon hegemony a common feature which linked South America with the Latin countries of Europe.[3] It was a common struggle against what Guilaine in 1928 called 'Anglo-Saxon expansionism'. The cleavage was deeper than was often realized and went below the political and economic layers, for much of the twentieth century way of life had, indeed, assumed Anglo-Saxon rather than Latin characteristics. The only country of the English-speaking world which sympathized with the Latin point of view was Ireland, where imperialism has stood for the detested rule of the British.

During the years 1918–45, therefore, imperialism became the symbol of a hated world order in the eyes of its opponents, communists, Germans, Italians, Continental nationalists and Right-wing Europeans, Roman Catholics, Japanese, and Latin Americans. They all were united by that word in condemning the economic, social, and political power of the English-speaking world. Many hoped to find a powerful ally among the colonial peoples of Asia and Africa. The political word, which at the beginning of the century had existed mainly in the vocabulary of the opposition inside the Anglo-Saxon countries, had by 1940 become the rallying-cry of an opposition outside the English-speaking part of the world and was directed against Anglo-Saxon world leadership.

XII

THE SLOGAN OF IMPERIALISM AFTER THE SECOND WORLD WAR

The First World War made many of the warring nations world-order conscious. It was felt that a new world would and should emerge from the general blood-bath. When the end came, the British Commonwealth and Empire together with the United States of America had gained a position of world hegemony. Their opponents maintained that the acquisition of that hegemony had been the deliberate design of the Anglo-Saxons. Many expected Britain and America to impose their 'dy-archy' on the whole world. Those on the Continent of Europe who wanted more power for themselves believed that the Anglo-Saxons were the most consistent and the most successful power-seekers in the world, that their whole way of life was shaped in the interest of their supreme political design, viz. world domination, imperialism. The peoples of the English-speaking world and their governments, however, wanted nothing more than to be left in peace and to restore things as quickly as possible to what they had been before the calamity of the war occurred. In America in particular no idea was more abhorrent to the man in the street than the assumption of responsibility for the law and order of the whole planet. At their moment of victory in 1918 the Anglo-Saxon peoples hoped to find the general co-operation of the other nations in the restoration and maintenance of constitutional freedom, law, and order in every part of the world, not realizing to what extent those concepts were peculiar to their own way of life. They did not then have to ask themselves whether their ideas and their civilization could be upheld, if others should gain a considerable share in world power. The 'have-nots' had, in fact, different values and political aims. In Italy, Germany, Russia, and Japan, power was sought for a totally different order of the world. The Second World War was waged in part by some of those 'have-nots' against the Anglo-Saxon economic, social, and political world. Once more the United States and the British

301

Commonwealth and Empire emerged victorious. This time their sense of responsibility for world leadership was greater than in 1919 but, unlike in 1919, their actual world power was greatly diminished and their control confined to only one portion of a divided world.

As in the period after the First World War, opposition against Anglo-Saxon power was much in evidence after the second. The challenge came from the same three groups. The white peoples of South America and the Continent of Europe continued to regard the Anglo-American hegemony with a mixture of hope and suspicion. The communist powers and the coloured races of Africa and Asia opposed it more violently and with a vastly increased political weight. Imperialism, therefore, remained the main political slogan of those three groups in their struggle for political gain and influence. It was natural that the new distribution of power within the English-speaking world after the Second World War should be reflected in the meaning and use of imperialism as an anti-Anglo-American slogan. More often than during previous periods in the present century the slogan stood for and was directed against the political and economic power of the United States. This did not prevent Americans from using the term against their own political rivals and enemies, the Soviet Union and China. There were more signs that imperialism lost a good deal of meaning from too frequent and too wide a use at the turn of the mid-century.

A slogan like any other word can be over-worked and eroded. As the precise meaning of a word begins to fade, its emotive force, nevertheless, increases. The political vocabulary of every party contains such emotive words whose precise meaning is no longer clear. In most cases it is the emotive impact rather than the factual connotation which political propaganda desires to employ. Adjectives like 'reactionary', 'progressive', 'capitalist' today belong to the political language of every country, just like 'imperialist'. Their purpose is agitation, not information. As a global propaganda slogan imperialism has suffered a good deal of erosion. A survey of its use after the Second World War, however, shows that it is still the symbol of opposition against America and Britain and their influence in world affairs, a powerful word in the linguistic arsenal of power seekers.

In Latin America imperialism has remained the main political slogan in the struggle against Britain and North America. It was employed in British Guiana and in the agitation against British Honduras which emanated from Guatemala. But those were minor centres of irritation compared with the highly vocal opposition directed against 'the Yankee imperialism'. Many Latin American countries resented the fact that they were economically tied to the North and dependent on the market of the United States. They complained of being economically exploited and neglected by the North Americans. They disliked North American control of Panama and pointed to the undemocratic policy adopted by the United States in Guatemala, Venezuela, Colombia, the Dominican Republic, and Cuba where dictatorships had been backed by the North. Neither Britain nor the United States were inclined to tolerate 'a people's democracy' in South America, however democratically elected, and seemed to give preference to any dictator, provided he was anti-communist. Yet anti-Anglo-American agitation in South America was more nationalist than communist. Nationalist sentiment was the cause and communist sympathy the effect. For that blend of emotions anti-imperialism remained the most forceful and typical expression. Neutralism was another form of South American nationalism. It became the official policy of Peron's Argentina. Argentinian writers justified their country's policy on the grounds that both the United States and the Soviet Union were imperialist. Imperialist power blocs, they maintained, must lead to wars.

The theory of neutralism, based on a principle of opposition to imperialism, was expounded in a book on the culmination and crisis of imperialism. Its author defined imperialism as the political action undertaken by a state to extend its power, 'un sistema de acción política que tiende a multiplicar el poder, extiendo la dominación de un Estado . . .'.[1] Despite that definition, however, the term was in fact mainly directed against British and American power. Anglo-Saxon imperialism was the main theme of the treatise. It was presented as the main villain of the political world. Anglo-Saxon imperialism, the book declared, had thriven on wars since the days of Cromwell, but it had never settled any political question. It had fought Austria, Germany, Turkey, Russia, Japan, Italy, enchained other countries with its dollars and pounds, and threatened to wage a third world war against the communists.

Imperialism was dangerous to the peoples of Latin America in the Anglo-Saxon or in the Russian form. In October 1959 students in Argentina even rejected the aid offered by the United States to fellow students and academic institutions as 'cultural imperialism'.[1] The violent anti-imperialist demonstrations which accompanied Vice-President Nixon's good-will tour to Latin America in May 1958 were another expression of the deep-rooted opposition to North American influence and power. Anti-American outbursts were weaker in 1960, when President Eisenhower went on another good-will mission, but they were still very much in evidence. By that time Castro of Cuba had made himself the political leader of a campaign against 'Yankee imperialism'. Havana radio broadcasts and newspapers attacked North American imperialism almost every day.

In Western Europe opposition to Anglo-American power did not come to an end with the downfall of the Axis Powers; but as the Continent depended on America for its protection and economic recovery, that opposition was not allowed to find official and public expression. It assumed more subtle forms than open anti-imperialist campaigns except in Iceland and Ireland. Although official relations between the British and the Irish governments were unperturbed after the Second World War, Irish agitation against Britain continued. Acts of terrorism were supported by anti-British literature militating against what Irish nationalists called 'the six county government' of North Ireland. Raiders of the Irish Republican Army started an 'offensive' at the end of 1956. Britain was accused of exaggerating the religious differences between the Protestant North and the Catholic South so as to keep Ireland divided. To keep the Ulster Protestants in the North thinking that a united Ireland would mean rule by the Catholic Bishops 'is good policy from the point of view of British Imperialism', pamphleteers declared.[2] For the career of imperialism as a political slogan, however, Eastern Europe became more significant towards the mid-century. It soon resumed the tradition which Nazi propaganda against Britain and America had developed before, including its anti-Jewish variations, for in 1947 Stalin revived his policy of relentless struggle against the power of the Anglo-Americans, particularly in Europe and in the Middle East.

The economic recovery of Europe after the Second World War astonished even many economists of the capitalist countries. It left Marxists without the comfort of a Marxist explanation. The absence of a major economic crisis and the high rate of employment, together with the implementation of social welfare on a large scale, appeared to promise the economic system of private enterprise modified by social needs, as it was practised in West Europe, a new lease of life. No propaganda effort could present it as a dying economic system. But Stalin was not interested in economic theory. His main obsession was the use and direction of political power. Lenin and he had based their policy on the assumption that sooner or later the Soviet Union would be attacked. That assumption had proved to be correct. During the Second World War Stalin was haunted by the fear that his Anglo-Saxon allies were deliberately delaying a decisive counter-blow in the West in order to weaken Russia. When the war was won he was unable to co-operate with Britain and America and thought it safer to treat all power outside his own as potentially hostile; and so he returned to his life-long view of the divided world, the one part where he was the master, the other where the Anglo-Saxons were the masters. At some stage in the late 1940's he must have become convinced again that sooner or later Russia would be attacked once more by the imperialist world. So he devoted the rest of his life to the struggle for world power in the knowledge of the tremendous losses Russia had suffered in the course of the German invasion and the advantage gained by America in the field of nuclear weapons. Press and radio were engaged in a new propaganda campaign against Britain and America.

The Marshall Plan was the first major object of Russian invectives. It was depicted as a plot to enslave Europe, to chain her to America, an instrument of American imperialism. In the Middle East Glubb Pasha was credited by the Russians with the power of a master-plotter, who was in the confidence of predatory, deceptive British imperialism.[1] By the early 1950's imperialism had regained the position of the first slogan of communism. Imperialism was seen at work as one uniform and co-ordinated force operating against the socialist camp. It was at that time that Hobson and his theory of imperialism were given new prominence. Hobson was acclaimed by the Soviet press as 'one of the greatest

English historians'.¹ Imperialism was seen to triumph even in the socialist republic of Yugoslavia. As soon as the Yugoslavs ceased to obey the writ of the Kremlin, they were denounced as ' accomplices of the imperialists'. The victory of the British Conservative Party in 1951 was regarded as another sinister advance of imperialism.²

Imperialism became a prominent subject in Russian historiography again. Britain and America were depicted by Russian historians, in the way they had been described by hostile German writers in earlier periods, as plundering, exploiting, and pirating countries. Russian historical articles carried titles such as 'The Imperialistic Policy of the U.S.A. in Mexico 1913–1914', and 'How the American Imperialists seized Panama'.³ S. F. Naida, the editor of the journal *Voprosy Historii*, writing on Russian history during the years 1917–20, managed to use the phrase 'American imperialists' no less than eighty times in thirty-five pages.⁴ The official history of the Russian Communist Party gave similar prominence to the slogan of imperialism,⁵ and so did the *Great Soviet Encyclopaedia*. Its article on imperialism, written in 1952, restated Lenin's theory of imperialism as the highest stage of capitalism. It described the wars of the preceding sixty years as the result of that capitalist stage, dwelt on the exploitation of colonies by Britain, the United States, France, and Germany, and depicted the rise of Fascism and Nazism as forms of imperialism which developed after the first imperialist world war.⁶ The Second World War, the article informed its readers, must be attributed to the imperialists of America, Britain, and France. Those powers had consistently followed a policy of expansion and were interested in a long drawn-out war in order to weaken Germany and Russia at the same time. After the Second World War American imperialism used the Marshall Plan to win control over Europe and unleashed the Korean War. The British Empire was treated by the Encyclopaedia as if it was the possession of the British people, a possession, however, which was no longer in their safe grip, because their American rivals were slowly pressing the British out of their dominions and colonies.⁷ The role of imperialism was made more sinister by its alleged alliance with the Jewish capitalists and the world-wide network of Jewish finance. The Soviet Encyclopaedia's article on the history of Palestine in the twentieth century presented the conflicts of the period of the British Mandate as the result of the league between the Jews and the imperialists in a way which made those paragraphs undistinguishable from earlier Nazi publications.[1] In its political approach to the Middle East, Russian anti-imperialist propaganda continued where it had left off in 1941, and where the Germans had left off in 1945.

In Persia, Palestine, and Egypt, British policy was attacked by the Russian radio service containing words like imperialism dozens of times.[2] A strong anti-Jewish flavour was given to anti-imperialist broadcasts emanating from Russia in Arabic. But even Russian publications intended for a smaller number of serious readers inside Russia made imperialism a main theme in the presentation of economic and political topics connected with the Middle East. The leading Russian journal on economic questions reviewed the Persian situation at the beginning of 1952 with the words: 'The British imperialists have long pursued a bare-faced policy of colonial plunder and oppression in Iran.'[3] The Russian academician and noted expert, I. P. Belyaeff, in a study of 'American Imperialism in Saudi Arabia' stressed the importance of a study of the Arab countries. Those were a part of the great anti-imperialist movement which, in the eyes of the author, embraced all the peoples of Asia and Africa. Saudi Arabia was, therefore, studied as a chapter of the struggle against American imperialism.[4] The struggle against the hostile world of imperialism was the main political theme which pervaded Russian thinking about foreign affairs. Communism had, in fact, ceased to fight for a new economic system on the international stage. It fought against a political system of a highly imaginary nature. Imperialism had become more than a slogan. Stalin had elevated it to a negative creed. It was charged with emotion and coloured communist ideas about the political world outside the communist camp. Its political function was to curb the power of the West and to ally the struggle of the nationalists in Latin America, Asia, and Africa with the communist countries in a world-wide opposition against America, Britain, and their allies. In February 1960 Khrushchov declared in the Indian Parliament that the Soviet people rejoiced at the successful liberation struggle of the peoples of Asia, Africa, and Latin America. He pledged Soviet sympathy with and assistance to all nations in their struggle for independence.

Some of the Western countries were advanced, Khrushchov explained, merely because those of Asia, Africa, and Latin America were underdeveloped.[1] Communists retained the idea that events and conditions in the outside world of capitalism occurred by the design of the one evil power. Imperialism had intended the peoples of Asia and Africa to remain on a low standard of living, designed their exploitation, and fostered mutual strife and wars. It is difficult to discern how much of that interpretation was invented for agitation, and how much was genuine belief and public paranoia emanating from the Stalin period. After all, the English Liberals in the days of Lord Palmerston believed that every constitutional government and independent nation of Europe would be another step towards progress and would also become a natural ally of Britain. Russian communists viewed the struggling nations of Asia and Africa in a similar light and regarded them as natural allies in the common struggle against imperialism. They were not wholly right in that belief just as history has proved the English supporters of Italian independence wrong. The nations of Europe desired the diplomatic and naval assistance of Britain. Those of Africa and Asia welcomed Russian aid and technicians. But at the same time young nations are jealous guardians of their freedom of action and full national sovereignty.

In the nineteenth century Britain was too secure to fear almighty plotters and omnipresent fiends. Such collective fear, however, was much more in evidence and justified in the reign of Queen Elizabeth I, when the doctrinal division of Europe and political plots cast their shadows across the British Isles. After two devastating wars fought in this century on Russian soil the spectre of an almighty imperialist foe undoubtedly reflected a genuine collective fear, for Russia's position was not as secure after the Second World War as Britain's had been in the nineteenth century. Then it was Lord Palmerston who was regarded as the all-powerful revolutionary schemer by his Continental opponents in Germany and in Austria. Lenin's and Stalin's doctrine regarding imperialism meant that after their victory in the Second World War the Russian people continued to live in fear of a new war and regarded the world outside the communist camp with suspicion and hostility. Imperialism assumed a new meaning inside Russia. It spelt the inevitable advent of a third war of aggression against the Soviet Union. The new post-Stalinist doctrine of peaceful co-existence was a contradiction of the older concept. It maintained that capitalism was shrinking and would be overtaken by socialism even without war. This was adopted by the Twentieth Soviet Congress and confirmed by the Twenty-first Congress and once again in Khrushchov's speech addressed to the representatives of world communism in Bucharest in June 1960. Imperialism thus became a topic of political theory and debate of the highest importance within the communist camp. The new theory of co-existence was not accepted by Russia's allies. China and the German Democratic Republic, to judge by official pronouncements, remained more closely wedded to Stalin's interpretation of imperialism and the belief in the inevitable approach of a third world war between socialists and imperialists. And so that slogan assumed a new overtone of opposition to a policy of peaceful co-existence and—one suspects—to Russia's reluctance to share her nuclear weapons with her mighty communist neighbour. Agitators in China spoke out against imperialism when they really meant to voice criticism of Khrushchov's attempts to reach a modus vivendi with the United States. The different uses of the word within the communist camp revealed two different states of mind. No other political word has ever been fraught with such power and kept the peace of mankind in such fateful balance. In 1960 China and the German Democratic Republic in their public utterances appeared to be more militant in their anti-imperialism than the Soviet Union. The East German Government was in no mood to relax the cold war.

By 1960 Germany was divided in doctrine and politics as never before since the Reformation. The two German states on either side of the iron curtain were hostile to each other; and their leading intellectuals, if they met at all at international conferences, astonished other conference members by their bitter enmity. The only thing the two German governments had in common was their undoubted gain of power and influence within their own camp, which was derived from international tension. In the last years of Stalin's rule the Government of the German Democratic Republic appeared to be more Stalinist than Stalin. Their press did not hesitate to revive Nazi cliché and propaganda. Their attacks against the West—in the days of the notorious 'doctors plot'—hinted at the connexion between Jewish capitalists and American policy. Uncle Sam was given prominent Jewish features by cartoonists. He was depicted as the parasite who profited by wars, while other nations bled for his dollars.[1] East German radio stations at that time gave American voices a slightly Jewish accent or presented American speakers who spoke Yiddish for purposes of political caricature and ridicule. Dealing with subjects of the Middle East, German communist writers pointed to the alleged alliance between imperialism and international Jewry.

In July 1952 Walter Ulbricht presented the official view of the world situation. Its main theses were adopted by the Conference of the Socialist Unity Party. It began with the fundamental thesis of the divided world. 'Die Welt ist in zwei Lager gespalten, in das Lager des Friedens, der Demokratie und des Sozialismus und in das Lager des Imperialismus.'[2] The antithesis implied in the denominations, the camp of peace on the one hand and the camp of imperialism on the other, is clear. The camp of imperialism is the camp that is preparing for a new war. The term condemned the whole world as far as it had not yet become communist. Imperialism, Ulbricht explained, plundered the colonies and organized new wars, for wars were good business. He mentioned Britain, France, and the United States but reserved his sharpest attacks for the latter. American imperialism was the worst enemy of the peoples of Europe. It was the policy of the American war industry to undermine the national tradition and culture of the Germans, so as to remove the threat of national resistance against the Anglo-American policy of enslavement.[3] Another imperialist war, Ulbricht added, would, however, result in the downfall of capitalism and imperialism. Imperialism, in fact, carried its own destruction just like capitalism. After each imperialist war the camp of socialism emerged stronger and the camp of imperialism weaker. That theory was given special prominence in June 1955, when Ulbricht offered the Central Committee of his Party his version of co-existence. The obvious question was why the communists should not welcome a development leading towards a third world war and the final liquidation of imperialism. Ulbricht's answer was in keeping with the new official communist theory that the superiority of the communist system would be established by peaceful means, and that another world war would prove too costly in human lives and material wealth.[1]

The prospect of an American-Russian détente and a summit conference in 1959 and early in 1960 must have been viewed with misgivings and opposition in the German Democratic Republic. Its anti-imperialist agitation went on unrestrained. It continued to view the struggle against imperialism as the paramount world issue. A leading trade unionist suggested closer relations between the German Democratic Republic and the 'Arab-African nations' on the basis of a common struggle 'against imperialism and colonialism'.[2] Imperialism formed the main subject of a theoretical conference convened in January 1960. A thousand secretaries of the Socialist Unity Party and other communist functionaries of East Germany took part.[3] The struggle against imperialism on a global scale, which figured in their discussion and resolution, was a theme oddly at variance with the official Russian policy at that time and pointed to a closer harmony with the more aggressive views which were then entertained in China at the other side of the communist continent.

The triumph of the Chinese communists under the leadership of Mao Tse-tung after the Second World War was likened to the triumph of the Russian communists under the leadership of Lenin after the First by those who argued that communism had nothing to lose by imperialist wars but everything to gain. Mao Tse-tung adopted imperialism as a main slogan in the civil war and identified it with the power of the United States. He called for an anti-imperialist front with the Soviet Union and declared that U.S. imperialism had taken the place of fascist Germany, Italy, and Japan as the world's greatest menace.[4] Stalin's view of the divided world was whole-heartedly adopted by the Chinese. Chinese descriptions of the 'anti-democratic camp of imperialism' mentioned a plot to dominate the world and to push innocent people into the abyss of poverty and darkness. A strong flavour of Asian nationalism was injected into communist arguments. Stalin's radical and simple image of the divided world and the unabated world struggle was retained in China after Stalin's death, and so the Chinese communists began to view the international scene in a more radical and aggressive frame of mind than the Russians. To them a theory of peaceful co-existence with imperialism made no sense. The divergence of views between Peking and Moscow was reflected during the anniversary of Stalin's eightieth birthday in 1959, which was widely celebrated in China but not in Russia. It was significant that the Chinese communists praised Stalin as 'the implacable enemy of imperialism', as the leader who had stressed the need for maintaining a high degree of vigilance against imperialism and exposing imperialist intrigues. His message, official sources emphasized, had remained important. Imperialism was still the source of wars and dangerous plots. Here there was often a hint that Khrushchov was not fully alive to the danger of war-mongering imperialism. A Western traveller reported in 1959 that the term 'imperialists' could evoke fierce hatred in the hearts of the Chinese.[1] On the occasion of the tenth anniversary of the signing of the Sino-Soviet Treaty of Friendship early in 1960, all the Chinese made prominent mention of the determination of China and Russia to oppose the alleged strategy of the imperialists to split the socialist camp.[2] Celebrating Lenin's anniversary in April 1960 on the eve of the suspect summit conference in Paris, the Chinese did not conceal their quarrel with their Russian comrades over the central idea of the struggle against imperialism.

An editorial article published in the paper *Jenmin Jih Pao* dwelt at length on Lenin's principle that imperialism was the source of modern war. The article then declared that, despite the fact that the summit conference was about to begin, China could not see any substantial change in the war policy of U.S. imperialism. The paper urged its readers to spread Lenin's theory of imperialism and to expose the tricks adopted by imperialists. The paper concluded: 'Let the Chinese people and the other peoples of the world work together to secure even greater victories for Leninism, the Marxist theory of the epoch of imperialism and proletarian revolution, in the period of history that is now ensuing!'[3] On the same day at a rally held in Peking, the major address denounced the 'revisionists' who called adherence to Marxism-Leninism dogmatic. The speaker, Vice-Premier Liu Ting-yi, demanded an undiminished struggle against imperialism, U.S. imperialism in particular, 'the most vicious and cunning enemy of the people's revolution in all countries, of the national liberation movement, and of world peace. . . . If the proletariat in the capitalist countries is to win emancipation, if the peoples of the colonies and semi-colonies are to obtain national liberation, if the people of the world are to safeguard world peace, the spearhead of the struggle must be directed against U.S. imperialism', he said.[1] The Chinese uncompromising rejection of peaceful co-existence must have gained support within the communist camp after the events of May 1960 and the breakdown of the summit conference. Detailed information is still difficult to come by, but it is quite possible that the Chinese interpretation of the nature of imperialism was a factor in the situation.

During the following weeks the Chinese Government made it quite clear that China had not shared Khrushchov's optimism and did not believe in the possibility of peaceful co-existence with imperialism. The sooner imperialism was crushed the better. The *Red Flag*, the theoretical journal of the Chinese Communist Party, felt confident that after a nuclear war a communist world would be built 'on the debris of a dead imperialism'. Mao Tse-tung expressed himself in a similar way.[2] While *Pravda* opposed such radical and devastating views, the *Red Flag* in June 1960 took the Russian leaders to task. They were guilty of wishful thinking in supposing that communism could go on living side by side with imperialism. 'Imperialism', the Chinese paper wrote, 'will never change its nature till doom. The people have no alternative but to wage a struggle against it to the end.'[3] It was, therefore, quite wrong to suggest a policy of disarmament. The Chinese believed it would weaken the determination of the people to fight the enemy. China's policy of a forced pace in the increase of her industrial wealth was motivated by the desire to reach the status of a nuclear and technological world Power as quickly as possible so as to make her struggle against imperialism and her bid for communist leadership more effective.

When the first secretaries of the communist parties and other communist delegations arrived in Bucharest in June 1960 to take part in the Russian party congress, the dispute over the nature of imperialism and peaceful co-existence was already very prominent. It was not resolved in Bucharest. East Europe followed the Russian theory that a policy of peaceful co-existence was possible and preferable. The Chinese delegate, on the other hand, gave his endorsement of the

Moscow declaration of 1957 regarding peaceful co-existence with a comment that virtually opposed it. He said that American imperialism was aggressive, he opposed 'revisionists', and called for a united front in a struggle against imperialism, which should embrace not only the socialist camp but also the peoples of Latin America, Africa, and Asia.[1] Already in 1958 Mao Tse-tung had stressed the need for a united anti-imperialist struggle of the Afro-Asian and Latin American peoples and the communists. But was this, in fact, a common struggle? It is evident that ever since the days of Stalin imperialism had been more than a slogan, more even than an economic theory. It had been the main conceptual model of the nature and purpose of Anglo-American political and economic power which the communists possessed. It had been Stalin's political working hypothesis during the last years of his life. The Chinese fully upheld it while the Russians did not. The inter-communist dispute was, therefore, not a quarrel over a mere political slogan but a quarrel over the interpretation of political reality. One section of the communists argued, in fact, that the model had become a dangerous delusion in a world parts of which could be made un-inhabitable within a few seconds.

The history of the German people has demonstrated how a conceptual model easily deludes its own creators. Biological metaphors and racial theories prompted many German thinkers, including Nietzsche, to view Britain as a declining power. There was the model of the Western nations being old and decaying, Germany being young and rising; Britain and America were seen as declining because of their alleged inability to keep the Anglo-Saxon race free from the dangerously weakening admixture of Jewish blood. This led to the belief that the future of the world belonged to a pure Nordic master-race. For a con-siderable time many Germans were unable to regard the evolution of the British Commonwealth in any other light but that of the decline of British power, of defeat and retreat. Communist misjudgement of the Commonwealth had a similar origin. To a mind that is pre-occupied with the acquisition of greater power it is hard to believe that other minds are not similarly pre-occupied. Nationalism and communism both wanted political power and were rarely satisfied with the power they possessed but wanted more. The Continent of Europe has given birth to that insatiable hunger for power in its nationalist form as well as in its communist form. It lacked the experience and political tradition which the Anglo-Saxons possessed in the field of political co-operation, in compromise and improvisation. It was prestige-ridden. The nationalist power-seekers of Europe failed to develop any system of co-operation. The communist power-seekers have remained essentially political Bonapartists. Centralized state-control is a characteristic feature of their system together with planned efficiency and directed popular opinion. They show no ability of co-operating with the rest of the world, nor have they any plans about co-operation on a global scale, apart from the negative concept of the struggle against imperialism. This does not mean that their criticism of the use of Anglo-American power has always been unjustified, or their suspicion of the existence of aggressive elements inside the United States and the Federal Republic of Germany unfounded. Future historians reviewing the events of 1960 may perhaps reach the conclusion that the enemies of peaceful co-existence on either side of the iron curtain were tragically allied in that year. Nevertheless, the imperialist obsession led the communists to a mistaken view of reality on numerous occasions.

Could imperialism be imagined to surrender its power voluntarily? Could monopolist capitalism ever agree to contract its markets rather than expand them? According to communist belief that was a contradictory thought. What then was the explanation communists had to offer for the post-war development of the British Commonwealth? At first it was maintained, as we saw earlier in this chapter, that British imperialism was being taken over by American imperialism. Again, this was partly true. Britain did hand over political control to the United States in the Mediterranean and in the Middle East. It did not, however, result in any serious clash between British and American interests, nor did that view reveal another important part of the truth, the deliberate development of a self-governing family of Commonwealth nations by Britain. That phenomenon was totally unintelligible to communists. Their reaction was curiously German—so much in Russian political thought is either French or German. They called the Commonwealth idea a British trick to fool foreigners. The Germans had said exactly the same about British liberalism earlier in the century and during the anti-liberal campaign in the days of Treitschke. Stalin could not believe that India had become an independent nation, set free by the British imperialists. Such a thing did not make sense in communist eyes and, therefore, could not exist. Chinese communists reacted in exactly the same way. Nehru was at first an imperialist puppet in their eyes. A few years later the Chinese recognized the fact that India was truly independent of Britain, although they did not attempt to explain that process. They hailed India's neutralism and welcomed India as great fellow-Asians whenever Nehru opposed British or American political ideas and moves. No sooner did Indian interests clash with Chinese, however, than India was declared an imperialist. In spring 1959 anti-Indian feelings ran high in China over India's attitude in Tibet. The May-Day slogans, therefore, ran: 'American, British and Indian imperialists are siding with the rebels.'[1] This was the Stalinist approach to international affairs again. Imperialism stood for any power which was unfriendly to communist policy. Communist expansion was liberation. Opposition to it was imperialist. The rise of an African nation was a welcome struggle against imperialism, the rise of an East European nation was a damnable instigation of imperialism.

The division of the world into imperialist and anti-imperialist halves by communist theorists implied that the Afro-Asian nations and the communists fought a *common* anti-imperialist struggle. This has been another delusion wrought by semantics. At best it was wishful thinking on the part of the communists. In 1948 the Zionists accepted Czech arms and Soviet support in the United Nations. They genuinely sought Russian friendship, and many Zionist leaders were East Europeans, who had been brought up on socialist ideas. As soon as their interests ran counter to those of the Soviet Union, however, they were no longer fighters against imperialism but, in communist nomenclature, its stooges. Afro-Asian and Latin nationalism, in fact, did respond to the anti-imperialist call in the post-war era. It was prepared to accept moral and material support from any wealthy and influential power, but domination from none. It was a communist illusion to believe that each colonial nation struggling for liberation was its ally. Even Europe contained a number of nations that did not fit into the communist picture of the divided world. Sweden, Switzerland, Ireland, and Finland had kept aloof from military alliances, and some of them had proved their readiness to fight against domination of the West or the East. The coloured colonial peoples fought against the rule of the white man, any white man. Their struggle was by no means identical with communism despite the wish of the communists to make it so, despite the frequent American and British misinterpretations that it was so, and despite the widespread use of imperialism as political slogan by the Afro-Asian nations.

Before the Second World War agitation against colonial rule was led by socialists and communists. It was conducted on behalf of the colonial peoples rather than by the colonial peoples. During the late 1930's that agitation was reinforced by Italian and German propaganda for the purpose of weakening British and French political power in Africa and the Middle East. For a long time Germans had been reluctant to stir a colonial people against the rule of a white European country. It was only in 1939 that Nazi propaganda in the Middle East and in Africa assumed the dimensions of a virulent campaign conducted on a large scale.[1] Many Africans and Asians were politically trained in Britain, Germany, and Russia before the Second World War. Their anti-imperialist agitation at home, therefore, blended British, German, and Russian ideas and employed them for their own political ends.

Occasional Indian voices against imperialism were raised even before the First World War,[2] but the massive use of imperialism as a slogan in the mouth of a coloured political leader became a general phenomenon only after the Second World War. The emancipation of the Afro-Asian nations has not been achieved without conflict and bloodshed. Western statesmen had their share in the responsibility for the outbreak of violence in Palestine, Egypt, India, Algeria, and the Congo. Propaganda, however, is not interested in fair judgement and lays all the blame at the door of the political enemy. The pattern of an alleged imperialist conspiracy was often adhered to as the most effective way of creating and influencing public emotions. The partition of India was attributed to imperialist intrigue just as the partition of Palestine was presented as a device to guarantee the continuation of British power in those regions. Jews as well as Arabs blamed British imperialism for many of their misfortunes. Jews often argued that the disturbances of the 1930's and the hostility of the Arabs were the work of British imperialist interests. Many were convinced after the Second World War that Jews and Arabs would be able to get on together much better once British power had been removed from Palestine. In the eyes of the Arabs, on the other hand, Zionism was the expression of Anglo-American design on their lands. Theirs was the illusion that all history occurs by design and plan.

Gamal Abdul Nasser conceived history as a plot and vividly personalized imperialism, reflecting on the deeper meaning of the struggle in Palestine. '...All our peoples', he wrote, 'seemed to be victims of a well-knit conspiracy which deliberately suppressed the realities of what was happening....'[1] Imperialism, Nasser believed, was the prime force in history, 'the great force that is imposing a murderous, invisible siege upon the whole region, a siege one hundred times more powerful and pitiless than that which was laid upon us in our trenches at Faluja'.[2] Imperialism means to Nasser the assertion of superior foreign power over the Arabs and over the peoples of Africa, for Egypt is both Arab and African. Since the Revolution of July 1952 anti-imperialist propaganda has been the key-note of the Egyptian press and radio. There has been hardly a day when the slogan of imperialism has been omitted by Egyptian broadcasters and public leaders.

The Voice of the Arabs would inform its listeners that in Aden British imperialism was fighting its last battle in the Arab South. The Cairo Home Service predicted the doom of imperialism in Egypt, Algeria, and the Sudan and deplored Bourguiba's or King Hussein's alleged subservience to French and British imperialist masters. Cairo Radio did not confine its broadcasts to the Arabs but addressed the peoples south of the Sahara in their native languages militating against the stooges of European settlers in Kenya and threatening 'to bury them in the same hole with imperialism'. Cuba's conflict with the United States was given prominence and sympathetic treatment by the Egyptian press and radio as a struggle against imperialism. The Shah of Persia was severely attacked for recognizing Israel, as a man 'who sold himself to his masters, imperialism and Zionism'. The link between imperialism and Zionism was an established fact in Egyptian political theory. It had been seen at work in 1956 when France, Britain, and Israel attacked Egypt.

Israel, Egyptians argued, could not have been founded and maintained as a viable state without the assistance of the United States, France, and Britain. Imperialism used Israel for its own interests not only in the Middle East but also in Africa. As the imperialists had to withdraw from Africa they employed Israel, for they assisted Israel, and Israel assisted African nations. Thus through the political influence in Africa, Egyptians argued in 1960, Israeli interests were advanced and with them imperialist interests, too.[1] That was the 'masked imperialism' of foreign aid. The image of the imperialist was given the features of the Jewish mask behind which lurked an American, Briton, or Frenchman. Essentially, the imperialist was anti-Arab. He wished to divide the Arab world. Speaking at Latakia in February 1960 President Nasser put his main political theme into these words: 'The imperialist stooges and agents have always tried to divide the Arab people into small countries and emirates. Syria faced this threat from France. The target of these imperialist attempts was not Syria alone, but the destruction of the entire Arab homeland, every part of Arab nationalism.'[2] The political intention of those words is not hard to detect. Nasser's anti-imperialist propaganda was used in support of his attempt to federate the Arabs under his leadership. The 'imperialist stooge' was a name bestowed on any Arab leader who opposed Nasser's bid for more power. It did not take other Arab leaders long to return that propaganda in the same fashion. Some Arab governments began to speak of 'the new imperialism which Cairo is seeking', and to accuse the United Arab Republic of plotting with Zionists and imperialists.[3]

The anti-imperialist propaganda voiced in Iraq did not differ much from that heard in Egypt, except, of course, when President Nasser was presented as an imperialist agent or ally. Leninist tradition blended with Nazi tradition in several curious ways. During the political trials of 1959 in connexion with an attempt to overthrow the rule of General Kassem, the president of the court, Colonel Mahdawi, made a name for himself as anti-imperialist. In January 1960 he declared in the tradition of Lenin that imperialism was the final stage of capitalist monopolism. Imperialism had received the Arab countries as part of the booty after the First World War. It then used religion as a pretext to divide the Arabs. American, British, and French imperialism desired to enslave the

319

Arabs because it desired their oil.[1] Another time the anti-imperialist tirade exhibited Nazi features. Imperialism was depicted as the tool of freemasons and Jews, who were said to work in close political alliance with the British. Iraquis were told—in the style of Dr Goebbels—that freemasons were organized as 'an imperialist society which serves world Jewry—that is, a Zionist society, and we know that the honorary president of this society is the British sovereign'.[2]

In the 1950's imperialism became more closely linked with Hobson's second anti-imperialist slogan, colonialism. Among the Arabs and other colonial peoples those two expressions became synonymous. Many educated Arabs, when asked to translate the corresponding political term, *Ista'amar*, into English, would call it imperialism, while others offered colonialism or both as their version of the Arabic term. Colonialism is, in fact, the correct translation, but the two terms had become so closely associated in their minds that many Arabs regarded them as identical.

While the anti-imperialist campaign was being waged by the Arabs, who regarded Israel as the creature of Western imperialism and one of its bridge-heads in the Arab East, there were at the same time Israelis on the other side of the barbed wire, who hoped to achieve a 'Semitic Federation'. They declared the political *raison d'être* and mission of such a federation to be a common Arab-Israeli struggle against imperialism.[3]

In Persia imperialism was a prominent slogan of Persian nationalism, particularly under the leadership of Dr Mossadegh during the Anglo-Persian conflict of 1951. In the foothills of the Himalayan Range the magic word was uttered in every valley. The Premier of Nepal hailed Mr Nehru with the words: 'You have inspired the world with your efforts for world peace and the struggle against colonialism and imperialism', when Nehru visited Katmandu in summer 1959. In India and South East Asia the effects of Nazi propaganda on anti-imperialist ideology are no longer in evidence. There nationalism derived its anti-imperialist ideas from European communism and adapted it for its own agitation. This did not mean that nationalism was ideologically linked with communism. In Malaya nationalism fought against 'British imperialists' and 'left wing adventurers', declaring both communists and 'colonialist imperialists' to be the enemies of national liberty.

The Slogan of Imperialism after the Second World War

In Singapore, the Prime Minister declared in August 1960, that his government was aware of the hostile intentions of the British and the communists. If a collision took place between communists and 'colonialist imperialists', the People's Action Party Government, he said, would let them break their heads on each other.[1]

The political arguments voiced by the leaders of Indonesia's Guided Democracy showed a similar blend of nationalism and anti-Westernism. During their struggle against the Dutch, Indonesians argued that the Netherlands would not be able to oppose the Indonesian struggle for national independence but for the assistance it received from America and Britain. Marshall Aid was, in Indonesian eyes, an imperialist design to enable the Netherlands to uphold their hated domination in the Indonesian archipelago. Dr A. Sukarno developed his own theory of imperialism. He believed that imperialism had systematically subjected all the peoples living along the highway that led from the Atlantic Ocean to the Indian Ocean and the South China Sea. He called it 'the Life-line of Imperialism'. The Indonesian Republic was proclaimed in August 1945, but as it was situated on the imperialist highway, imperialism attempted to strangle the national liberation. Post-war history, as interpreted by Dr Sukarno, witnessed the struggle against imperialism not only in Indonesia but along the whole line of colonial rule, from Gibraltar, Cyprus, the Suez Canal, the shores of the Red Sea, Aden, India to West Irian—the Indonesian name for West New Guinea. Those peoples had the experience of colonial rule in common as well as the desire for national self-determination. It was in Bandung, south of the Indonesian capital of Djakarta, where in April 1954 Dr Sukarno was pleased to welcome the delegates to the first Asian-African Conference, to recall their common struggle against imperialism, and to refer to his 'Life-line of Imperialism' triumphantly as a thing of the past.[2]

At the Bandung Conference Asian and African delegates were inspired by the new independence their countries had won. They all expressed their opposition to foreign domination, condemned colonialism as an evil, and affirmed the principle of national self-determination. But if communist delegates derived any satisfaction from the anti-imperialist tone of the conference, their gratification was only partially justified.

321

Among the peoples of the 'imperialist life-line' imperialism did not mean the same thing as in communist countries. In communist countries the political antithesis to imperialism was socialism. At Bandung the political antithesis to imperialism *qua* colonialism was national independence and the right of every small nation to live its own life and decide its own destiny. Communism cannot concede that right, as Stalin had shown before, and Mao Tse-tung proved afterwards. The semantic illusion of the common anti-imperialist front, which was still powerful at Bandung, was soon dispelled by events in Hungary and in Tibet. The communist powers have never admitted the right of small nations to oppose the decisions of Moscow and Peking.

The voice of the African peoples south of the Sahara Desert was not yet very strong at the Bandung Conference. During the following years the struggle for national freedom shifted to the Dark Continent, the darkest of all continents in a political sense. There the oppression and exploitation of Africans by Europeans, unresolved racial conflicts, the clash between tribal traditions and science, the work of disease and ignorance, and a nature often hostile to human habitation were open for all to see. To the ears of the Algerians engaged in a struggle against France, the politically conscious Africans of Nyasaland and Southern Rhodesia, the victims of Afrikaner racialist oppression in South Africa, the claims of Western statesmen to represent a free, democratic world sounded worse than empty propaganda boasts. They sounded like a patent lie and bitter mockery. Imperialism and colonialism were no vague words in areas where a small number of white men attempted to deny political and human rights to millions of Africans. African political literature, African party organization, and African leadership are young and under-developed. Illiteracy is still very high. Though millions of Africans cannot read, they can understand what their leaders mean by imperialism. In the post-war period the word has been echoed in the smallest desert oasis and in remote bush villages. It has been drummed through the thick forests and carried across the rift valleys. It always meant foreign rule. Its antithesis has always been freedom. South of the Sahara neither Nazi nor communist ideology had any important effect on the connotation of the word. No propaganda emanating from Moscow or Peking could match the pass laws of South Africa or the

French atomic explosions in the Sahara. They spoke a stronger language. African leaders did not elaborate economic and political theories of imperialism. When they addressed their people in English or in a native tongue, they attacked racial discrimination and foreign domination and were understood. The hostility against Britain and America, which accompanied anti-imperialist agitation in other parts of the world, played only a minor part in Africa where the active sympathy of the United States and the United Kingdom with the aspirations of African nationalism and the assistance of the British people towards the progress of African self-government, had been the practical experience of African civil servants and politicians alike. The peoples of Nigeria could pronounce imperialism without a feeling of hatred against Britain, for they knew and acknowledged the friendship of the British and accepted the Commonwealth, dedicated as it was to the rule of law, multi-racial society, tolerance, self-government, and freedom of expression. In a world that was still unsafe and inexperienced in the management of power and economics on a global scale, the Commonwealth offered a vast fund of administrative experience, opportunity for consultation and economic development as well as an important measure of military security. So in 1960 a Nigerian could be a staunch anti-imperialist and an equally staunch friend of Britain and the Commonwealth. There was hope that by 1970 this would be true of many more African nations. The Commonwealth alone in the world possessed a skill and tradition in one political art which could not be found elsewhere in the the world, the separation of powers—not only in its common traditional meaning of separation between the power to legislate, to administer, and to judge, but also in another equally important sense, the separation of power from the whims of mass emotion. And there are other political arts in which the Commonwealth has no rival. It is the accumulated wisdom necessary to ensure a smooth and universally accepted way of political criticism, the preparation of an alternative government, and the handing over of power without violence. At present the overriding preoccupation of the Africans is still the struggle against foreign domination and racial discrimination, the fight against imperialism as they understand it. Once self-government and freedom have been fully achieved, the real problems involved in the art of government will become more apparent and with it the need for political models which no other association of free peoples can provide in like manner as the Commonwealth. Emancipation from imperial rule alone does not solve all problems of Africa and may create many new ones.

The greatest evil of imperialism as a political slogan has been wrought in the minds of men, because it was so often employed as a toxicant. It could whip up emotions, but at the same time it diminished reason and judgement. It obscured the genuine political problems which are bound to follow the liquidation of imperial government and the universal installation of national independence, problems of the use, distribution, limitation, and administration of power in a national state. Can it be, one is tempted to ask, that in 1960 those problems are still approached by the young nations of Asia and Africa in the tradition of an era which is beyond recall, that some have copied European masters so well that they themselves should wish to expand and dominate?

We have come to the end of our study of the most prominent political slogan the world has ever known, at a time when the end of its life is not yet in sight. In the course of its astonishing career it has changed its meaning many times. We ignored its first meaning and appearance in the seventeenth and eighteenth centuries, when 'imperialist' was occasionally used to denote a politician and supporter of the Habsburg Empire and the political interests of Vienna, because such an occasional reference could not prove a genuine ancestry. We found the birth of our slogan in France, where it meant the desire to restore the glory of the Empire, and where later on it stood for the pompous pageantry, the personal rule, and adventurous foreign policy of Napoleon III. We saw how this expression of imperialism was transferred to Britain, and how it became a slogan directed against Disraeli's government, meaning an alleged bombastic personal rule coupled with jingoism and a foreign policy of military threats and conquests. Within a short time imperialism changed its meaning again and became allied with the British desire to establish closer ties with kinsmen overseas. Towards the end of the last century imperialism incorporated other political and moral sentiments such as social progress at home and an imagined Anglo-Saxon mission to educate colonial races in Africa and Asia. This was the era of Joseph

Chamberlain, which evoked a strong liberal and radical opposition. Again imperialism was turned into a slogan of political opposition against the Boer War and against all military expansionism. This time the opposition was not confined to Britain, but united liberal opinion in Europe and America. It gave rise to an economic theory concerning the new and dangerous phase of expanding capitalism, which originated in Britain and was adapted to Marxism by European socialists and to an historical interpretation of events which led to the outbreak of the First World War. We then saw how Europeans identified imperialism with the notion of Anglo-American world domination, and how the term assumed new shades of meaning after the Second World War, when it served the political propaganda of the cold war, opposition to American influence and to colonial rule, and even assumed new overtones of opposition within the communist fold.

In the nineteenth century imperialism reflected a deeper undercurrent of political sentiment. It was a symptom of the attitude adopted by the British people towards their own Empire and was closely connected with imperial issues. Now that the term has come into global use, the question arises whether it reflects deeper problems which underlie the frequent exchange of abuse among political writers and statesmen. We suspect that this is, indeed, the case. Anti-imperialism reflects a genuine national desire to be free from all outside interference and domination, while the world of 1960 is unable to fulfil that desire and will be even less likely to do so in the future. The quest for national self-determination and world-order in a post-imperial era is not free from inherent contradictions and confused political thought. Colonial empires may be dissolving, but a good many other things are dissolving with them without which the new nations cannot prosper.

XIII

SELF-DETERMINATION AND WORLD ORDER

Behind imperialism as a political slogan there lies hidden a pressing problem of world order, which is likely to occupy the minds of many generations to come. It is improbable, therefore, that the slogan has reached the end of its career in 1960. It is possible to predict its continued existence as the struggle for a new world order continues. The cry of imperialism is likely to be heard again and again with every attempt to bring the establishment of an effective world government a step nearer. In the early stage of its English career imperialism was essentially the expression of a protest against the real or imagined expansion of political power at home. Other expressions used in that connexion were Caesarism and despotism. By the end of the last century imperialism had become the expression of a protest against the expansion of political power abroad. Those who first voiced the protest were citizens of the expanding states themselves, Britons and Americans. Liberal opinion demanded not only respect for the rights of the individual but also respect for the rights of the Filipinos and the Boers, for the right of each nation to government by consent. Absolute rule and centralized universal dominion were two features of the Roman imperial tradition which the Victorian Liberal rejected, despite the sentimental idealization of the Roman tradition given to him by his educators. British policy in the nineteenth century gave constant encouragement to small nations in their struggle for independence in South America and on the European Continent. Sympathy for the Greeks and the Poles had been a mark of European liberalism. The French Revolution had proclaimed liberty, equality, and fraternity as principles governing the political relationship among individuals. British Liberals desired to see the same principles applied to nations as well as to individuals. Gladstone's scheme of 'a sisterhood of nations, equal, independent'[1] reflected an ideal of world order which Victorian Liberals hoped to achieve. It explicitly rejected the Latin tradition, the *imperium* in its modern shape in nineteenth-century France. It regarded the vision of universal dominion as 'detestable'. Mr Gladstone did not say whether he thought universal power would be merely corrupt or also inefficient. Europe's experience of Napoleonic power was that it proved oppressive, while the strong men of Germany, Austria-Hungary, South Europe and South America were often as corrupt and inefficient as they were oppressive; and equally dangerous to their neighbours in their desire for military expansion. The British Liberals of Gladstone's days found few European countries whose government could appeal to them; American Liberals even less so, being either refugees from European oppression themselves or their children. They were, therefore, all the more shocked when they found their own countries shattering the ideal of a 'sisterhood of equal and independent nations' by the employment of force against the Boers and the Filipinos. They could accept the First World War only as a war fought to restore, realize, and safeguard that ideal. The fate of the Belgians and the Serbs stirred David Lloyd George. He himself belonged to a small nation. The world, he pointed out in one of his emotional addresses at the beginning of the war, owed a good deal to the small nations.

In the nineteenth century Britain's support of the cause of national emancipation had gained her important friends in South America and in the Mediterranean. By adhering to 'the principle of nationality' in the First World War British statesmen hoped to win more friends in Central Europe and in the Levant, weakening at the same time the resources of the Powers which were fighting against the allies.[1] In the case of Balfour and Lloyd George there is little room for doubt that their enthusiasm for national self-determination was not dictated by political expediency alone, but by a deeply-felt belief in the right of all nations to determine the form of their government and their political status. Wilson knew that he would not obtain the support of the American people for an imperial war. More than any other statesman in the West he established the recognition of the principle of national self-determination. During the war his eloquence pleaded for the rights of the Czechs, Croats, Magyars, Rumanians, Serbs, Armenians, 'the rights of peoples, great or small, weak or powerful—their equal right to freedom and security and self-government and to a participation upon fair terms in the economic opportunities of the world'.[2] In an address to Congress, which dealt with German and Austrian peace terms, in February 1918 Wilson stressed what he believed was the real cause of the war. 'This war had its roots in the disregard of the rights of small nations and of nationalities, which lacked the union and the force to make good their claim to determine their own allegiances and their own forms of political life.' Again Wilson gave special prominence to the principle and name of self-determination when he said: 'National aspirations must be respected; peoples may now be dominated and governed only by their consent. "Self-determination" is not a mere phrase. It is an imperative principle of action, which statesmen will henceforth ignore at their peril.'[1] A few weeks later the American President, speaking at Baltimore, contrasted the German military empire and its ideals of power, the principle that the strong must rule the weak, with the American ideals of justice, humanity, liberty, and 'the principle of the free self-determination of nations upon which all the modern world insists'.[2] For Wilson imperialism was the very negation of national self-determination. Imperialism was embodied in his eyes in the colonial empires of his allies but also in the multi-national empire of his enemies. He was convinced that the world would be a happier place to live in, if the nations of the Ottoman and the Danubian empires would be allowed to govern themselves. Lenin was in fundamental agreement with Wilson on that issue. For Americans and Bolshevists alike self-determination and imperialism were mutually exclusive political principles. In 1918 both hoped to establish a new world order to safeguard the former and destroy the latter. In the judgement of the Bolshevists, however, the destruction of imperialism implied the destruction not only of the Austrian, the German, and the Ottoman empires but the destruction of capitalism as well. Wilson had spoken of the right of the small nations to freedom and security. Did national sovereignty bestow on a people greater security? How was it possible to gain both national self-determination *and* security, if Europe was to be broken up into many more bellicose, quarrelsome nation-states, if the Continent was to be divided by many more miles of uneasy and disputed borders?

Wilson had never envisaged the principle of self-determination to be realized in isolation. He had always insisted on world security to be derived not from national self-determination but from international organization. He hoped to see a new world order arise in which there would be not only free nations but also a physical security force in existence, powerful enough to enforce international law. He realized that the maintenance of international order would require the partial abolition of state sovereignty. Champion of national self-determination as he was, Wilson never regarded national absolutism as desirable or as compatible with world order. The organization of peace which he wished to see established would combine the military forces of the free nations for the purpose of police action anywhere in the world. His early pronouncements on that subject made during the war were couched in a stronger and more definite language than his post-war pronouncements on an international force which already reflected his awareness of a growing resistance to his ideals in Europe and in America. In 1917 he declared that mere agreements were no guarantee for a secure peace, unless they were backed by a force greater than the force of any big nation or combination of nations.[1] In 1918 he still dwelt on the need for an armed force. He wanted the nations to govern themselves, but he also wanted them to consent to be governed by the law, by a law that could be enforced, if needs be, through an international organization. His concept of a league of nations never lost sight of the moral and the physical force on which the projected league should rest. 'Armed force is in the background in this program,' he commented in February 1919, 'but it *is* in the background, and if the moral force of the world will not suffice, the physical force of the world shall.'[2] Wilson's opposition to imperialism, therefore, did not mean objection to the employment of superior force in the interest of global order. He desired to move the control of military force from the empires to a higher level of a global organization. He did not believe the world could have security without the existence of such a superior force. His concept of world order also implied that a defaulting nation could be brought to justice by coercion. 'What we seek is the reign of law, based upon the consent of the governed and sustained by the organized opinion of mankind.'[3] That was Wilson's formula. National self-determination was conditional, not absolute. Respect for the law and for its neighbours precluded a state from the possession of absolute power and sovereignty.

In the tradition of English political philosophy and American communal life Wilson believed that a nation, upon entering the supreme organization of civilized mankind, gained security of existence as a legal right at the price of losing its absolute sovereignty as its natural right. He said at Indianapolis in September 1919: 'Every man who makes a choice to respect the rights of his neighbours deprives himself of absolute sovereignty.'[1] No American president has ever before or since been so insistent that American world leadership demands clear operational ideas about world order and global objectives as Wilson was in the last active years of his tragic career. Stalin, we saw, solved the problem of conditional national self-determination in a cruder and more brutal way. Wilson's successors and colleagues in other countries abandoned any solution and hoped for the best. They partially incorporated the principle of national self-determination but failed to provide the essential complement to national freedom—international, enforceable law. General Smuts had his early misgivings and warned against such a course of action. He feared Europe was being turned into a Balkans on a vaster scale. In October 1918 he prophesied: 'With the creation of an "independent" Poland, there will be a chain of these discordant fragments right across Europe, from Finland in the north to Turkey in the south. No league of Nations could hope to prevent a wild war-dance of these so-called free nations in the future. . . .'[2]

The record of the new nation-states during the period between the two world wars was, indeed, full of set-backs and strife. Smuts' gloomy foreboding proved justified. The early 1920's were filled with angry border disputes among the new countries themselves or along the borders between the new countries and the old. Almost every month Europe had the name of another border town as a household word of crisis; Fiume, Vilna, Teschen, Klagenfurt, Temesvar, Memel, the Burgenland, Upper Silesia, the Corridor, and the Ulster boundary aroused national passion somewhere. Some European nations had failed to obtain a state of their own in 1919 and became restive. Ruthenians, Ukrainians, Slovaks, Croats, Slovenes, and even the Flemings showed signs of dissatisfaction with their political status. In some new states the position of the national majority was so precarious that the ruling nationals believed they could maintain their state only by a policy of intolerance towards other national minorities. Lack of security along the border was matched by lack of stability within the states themselves, many of which turned into dictatorships. As soon as world trade took a turn for the worse, the small national states, in their constant but vain quest for economic self-sufficiency, suffered more than the larger federations and empires. This in turn increased national and racial tension within. The basic fault of inter-war Europe was national absolutism, which led to the natural law of the jungle. National aspirations were not restrained but were occasionally encouraged for political ends by mightier friends. Polish expansionism by force, for example, had the tacit approval of France. In post-imperial Europe, in fact, each new national state tended to become the centre of expansionist aspirations, which were democratic and often in keeping with the principle of self-determination but essentially based on the rule of force. The law of the jungle was not always so clearly visible in the West, where a false belief in the power of the League of Nations was widespread, especially in the English-speaking world. However, nobody could have had any illusions any more in 1938, when from all the sides vultures assembled to tear apart the dying state of Czechoslovakia. The independent Irish state on the other end of Europe, depressed and poverty-ridden, very much like Poland, by its own weakness and policy of non-co-operation during the critical years of the Second World War, proved to be a security risk to Britain and the United States right to the invasion of Normandy in 1944. National absolutism made Europeans blind to regional considerations. They never asked whether a foreign province was prosperous and well-governed, and if so were content to leave it at that. They asked: 'Did it ever belong to *us*? And why does it not now?' When in the 1930's it had become clear that the many national states of Europe could secure for their citizens, apart from sentiment, neither security nor prosperity or freedom, a new scramble for Europe began, which led to the Second World War. Once more an American President won the hearts and the hopes of millions.

F. D. Roosevelt conveyed a public image of himself and handled political issues in a way which made him more endearing than Wilson; but he lacked the profoundness of Wilson's political thought and global vision. He was a better public figure and statesman but an inferior thinker. His utterances were often of a calculated, pleasing vagueness, comforting but meaningless. He said he hoped to see the world secure, disarmed, and all the small nations free and independent; a vision full of incompatible and contradictory thought. Stalin was more brutal than President Roosevelt and more consistent. He saw that Soviet security permitted only a limited measure of national sovereignty to the nations under his control. Russians and Americans were equally opposed to Wilson's federal solution of the world security problem. Stalin and Roosevelt and their political advisers insisted on the retention of absolute sovereignty. Wilson's bitter political failure was so much in Roosevelt's mind that he hesitated to be too precise and specific about possible American international obligations arising out of a projected world-order. In his declaration on the Four Freedoms he proposed to achieve freedom from fear by such a thorough disarmament 'that no nation will be in a position to commit an act of physical aggression against any neighbour—anywhere in the world'.[1] He did not say how such a general disarmament was to be brought about and to be maintained. Nor did he make it clear how real freedom from fear could be gained by such a method. Would the world be safer against outbreaks of collective crime without armed forces? Who would control and guarantee disarmament and how? Concrete, operational ideas were not to be found in Roosevelt's public utterances on the post-war world. The Atlantic Charter of 1941 was kept equally vague and comforting. The British Prime Minister had favoured a reference to an effective international organization. President Roosevelt favoured a security system in which Britain and the United States took over the policing duties, but he was aware of the strong suspicion many Americans had of international commitments.[2] The result was a declaration which embodied the right of national self-determination and the prospect of general disarmament. What if a nation refused to disarm, or if it determined to commit such a crime as the extermination of a racial or religious minority? In a radio address delivered in February 1943 the President answered that question in the following words: 'The right of self-determination included in the Atlantic Charter does not carry with it the right of any government to commit wholesale murder or the right to make slaves of its own people or of any other peoples in the world.'[3]

He saw, therefore, that national governments would have to recognize certain definite limits to their power, and that they might become guilty of a crime. Who could convict them and restore the law? The federal system of the United States as a legal and physical limitation of state power was not accepted as a model. Senator Vandenberg confessed his relief when he learned that the administration did not have a federal structure for a post-war world in mind. He disliked the idea of a world state and the use of an international force in the maintenance of world order.[1] Without such a force world security could be achieved only by the continued joint exertion of the war-time allies. Hull and Roosevelt first had such a solution in mind, which was also referred to as the Four Policemen Method. The United States, the Soviet Union, the British Commonwealth, and China were to police the world jointly. Small states would be revived at the same time on the basis of regional plebiscites.[2] This was an imperial solution in the sense that the big Powers were to make their contribution towards world peace and stability as sovereign Powers extending their influence *beyond* their own territory; each contributing policing Power at the same time remained its absolute master in its own house. Their policing control would effect only other, smaller nations. This imperial scheme of world order had the advantage of utilizing the existing machinery of government and armed forces. On the other hand, it provided no recognized vote for other nations in the administration of global security and could only work as long as the major Powers remained in fundamental agreement with one another. In 1944 Roosevelt modified his view in favour of a more federal scheme, with the United Nations as the supreme enforcing authority. Isolationist suspicion in the United States had decreased to such an extent as to enable President Roosevelt to be blunt. In a radio address on foreign policy in October 1944 he declared: 'The Council of the United Nations must have the power to act quickly and decisively to keep the peace by force, if necessary.' The accent of that declaration was on the word quickly. Quick action precluded making it dependent on national parliaments and on Congress. Having possible isolationist objections in mind Roosevelt continued:

A policeman would not be a very effective policeman if, when he saw a felon break into a house, he had to go to the Town Hall and call a town meeting to

333

issue a warrant before the felon could be arrested. So to my simple mind it is clear that, if the world organization is to have any reality at all, our American representative must be endowed in advance by the people themselves, by constitutional means through their representatives in the Congress, with authority to act. If we do not catch the international felon when we have our hands on him, if we let him get away with his loot because the Town Council has not passed an ordinance authorizing his arrest, then we are *not* doing our share to prevent another world war.[1]

In the same address, however, Roosevelt warned that the development of such a world organization would take time and that in the meantime the effective conduct of the war and the peace must rest on the co-operation of the four great Powers. Yet by 1947 the war-time alliance of the Big Four had disappeared, before the United Nations Organization had developed a capacity for policing the world, paralysed as it often was by the veto of a major Power. It was merely an association of absolute sovereignties and possessed as much effective power as its members were willing to give it. At times it was completely powerless. That was President Truman's dilemma. He found little reason to hope that either the imperial or the federal scheme of world order would work, but he preferred the federal ideal of Wilson and exerted American influence through the United Nations rather than outside it. He could not rely entirely on the United Nations Organization, however, as the rift between East and West widened and so had to devise with his Western allies a number of regional pacts such as NATO. Stalin re-inforced the imperial power of Russia inside the Communist bloc. Truman, on the other hand, wanted to see the withdrawal of imperial control not only on the part of Russia but also on the part of Britain.

The withdrawal of imperial forces from a country is by no means a guarantee for a new golden age. In the past interested writers have exaggerated the evils of imperial rule and over-stated the benefits of national self-determination. The slogan of imperialism has done a disservice to political thought by confusing the issue. Unless national policy and national aspirations can be effectively prevented by a superior force from degenerating into collective crimes, the newly-gained freedom is of questionable content and often gives way to licence. Personal security and economic prosperity, the rights of minorities to their own collective existence, and the safety of the whole region are not necessarily better looked after when all imperial control is gone. Those can be lost in a national state, where a crippling military burden and national or religious intolerance make a mockery of the officially proclaimed new era of national freedom and glory. When British imperial power and protection were withdrawn from India, the door was opened to communal strife. Reliable figures of the ensuing massacres are hard to come by, but the number of refugees who had to leave their homes exceeded eight millions. In 1900 world sympathy was on the side of the Boers. In 1960 the picture has changed, and it has become clear that the abolition of Pax Britannica has not improved the lot of South Africa. Nor was the triumph of the principle of self-determination in Palestine an unqualified success. The partition of India produced a state composed of two parts, one a thousand miles away from the other. Partitioned Palestine blocked all plans for an integrated economic development of the whole region. In November 1947 the General Assembly of the United Nations adopted the partition of the country into an Arab and a Jewish state, with the proviso that those states should remain an economic union. Jerusalem was not included in that partition but was set aside as a 'corpus separatum' to be administered by a United Nations governor under the Trusteeship Council. By adopting the partition of Palestine the United Nations assumed the political responsibility for the country without possessing any real executive power which could be used during the transitional period. Lacking the military force to implement the November resolution on partition, United Nations delegates approached Britain with the request to employ her troops in the interest of an orderly handing-over of power. This Britain refused to do. The humiliating position of a powerless political world organization was soon apparent. The resolution of the General Assembly began to look like an act of collective irresponsibility as fighting broke out in the country, which was eventually partitioned not by the United Nations but by the decree of battle. The divided City of Jerusalem has remained as a reminder that global order and planning requires much more than resolutions of the General Assembly. The partition of Palestine created a new problem of refugees as fast as it solved one, providing new homes for 900,000 oppressed Jews, while some 700,000 Arabs lost their old homes. The whole area was turned into a political volcano with quiescent periods and days of eruptions. Many Russians and Americans were satisfied that one more area had been freed from British imperialism. The British troops went, but security and economic viability did not come. 'I had hoped', President Truman wrote, 'that some day we could build an international organization that would eventually work on the same basis as the union of the United States.'[1] The basis of the United Nations, the Palestine case had demonstrated, was in fact closer to that of the Confederation set up in the early days of American independence, when each of the thirteen states retained its absolute sovereignty and freedom of action. That basis had soon proved to be unworkable.

While imperial control was rapidly dismantled throughout the British Empire after the Second World War, it was not followed by an authority powerful enough to fulfil all its previous military, legal, and economic functions. Fifteen Asian countries and eight African countries gained their independence between 1948 and 1956. Several more African countries were about to become independent states in the early 1960's. Some 800,000,000 Afro-Asians will have received self-government by 1962. Endowed with unaccustomed absolute power, the new states are like so many inexperienced drivers put into new, powerful cars and let loose on public highways without a recognized highway code in force and without traffic police on duty. The new face of independent Africa might look like the old face of Latin America before long. In many states strong men assure cheering crowds that they are at last free from imperialist intervention, but the 'free' citizens are not always safe against dictatorial outrages, when there is no legal authority to appeal to, and dictatorial whim shapes the law as well as the economy of the country. Fortunately, the record of the 1950's was not always discouraging for the supporters of international authority.

The invasion of South Korea in June 1950 proved another testing point for the United Nations. This time President Truman helped to organize the military resistance to the invaders as an international enterprise on a large scale. Again, United Nations armed intervention was successfully accomplished in the case of the Israeli–Egyptian conflict of 1956. Truce was restored and effectively maintained in that area for a number of years. This action did not remain isolated. It was accompanied by American pressure exercised on Israel with the object of bringing about a speedy evacuation of Israeli forces from the Sinai Peninsula, a pressure which Ben Gurion, the Israeli Prime Minister, was unable to resist.[1] President Eisenhower and his American advisers in this case combined a policy of federal execution through the United Nations with a policy of imperial control through direct action. While they were using the superior power of the United States in the Middle East, Russian military intervention in Hungary at that time and Chinese intervention in Tibet in summer 1959 produced a world reaction which demonstrated that imperialism had ceased to be regarded as associated with the policy of Great Britain and America and was not acceptable in Asia even if practised by an Asian country. It was easier, however, to use an international police force in regional conflicts which involved small nations like Israel and Egypt than in conflicts in which Powers like the Soviet Union and China were implicated. Even in regional strife of local character, which threatened to spread, prompt action of the United Nations was not always forthcoming. After 1956 events forced the United States and Britain to act as policemen in the Middle East. In June 1958 a rebellion in Lebanon upset the delicate balance of the whole state. The rebels were in sympathy with the United Arab Republic and were reported to have been reinforced from Syria. United Nations Palestine Truce observers were sent to the Syrian border to investigate the extent of foreign infiltration into Lebanon, and the Lebanese Premier, Sami es-Solh, requested United Nations armed intervention. It did not materialize, and in July the country was preserved from anarchy by the landing of U.S. marines. Prompt action was also required to save Jordan a few days later after the revolution in Iraq. King Hussein invited the British to land in Jordan. The collapse of Jordan and the Lebanese Republic would have led to large-scale war-fare in the whole Middle East. American and British intervention once more gave rise to protests against imperialism, voiced by political opponents of the *status quo*, whose own political designs had been frustrated by superior military force. The designers had been political gamblers and adventurers. Such political gamblers and adventurers are always at work. Some hope to profit from East-West tension. In the absence of an institutionalized world security authority which commands a federal, executive force, the world cannot yet dispense with imperial action of that kind, and world peace still depends on direct contact and co-operation between the leading world empires, each exerting a restraining and controlling influence on its own allies, each respecting, as in the past, a zone of influence. Imperialism—in the sense of the exercise of political power beyond its territorial confines—is a political necessity in the present as it was in the past. Its absence would make instant warfare a certainty. Its presence in the given form, however, cannot be regarded as desirable or acceptable. Imperialism, therefore, is still a problem. It is the problem of world order.

What cannot be obtained any longer is absolute sovereignty. Even the United States and the Soviet Union no longer possess an absolute freedom of action. The conception of the United Nations Organization as an association of absolute sovereignties still belongs to the pre-atomic era. It requires serious revision. Problems of security, economic prosperity, and human rights cannot be solved on a national basis. They are global problems demanding global solutions. There is a limit to the economic waste a population is able to indulge in for the gratification of its own national sentiments. That limit has not been reached yet, it seems. People are still prepared to vote the money needed for a national air force, national prestige, for a national economy which is as romantic as it is inefficient and costly, for national air-lines and shipping lines, which have no genuine economic place in the world, for a national government whose large and costly administrative hand rests heavily on the productive population. The rising burden of national administration and the apparent wastefulness of national economy will sooner or later induce nations to develop forms of regional co-operation and development. In a sense all nations will partake of imperialism in the future in so far as they will be able to share in the military, economic, scientific, and cultural effort of their region and of the whole world *beyond* the national borders and so extend their influence, while at the same time admitting the assistance and influence of other nations for the benefit of their own people. Imperialism might thus become indistinguishable from international co-operation. The revulsion against imperialism has been an expression of the contradiction inherent in the current concepts of security and sovereignty, economic development and national independence. This led to paradoxical reactions which made little sense. Nations request strong protection and effective guarantees and reject them at the same time. Economic aid is invited and simultaneously spurned. Nationals often groan under the yoke of their own government but resent outside intervention offering redress. They want many tourists to come and see their wonderful country but resent the public use of foreign languages without which the tourist is often uncomfortable. They wish to see a rapid economic development of their natural resources but dislike the influx of foreign workers and technicians who would be required to accomplish that task. They desire to see their country take a lead in science but insist on the exclusive use of their national language in schools, colleges, and universities as the medium of instruction and publication. In the past imperial power was abused by alien administrators. In the present time abuse and exploitation have not ceased under the new rule of national taskmasters, who often seek short cuts to industrial and political might. The author of *The End of Empire* and the process of British 'disimperialism' welcomed the development of imperial dissolution believing that all imperial rule and influence by aliens was wasteful to the alien people and was coming to an end.[1] But it is not true that all imperial control is vanishing in the world either in the West or in the East and it is a delusion to think that a system of over one hundred sovereign nation states, each a law to its own, would be less wasteful or less dangerous to human survival. It would spell economic stagnation, international lawlessness, and collective insecurity. It would make atomic warfare in the future even more certain than it is at present. If a nation is anxious to secure its survival and economic prosperity, it will in future have to submit to a measure of control and planning by foreigners. From a point of view of regional health it is not important whether a province is administered by this nation or the other nation, but whether the people of that province are offered the conditions conducive to physical and mental health. The same principle applies to social welfare and military security. Nationalists who demand absolute sovereignty are irrational in their demand and indulge in a sentiment which in the world of today must lead their own people to extinction or new serfdom. The destruction of the sovereign nation-state is being relentlessly promoted by the passage of time. Both economic development and military security require regional control and co-operation, unless a world is desired in which each African tribe possesses its own currency and its own atomic bombs. It is unlikely that such a state of affairs 'will pay' the nations and tribes concerned or the former imperial races. Though more and more peoples in Africa and Asia have reached the status of nationhood and self-government, the nuclear and electronic age will not favour their survival unless they develop forms of regional co-operation.

In the absence of a global security authority, organized on a federal basis, the world will for many years to come continue to depend on the co-operation of the four great empires for the maintenance of order, unwelcome though such an 'imperium mundi' may be to most people. The dyarchy of the United States and the Soviet Union is not even popular among their allies on either side of the red border. The belief that the world could dispense with all supreme authority, however, is as unjustified as the opinion that all supreme authority must be vested in the hands of one strong man or one group of men. Contemporary political and economic existence is too complex even for the intelligence of the most talented statesman. Efficient government by one dictator residing in one place has become impossible. The best global government would be decentralized, federal, anonymous and yet ubiquitous; but global government and authority there must be. It is necessary to hold in check the destructive forces threatening man from within himself and from without. The conflicts and the hostile forces that lurk in one person and in a group of persons, the destructive powers of nature which surround and constantly challenge human existence, can all be mastered, if at all, by a co-operative and rational effort alone. Taking future conflicts and natural catastrophes for granted, and preparing for such contingencies, is the only way of making the world safe for pessimists after the optimists so patently failed in the previous age. But then we also take the fire department and the criminal investigation department in every city for granted. If in some future time only few people are able to call to mind the name of the chairman of the world security authority or the names of members serving on a global development committee, imperial power will be more competent and more acceptable to all; security will become rooted in routine rather than in emotion, and the civil limits of individual and collective freedom will be better understood. Then the angry protests against imperialism will be heard no longer and a new substance will be given to Disraeli's famous classical misquotation of IMPERIUM ET LIBERTAS.

NOTES

PAGE vii

1 'The Concept of Economic Imperialism', *Econ. Hist. Rev.*, 2nd ser., vol. II, no. I (1949); '*The Emergence of the Concept of Imperialism*', *Cambridge Journ.* vol. V, no. 12 (September 1952).

PAGE xiii

1 For a detailed article on the subject see R. Koebner, 'Semantics and Historiography', *Cambridge Journ.* vol. VII, no. 3 (December 1953). Some passages relevant to the book have been incorporated with the kind permission of the editor.

PAGE xv

1 For a detailed study combining the historical with the laboratory method see H. D. Schmidt, 'Bigotry in Schoolchildren', *Commentary* (New York, March 1960), pp. 253–7.

PAGE xvi

1 H. D. Schmidt, 'The Idea and Slogan of Perfidious Albion', *Journ. History of Ideas*, vol. XIV, no. 4 (1953), pp. 612 ff.

PAGE 2

1 F. Raymond, *Supplément au dictionnaire de l'Académie française* (1836), has the entries: *Bonapartiste*, partisan de Bonaparte, du gouvernement de Bonaparte; *Bonapartisme*, opinion des bonapartistes; *Impérialiste*, partisan du gouvernement impérial; *Impérialisme*, système opinion, doctrine des impérialistes. *Impérialisme* has an asterisk, signifying that the word has not been noted by any earlier dictionary. Louis Barré, *Complément du dictionnaire de l'Académie française* (1842), approximately reiterates these definitions although in the preface Raymond's work is declared to be 'au dessous de toute critique sérieuse'.

2 *La Quotidienne, Moniteur de l'Avenir* (21 December 1840). The paper had 3000–5000 subscribers; it was run by young fanatics. Cp. E. Hatin, *Histoire . . . de la presse en France* (1861), vol. VIII, pp. 571, 590.

PAGE 3

1 Letters to the *Augsburgische Allgemeine Zeitung*—later republished under the title *Lutezia*, but partly suppressed in the first edition of 1854—nos. 10, 20, 22. The shortlived *Revue de l'Empire* (1842–5), dedicated 'à toutes

les gloires du Consulat et de l'Empire', deprecated being considered as an organ of *Bonapartistes* and prided itself on having the King among its subscribers. 'Echo impartial de toutes les gloires du Consulat et de l'Empire notre Revue sera purement historique.' The editor, Charles-Edouard Temblaire, soon belied this claim. Communications concerning the Bonaparte family and the prisoner of Ham became regular items of the *Revue.*

2 *Œuvres de Louis Napoléon Bonaparte*, publiés par Ch.-Ed. Temblaire (1848), vol. I, p. 19 (letter to Armand Laity), pp. 25, 28 (address to the Chambre des Pairs).

3 *Ibid.* vol. I, pp. 19, 279; vol. III, p. 234.

PAGE 4

1 *Ibid.* vol. I, pp. 59 ff. *Correspondence and Conversations of Alexis de Tocqueville with Nassau William Senior II*, p. 11.

2 *La France Parlementaire*, vol. V, p. 469.

PAGE 5

1 *Discours du président* ... *à Lyon* (15 August 1850): 'Je suis, non pas le représentant d'un parti, mais le représentant de deux grandes manifestations nationales qui, en 1804 comme en 1848, ont voulu sauver par l'ordre les grands principes de la révolution française.' *La Politique Impériale exposé par les discours et les proclamations de l'Empereur Napoléon* ... (1868), p. 66; see also pp. 45, 60. Comte Huebner, *Neuf Ans de Souvenirs d'un Ambassadeur* (1901), I, p. 8; *Dictionnaire Politique Napoléonien*, par Alfred d'Alembert (Paris, 1849), p. 7, and items Napoléon, Empire, Parti napoléonien, opinion napoléonienne.

2 Lamartine, *La France Parlementaire*, vol. VI, pp. 540 ff. *Revue des Deux Mondes*, vol. XII, p. 379 (14 October): 'Ce n'était pas qu'elles (la campagne et les villes) eussent du goût pour le régime impérial; c'est qu'elles avaient une revanche à prendre sur le régime républicain des conquérants de février.'

PAGE 6

1 *Ibid.* 31 October 1851: 'Qui ne se rappelle avoir entendu vanter les merveilles promises à la France par le mariage de l'idée napoléonienne avec l'idée démocratique? Nous le disons du fond de l'âme, ... nous parlons avec la sérieuse d'une tristesse qui n'est pas jouée: si c'est par hasard ce mariage-là que rêve le président, c'est qu'il n'habite qu'avec des fantômes ... Ainsi l'on voit comment le régime napoléonien, déjà si souvent transfiguré par les fausses poétiques, pourrait encore se transfigurer une

fois de plus et prendre pour l'avenir aux yeux d'esprits sans justesse, je ne sais quel aspect de dictature humanitaire' (p. 572 ff.).

2 'Pourquoi ne tenterait-on pas de recommander ainsi l'impérialisme ressuscité?' (*ibid.* 14 November, p. 755).

PAGE 7

1 *Ibid.* p. 975.

2 *Mémoires du Comte Horace de Vieil Castel* ... *1851–1864* (Paris, 1881), vol. I, pp. 249 ff; vol. II, p. 29. The abbreviated translations given above may be excused for not being completely literal. The Comte had even harsher words for the *bourgeoisisme*, 'qui a longtemps conduit nos affaires' (vol. III, p. 20).

3 Vol. I, pp. 67, 76 ff. Cf. also p. 46 on Louis Napoleon himself, 'son sac de voyage tout plein de projets, ... tous imbus de traditions impérialistes ...'.

4 On the ambiguous situation of this concept under the Second Empire see A. Momigliano, *Cesare nel Bimillenario della Morte*, Ed. Radio Italiana, pp. 234 ff.

PAGE 8

1 The preface of the translator, Derosne, suspiciously abounds in deprecations. The pages referred to in the fifth chapter are pp. 277, 280. The status of the term was not changed much by the episode of 'l'Empire libéral'. Emile Littré (himself an opponent of the regime) in his *Dictionnaire* of 1869 asserted its topical significance by the entries: '*Impérialisme*: Opinion des impérialistes. *Impérialiste* 2°: Partisan du régime politique de l'empereur Napoléon Ier et de sa dynastie.' The legitimist, Victor de Laprade, in his preface to Chateaubriand's *De Bonaparte et des Bourbons*, p. 40, wrote: 'Dieu sait combien toutes ces infamies contre la patrie et contre Dieu même ont été habilement exploitées pour donner à l'impérialisme un vernois libéral' in 1872, but has *bonapartisme*—'the worst of Bonaparte's deeds'—as its butt and uses the old terms of *despotisme* and *Machiavellisme* to denote the atrocious character of the system. The French committee which has recently compiled references to *imperialism* for the Terminology Section of the *International Social Science Bulletin* (ed. UNESCO, vol. VIII, p. 1; 1956) has stated: 'Le mot d'impérialisme apparaît sous le Second Empire au sens d'opinion favorable au régime impérial' (p. 136). Based on Littré's definition this statement, inaccurate in almost every word, demonstrates what may result from using dictionaries for historical purposes for which they were not meant.

2 *The Times* (19 August 1850); quoted together with similar references by F. Ch. Palm, *England and Napoleon III* (Duke Univ. Press, 1948), pp. 49–58.

3 For instances of this application see *O.E.D.*, article *Imperialist*. The quotation from the *Monthly Magazine*, vol. VIII (1800), given at that place, does, however, not refer to Napoleon Bonaparte, but orginated from an article on the Jesuits, published in September 1799. The 'cryptarchs' of the order are called 'imperious imperialists'; the singular metaphorical application of the word might be the result of a misprint. Later in the century the name was constantly used in the description of Chinese affairs; cf. for instance, the *North China Herald*, as quoted by Cobden on 1 August 1862 (*Speeches*, vol. II, p. 269).

PAGE 10

1 *North British Review*, vol. xv, article 1 (Edinburgh, May 1851). 'France since 1848', pp. 4, 10–23, 28, 31. Italics mine. Mentioned, like some of the following references, in *O.E.D.* No item *Imperialism* was provided for the first edition of the Imperial Dictionary of English, the most circumspect of its time. This fact goes far to prove that the term was a neologism when applied to the career of Louis Napoleon in 1851. The name of that Dictionary, needless to say, was only a claim to its excellence, not an allusion to the British Empire.

2 *North British Review*, vol. xvi, article x (February 1852), 'France in January 1852', referring to *Œuvres de Louis Napoléon Bonaparte* and to *Des Idées Napoléoniennes*, pp. 587 ff.

PAGE 11

1 *The Times* (8 December 1851; reprint in Sir James Marchant, *History through 'The Times'* (1937), pp. 139 ff.); 26 December 1851, 3, 14, 16, January 1852; see also the expressions in H. Reeve's and Delane's correspondence with Lord Granville, *The History of the Times*, vol. III, pp. 149 f. *Quarterly Review* (December 1851), vol. xc, pp. 257–83, esp. pp. 258, 275. *Annual Register for 1851*, pp. 271 f. Complacency was not wholly restricted to the 'base exception' (so *The Times*, Marchant, p. 144) of the *Morning Post*, Palmerston's paper. Walter Bagehot let the *Economist* opine that 'it was only by such an absolute and military authority ... that trade in France and England can be preserved and property respected'. Palm, *op. cit.* p. 67—who needlessly asks for particular interests influencing the attitude of *The Times*. Palmerston preferred Louis Napoleon's ascendancy to the alternative of a Bourbon or Orleanist restoration; cf. Seton Watson, *Britain in Europe*, p. 290.

PAGE 12

1 Vol. xvi, pp. 587 f.

1 Karl Marx, *Der 18. Brumaire des Louis Buonaparte* (reprint, Berlin, 1921), p. 108. The cramped style of the pamphlet defies adequate translation. The rendering attempted above, however, keeps closer to the original than the English edition by Eden and Cedar Paul (London, 1926), p. 140. The passage quoted had, of course, no influence on Marx's disciples when they, fifty years later and in quite a different meaning, borrowed the term imperialism from English liberal phraseology.

2 'Styles, American and Foreign. Carlyle and his Imitators', *The American Whig Review*, vol. xv (April 1852), pp. 349–56, esp. pp. 354 f. As in the *North British Review* so in this article—to which my attention was drawn by Dr Joshua Arieli—*despotism* is incriminated first, until the reference to the Napoleons let *imperialism* spontaneously take its place. Dr Francia was the dictator of Paraguay of whom Carlyle approved.

PAGE 14

1 The *North British Review* had, after the establishment of the Empire, come round to the chorus of unqualified condemnation and distrust in the regime's durability: 'We can never be apologists of a Tyrant, even where the tyranny is welcomed by millions.... In a despotism so stern, indiscriminate and inglorious as this she (France) *cannot* ultimately acquiesce' ('The Prospects of France and the Dangers of England', February 1853, vol. xviii, p. 350). One year later, however, the same paper imputed Nicholas' confidence that no Anglo-French alliance was possible to 'the language of journals'. For the attitude of the Radical press towards the Crimean War see Maccoby, *British Radicalism*.

PAGE 15

1 *Pariser Kaiserskizzen*, parts i and ii (Berlin, 1857), preface. The author apprehends that many of his readers will think him going too far in making Imperialism responsible for so many things—'Manchem wird es gewiss zu weit gegangen sein, was diese Skizzen dem Imperialismus Alles in die Schuhe schieben'—but takes it as an axiom 'that the life of a great nation ... is every point so much of an indivisible and coherent whole that the personality inhabiting the Tuileries and possessing the French throne must leave its unmistakable imprint on every new vaudeville of a boulevard theatre'.

2 H. B. Oppenheimer's *Demokratische Studien* (1860), from which a passage (p. 54) is quoted in O. Ladendorf's *Historisches Schlagwörterbuch* (1906, p. 133), distinguish between the 'Imperialismus' of the imperial government and the response of the people—very much in the vein of English comments, mentioned below, only to arrive at a more sceptical

result. Influence through the medium of English usage is not out of the question. The publication of Napoleon's *Histoire de Jules César* was used as an occasion by an enthusiastic admirer for a dithyrambic recommendation of *Der Imperialismus und die Congress-Idee* in 1865 (Leipzig, Matthes). The author expatiates on the 'universal genius' of the Emperor and proclaims the 'sublime interpretation of Imperialism' ('im geläuterten Begriffe vom Imperialismus', p. 22) as the 'perfection of free activity of man in political life, ... coordination of law and power'. On the other hand, a critical examination of Napoleon's politics as expressed in H. v. Treitschke's *Frankreichs Staatsleben und der Bonapartismus*, written in the same year (reprint *Historische und politische Aufsätze*, vol. III), made no use of the term. The re-edition of J. C. A. Heyse's *Fremdwörterbuch* (1873) has 'Kaiserherrschaft' and 'Despotism' as alternative explanations of 'Imperialismus', but gives no special reference to France, while the entry 'Imperialist' has 'ein Kaiserlicher' adding 'bes. in Frankreich = Bonapartist, entg. den Royalisten'.

PAGE 16

1 *Pariser Kaiserskizzen*, vol. I, pp. 3, 14, 34, 39 ff. (quoted in Hans Schulz, *Deutsches Fremdwörterbuch*, 1914) also p. 63 (stock-jobbing), vol. II, p. 29.
2 *Hansard*, 3rd ser. vol. CXLVIII, pp. 957 f., 963, 1819 (8, 9, 19 February 1858).

PAGE 17

1 *The Westminster and Foreign Quarterly Review*, vol. XIV (1 October 1858), article 1, pp. 301–50.
2 *Op. cit.* pp. 311–33.

PAGE 19

1 *Op. cit.* pp. 335, 340, 344. The last quotation is mentioned in the *O.E.D.*
2 The Earl of Clarendon reported from Paris in October 1858: 'Tout respire la prosperité et la tranquillité & the surface is as smooth as possible —beneath it the usual elements of disorders are at work but even Thiers with whom I had a long talk admitted that there was now no reason why the Empire shd not last as it was in sufficient harmony with the indifference & profond égoisme of the people.' '*My Dear Duchess*'. *Social and Political Letters to the Duchess of Manchester, 1858–1869*, ed. A. L. Kennedy, (1956), p. 30. Two years later W. Nassau Senior was advised by Kergoley that the 'Imperialists', were as little as the Legitimists and Orleanists 'loyal in the old sense of the term—neither of them has the personal devotion which you have towards your Queen'. *Conversations with Distinguished Persons from 1860–1863*, ed. M. C. M. Simpson, vol. I, p. 8.

PAGE 20

1 Cf. Lords' Debates, 1 and 5 July 1859, *Hansard*, 3rd ser. vol. CLIV, esp.
p. 517 (Lord Howden), (Lord Granville's declaration)—on the other hand
Clarendon's letters of 27 April and 3 May 1859 (*My Dear Duchess*,
pp. 53, 56) and his aphorisms one year later: 'France at the moment is
nothing else than L. N. with his passions and ambition and resentment';
Palmerston and John Russell are 'enraged at finding that L. N. is a much
cleverer conspirator than either of them and that a Gambler with 600,000
bayonets and no responsibility is stronger than a divided Cabinet' (27 May
1860; *op. cit.* pp. 105, 107). Queen Victoria's deep concern to find a clue
to Napoleon's character and intentions appears from her letters and diaries.
In January 1861 Clarendon found her regrettably 'tormented by a succes-
sion of Imperial Nightmares of the Anglo-Germanic breed' (*op. cit.* p. 131).
About the same time a spate of apocalyptic pamphlets tried to convince
English believers that the Emperor was the Antichrist in person. Cobden's
unshakeable belief in Napoleon's benevolent intentions is in the sentence
quoted above (*The Three Pansies*, 1862, *Political Writings*, 4th ed.) imputed
to the industrialists and other reflecting men who witnessed his personal
interest in the Commercial Treaty. This made him notorious to Clarendon
(letters of 14 Sept. 1862, 18 April 1865, *op. cit.* pp. 203, 233).

2 *Irish History and Irish Character* (1861), p. 18 (quoted in *O.E.D.*).

PAGE 21

1 The secret of the authorship has been well kept. None of the guesses
collected in the dictionaries of pseudonyms is based on reliable evidence—
least of all that which attributes the authorship to the Earl of Clarendon.

PAGE 22

1 *Op. cit.* esp. pp. 58 f., 65 f., 75, 83, 105, 157, 167.

PAGE 23

1 *Op. cit.* pp. 172, 186 f., 204, 212, 221.

PAGE 24

1 Edition 1868, vol. II, p. 367.
2 *Op. cit.* p. 380. Dilke very incautiously adds: 'and are commencing to see
in Russia.'
3 R.H.S., Introduction to John Bright's *Speeches on the Public Affairs of the
last twenty Years* (1869), p. xiv: '... if we live in an atmosphere where free
thought is not stifled by imperialism nor free action by Oriental sluggish-
ness ... let us honour the great patriots and liberal leaders ....' Louis
Mallet, a more prominent Cobdenite, insisted on maintaining his master's

sympathetic attitude to Napoleon III, whose setting aside for a time of other forms of liberty in France counted for little in view of his attempts at material reform (introduction to Cobden's *Political Writings*, 4th ed. vol. I, p. xxv).

PAGE 25

1 '*The Use of Goldwin Smiths in Parliament*', vol. XLI, p. 38 noted by C. A. Bodelsen, *Studies in Mid-Victorian Imperialism* (Copenhagen, 1924), p. 100, as the earliest occurrence of a reference of the term in connexion with the British Empire.

2 'A Fallen Star' (i.e. the *Morning Star* and the *Evening Star*), 16 October 1869, vol. XLII, p. 1203.

PAGE 26

1 *The Times*, 15th October 1869, on the occasion of the tumults in Folies Belleville two days earlier: '... there is hardly any Imperialism, or, indeed, any worse form of despotism, into the arms of which France would not, at all times, throw herself as a refuge against revolutionary excesses.' The resolution of a meeting expressing 'delight at the downfall of Imperialism in France and the proclamation ... of the Republic' was reported in the *Daily News* of 8 September 1870. Both quotations in *O.E.D.*

PAGE 29

1 This reference applies, first of all, to the two comprehensive surveys, to which every study touching upon the British Empire in the Early Victorian Age is highly indebted, viz. C. A. Bodelsen, *Studies in Mid-Victorian Imperialism* (Copenhagen, 1924), and Robert L. Schuyler, *The Fall of the Old Colonial System. A Study in British Free Trade 1770–1870* (1945). Bodelsen's book begins with explicit reservations concerning the use of the term Imperialism. Its section I is mainly a study of 'separatist' public and private opinion; it does not use the term Anti-Imperialism. This expression, on the other hand, looms large in Schuyler's studies, now incorporated in the book mentioned above, which in contradistinction to that by Bodelsen, lets the history of opinion serve only as background to the development of commercial legislation. For the constitutional development and administrative matters cf. the relevant chapters in the *Cambridge History of the British Empire* (*C.H.B.E.*), vol. II, chs. VIII, X, XIX (by Paul Knaplund, J. R. M. Butler, and E. A. Benians respectively) and W. P. Morrell, *British Colonial Policy in the Age of Peel and Russell* (1930).

PAGE 30

1 *Russia, Political Writings*, 4th ed., vol. I, p. 153.

PAGE 31

1 *How Wars are got up in India* (1853), vol. II, p. 458. Letters 23 December 1848, 4, 27 August 1860; John Morley, *Life of Richard Cobden*, vol. II, pp. 4, 354 f: '. . . the pride of territorial greatness will prevent our loosening our hold upon them' (our 'possessions' in the East). 'Shall we never learn to live at peace and be content with the honest possessions with which God has so bountifully blessed our island?'

PAGE 32

1 *Speeches on Questions of Public Policy*, ed. Bright and Rogers, vol. I, p. 363 (On Free Trade), vol. II, p. 315 (American Civil War)—Cobden's religious convictions are most distinctly laid down in his great letter to George Combe (1 August 1846), Morley, *op. cit.* vol. I, pp. 216 ff. His primary interest in 'education' was appropriately stressed by Sir Louis Mallet, the first commentator of his *Political Writings*, introd. p. xxviii.

2 *The Empire* (1863), letter I ('Colonial Emancipation'), p. 8; letter IV ('Colonial Expenditure'), pp. 74, 77.

PAGE 33

1 *Op. cit.* p. 32. Quotation from *The Times*, leader (4th February 1862): 'Is, then, Mr. Goldwin Smith really persuaded that England, deprived of her Colonies and of India, would wear before the world the same air of grandeur with which she is now invested? Grant all he writes as to worthlessness of this dependent Empire calculated in money, and it has still to be shown that augmentation of wealth and strength which he promises us from its sacrifice is likely to impose on mankind as majestically as does at present the possession of merely apparent power.' Smith's comment was: 'Wooden artillery has been useful as a stratagem in war; but I never heard that it was useful, or that anything was risked by a wise commander to preserve it, after the enemy has found out that it was wooden.'

PAGE 34

1 For tirades under these heads see *The Empire*, pp. 29, 32, 93. Against the reproach that he was 'neglecting "sentiment"', and looking only to advantage', Goldwin Smith argued: 'I reply that political confederations are not religious communities and that reciprocal advantage, not sentiment, must be their basis if they are intended to endure. None but a cynic would despise sentiment; none but a fool would build on it' (p. 35).

2 *Op. cit.* pp. 9 f.—A remark 'joyfully withdrawn' in a footnote to the book edition, after 'the adherents of Lord Palmerston as well as the writer have been surprised by the determination of his Government to cede the Ionian Islands'.

PAGE 35

1 *Hansard*, 3rd ser. vol. CXLIV (February 1857), pp. 1155 (Derby), 1394 f., 1421, 1476 (Cobden and Russell).

PAGE 36

1 *Loc. cit.* p. 1421.
2 *Loc. cit.* pp. 1833, 1840 (3 March).
3 Vol. XXXII, p. 101 (7 March 1857), 'Essence of Parliament'.
4 The combination of these motives had some interesting bearing on the first debate in the House of Lords—The Foreign Secretary, the Earl of Clarendon, warned: 'I trust that your Lordships will not agree to a Resolution which will fetter the discretion and tie the hands of His Majesty's servants in China, which will cast disgrace upon our name and our flag . . . .' Lord Lyndhurst, answering for the Opposition, took special exception to an address from an association of traders, who demanded a forcible revision of the Chinese commercial tariff: 'I most heartily and sincerely wish that that association, whatever might be the respectability of its members, may not, in their anxiety for gain, exercise such an influence over the Government as to induce them to persevere in the unfortunate course in which they are at present engaged,' *Hansard*, vol. CXLIV, pp. 1212, 1220.

PAGE 39

1 Leitch Ritchie, *The British World in the East* (1847).
2 *Op. cit.*, C. P. Lucas' edition (1891), pp. 73 f. For confirmation of his definition George C. Lewis referred to Burke's Speech on American Taxation—not to the definition Burke included in his Conciliation Speech, 'the aggregate of many *states* under a common head'. As an example of the literary renown of the passage quoted, cf. *Edinburgh Review*, vol. LXXXIII (1846), p. 518.

PAGE 40

1 *Op. cit.* pp. 311, 316–26, for the greater part reprinted in *The Concept of Empire, Burke to Attlee*, ed. George Bennett (1953), pp. 165 ff.
2 *Op. cit.* p. 289.

PAGE 42

1 *Edinburgh Review*, vol. CIX, no. 222, article X (April 1859), commenting on 'L'Empereur Napoléon III et l'Italie', and other pamphlets, pp. 563–5.

PAGE 43

1 For English diplomacy in the Italian question see R. W. Seton-Watson, *Britain in Europe, 1789–1914* (1937), pp. 384, 395 f., 406. A. J. P. Taylor,

The Struggle for Mastery in Europe, 1848–1918 (1954), pp. 102, 108 f., 113, 117 f., 123 f. H. Temperley and L. M. Penson, *Foundations of British Foreign Policy*, Documents 54–68 and the Introductions; especially Document 58, pp. 203, 214. Still in August 1859 Russell spoke of the unification of the whole of Italy as a 'wild and foolish' idea.

2 John Earl Russell, *Recollections and Suggestions, 1813–1873* (1875), pp. 280 f.; Temperley and Penson, *op. cit.* Doc. 68, p. 223.

PAGE 44

1 '*A Few Words on Non-Intervention*', *Fraser's Magazine* (1859), reprinted in Mill's *Dissertations and Discussions* (1875), vol. III, esp. pp. 167–71.

2 Cf. *supra*, pp. 58–60 and *The Empire*, ch. XVIII. But this chapter culminated in the statement: 'India is not a Colony or a nation but an Empire . . .', p. 297. Like all advocates of the abandonment of imperial ties (cf. H. J. Habbakuk, *C.H.B.E.* vol. II, p. 752) he denied the possibility that Britain could surrender her responsibility of governing India (p. 292). Sir William Molesworth had asked: 'Should we despond over our mighty empire in the East?' when deprecating the cry *Emancipate your colonies* in the House of Commons on 6 March 1838; but he did not join both issues under the head of 'the British Empire'. (Speech in moving a vote of censure on Lord Glenelg, *Selected Speeches*, pp. 2 f.; Bennett, *op. cit.* pp. 131 f.)

3 One example must suffice to stand for many, a letter, written by the engineer Richard Baird Smith during the Mutiny: 'As to the empire, it will be all the stronger after this storm . . .' (30 May 1857, quoted in *D.N.B.* vol. LIII, p. 106). After the Second Sikh War, on the other hand, Lord Dalhousie used the term in a wider meaning in a letter to Lord John Russell which included the remark: 'I truly hope you may find a way through the graver difficulties which surround the Empire. These are hard times for Prime Ministers.' *The Later Correspondence of Lord John Russell*, ed. G. P. Gooch, vol. I, p. 281 (2 March 1849).

4 *The Administration of the East India Company. A History of Indian Progress*, 2nd ed. (1853), p. 7. Similar phrases could be quoted from the 'Introductory Remarks' and 'Concluding Remarks' of the book, pp. 658 ff.

PAGE 45

1 Everyman's edition, p. 211. See also R. Koebner, *Empire* (Cambridge 1961), pp. 294–5.

2 *Op. cit.* vol. I, pp. 594. The preface refers to Chamberlayne's antiquated *State of Great Britain and Ireland* as the latest work of the kind and takes the fact for granted that 'a statistical account of the British Empire' means the same as 'a fair representation of the present condition of the United Kingdom'.

PAGE 46

1 The fourth edition was published in 1854 under the title *A Descriptive and Statistical Account of the British Empire.*

2 *Addresses and Pamphlets* (1832–7), quoted in Monypenny and Buckle, *Life of Disraeli* (two volumes edition), vol. I, pp. 212, 222, 225, 231, 278, 287, 325, 415; letter to Ch. Atwood and Speech at Shrewsbury, 1840, *op. cit.* pp. 486 f., 540; *Coningsby*, bk. III, ch. 15, Everyman ed., p. 206. *Imperium et Libertas* (1851), *Life*, vol. I, p. 1099. Our earlier study of the concept of Empire already mentions the misquotation of *imperium et libertas*, cf. *Empire, op. cit.* p. 325.

3 In a system of proportional representation 'the elector would have the opportunity, if he chose, of tendering his vote for the ablest and best man in the Empire who is willing to serve'. J. S. Mill, 'Recent Writers on Reform', *Fraser's Magazine* (April 1859); *Dissertations and Discussions*, vol. III, p. 89.

4 Seventeen years earlier *The Times* had, in the first China conflict, taken exception to people who countenanced the disregard of justice or mercy 'for the interests of civilization, or of the East India Company, or of the British empire, or for some other equally sufficient reason', Leader (6 November 1840), Sir James Marchant, *History through The Times*, p. 107.

PAGE 47

1 In actual fact, the unification of Italy had reduced the strategical value of Corfu to a minimum; the objection that the Greeks, once having been satisfied on the point of the Ionian Islands, would press for further annexations, had more weight. Cf. Seton-Watson, *op. cit.* pp. 426–8; Carrington, *The British Overseas*, p. 537.

2 5 February 1863, *Hansard*, 3rd ser. vol. CLXIX, pp. 95 f.

PAGE 48

1 A preliminary summary of his attitude is found in Letter I, *Empire*, pp. 6 f. A detailed treatment follows in Letters XIII, XV, XVI.

2 Carrington, *op. cit.* pp. 464 f.

3 John Stuart Mill regretted it especially as giving colour to foreign denunciations of British selfishness. '*A Few Words*' etc., *op. cit.* pp. 162–6.

PAGE 49

1 *Hansard, ibid.* pp. 104 f. (Lord Robert Montagu), 127 f. (Palmerston); *Spectator*, 7 February 1863, vol. XXXVI, p. 1601. Concerning public opinion at that time a remark by John Morley made about the time of the Crimean War also holds good for this occasion: 'We must remember that even the modern Road-to-India argument for the defence of Turkey had

not then been invented.' (*Life of Cobden*, vol. II, p. 124, footnote written in 1881.)

PAGE 50

1   'Empire' was not a prominent term in the arguments for and against slavery. Wilberforce addressed his '*Appeal to the Religion, Justice, and Humanity of the Inhabitants of the British Empire*' to the British West Indians in particular (1823; Bennett, p. 102); but official language used in 1832–3 declared slavery abolished 'throughout the British dominions' or 'throughout the colonies' (Harlow-Madden, *British Colonial Developments*, pp. 587 f.). A Jamaican protest at that time was voiced against certain parliamentary debates 'having been industriously circulated . . . throughout this island as well as the British Empire' (Harlow-Madden, p. 584) which proves that the colonists, too, identified the *Empire* with the *United Kingdom*. A similar interpretation of Empire is also found in the *Report of the Parliamentary Select Committee on Aborigines (British Settlements)*, reports from Committees, vol. VII (1837), p. 76; Bennett, p. 105.

PAGE 51

1   Carrington, *op. cit.* pp. 128 ff., 501, 506.

PAGE 52

1   *Selected Speeches on Questions relating to Colonial Policy*, ed. H. E. Egerton (1903), p. 314. No echo was evoked by the lonely meditations of the tireless compiler and statistician, R. Montgomery Martin, in the preface to his *History of the British Colonies* (completed 1831, published 1834), dedicated to King William IV 'sovereign of the greatest colonial empire in the world'.

PAGE 53

1   The debates fill hundreds of pages in *Hansard*, 3rd ser. vol. XL. Extracts containing the significant utterances of Peel and Russell (pp. 41, 69 f., 469) in Bennett, pp. 115–24. Molesworth's terminology was consistent and still widely remote from the language chosen by him twelve years later in the Australian debate. He stated that Lord Durham was sent to Canada 'to recall the revolted subjects of the empire to their allegiance' and had misgivings as to what 'the colonial policy of the Empire' would become in the hands of the opposition (*Hansard*, pp. 358, 361). In the House of Lords the Colonial Secretary, Lord Glenelg, used the term vaguely when he recommended the Bill as 'affecting the interests and prosperity of the Empire' (*Hansard*, p. 163); in reply to a disparaging remark made by Brougham the Prime Minister maintained that the 'present proceedings . . . involve . . . the honour and integrity of this country . . . and its character as a great empire' (*Hansard*, p. 223; Bennett, p. 119).

2 *Lord Durham's Report*, ed. C. P. Lucas (1912), vol. II, pp. 65 f., 283, 286. Most of the passages quoted here are also contained in Sir Reginald Coupland's abridged edition and in A. Berriedale Keith, *Selected Speeches and Documents on British Colonial Policy, 1763–1917*, vol. I, pp. 113–72.
3 *Report*, vol. II, pp. 13, 330, 333.

PAGE 54

1 *Ibid.* p. 284.
2 *Ibid.* p. 285.
3 *Ibid.* pp. 288, 291.

PAGE 55

1 *Ibid.* pp. 304, 309 f.
2 *Ibid.* pp. 62, 272, 310 f.

PAGE 56

1 Huskisson, H. of Commons, 21 March 1825, *Speeches* (1831), vol. II, p. 322; cf. Schuyler, p. 123, Bennett, p. 88 (using the phrase 'in the progress of human events' reminiscent of the Declaration of Independence). Russell, H. of C., 16 January 1838, *Hansard*, 3rd ser. vol. XL, p. 41, Bennett, p. 115. Lord Melbourne imitated Lord Durham's proviso in his speech of 30 June 1840 (*Hansard*, 3rd ser. vol. LV, p. 228) quoted by Schuyler, p. 77.
2 The sentence is found inserted in the passage which recommends responsible government as an antidote to the influence of the United States, *Report*, vol. II, p. 310. For other passages, using or supposing the notion of 'portions of Empire' cf. pp. 170, 259, 329.
3 P. 282: 'A perfect subordination, on the part of the Colony, on these points, is secured by the advantages which it finds in the continuance of its connexion with the Empire'; 'Imperial interests', p. 286.

PAGE 58

1 Letter of 11 October 1839, reprinted in Lucas' edition of *Lord Durham's Report*, vol. III, pp. 334 f.; Berriedale Keith, *op. cit.* pp. 177 f. For Lord Durham's argument see *Report*, pp. 278 f.; Berriedale Keith, *op. cit.* p. 136.
2 To Melbourne, 6 September 1838: 'Our Empire grows every day internally and becomes every day more difficult to control' (Early Correspondence, ed. R. Russell, p. 222). This letter betrays Russell's impatience with Glenelg's handling of the Secretaryship as does, still more explicitly, that of 2 February 1839 (p. 244 f.), in which he threatens his resignation, because 'the destinies of our Colonial Empire could no longer be continued in their present hands'. In his memoirs (Introduction to *Speeches and Dispatches* (1870), p. 153), (*Recollections and Suggestions* (1875), p. 198)

he, indeed, dated his interest in colonial affairs only from his accession to the office in September 1839. Concerning his attitude to Australia and New Zealand, cf. *Recollections*, pp. 198, 203; Carrington, *op. cit.* pp. 360, 382.

PAGE 59

1 On Buller and Stephen, cf. P. Knaplund, 'Mr. Over-Secretary Stephen', *Journ. of Mod. History*, vol. I, pp. 40 ff.; on Buller and Durham see Carrington, *op. cit.* p. 344.

2 Sir William Molesworth, *Selected Speeches on Questions Relating to Colonial Policy*, ed. H. E. Egerton (1903), p. 176. 'Every other nation has attempted, in some shape or form, to draw tribute from its colonies; but England, on the contrary, has paid tribute to her colonies. She has created and maintained, at an enormous expense, an extensive colonial empire for the sole purpose of buying customers for her shopkeepers.'

PAGE 60

1 Lord Howick, H. of C., March 1842, *Hansard*, 3rd ser. vol. LXIII, pp. 515 f.; W. P. Morrell, *British Colonial Policy in the Age of Peel and Russell* (1830), pp. 173 f.; Schuyler, *op. cit.* pp. 134 f.

2 *Hansard*, 3rd ser. vol. LXIII (March 1842), pp. 533, 535.

PAGE 61

1 *Ibid.* vol. XII, p. 1105; Huskisson, *Speeches* (1831) (speech made on 21 March 1825).

2 *Hansard*, 3rd ser. vol. LXIII, p. 546. In the detailed summary of the debate published by the *Annual Register* early in the following year neither appeal was thought worth mentioning.

PAGE 62

1 Charles Buller, in a vain attempt to win the Cobdenites for the cause of 'systematic colonisation', declared: '... in the principles and objects of the friends of Free Trade I fully concur' (6 April 1843, Bennett, *op. cit.* p. 142).

2 Cf. Morrell, *op. cit.* pp. 175–9 (quoting Lowe after A. Patchett-Martin's biography).

PAGE 63

1 *Hansard*, 3rd ser. vol. LXXX, pp. 292–340, H. of C. debate, 8 May 1845, on the motion of W. Hutt, esp. pp. 303, 340 (Hutt's perorations), 310 (Captain H. J. Rons, denouncing the spirit of bigotry and selfishness which 'weighed down the energies of this mighty Empire'), 334 (Lord Howick

challenging Stanley on the rights of 'an integral part of the British Empire'). For other passages in Hutt's speeches cf. Schuyler, *op. cit.*, pp. 144 f.

PAGE 65

1 *Hansard*, 3rd ser. vol. LXXXVI, H. of C., 14 and 15 May, pp. 553 ff. (Bentinck), 670 (Disraeli), 685 (Russell); Lords, 25 and 28 May, pp. 1165 f. (Stanley), 1307 ff. (Grey); for the topic of the 'Zollverein' cf. Morrell, *op. cit.* p. 174 (*The Times*, 31 March 1842), Schuyler, *op. cit.* p. 147 (Sir Howard Douglas in Repeal debates). Opposition to the new commercial policy and advocacy of the promotion of colonial settlements are in an exceptional manner combined in a pamphlet written by 'A Liverpool Merchant' entitled *Our Free Trade Policy Examined* (London, 1846).

PAGE 66

1 Schuyler, *op. cit.* pp. 151–7, Russell's speech, p. 155; cf. *Hansard*, 3rd ser. vol. LXXXVII, pp. 1324 f.

PAGE 67

1 Schuyler, *op. cit.* pp. 158–160 (authorization of colonial repeals of protection), 182–95 (abrogation of the Navigation Laws). Speeches and papers quoted: *Hansard*, 3rd ser. vol. LXXXVIII, pp. 743 f., 907; vol. XCV, p. 14; *Parl. Papers* (1847–8), vol. LIX, pp. 4 f.
2 Earl Grey, *The Colonial Policy of Lord John Russell's Administration* (London, 1853), vol. I, pp. 209–13.
3 New Zealand Debate, June 1845. *Hansard*, vol. LXXXI, p. 807.

PAGE 68

1 *The Elgin-Grey Papers, 1846–1852* (Ottawa, 1937), vol. II, p. 538. (Town Hall Meeting at Cobourg, 30 October 1849.)
2 *Ibid.* p. 522 (letter to Grey, 14 October 1849).

PAGE 69

1 *Hansard*, vol. LXXXI (June 1845) (New Zealand Debate), p. 947; *The Later Correspondence of Lord John Russell, 1840–1878*, ed. G. P. Gooch, vol. I, p. 198 (18 December 1849, to the Duke of Bedford).

PAGE 70

1 *Elgin-Grey Papers*, vol. II, pp. 586–90. Extracts from London dailies were reprinted and commented on by the *Montreal Herald*.

PAGE 71

1 *Hansard*, 3rd ser. vol. CVIII, pp. 535–67 (8 February 1850).

PAGE 72

1 *Ibid.* pp. 567–79 (immediately following Russell's speech); pp. 1001–7 (Australian Colonies, Government Bill, second reading, 18 February).
2 *Empire, op. cit.* pp. 108–9.

PAGE 73

1 *The Elgin-Grey Papers*, vol. II, pp. 610, 611.
2 *Ibid.* pp. 616, 617 (quoting *The Times*); comments in the *Spectator* and *Morning Star*.

PAGE 74

1 *Edinburgh Review* (April 1851), vol. XCIII, pp. 476–98.

PAGE 76

1 Earl Grey, *The Colonial Policy of Lord John Russell's Administration* (London, 1853), vol. I, pp. 1–49.
2 *Ibid.* vol. II, pp. 299–305.

PAGE 77

1 W. Childe-Pemberton, *Life of Lord Norton* (1909), p. 178.
2 *Hansard*, 3rd ser. vol. CLXIII, p. 1525 (24 June 1861).

PAGE 78

1 Sir Charles Bowyer Adderley, *Letter to the Right Hon. Benjamin Disraeli, M.P. on the Present Relations of England with the Colonies* (1861). In 1862 a new edition was published which carried a preface dealing with Canadian affairs and an appendix of extracts taken from the evidence submitted before a select committee on colonial military expenditure.

PAGE 79

1 R. L. Schuyler, *The Fall of the Old Colonial System* (Oxford, 1945), pp. 226, 227.
2 *Hansard*, 3rd ser. vol. CLXXVIII (23 March 1865), cols. 109 ff.

PAGE 81

1 *Destiny of the British Empire as revealed in the Scriptures* (London, 1865).
2 Disraeli writing to Adderley, 13 September 1864. Childe-Pemberton, *Life of Lord Norton* (1909), p. 188.
3 H. Thring, *Suggestions for Colonial Reform* (London, 1865), p. 12.

PAGE 83

1 Viscount Bury (W. C. Keppel), *Exodus of the Western Nations* (1865), preface, p. iv; main thesis and its defence, vol. II, pp. 451–89.

2 Despite the misleading heading of the chapter '*The climax of Anti-Imperialism*', R. L. Schuyler, *op. cit.* offers an informative synopsis of views advocating colonial separation.

3 That poem was first published in *New Poems* (1867).

PAGE 84

1 *The Times*, 4 January 1866, p. 9. In the same issue the action of the Governor was defended. Bright's views were opposed in the following days, 8 January, p. 8, 13 January, p. 8. A change of attitude began on 27 January, p. 8, and the Governor came in for more criticism on 7 February.

2 *Spectator*, 6 June 1868, vol. XLI, pp. 665, 666.

PAGE 86

1 Joseph Howe, *The Organization of the Empire* (1866), opening lines and pp. 16–32.

PAGE 87

1 Louis Mallet, *The Political Opinions of Richard Cobden*, reprinted from the *North British Review* as introduction to *The Political Writings of Richard Cobden* (ed. 1869); quotations according to the second edition of 1878, esp. pp. xiii, xvi, xix, xx.

PAGE 88

1 C. W. Dilke, *Greater Britain*, ed. Philadelphia (1869), vol. I, preface and pp. 36–8, 232, 259, 260; vol. II, pp. 314–48.

PAGE 89

1 *Ibid.* mainly in vol. I in ch. VI on 'Canada', and in vol. II in ch. XV on 'Colonies', whose last sentence is quoted above.

PAGE 90

1 Bodelsen, *op. cit.* p. 71.

PAGE 91

1 The history of the preliminary meetings and details about the inaugural dinner speeches in A. Folsom, *The Royal Empire Society* (1933), ch. II, pp. 36 ff., dinner speeches reported pp. 46 ff.; for the discussions at the inaugural meeting see *Royal Colonial Institute* (*Colonial Society*), Proceedings, vol. I, p. 5, Chichester Fortescue on the difference of the colonies except 'in their attachment to the great empire to which we all belong' and p. 63 on integrity, Lord Bury's speech, pp. 51 f.; see also Childe-Pemberton, *op. cit.* p. 209.

PAGE 92

1 C. B. Adderley, *Review*, etc. (London, 1869), pp. 5, 10.

PAGE 93

1 *Ibid.* p. 25.

PAGE 94

1 *Selections from Speeches of Earl Russell 1817–1841*, etc. (London, 1870), vol. I, pp. 151–4.

PAGE 95

1 J. A. Froude, Rectorial Address in W. Knight, *Rectorial Addresses, delivered at the University of St. Andrews* (1894), pp. 101, 102.
2 *Spectator*, 11 January 1868, p. 38; see also ch. 1.

PAGE 96

1 *Accounts and Papers, 1868/9*, vol. XLIV, pp. 625–9.

PAGE 97

1 *Spectator*, 24 July 1869, vol. XLII, p. 868.

PAGE 98

1 *Transactions of the National Association for the Promotion of Social Science* (1870), 1st subject of Bristol meeting in autumn 1869, pp. 6, 7.
2 *Ibid.* pp. 112–18.

PAGE 99

1 John Ruskin, *Inaugural Lecture*, Oxford, 1870, pp. 28, 29.

PAGE 100

1 Bodelsen, *op. cit.* p. 106 ff.; G. Bennett, *op. cit.* pp. 245–7.
2 *Hansard*, vol. CXCIX, pp. 193–233, esp. pp. 209–13.

PAGE 101

1 *Hansard*, 3rd ser. vol. CC, pp. 1817 f. (Motion for a Select Committee, 26 April 1870).

PAGE 103

1 Disraeli, *Speeches*, ed. Kebble, vol. II, p. 531; also G. Bennett, *op. cit.* p. 258.

PAGE 104

1 *Annual Register* (1870), pp. 113, 114.

PAGE 105

1 *Spectator*, vol. XLII, p. 868 (24 July 1869).

PAGE 106

1 E. Jenkins, *An Imperial Confederation*, Contemporary Review (April 1871), vol. XVII, pp. 60 ff.

2 Epilogue to *Idylls of the King* (added in 1872), G. Bennett, *op. cit.* p. 256.

PAGE 108

1 T. E. Kebbel, *Selected Speeches*, etc. (1882), vol. II, p. 521.

PAGE 109

1 *Ibid.* pp. 523 ff.

PAGE 110

1 C. A. Bodelsen, *Studies in Mid-Victorian Imperialism* (Copenhagen, 1924), p. 121.

2 Monypenny and Buckle, *The Life of Benjamin Disraeli*, vol. I, p. 1099.

PAGE 111

1 Sir Robert Borden, *Selected Speeches and Documents on British Colonial Policy*, ed. A. Berriedale-Keith, vol. II, p. 378.

PAGE 112

1 *Hansard*, 3rd ser. vol. CCXXI, cols. 1264–91 (4 August 1874), Annexation of Fiji Islands.

PAGE 113

1 *Ibid.* vol. CCXXII, cols. 4, 5 (2 February 1875), Speech from the Throne.

PAGE 114

1 Monypenny and Buckle, *op. cit.* vol. II, p. 1286 ff. (20 September, 15 October 1876).

2 Monypenny and Buckle, *op. cit.* vol. II, p. 1288 (April 1877) and p. 1291 (Montagu Corry, 13 May 1878).

PAGE 115

1 *Edinburgh Review*, vol. CXLIII, p. 272.

PAGE 116

1 *Hansard*, 3rd ser. vol. CCXXVII, cols. 54, 56, 58, 65, 66, 67, 94, 102 (the last being Disraeli's concluding sentences quoted above).

PAGE 117

1   *Daily Telegraph,* 10 February 1876, p. 5a; 14 February, p. 4e; 14 March, p. 4h.

PAGE 118

1   *Punch,* 6 March 1875.
2   W. E. Forster, *Our Colonial Empire*; G. Bennett, *op. cit.* pp. 259–63.
3   *Letters of Queen Victoria,* 2nd ser. ed. G. E. Buckle, vol. II (1926), pp. 238, 438, 440. (Disraeli's letter to the Queen of 21 January 1876 showed that the Queen would have preferred to give the title of Empress a more general significance.)

PAGE 119

1   *Hansard,* 3rd ser. vol. CCXXVII, cols. 408–10.
2   R. Lowe and W. Forster spoke after the Prime Minister, *ibid.* cols. 411–20.

PAGE 120

1   *Punch,* 26 February 1876, p. 74.
2   *Ibid.* 4 March 1876, p. 82.
3   *Letters of Queen Victoria, op. cit.* vol. II, pp. 450 ff. (letter to Theodore Martin, 14 March).

PAGE 121

1   *Hansard,* 3rd ser. vol. CCXXVIII, cols. 130, 131.
2   *Punch,* 8 April 1876, letter to the Editor; 22 April, p. 161, Imperialism triumphant; 6 May, p. 184, Disraeli's newly acquired Imperialism.

PAGE 122

1   *Spectator,* 11 March 1876, pp. 328, 329; 25 March 1876, p. 392; the article headed, English Imperialism, was published in the issue of 8 April 1876, p. 457.

PAGE 123

1   *Fortnightly Review,* 1 April 1876, pp. 617–19.
2   This modifies an earlier report in which we stated that the modern career of the word Imperialism in its relation to Great Britain began in October 1878. See R. Koebner, 'The Emergence of the Concept of Imperialism', *Cambridge Journ.,* vol. V, pp. 726–41 (September 1952). Other parts of that article have been incorporated in the following pages with the permission of the editor.

PAGE 124

1   *Stafford Northcote Papers*, P.R.O. 4/700 and 4/701.
2   *Ibid.* 4/369.

PAGE 125

1   W. M. Thorburn, *The 'Great Game'*: A Plea for a British Imperial Policy. A short statement of the ultimate objective of imperial policy is found in the preface to the second edition.

PAGE 126

1   T. E. Kebbel, *Selected Speeches*, vol. II, p. 160.
2   Buckle, *op. cit.* vol. II, p. 964.
3   Madame Olga Novikoff, *Reminiscences and Correspondence*, ed. W. T. Stead (1909), vol. I, p. 265 (27 November 1876).

PAGE 127

1   Hughenden Archives, XVI, 10.

PAGE 128

1   *Punch*, vol. LXXII, p. 210 (12 May 1877); vol. LXXIII, pp. 42, 54, 59, 73.
2   *Ibid.* vol. LXXIII, p. 126 (22 September 1877).
3   Hughenden Archives, XV (Corry to Beaconsfield, 21 May 1877).
4   *Ibid.* (Corry to Beaconsfield, 19 April 1877).

PAGE 129

1   Buckle, *Life of Disraeli*, vol. II, p. 1030 (29 July 1877).
2   *Stafford Northcote Papers*, P.R.O. 3/548.   (To Derby, Paris, 26 May 1877.)

PAGE 130

1   *Hansard*, 3rd ser. vol. CCXXXIV, cols. 408–14 (7 May 1877, Resolutions, Mr. Gladstone).
2   *Ibid.* cols. 646, 771.
3   *Nineteenth Century* (July 1877), vol. I, p. 872.
4   Buckle, *Life of Disraeli*, vol. II, p. 1089 (Queen Victoria to Beaconsfield, 10 January 1878).

PAGE 131

1   *Hansard*, 3rd ser. vol. CCXXXVI, col. 820 (14 August 1877, Prorogation of the Parliament).
2   *Ibid.* vol. CCXXXV, col. 995 (9 July 1877, South African Bill).
3   'The Royal Colonial Institute', *Proceedings*, vol. VI, pp. 36–9.
4   In a paper read to the Institute in 1881, see Bodelsen, *op. cit.* p. 127n.

PAGE 132

1 J. Vogel, 'Greater or Lesser Britain', *Nineteenth Century*, vol. I, pp. 809–31 (July 1877).
2 J. S. Little, *A World Empire* (London, 1879). (The essay had been composed during the years 1876–77.)

PAGE 133

1 E. Dicey, *Nineteenth Century*, vol. I, pp. 665–85; vol. II, pp. 3–14, 292–308.

PAGE 135

1 *Stafford Northcote Papers*, P.R.O. 4/232 (15 December 1877).
2 *Gladstone Papers*, Brit. Mus. Add. MS. 44303, fols. 282 and 283 (25 and 27 January 1878).

PAGE 136

1 S. Maccoby, *English Radicalism 1833–1886*, p. 230; based on *London Illustrated News*, 2 March 1878.
2 Monypenny and Buckle, *op. cit.* vol. II, pp. 1138–43.
3 *Ibid.* pp. 1133, 1138.
4 *Annual Register* (1878), p. 35.

PAGE 137

1 T. E. Kebbel, *Selected Speeches*, vol. II, p. 177.

PAGE 138

1 *Nineteenth Century* (April 1878), pp. 617–33.

PAGE 139

1 *Punch*, vol. LXXIV (25 May 1878), pp. 234, 235 (cartoon).
2 *Ibid.* 1 June 1878, pp. 246, 247.
3 *Ibid.* 8 June 1878, pp. 258, 259, 261.

PAGE 140

1 *Spectator*, 20 April 1878, pp. 493, 494. (The Despatch of Native Troops to Malta.)
2 *Hansard*, 3rd ser. vol. CCXL, cols. 264 ff. (20 May 1878).
3 *Ibid.* cols. 290–2.
4 *Ibid.* col. 559 (the speech made by W. E. Forster).

PAGE 141

1 *Stafford Northcote Papers*, P.R.O. 4/246, letter to Sir John A. Macdonald, 25 May 1878.

PAGE 142

1 T. E. Kebbel, *Selected Speeches*, vol. II, pp. 179–202.

PAGE 143

1 *Annual Register* (1878), p. 99. *The Times*, however, had 'England's old Imperial position' instead of tradition (1 August 1878), p. 10.
2 *Daily News*, 23 July 1878; 29 July (The Knightsbridge Banquet); 2 August; 13 September; 23 September, in the editorials printed on page 4.
3 *Spectator*, 13 July 1878, p. 883.

PAGE 144

1 *A Selection from Goldwin Smith's Correspondence*, ed. A. Haultain (London), letter to Mr Winkworth, Toronto, 22 January 1878, p. 85.
2 *Hansard*, 3rd ser. vol. CCXLII, cols. 881–6.

PAGE 145

1 *Nineteenth Century*, vol. IV (September 1878), pp. 393 ff.

PAGE 146

1 *Nineteenth Century*, ibid. pp. 560–84.

PAGE 148

1 *Punch*, 17 August 1878, p. 61.
2 *The Times*, 3 September 1878, p. 6.
3 *Daily Telegraph*, 24 September 1878, p. 5.

PAGE 149

1 *Fortnightly Review*, vol. XXIV, p. 457 (1 October 1878).
2 *Ibid.* pp. 458–9.

PAGE 151

1 *Spectator*, 5 October 1878, pp. 1230, 1231.
2 *Daily Telegraph*, 1 October 1878, p. 4.

PAGE 152

1 J. L. Garvin, *Joseph Chamberlain* (London, 1932), vol. I, p. 267.
2 *Nineteenth Century* (October 1878), vol. IV, p. 585 ff.
3 Speech made in Birmingham on 19 October, *The Times*, 21 October 1878, p. 11. Other speeches in *The Times*, 22 and 23 October, p. 4 and p. 10 resp.

PAGE 153

1 *Daily News*, 21 October 1878, p. 5.
2 *Daily Telegraph*, 21 October 1878, p. 4.
3 *Punch*, 2 November 1878, vol. LXXV, p. 193.

PAGE 154

1 A report of the address was printed in the *Scotsman* (6 November), p. 5 and the address was printed with slight deviations from the original in the *Fortnightly Review* (December 1878), pp. 760–3; see also the *Spectator* (9 November), pp. 1388, 1389.

PAGE 155

1 *The Times*, 6 November 1878, p. 9.
2 *Nineteenth Century*, vol. IV, p. 797.

PAGE 156

1 *Ibid.* p. 793.
2 *Punch*, 23 November 1878, vol. LXXV, p. 233.

PAGE 157

1 *Hansard*, 3rd ser. vol. CCXLIII, col. 768 (13 December 1878).
2 *Spectator*, 14 December 1878, p. 1553.
3 *Annual Register* (1878), p. 256; concerning the change in editorship, possibly because of the revelation of a Liberal bias, see Monypenny and Buckle, *op. cit.* vol. II, p. 1268.

PAGE 158

1 *Contemporary Review*, vol. XXXVI, pp. 568, 571 (December 1879).
2 E. D. Wilson, 'The Government and its Critics', *Nineteenth Century*, (February 1879), pp. 380, 383, 384.
3 *Punch* (19 April 1878), p. 174; see also 25 January, p. 35; 1 March 1879, p. 95.
4 A collection of Liberal pamphlets is kept in the British Museum, B.M. 8139 b.3. *The Book of Benjamin, Our Spirited Foreign Policy, Who is your leader? The Instincts of Liberalism.* The prominent use of Jingoism and Imperialism is evident in all. *Plundering and Blundering*, A political Retrospect, 1874–9.

PAGE 159

1 James George Ashworth, *Imperial Ben* (1879), p. 75.
2 W. Sykes, *Before Joseph came into Egypt* (1898), p. 27; concerning Frere's Empire ideas, see T. W. Irvine, *British Basutoland and the Basutos* (London, 1881).
3 G. D. Campbell, Duke of Argyll, *The Eastern Question*, p. xiv.

PAGE 160

1 Nemesis (Alfred H. Robbins), *Five Years of Tory Rule* (London, 1879), p. 133.
2 Sir David Wedderburn, *Modern Imperialism in India* (London, 1879), p. 21 ff.
3 W. E. Gladstone, *Political Speeches in Scotland* (London 1879), vol. I, p. 128; Third Midlothian Speech, November 27.

PAGE 161

1 *Ibid.* vol. II, p. 175.
2 *Ibid.* vol. I, p. 128.

PAGE 162

1 *Nineteenth Century* (March 1880), p. 406.
2 *Contemporary Review* (November–December 1879), vol. XXXVI, pp. 398–431, 665–96.
3 British Museum, B.M. 8139 b.b. nos. 3–14; 8138 df. 7. '... No formula has ever been devised that so accurately expresses the theory of Napoleonic Imperialism as these words of Mr Disraeli's,' P. Baynes, *The Nation's Vote* (1880), p. 6.

PAGE 163

1 F. Seebohm, 'Imperialism and Socialism', *Nineteenth Century* (April 1880), vol. VII, p. 728.
2 *Ibid.* p. 730.

PAGE 164

1 *The Times*, 11 March 1880, p. 11.

PAGE 166

1 J. Shirley, 'A Last Word on Disraeli' (June 1881), *The Contemporary Review*, vol. XXXIX, p. 990.
2 *Fortnightly Review* (June 1880), vol. XXVII, pp. 867–70.

PAGE 167

1 J. A. Froude, *Lord Beaconsfield* (1890), p. 261.
2 G. Brandes, *Lord Beaconsfield* (1879), p. 358.
3 *Political Science Quarterly* (1921), no. 36, p. 315.
4 W. T. Stead, *The M.P. for Russia*, vol. I, p. 247, quoted in Seton-Watson, *op. cit.* p. 72.

PAGE 168

1 *Annual Register* (1880), pp. 5, 32.
2 *Annual Register* (1883), pp. 167, 178, 179.
3 Hammond, *Gladstone and the Irish Nation* (London, 1938), p. 404.

PAGE 169

1 *Ibid.* p. 476.
2 G. Smith, *Dismemberment no Remedy* (1886), p. 31.

PAGE 170

1 *Nineteenth Century* (January–June 1886), p. 784.
2 *Fortnightly Review* (May 1886), p. 701.
3 *Hansard*, 3rd ser. vol. CCCV, Government of Ireland Bill (10th May 1886), col. 586.

PAGE 171

1 E. A. Freeman, 'Prospects of Home Rule', *Fortnightly Review* (September 1886), pp. 319, 320. See also R. Koebner's comment on Freeman's ignorance about earlier meanings of the British Empire in R. Koebner, *Empire* (Cambridge, 1961), pp. 295–6.

PAGE 172

1 *Contemporary Review* (March 1887), vol. LI, pp. 305–21.
2 *Fortnightly Review* (May 1886), p. 602.

PAGE 173

1 Garvin, *op. cit.* vol. II, p. 164.
2 J. R. Seeley, *The Expansion of England*, ed. Macmillan, London (1925), p. 44.
3 *Ibid.* p. 89.

PAGE 174

1 *Ibid.* p. 127, 205.
2 *Ibid.* p. 212.
3 *Ibid.* Lecture VIII, pp. 340–1.

PAGE 175

1 *Ibid.* p. 346.
2 *Ibid.* p. 350.
3 *Fortnightly Review* (August 1896), p. 191.
4 *Westminster Gazette*, 15 January 1895, p. 2.
5 *Contemporary Review* (April 1884), p. 537.

PAGE 176

1 *Contemporary Review* (January 1884), vol. XLV, pp. 1–4. *Fortnightly Review,* vol. XXV, pp. 241–55; vol. XXXVI, pp. 339, 400.

PAGE 177

1 British Museum, *Gladstone Papers*, Add. MSS. 44142, fols. 25–7, Derby to Gladstone, 18 December 1883.

PAGE 178

1 *Imperial Federation*, Report of the Conference held 29 July 1884 at the Westminster Palace Hotel, London, p. 52.
2 *Ibid.* p. 37.
3 *Ibid.* p. 48.

PAGE 179

1 For press reactions see *ibid.* pp. 70–98.
2 *The Cambridge History of the British Empire*, vol. VII, part II, p. 213.
3 *Fortnightly Review* (March 1885), vol. XXXVII, pp. 338–51.

PAGE 180

1 *Spectator* (March 1885), vol. LVIII, p. 378.
2 J. Cowen, *Speeches on the Near Eastern Question*, etc. (ed. 1909), pp. 197–201.

PAGE 181

1 *Ibid.* pp. 325–6.
2 G. Bennett, *op. cit.* p. 293.

PAGE 182

1 *Ibid.* p. 295.
2 *Ibid.* p. 283.

PAGE 183

1 J. A. Froude, *Oceana or England and her Colonies*, 3rd ed. (London, 1886), p. 12.
2 *Ibid.* p. 211.
3 *Ibid.* p. 393.

PAGE 184

1 *Fortnightly Review* (August 1886), vol. XL, p. 270.
2 Sir George F. Bowen, *The Federation of the British Empire* (London, 1886), p. 5.

PAGE 185

1 *Ibid.* p. 16.
2 *Hansard*, 3rd ser. vol. CCCIX, col. 1350.

PAGE 186

1 *National Review*, vol. VI, p. 651, 'parochialism' is used in a derogatory sense while 'imperialism' is approved.
2 The Royal Colonial Institute, *Proceedings* (1887/8), Report on the Colonial Conference of 1887, p. 36.

PAGE 187

1 Garvin, *op. cit.* vol. II, p. 333; *Foreign and Colonial Speeches*, J. Chamberlain (1897), pp. 3 ff.
2 Ch. Dilke, *The Present Position in European Politics* (1887), p. 363.
3 *Ibid.* pp. 356–9.

PAGE 188

1 C. W. Boyd, *Mr. Chamberlain's Speeches* (1914), p. 322.
2 *Ibid.* p. 323.

PAGE 189

1 J. Willison, *Sir George Parkin* (1929), pp. 60–1.

PAGE 190

1 *Ibid.* pp. 63–72.
2 *The Times*, 3 August 1889, p. 7.

PAGE 191

1 C. W. Dilke, *Problems of Greater Britain* (London, 1890), pp. 273, 274.
2 *Ibid.* p. 628.
3 *Ibid.* pp. 643, 644.

PAGE 192

1 *Ibid.* pp. 280, 635.
2 *Fortnightly Review*, vol. LIII (June 1893), p. 895.
3 *Britannic Confederation*, ed. A. S. White (1892), pp. x, xiii, 49.
4 W. T. Stead, *Gladstone 1809–1898*, A Character Sketch, pp. 75–7.

PAGE 193

1 *Contemporary Review* (August 1894), vol. LXVI, pp. 192–209.
2 *Nineteenth Century*, vol. XXXV (March 1894), p. 375; see also *The Times*, 8, 11, 12 July 1895 in its reports about the election campaigns of A. J. Balfour and J. Chamberlain.
3 J. Scott Keltie, *The Partition of Africa* (1893), p. 202.

PAGE 194

1 *Contemporary Review*, vol. LXV, p. 465; *Fortnightly Review*, vol. LV, p. 713.
2 *Nineteenth Century*, vol. XXXVI, p. 498.
3 T. F. Coates, *Lord Rosebery* (1900), vol. I, pp. 324, 386; vol. II, pp. 552, 788; *Annual Register* (1893), p. 68.

PAGE 198

1 Gwynn and Tuckwell, *Life of Sir Charles Dilke* (London, 1917), vol. II, pp. 52 f. Of Dilke's letter to Grant Duff, 22 May 1884, a copy is preserved with the Gladstone Papers (Add. MS. 44149, fols. 215, 216); see also Derby's letter quoted in the previous chapter, (note 1, page 177). In it Derby suggested to announce that Zululand was to be governed '*ad interim—much as we do Egypt*'. See also Koebner's article on 'Economic Imperialism' in the *Economic History Review*, 2nd ser. (1949), vol. II, p. 8. This article has been incorporated into this and the following chapters with the kind permission of the editors.
2 *The History of The Times*, vol. III, pp. 20–38.
3 *Nineteenth Century*, vol. XVIII (1885), p. 1.
4 E. A. Walker, 'The Jameson Raid', *Camb. Hist. Journ.*, vol. VI (1941), p. 286.
5 *Scots Observer*, 25 May 1889, p. 11 ('Sir Hercules Robinson').
6 Cf. J. S. Cotton, *Colonies and Dependencies* (1883) (part of the textbook series, *The English Citizen*, as aptly emphasized by Dilke, *Problems, loc. cit.*), p. 114; Dilke's diaries, Gwynn and Tuckwell, *loc. cit.* p. 86.

PAGE 199

1 In the same year, 1884, The 'Empire Theatre' in Leicester Square opened its doors, but the name was then also the rallying-cry against the Irish demand for Home Rule and is not necessarily significant. For 'imperial spreadeagle policy' see *Hansard*, 3rd ser. vol. CCXCI, cols. 1050–1126, esp. col. 1054.
2 Dilke, *Problems of Greater Britain, op. cit.* p. 464.
3 'Manchester Chamber of Commerce'. Special meeting of members, 21 October 1884, etc. *Report of Proceedings*.
4 William N. M. Geary, *Nigeria under British Rule* (1927), p. 182.

PAGE 200

1 Joseph Hatton, *The New Ceylon* (1881), pp. 2, 30.
2 Geary, *loc. cit.* pp. 177, 183, 188–92.

PAGE 201

1 McDermott, *British East Africa or IBEA* (1893), p. 14.
2 *Fortnightly Review*, vol. CIII (1893), p. 148.

3 *Scots Observer,* 2 March 1889, p. 405.
4 Henley, *National Observer,* 18 April 1891, pp. 556 f. To Stead's enthusiasm Edmund Garrett's reports from South Africa, 1889–90, made an important contribution. Cf. J. A. Spender and Cyril Asquith, *Life of H. H. Asquith* (1932), pp. 1, 147. The passage quoted above is from the appeal 'To all English-speaking Folk', *Review of Reviews* (1891). The only disquieting element in 'the potentialities that lie hidden in this remarkable personality' was for Stead at that time that Rhodes was 'deficient in his appreciation of existing factors in our home politics'; he wished to improve upon the great man's erudition by providing him with instructive books and asked Gladstone for advice, which, of course, was withheld (Add. MS. 44303, fol. 462, 17 August 1891). Dilke's attitude to the same question was characteristically different; he was simply annoyed by Rhode's 'avowed intention of ultimately coming to England to take part in English politics'. (Gwynn and Tuckwell, *loc. cit.* p. 301.)
5 Cf. Chamberlain's speech in the Zululand debate, 1884, *Hansard,* 3rd ser. vol. CCXCI, pp. 1113 f. and H. H. Johnston, *The Story of my Life,* p. 223.
6 Letter to Stead, 28 May 1889, Add MS. 44303, fol. 406.

PAGE 202

1 Gardiner, *Life of Harcourt,* vol. II, pp. 151, 192, 195, 198, 227. Harcourt believed, so Balfour said, 'in the curtailment of the British Empire if he believed in nothing else'. (Fred. Whyte, *The Life of W. T. Stead,* vol. II, p. 31.)
2 Speech at the Royal Colonial Institute, 1 March 1893, when he looked forward to an Anglo-Saxon world; see also preceding chapter, p. 361.
3 *Hansard,* 4th ser. vol. X, pp. 547, 560.
4 *Fortnightly Review,* vol. CIII (1893), *op. cit.* In 1895 Dilke sold his South African Company shares, 'not thinking them things for a politician'. (Gwynn and Tuckwell, *op. cit.* vol. II, p. 496.)

PAGE 203

1 *Hansard,* 4th ser. vol. X (20 March 1893), col. 588.
2 *Ibid.* p. 592.
3 *Hansard, loc. cit.* col. 596.

PAGE 204

1 *Nineteenth Century,* vol. XXXIII (February 1893), pp. 220–34.
2 *Edinburgh Review* (April 1893), no. CCCLXIV, p. 283.

PAGE 205

1 *Spectator,* vol. LXX (May 1893), p. 631; vol. LXXI, p. 69.
2 *The Autobiography of Sir Henry Morton Stanley* (London, 1909), pp. 440–42.

PAGE 206

1 Garvin, *op. cit.* vol. II, pp. 452–6; *Foreign and Colonial Speeches*, *op. cit.* pp. 31–41.
2 A. Milner, *England in Egypt* (7th edition, London, 1899), pp. 160 f.
3 *Spectator*, vol. LXX (January 1893), pp. 83, 84.
4 *New Review*, vol. VIII, pp. 316, 317.

PAGE 207

1 *Nineteenth Century*, vol. XXXIX (April 1896), p. 547.
2 *Spectator*, vol. LXXIV (September 1895), p. 362.

PAGE 208

1 *Nineteenth Century*, vol. XXXVIII (September 1895), pp. 442–9.
2 G. Bennett, *op. cit.* pp. 313–16.
3 *Nineteenth Century* (July 1890), p. 4.
4 D. Wellesley and S. Gwynn, *Sir George Goldie* (1934), p. 65.

PAGE 209

1 *Nineteenth Century*, vol. XXXIX (May 1896), pp. 721–3.

PAGE 210

1 Speech at the Royal Colonial Institute, 31 March 1897, George Bennett, *op. cit.* p. 318.
2 Quoted in Baden Powell, *The Downfall of Prempeh*, pp. 18, 19.

PAGE 211

1 Kennedy Jones, *Fleet Street and Downing Street* (1919), pp. 144–6; W. L. Langer, *The Diplomacy of Imperialism* (1935), vol. I, p. 83.
2 *The Times*, 29 September 1897, p. 4.

PAGE 212

1 *Spectator*, 2 October 1897, p. 428.
2 *Contemporary Review*, vol. LXXII (August 1897), pp. 171–82.
3 J. Holland Rose, *The Rise and Growth of Democracy in Great Britain* (1898), pp. 198, 199.

PAGE 213

1 *Contemporary Review*, vol. LXXIII (April 1898), pp. 470–80.
2 *Nineteenth Century*, vol. XLIV (October 1898), p. 525.
3 For early comments, cf. the letter of W. H. Page quoted below (Burton J. Hendrick, *The Earlier Life and Letters of W. H. P.* (1928), p. 264); *New*

York Nation (July 1898); O. Flower, *The Arena* (Boston, 1898); F. Greenwood, 'The Anglo-American Future', *Nineteenth Century*, vol. xciv. In England Edward Dicey, the veteran of anti-Gladstonianism, became a most eloquent champion of the cause in 'The New American Imperialism', *Nineteenth Century*, *loc. cit.* pp. 487 ff.

4 Congress. Record, 55th Congress, 2nd Session, Appendix, p. 573. *Kölnische Zeitung* (21 June), p. 1.

PAGE 214

1 The discussion includes Bryan's speeches, Karl Schurz, 'American Imperialism' and, on the other hand, President McKinley's message to Congress concerning the annexations. It has given rise to important scholarly comment but deserves special surveying with regard to the concepts of 'empire' and 'imperialism'.

2 *New York Nation*, vol. lxxiv (15 July 1898), p. 74.

3 *Forum*, vol. xxvi (1898), pp. 177, 178.

4 *North American Review*, vol. clxviii (January 1898), p. 14.

5 *Spectator*, 21 January 1899, p. 77.

PAGE 215

1 *Die Grenzboten*, 58. Jahrgang, 1. Vierteljahr 1899, pp. 14 f. The first German student of the movement was, however, the socialist refugee M. Beer, who in the Jubilee year 1897 wrote an article, 'Der moderne englische Imperialismus', for *Die Neue Zeit*, Jahrg. 16, 1, pp. 300 ff.

2 *Imperialismo. La civiltà industriale e le sue conquiste*, Studii Inglesi (Milano, 1901), Prefazione. The book had been in preparation since 1898.

3 *Contemporary Review*, vol. lxxv (February 1899), esp. pp. 158–60.

PAGE 217

1 R. Kipling, *Collected Verse* (New York, 1907), Kitchener's School, 1898, pp. 113–15.

PAGE 218

1 *Contemporary Review*, vol. xxv (March 1899), pp. 306–9.

2 *Spectator*, vol. lxxxii (11 February 1899), p. 193.

PAGE 222

1 *Contemporary Review*, vol. lxxiv, esp. pp. 176–8, and 833, 834 (July–December 1898).

2 S. H. Swinny, *The Nemesis of Empire* (April 1898) (quoted in *Public Opinion*, 22 April 1898, vol. lxxiii, p. 487).

3 Speech at Brechin, *The Times*, 18 January 1899, p. 6.

PAGE 223

1 Among political speeches those of Hicks-Beach, Chamberlain, G. Wyndham, Asquith, 18, 19 and 28 January, and the address of Campbell-Bannerman to the National Liberal Federation on 8 March, are notable for being reported and commented upon copiously in the daily and weekly press. Sir R. Giffen's paper on 'The Relative Growth of the Component Parts of the Empire', read at the Royal Colonial Institute on 14 February and Rosebery's address at the Cromwell tercentenary belong to the series as well. Of articles in periodicals 'Imperialism' by J. L. Walton was already mentioned in the last chapter.

2 Cf. Fred, Greenwood, *Nineteenth Century*, vol. XLV (April 1899), pp. 538 ff., esp. pp. 541, 543.

3 And satirically by *Punch*, 24 May 1899: 'Private Views: Mostly Unpopular. No. II, Empire Makers.'

PAGE 224

1 Ritortus in *Contemporary Review*, vol. LXXVI (July, August 1899), pp. 132–152, 282–304, esp. pp. 145 f., 295 ff., where the author referred also to similar warnings of the *Financial News*.

2 Pp. 140, 172–8.

PAGE 225

1 *Contemporary Review*, vol. LXXV (June 1899), pp. 782–99.

PAGE 226

1 *West African Studies* (2nd ed. 1901), pp. 415 ff., esp. pp. 419, 423 ff. On Mary Kingsley's attitude towards colonial economics, cf. Hancock, *Survey*, vol. II, 2, pp. 332 f.

2 'The New Jingoism', *Spectator*, vol. LXXXI (8 October 1899), p. 480—preceded by an appeal for imperial concentration, *loc. cit.* (30 July), p. 137; the tendency of which is similar to that of Greenwood's article quoted above.

PAGE 227

1 J. A. Hobson, *The War in South Africa* (London, 1900), p. 226; see also the chapters on Johannesburg and the chapter 'For Whom are We Fighting?' pp. 189–97.

PAGE 228

1 Beatrice Webb, *Our Partnership* (London, 1948), pp. 190–4; A. R. Fry, *Emily Hobhouse* (1929), p. 74.

2 *Hansard*, 4th ser. vol. LXXVII, 17 October 1899, cols. 124, 125; 23 October, col. 524; 27 October, col. 783.

3 Add. MS. 46317, Brit. Mus. 10 October 1899.

4 *Review of Reviews*, vol. XX, 2 October 1899, p. 329; 1 December 1899, p. 554.

PAGE 229

1 *Ibid.* vol. XXI, May 1900, pp. 441–9.

2 *Canadian Historical Review*, vol XL (December 1959), J. O. Baylen, W. T. Stead and the Boer War, p. 304 ff.

3 *Contemporary Review*, vol. LXXVI (December 1899), pp. 775–88.

PAGE 230

1 *Contemporary Review*, vol. LXXVI (December 1899), p. 900 f.

2 *Hansard*, 4th ser. vol. LXXVIII, col. 218.

PAGE 231

1 Lord Rosebery, *Questions of Empire* (New York, 1901), p. 8.

2 B. Webb, *Our Partnership*, *op. cit.* p. 193.

3 *North American Review*, vol. CLXX (April 1900), pp. 523–6.

4 *Hansard*, 4th ser. vol. LXXVIII (6 February 1900), cols. 783–96.

PAGE 232

1 *Imperialism*, Independent Labour Party, Pamphlet No. 3 (May 1900), pp. 15 ff.

2 B. Shaw, *Fabianism and the Empire* (London, 1900), p. 1; a detailed study of the attitude of the Fabians towards Imperialism and of the nature of social Imperialism, particularly during the first decade of this century, is found in B. Semmel, *Imperialism and Social Reform* (London, 1960), esp. pp. 64–72 dealing with the Fabians.

3 *Monthly Review*, vol. I (1900), pp. 1–14.

PAGE 233

1 *Westminster Review*, vol. CLVII (February 1902), pp. 126–35.

2 G. Gale, *The Exploitation of the British Flag by Rhodes, Chamberlain, Milner & Co.* (Leeds, 1902), p. 28, B.M. 8138 i. 20, 17.

3 *Edinburgh Review*, vol. CXCV (January 1902), p. 256.

PAGE 234

1 Hirst in *Liberalism and Empire*, pp. 72–4.

2 Hirst, *loc. cit.* pp. 63 f. More sarcastically, Bernard Shaw, *Fabianism and the Empire* (1900), pp. 9 f.

PAGE 235

1 Hirst, *loc. cit.* pp. 43–57.
2 Beatrice Webb's diary entries of September and October 1901 (*Our Partnership*, pp. 220–3), compared with those of January 1900, p. 194, show how Socialist thinking at this time was not necessarily bound to take up an anti-Imperialist line. The closing pages of the book, pp. 488 f., are remarkable for mirroring the change of mind after the Great War.

PAGE 237

1 *North American Review*, vol. CLXVII (September 1898), pp. 326–39.
2 *Forum*, vol. XXVI, pp. 282–5.

PAGE 238

1 *Nation*, vol. LXVII (24 November 1898), p. 380.
2 *North American Review*, vol. CLXVIII (January 1899), pp. 5–13; second part, pp. 363–72.

PAGE 239

1 *Review of Reviews* (January 1899), p. 14.
2 C. Schurz, *American Imperialism* (January 1899), 34 pp., esp. p. 17.

PAGE 240

1 *Nation*, vol. LXVIII (15 June 1899), p. 450.
2 Commager, *Documents of American History*, p. 192, no. 351; C. Schurz, *Speeches*, etc. vol. V, p. 77 ff.

PAGE 241

1 *Nation*, vol. LXXI (5 July 1900), p. 7.
2 *North American Review*, vol. CLXX (June 1900), p. 769; *Forum*, vol. XXX (1900), pp. 105, 273, 283, 284.
3 *North American Review*, vol. CLXXI (October 1900), pp. 435–8.

PAGE 242

1 *Ibid.* (September 1900), pp. 289 ff.
2 *The Messages and Papers of Woodrow Wilson*, ed. New York (1924), vol. I, p. 470.
3 *The Listener*, vol. LXI (22 January 1959), p. 155.

PAGE 243

1 *Contemporary Review*, vol. LXXXIV (December 1903), pp. 764–74.
2 *Ibid.* p. 763.

PAGE 244

1 *North American Review*, vol. CLXX (April 1900), p. 462.
2 *Revue des Deux Mondes*, vol. LVII (February 1900), pp. 522–4.
3 *Ibid.* pp. 520–2.

PAGE 245

1 *La Revue de Paris*, vol. XII (April 1900), pp. 515–21; the same sentiments
   were presented in detail in a book by the author of the article, V. Bérard,
   L'Angleterre et l'impérialisme anglais (1900).
2 *Contemporary Review*, vol. LXXVII (June 1900), pp. 881–2.

PAGE 246

1 Heinrich Class, *Wider den Strom* (Leipzig, 1932), pp. 57–65; *Deutsch-
   Soziale Blätter* (15 Jahrg.), 4 January 1900, pp. 2, 26; 18 January 1900, p.
   26; 28 June 1900, p. 301; for a detailed presentation of the blending
   between anti-British and anti-Semitic sentiment in German thought cf.
   H. D. Schmidt, *Anti-Western and Anti-Jewish Tradition*, Leo Baeck
   Institute, Year Book IV, London 1959.
2 *Neue Zeit*, no. 7, 1899; *Preussische Jahrbücher*, vol. XCVIII (December
   1899), pp. 583–7.
3 A. Tille, *Aus Englands Flegeljahren* (1901), pp. viii, ix, 46, 47, 89.
4 *Die Gegenwart* (30. Jahrg. March 1901), p. 178.

PAGE 247

1 *Schweizerische Rundschau* (1. Jahrg. 1900), p. 220.
2 *Neue Deutsche Rundschau* (12. Jahrg. 1901), p. 673.
3 *Ibid.* pp. 679–84.

PAGE 250

1 J. A. Hobson, *The Psychology of Jingoism* (London, 1901).

PAGE 251

1 *Contemporary Review*, vol. LXXVIII (October 1900), pp. 541–52.
2 *Contemporary Review*, vol. LXXVII (January 1900), pp. 1–17; the article
   was reprinted in New York.

PAGE 253

1 *Contemporary Review*, vol. LXXXII (August 1902), pp. 228 ff.
2 *Ibid.* p. 227.
3 *Political Science Quarterly*, vol. XVII (1902), pp. 460–89.

PAGE 258

1 *Punch*, vol. CXXXIV (5 February 1908), p. 96.
2 Lord Cromer, *Ancient and Modern Imperialism* (London, 1910), p. 4.
3 E. Seillière, *Philosophie de l'Impérialisme, 1903/1908.*
4 G. v. Schulze-Gaevernitz, *Britischer Imperialismus*, etc. (1906), pp. 5–29, 54–6, 418.

PAGE 259

1 G. Schmoller, *Grundriss der Allgemeinen Volkswirtschaftslehre* (1904), part II, pp. 637–9; (ed. 1919), pp. 717–39.
2 E. Marcks, *Die imperialistische Idee in der Gegenwart* (1903), in *Männer und Zeiten*, vol. II (Leipzig, 1918), pp. 229 ff. (ed. 1912), pp. 267 ff.
3 *Ibid.* (ed. 1918), p. 226.

PAGE 260

1 A. Viallate, *La Crise Anglaise. Impérialisme et Protection* (1905), p. viii.
2 L. Hennebicq, *L'Impérialisme Occidental* (Paris/Bruxelles, 1913), pp. 10–19, 273.
3 E. Flourens, *La France conquise* (Paris, 1907).

PAGE 261

1 A. v. Peez, *England und der Kontinent* (8th ed. Wien, 1915), p. 13.
2 *Nineteenth Century*, vol. LXIII (January 1908), pp. 151–65.

PAGE 262

1 A. Milner, *The Nation and the Empire* (1913), vol. I, Introduction.
2 *Fortnightly Review*, vol. XCIII (January 1913), pp. 1–12.
3 *Socialist Review*, vol. VIII (October 1911), pp. 13–24.
4 *Ibid.* p. 125; see also B. Semmel, *op. cit.* p. 140, on the Fabians and the *New Statesman* and their positive attitudes towards Imperialism during the years 1911–13.

PAGE 263

1 *Ibid.* vol. X (December 1912), p. 244.
2 S. Olivier, *White Capital and Coloured Labour* (1910), Introduction.

PAGE 264

1 H. N. Brailsford, *The War of Steel and Gold* (3rd ed. 1915), pp. 51–81; definition of the term on p. 74.

PAGE 265

1 R. Luxemburg, *Reform or Revolution* (1899); K. Kautsky, *Die soziale Revolution* (Berlin, 1902), part I, pp. 34–6.

2 O. Bauer, *Die Nationalitätenfrage und die Sozialdemokratie* (1907), pp. 472–6.

PAGE 266

1 R. Hilferding, *Das Finanzkapital* (ed. Wien, 1923), pp. 390–477.
2 R. Luxemburg, *Die Akkumulation des Kapitals* (ed. Berlin, 1923), p. 361.

PAGE 267

1 *Ibid.*
2 *Sozialistische Monatshefte*, May 1912, p. 549.
3 *Ibid.* p. 555; p. 551 as definition of imperialism: 'Neigung die staatliche Herrschaft über Land und Leute zu erwerben oder zu behaupten.'
4 *Die Neue Zeit* (31 Jahrgang), December 1912, p. 346.

PAGE 268

1 *Sozialistische Monatshefte*, 27 March 1913, p. 333.
2 *Ibid.* p. 339.

PAGE 269

1 V. I. Lenin, *Collected Works* (New York, 1930), vol. XVIII, p. 61.
2 *Ibid.* p. 69; see also p. 145.
3 *Ibid.* p. 236.

PAGE 270

1 V. I. Lenin, *Imperialism* (ed. New York, 1939), p. 88.
2 *Ibid.* p. 111.

PAGE 271

1 A. Viallate, *La Crise Anglaise. Impérialisme et Protection* (1905). Cf. esp. p. viii.
2 *Economic Imperialism and International Relations during the last Fifty Years* (New York, 1923), pp. 62 f., 167 f.
3 American writing based on the concept has been reviewed by E. M. Winslow, 'Marxian, Liberal, and Sociological Theories of Imperialism', *The Journal of Political Economy*, vol. XXXIX (1931), pp. 737 ff. IV 'The Formula of Economic Imperialism and the Historians.'

PAGE 273

1 *Capitalism, Socialism, and Democracy* (1943), pp. 49–55; *Imperialism* (New York, 1955, American ed.), of an article published in German after the First World War.

2 Lately by W. K. Hancock, *Survey of British Commonwealth Affairs* (1940), vol. II, pt. I, pp. 26 f., and by Louis M. Hacker, *England and America: the ties that bind*, Inaugural Lecture, Oxford, 1948, pp. 19 f.
3 Hancock, *Survey*, etc. vol. II, pt. 2, pp. 300–2; Frankel, *Capital Investment in Africa* (1938), p. 28.

PAGE 274

1 E. Ludendorff, *Kriegsführung und Politik* (Berlin, 1923), p. 323; Admiral Tirpitz, *Erinnerungen* (1919), pp. 157/8, 222, 274/5; Kaiser Wilhelm II, *Ereignisse und Gestalten* (1922), p. 219.
2 *Heidelberger Akademie der Wissenschaften*, Sitzungsberichte, 2. Abh. 1922.

PAGE 275

1 F. Brie, *Imperialistische Strömungen in der englischen Literatur* (2nd ed. Halle, 1928), p. xiii.
2 E. Meyer, *Kleine Schriften* (Halle, 1924), vol. II, p. 559; *Die Vereinigten Staaten von Amerika* (Frankfurt a/M, 1920), pp. 172, 244, 284; F. Meinecke, *Nach der Revolution* (München, 1919), pp. 88–96. See also E. Troeltsch, *Spektator Briefe*; F. Schäfer, *Weltgeschichte der Neuzeit* (Berlin, 1920), pp. 449, 450; J. Hatschek, *Britisches und römisches Weltreich* (München, Berlin, 1921).
3 W. Dibelius, *England* (Leipzig, 1923), pp. 67–104.
4 G. Schmoller, *Grundriss der Allgemeinen Volkswirtschaftslehre* (ed. Leipzig, 1919), p. 732.
5 *Ibid.* p. 734.
6 O. Spengler, *Preussentum und Sozialismus* (München, 1920), pp. 33, 34.

PAGE 276

1 *Sozialistische Monatshefte* (25. Jahrgang, 28 April 1919), pp. 380/1.
2 H. Friedjung, *Das Zeitalter des Imperialismus, 1884–1914* (Berlin, 1919), vol. I, p. 5.
3 *Ibid.* p. 283.
4 *Ibid.* p. 387; vol. II, p. 300; Friedjung's book title was taken over by W. Goetz for the 10th volume of *Propyläen-Weltgeschichte* (Berlin, 1933) and by '*Peuples et Civilisations*', t. 17 which was called: *Du Libéralisme à l'Impérialisme* (Paris, 1939).

PAGE 277

1 R. Steiner, *Geschichte und Überwindung des Imperialismus* (Zürich, 1946), pp. 2, 13, 55.

PAGE 282

1 J. Stalin, *Works* (Moscow, 1953), vol. IV, p. 243; *Izvestia*, 22 February 1919; V. A. Yakhontoff, *USSR Foreign Policy* (New York, 1945), p. 24.

PAGE 283

1 *Pravda*, 5 December 1917.
2 J. Stalin, *Works*, *op. cit.* vol. IV, 'The October Revolution and the National Question', pp. 158–65.
3 *Ibid.* p. 168.
4 *Ibid.* p. 170; *Pravda*, 6 and 19 November 1918.

PAGE 285

1 G. Lenczowski, *Russia and the West in Iran, 1918–1948* (New York, 1949), p. 124; L. Trotsky, *Between Red and White* (London, English ed.) p. 86.
2 G. Lenczowski, *op. cit.* pp. 99, 107.
3 C. Brandt, B. Schwartz, J. K. Fairbank, *A Documentary History of Chinese Communism* (Cambridge, Mass. 1952), pp. 56, 71, 75.

PAGE 286

1 J. Stalin, *Works*, *op. cit.* vol. VII, pp. 276, 277.
2 *Geschichte der kommunistischen Partei Deutschlands* (Berlin, 1955), pp. 112–14,
3 *Die Rote Fahne*, 2 August 1925.

PAGE 287

1 *Die Rote Fahne*, 10 March 1927; Eleventh Party Congress of the Communist Party of Germany at Essen, March 1927.

PAGE 288

1 C. Brandt, etc., *A Documentary History of the Chinese Communist Party*, *op. cit.* pp. 128–34.
2 G. Lenczowski, *op. cit.* p. 333.
3 C. Brandt, *op. cit.* p. 184.; resolution of the Politburo, 11 June 1930.

PAGE 291

1 O. Spengler, *Der Untergang des Abendlandes* (München, 1920), pp. 517–21, 569; cf. with *Preussentum und Sozialismus* (München, 1934), pp. 75–8.
2 Moeller van den Bruck, *Das dritte Reich* (3rd ed. Hamburg, 1931), p. 58.
3 A. Hitler, *Mein Kampf* (English ed. Boston, 1943), p. 144.

PAGE 292

1 *Dokumente der deutschen Politik und Geschichte* (Berlin, 1951–56), vol. V, pp. 250, 363, 527.
2 W. Sombart, *Deutscher Sozialismus* (Berlin, 1934), p. 13.

PAGE 293

1 C. Brinkmann, *England seit 1815* (Berlin, 1938), p. 316.
2 *Illustrirte Zeitung*, 14 September 1939, p. 355.
3 *Illustrirte Zeitung*, 2 November 1939, report, p. 476.
4 Examples, S.S.-pamphlets, *Amerikanismus eine Weltgefahr; Roosevelts Weg in den Krieg* (Berlin, 1943), Archiv des deutschen auswärtigen Amtes, p. 8.
5 L. Reichhold, *Die Schicksalsstunde des Westens* (Hamburg, 1940), p. 258.
6 *Ibid.* p. 311.
7 E. Fleischer, *Europa und das neue Weltbewußtsein* (Stuttgart, 1942), p. 177.

PAGE 294

1 P. R. Rohden, *Seemacht und Landmacht* (Leipzig, 1943), pp. 150–2, 172–82.
2 For example, in his appeal to the students of Europe, *Popolo d'Italia*, 1 February 1936; B. Mussolini, *Scritti e Discorsi* (Milan, 1936), vol. x, pp. 35, 40.
3 P. Herre, *Deutschland und die europäische Ordnung* (München, 1941); H. Lufft, *Der britische Imperialismus* (Berlin, 1940), *England und Europa*, ed. P. Meissner (Stuttgart, 1941).
4 K. H. Pfeffer, *England* (Hamburg, 1940), pp. 225–61.

PAGE 295

1 S. Nearing, *Dollar Diplomatie* (German ed. Heidelberg, 1943), pp. 274–8.
2 *Ibid.* introduction to the first edition.

PAGE 296

1 More details concerning the development of the Nazi Party in the Levant were given in my article on 'The Nazi Party in Palestine and the Levant, 1932–1939', *International Affairs*, vol. xxviii (October 1952), pp. 460–9.
2 W. Z. Laqueur, *Communism and Nationalism in the Middle East* (New York, 1957), p. 182.

PAGE 297

1 I. Kirchner, *Der Nahe Osten* (Brünn, München, Wien, 1943), pp. 563–661, 723.
2 W. Z. Laqueur, *op. cit.* p. 105.
3 A. Sanders, *Die Stunden der Entscheidung* (München, 1943), pp. 14, 22, 34–8, 94, 101–7, 142, 194.

PAGE 298

1 J. Polonski, *La presse, la propaganda et l'opinion publique sous l'occupation* (Paris, 1946), p. 99.

2 Kinoaki Matsuo, *How Japan Plans to Win* (English ed. London, 1942), p. 55; the book was originally published in 1940.

3 *Contemporary Japan*, vol. x (March 1941), p. 285.

PAGE 299

1 *Ibid.* p. 293.

2 H. B. Fombona, *Crimenes del Imperialismo Norteamericano* (Mexico, 1927), preface.

PAGE 300

1 A good example of that type is Pedro Muñiz, *Penetración Imperialista* (Santiago de Chile, 1935), pp. 6, 21, 50.

2 D. Aikman, *The All-American Front* (New York, 1942), p. 275.

3 L. Guilaine, *L'Amérique Latine et l'Impérialisme Américaine* (Paris, 1928), pp. 264, 265.

PAGE 303

1 V. Rojo, *Culminación y crisis del Imperialismo* (Buenos Aires, 1954), pp. 101, 113, 115, 122, 128, 137–9.

PAGE 304

1 *The New York Times*, 26 October 1959.

2 J. Mc Garrity, *Resistance* (Irish Freedom Press, 1957), pp. 15–17 and preface may serve as an illustration of the Irish use of imperialism as a slogan.

PAGE 305

1 Examples can be found in *Pravda*, 22 November 1947, the *New Times*, 12 February 1948 and in the recorded monitoring of the U.S.S.R. Home Service, 13 February 1949.

PAGE 306

1 *Soviet Press Translations* (Washington, 1949), p. 597.

2 Vienna Radio, *Russian Hour*, 31 October, 1951.

3 List of contents in *Voprosy Istorii* (1950–51).

4 *American Historical Review*, G. F. Kennan, 'Soviet Historiography' (January 1960), vol. LXV.

5 German edition (Berlin, 1953).

6 *Bolshaya Sovietskaya Encyklopedia* (ed. 1952), vol. XVII, pp. 568–80.

7 *Ibid.* vol. XXXLX (ed. 1956), survey of American history, pp. 597–610.

PAGE 307

1 *Ibid.* vol. XXXI (ed. 1955), pp. 601, 602.

2 For example, the monitored Russian Near-East Service broadcasting in Arabic on 1 November 1951.

3 *Voprosy Ekonomiki*, no. 9 (1 January 1952), p. 3.
4 I. P. Belyaeff, *Amerikansky Imperialism v Saudovsoy Araby* (Russian Academy of Sciences, Moscow, 1957), pp. 18, 159, 175, 188, 189, 193–9.

PAGE 308

1 *The New York Times*, 12 February 1960, p. 4.

PAGE 310

1 *Neues Deutschland*, 18 January 1951, 16 February 1951, 3 March 1951, 21 August 1951; *Tägliche Rundschau*, 18 December 1951, may serve as examples of that propaganda line.
2 W. Ulbricht, *Die gegenwärtige Lage*, Parteikonferenz der S.E.D. Berlin, 1952, p. 7.
3 W. Ulbricht, *Der Friedensvertrag und die nationalen Streitkräfte* (Berlin, 1952), p. 21.

PAGE 311

1 24. Tagung des Zentralkommittees der S.E.D. 1955, W. Ulbricht's address, p. 12.
2 Radioteletyped from East Germany, 13 February 1960.
3 *Neues Deutschland*, 7 February 1960; radioteletyped report, 30 January 1960.
4 Mao Tse-tung, *Imperialism and All Reactionaries are Paper Tigers* (Peking, 1958), pp. 21, 22, 23.

PAGE 312

1 *The Listener*, 14 May 1959, talk by Tibor Mende; monitored Peking radio broadcasts during the second half of 1959 contain many variations of the same theme; cf. also *The Manchester Guardian Weekly*, 24 December 1959, p. 3.
2 Radio Peking, 13 February 1960 and Radio Sofia on the same day; cf. also *The New York Times*, 15 February 1960, p. 2.
3 *Jenmin Jih Pao*, 22 April 1960, English version in the B.B.C. Monitoring Report, 23 April 1960.

PAGE 313

1 *Ibid.* 25 April 1960.
2 *The Observer*, 19 June 1960, report by Robert Franklin from Hong Kong.
3 Quoted by *Time*, 27 June 1960.

PAGE 314

1 *The Times*, report of the special correspondent from Bucharest, 24 June 1960; B.B.C. Monitoring Report, 24 June 1960.

PAGE 316

1 Report in *The Manchester Guardian*, 4 May 1959.

PAGE 317

1 H. D. Schmidt, *The Nazi Party in Palestine and the Levant, 1932–1939*, *International Affairs* (October 1952).

2 *The Socialist Review* (November 1912), p. 208; G. D. Overstreet, *Communism in India* (Berkeley, 1959), p. 56.

PAGE 318

1 Gamal Abdul Nasser, *Egypt's Liberation* (Washington, 1955), p. 97.

2 *Ibid.* p. 103.

PAGE 319

1 This summary of Egyptian views was gleaned from the Egyptian and Western press as well as from monitored broadcasts which are available in print. Examples are found in *Jewish Observer*, 26 December 1958; *Al Ahram*, 27 October 1959; *The New York Times*, 8 March 1960. Speeches made by the delegates of the U.A.R. in the assembly of the United Nations, e.g. September session 1960, *The Times*, 27 July 1960; Cairo and Damascus broadcasts on 19 and 26 May, 30 September 1960; *The Jewish Observer*, 1 July 1960.

2 Damascus Radio, live broadcast, 14 February 1960.

3 *The Christian Science Monitor*, 21 October 1959; Tunis Home Service, 4 February 1960; *The Manchester Guardian*, editorial, 6 June 1959. Mr Anthony Nutting was described as a known friend of 'the Nasser of Imperialism' by hostile Iraquis.

PAGE 320

1 Baghdad Radio, Home Service, 30 January 1960.

2 *Ibid.*

3 *Ha'olam Hazzeh*, 18 November 1959.

PAGE 321

1 *The Times*, 4 August 1960.

2 Institute of Pacific Relations, *Selected Documents of the Asian–African Conference* (New York, 1955), pp. 3–6.

PAGE 326

1 In his Midlothian Campaign, quoted already in chapter VI.

PAGE 327

1 See the Memorandum on the peace settlement in Europe, drawn up by Balfour in November 1916; B. E. C. Dugdale, *A. J. Balfour* (New York, 1937), p. 329.
2 *The Messages and Papers of Woodrow Wilson* (New York, 1924), p. 423.

PAGE 328

1 *Ibid.* p. 475.
2 *Ibid.* p. 483.

PAGE 329

1 *Ibid.* p. 351; in 1918 similar statements were made by him, cf. pp. 476, 584.
2 *Ibid.* vol. II, p. 634.
3 *Ibid.* vol. I, p. 501.

PAGE 330

1 *Ibid.* vol. II, p. 728.
2 D. Lloyd George, *War Memoirs* (London, 1933), vol. VI, p. 3307–8.

PAGE 332

1 *Nothing to Fear*, the selected addresses of F. D. Roosevelt (ed. B. D. Zevin, 1946), p. 266.
2 R. B. Russell, *A History of the United Nations Charter* (Washington, 1958), pp. 38, 39.
3 *Nothing to Fear*, *op. cit.* p. 259.

PAGE 333

1 *The Private Papers of Senator Vandenberg* (ed. Boston, 1952), pp. 56, 95–8.
2 R. B. Russell, *op. cit.* pp. 43, 199, 236.

PAGE 334

1 S. I. Rosenman, *The Public Papers and Addresses of Franklin D. Roosevelt*, vol. 1944–45 (New York, 1950), p. 350.

PAGE 336

1 Harry S. Truman, *Memoirs* (ed. 1955), vol. I, p. 270.

PAGE 337

1 The Israeli Premier revealed the extent of American pressure brought to bear on the Israeli government three years later; cf. *Ha'arets*, 8 October 1959.

PAGE 339

1 John Strachey, *The End of Empire* (London, 1959).

INDEX

Absolutism, 280

Adderley, Sir Charles Bowyer, Colonial Reformer, 77, 78, 91–3

Aden, 318

Administration, instead of politics, as an issue in French politics, 6

Adrianople, 135

Aegean Sea, 135

Afghan-British relations, 1878, 156–7

Afghan campaign in 1879, 157

Afghanistan, 153, 158, 159, 160, 166
  crisis, 151–2

Africa, 180, 198, 207, 226, 233, 267
  impact on British outlook, xvii
  and Empire planners, 178
  predicted to be civilized by Britain, 181
  and Empire, 195–220
  civilizing tasks in, 205, 210, 225, 233

African colonies, 215

African conquest for the Africans, 216

African nationalism, 322–3

African policy, and Christian missionaries, 203–4

African politics, 193

Afrikaner racialism, 322

Afrikaner support for Rhodes, 198

Afro-Asian Conference 1954, 321–2

Afro-Asian independence, 336

Afro-Asian nationalism, 324

Afro-Asian nationhood, 340

Afro-Asian struggle against white rule, 317

Afro-Asian struggle, East German view, 311

Afro-Asians, 219, 278
  and Anglo-American power, 302
  and communists, 316
  exploited, 266
  anti-imperialist movement, 307
  and Russian help, 308

Age of crisis, as historical notion, xvii

Age of imperialism, xviii, xxiv, 255, 256, 276, 277
  eschatology, 278

Age of Imperialism, The (H. Friedjung), 276–7

Age of liberalism and nationalism, 276

Agents-general, 179
  council of, 191

Agricultural labourers, 122

Alabama arbitration, 108

Albania, 136

Albert, Prince Consort, 120

Alexandria, 48

Algeria, 317, 318, 322
  French campaigns in 1840s, 21

Alien dependencies, 177

Alien peoples, and Empire, 92

Alien races, 90, 241
  and the Empire, 87
  rule over, 116
  within the Empire, 161

Aliens, not to be ruled by Britain, 146

Alsace, 132

Amadore-Virgili, 260

America, 88, 92, 234
  home of freedom, 88
  and Britain, 146
  and British Empire union, 188
  a revolutionary society, 284
  as rival of Britain, 95
  through Russian eyes, 306
  See also United States of America

American Anti-Imperialist League, 240

American capitalism, 253

American colonists, 160

American communal tradition, 330

American democracy, 284

American democrats denounce imperialism, 239

American distrust of Europe, 272

American expansion, desirable and undesirable, 238

American expansionism, 214, 236

American anti-imperialism, 270

American ideals, 328

American imperialism in communist language, 305

Index

Index

Index

394

Index

British Empire—*contd.*
its future, 150–1
and Indian economics, 152
Britain's responsibility, 152
and Britain, 153
its true strength, 154
military conception of, 159
based on consent, 161
as election topic in 1879–80, 160–2
the right and the wrong evolution, 161–2
public attitude towards, 165
fundamental issues of, 165
contrasting attitudes, 165
and the administration of its power, 169
old meanings, 171
and forms of authority, 172
meeting modern requirements, 175
as one state, 184
and world peace, 185
a novelty, 191
weakness and strength, 192
the most beneficent in history, 216
and the Jews, 296
Russian view, 306
awareness, 325
See also Empire, Colonial Empire
British Empire, The (J. Vogel), 138
British fleet, and Canadian defence, 79
British foreign policy, and imperial defence, 115
British government, in India, 23–4
and the Maoris, 95–6
British Guiana, 303
British history, problems of interpretation, 165
British Honduras, 303
British imperial affairs, and its critics, 29
British imperialism, 234, 277, 317
admired in Germany, 291
German version, 293
in the Middle East, 305
See imperialism
British institutions, and coloured subjects, 84
British interests, 128, 129, 130, 136, 138
in the East, 46
in the Mediterranean, 48
'British interests', suspect as a phrase, 126
as slogan, 127, 147, 152

British journalists, observing a truce in 1853–58 concerning Napoleon III, 14, 16
British landed gentry, 63
British liberties, 55
British maritime interests, 141
British merchants, 261
British mission, 146
and human progress, 201
murdered in Kabul, 160
British monarch, of an Empire or of Britain? 73
British monopoly, as principle of trade, 59
British monopolies in the colonies, 66
British Museum, 225
British nationalism, 246–8
British nations, the sole depositories of liberty in Europe, 16
British naval supremacy, 128
British North America, 50, 57, 83, 175
in the Durham Report, 56
British North Americans, 54, 55
British opposition party, misunderstood abroad, 160
British plot, alleged, and imperialism, 274
British policy, and the national principle, 42
in the Mediterranean, 45
its double standard, 151
criticized in 1880, 163
and imperial policy, 170
suspect, 242
explained by Germans, 274–8
in the Middle East, the communist view, 307
in the nineteenth century, 326
in the first war, 327
British political life alert, 155
British politics, misunderstood abroad, 160
British power, 133
and the colonies, 75
and emigration, 99
and global empire, 106
in the Pacific, 112
resented, 243–6
suspect in Germany, 257
explained, 258
explained in Austria, 260

395

Index

Index

Commonwealth—*contd.*
idea, the communist view, 315
ideals, 323–4
See also British Commonwealth
Commune, 163
Communism, 278
and colonial policy, 288
suppressed, 288
and Germany, 290
and reality, 315
and Bonapartism, 315
and national independence, 322
Communist agitation, 287
in Germany 286
against colonial rule, 317
Communist expansion, 316
Communist policy in Asia and Europe, 286
Communist propaganda, 282
in Latin America, 299–300
and Nazi tradition, 304
Communist theory on divided world, 316
Communists, 278
and imperialism, 272
and colonial nationalism, 286
and Anglo-American power, 302
and self-determination, 328
Complément du dictionnaire de l'Académie française (Louis Barré), n. 342
Conan, C. A., 236–7
Concentration camps, 233
Concept of Economic Imperialism, The (R. Koebner), vii, n. 342
Conceptual political models, 314
Concordances, their limitations, xvi
Congo, 199, 317
Congregational Union of England and Wales, 203
Congress of Berlin 1878, 140–1, 147
Congress in Washington, as a model, 184
Coningsby (Benjamin Disraeli), 110
Conservatism, and Empire, 111
Conservative Party, 46, 202
election campaign, 161
Conservative victory 1951, 306
Conservatives, 193, 198
opposed to Far East policy, 35
and the Corn Laws, 63
and the Empire, 132
accused of imperial language, 164
and African policy, 203

'Conspiracy to Murder Bill' 1858, 16
Constantinople, 127, 129, 136
Constitutionalism, inherent in the Teutonic races, 20
Contemporary Review, 103, 157, 162, 213, 245, 250
Contiguous, as significant American epithet, 238
Continental despotism, 154, 232
Continental imperialism, 163
Continental men of letters viewing imperialism, 261
Continental theories of imperialism, 262
Continental tradition and Anglo-American thought, 280
Coolie labour, 154
Corfu, isle of, 47
Corn Laws, 63
repeal of, 28
Correspondence and Conversations of Alexis de Tocqueville with Nassau William Senior, n. 343
Corruption in France, 9
Corry, Montagu, Disraeli's secretary, 127, 128
Corsica, 41
Cotton duties, repealed in India, 157
Coup d'état, in France 1851, and imperialism, 21
Courtney, Leonard H., English politician, 223, 225, 228, 229, 244
Cowen, Joseph, M.P. and editor, 180
Crimean War, 14, 46, 78, 123, 125
Croats, 327, 330
Cromer, Lord, Evelyn Baring, British statesman, 211
comparing old and modern imperialism, 258, 262
Cromwell, 174, 182, 262
as imperialist, 258
Crown, the British, and the Colonies, 132
Crown, allegiance, 154
Crown colonies, 85, 97
distinguished from English settlements, 92–3
in the tropics, 207
Cyprus, 136, 141, 142, 143, 145, 151, 153
its ethnic character, 146
Cyprus Convention 1878, 147, 156

400

Index

Index

Eastern Question, 116, 129, 130–1, 132, 147, 156, 167
East Europe and co-existence, 313
East India Company, 27, 44, 117
East Indian possessions, 65
East-West division, 283
Eckstein, South African financier, 288
Economic advantages of federation, 178
Economic arguments in favour of expansion, 208
Economic crises explained, 236–7
Economic crisis, 288
Economic depression, (1876) 124, (1878) 151, 157
Economic development, 252
Economic expansionism, 215
Economic injustice, 298–9
Economic imperialism, 200, 236, 255–6, 270–3, 325
  described, 264
  denounced by the Pope, 299
  See also Imperialism
Economic interests, in Africa, 199
  and Empire discussed in 1899, 223
  and imperialism, 251–2
Economic motives, in African policy, 202–3
  in Africa, 205
  and colonial policy, 206
  to the fore, 207
  for American expansion, 236
  of imperialism, 260
Economic nationalism, 256
Economic power, 259
Economic Imperialism (Leonard Woolf), 271
Economic Taproot of Imperialism (J. A. Hobson), 252–3
'Economists' opposed to 'imperialists', 144
Edinburgh Review, 41, 43, 44, 73–4, 115, 205
Edward VII, 281
  Prince of Wales, 185
  as Prince of Wales, tour to India, 115
  as Prince of Wales, and Empire value, 199
Egypt, 48, 129, 132, 147, 177, 180, 197, 198, 205, 206–7, 251, 286, 288, 317, 318
  and British policy, 307
  and Israel 1956, 318–19

Egyptians, 225
Eighteenth Brumaire of Louis Buonaparte, The (Karl Marx), 12
Eire, and Atlantic security, 331
Eisenhower, Dwight, U.S. President, 304
Elgin, Lord, Governor of Canada and Empire sentiment, 68
  quotes Robert Baldwin, 72–3
  formulates Empire issue, 72–3
Elizabeth I, Queen of England, 247
Emergence of the Concept of Imperialism, The (R. Koebner), vii, n. 342
Emigration, campaign in 1870, 98
  to the U.S.A. deplored, 99
  and Empire, 183, 194
  and social problems in England, 207
Emotionalism, in British politics, 155
Emperor, associations, 118
  the Roman version, 118
  as a name, 119
  as title, 120, 121
  use of the term in England in 1898, 214
Empire, 25, 173
  as expression of historical thought, xvii
  its meaning in the 1830's, xxv
  symbol of the French national cause, 3
  embodying an idea in France, 5 (see also système impérial)
  heralded by Louis Napoleon, 7
  as French translation of imperialism, 8
  in France ridiculed, 11
  as name in France, 23
  and the Colonial Reformers, 24, 58
  as title of the British dependencies, 27
  of Louis Napoleon, 27
  of Napoleon III, 28
  monstrous, 30
  notion, rejected by Cobden and Smith, 30
  not used as an indictment of British rule, 31
  pride in, 32, 33, 34
  term with a stigma, 32–3
  meaning the United Kingdom, 33, 37, 39
  meaning all that the nation holds, 33
  lack of definite meaning, 37
  meaning the system of imperial connexions, 37, 39
  the glory of England, 42

Index

Index

European salvation, the German appeal, 284
European scholars, 258–60
Europeans, and Africans, 218
Evening News, 211
Exodus of the Western Nations, (Viscount Bury), 82–3
Expansion of England (John R. Seeley), 173–5
Expansionism, 209, 261, 265, 176, 325, 326
  in Africa, 202
  after 1895, 206
  as an evil, 222
  deplored, 225
  denounced, 229
  and capitalism, 234–5
  in the U.S.A., 237
  in Germany, 291
  in Europe, 331
Eyre, Edward, Governor of Jamaica, 84

Fabian Society, 231
Fabians, 235, 262
  and imperialism, 232
  and Hobson, 271–2
Fabianism and the Empire (Bernard Shaw), 232
Far East, policy of Lord Palmerston, 34, 35
  in 1874, 112
Farrer, Lord Thomas H., Lt. Baron, English civil servant, 221, 231
Fashoda, 196, 212, 213, 215, 222
Federal assembly, proposed, 184
Federal principle, 175
  defeated in 1886, 171
Federal Republic of Germany, 315
Federal system, 175
Federal union, 175
Federal world government, 334
Federalism declining, 190
Federation, 177–93
Federation of the British Empire (Sir G. F. Bowen), 184–5
Feudalism, 224
Fiji Islands, 113, 132, 145
  annexation in 1874, 112
Filipinos revolt, 239–40, 241
Finance capital, 270

Financial power, 251–2
Finanzkapital, Das (R. Hilferding), 265–6
Finland, 316–17
Fisher, H. A. L., historian, 175
Flâneur, 21, 23, 26
  English, in Paris, 8
  See also Ten Years of Imperialism in France, 22
Fleischer E., German writer, 293
Flemings, 330
Florence, 180
  as a power, 175
Flourens, Émile, French agitator, 260
Force, British doctrine of, 248
Förster, F. W., Swiss philosopher, 247–8
Foreign domination, in Africa, 323
Foreign policy, and colonial influence on, 178
Foreign Policy of Great Britain (W. R., Grey), 144–5
Forster, W. E., 132, 177, 178, 179, 181–2, 183, 184
  his concept of Colonial Empire, 118
  on the meaning of imperialism, 158
  chairman of the Imperial Federation League, 172
Fortescue, Chichester, 91
Fortnightly Review, 122–3, 148, 151–7, 166, 179, 184
Four Freedoms, 332
Four Policemen, 340
Four Policemen Method, 333
Four Power co-operation, 334
France, 41, 48, 94, 114, 118, 125, 129, 154, 173, 180, 187, 196, 201, 207, 208, 213, 215, 233, 243, 256, 258, 259, 262, 270, 274, 282, 318–19, 322
  revival of the 'imperialist' spirit in 1840, 2
  her organization of despotism and free institutions, 9
  unqualified for representative institutions, 9
  morally vulnerable exposed to political convulsions, 9
  diagnosed in Britain, 10
  criticized by the British press, 11
  in 1858, 17
  allied with Britain in 1860, 20
  intellectual life, 22

Index

German men of letters, 160
German middle-class opinion, 268
German militarism, 234, 265
German military might, 118
German moral rearmament, 278
German nationalists, and post-war history, 281–2
  view of post-war history, 290–2
German naval armament, 261
German navy, 262
German occupation of North East New Guinea, 181
German philosophy, 280
German promises to Latin America and the Arabs, 296
German propaganda, 290–7
German reply to British ultimatum 1939, 293
German rule, 327
German and Russian slogans similar, 294
German scholars, describing imperialism after 1918, 274–6
  describing Britain, 258–9
German socialists, 264
German-speaking socialists, 265–8
German states after 1945, 309
German trade, 257
German view of Britain, 314
German war guilt, 275
Germanic-Romance Europe, 295
Germans, in Africa, 200
  and Boers, 243
  and Europe, 295
Germany, 94, 100, 114, 125, 132, 180, 187, 189, 196, 201, 207, 208, 234, 243, 256, 257, 258, 260, 262, 270, 282, 289, 301
  rise of military power, xvii
  as a model, 184
  a warning to Australia, 190
  in Africa, 193–199
  as world power, 268
  after 1918, 174, 278
  her advance opposed, 276
  and Russia, 286
  in the League of Nations, 287
  encircled, 290
  victim of Jewry, alleged, 292
George III, King of England, 232
Georgia, 284–5
Gibraltar, 30, 82

Gisborne, 178
Gladstone, William E., British statesman, 25–6, 132, 135, 143, 145–6, 172, 224, 229, 235, 326, 327
  protests, 16
  and the abolition of colonial preferences, 66
  addressing the Colonial Society in 1869, 91
  defining his attitude to the colonies in 1870, 101–2
  and the Colonial Reformers, 102
  defending Empire unity, 104, 168
  annoyed at demand for preferential duties 104
  and the Eastern Question, 126
  criticizing 'British interests', 129–30
  opposed to Disraeli's concept of Empire, 130
  cartoon, 139
  depicted as anti-imperialist, 147
  makes Imperialism a slogan in 1879, 147
  against imperialism, 157
  and the election campaign of 1879–80, 160–2
  and colonial policy, 166
  and empire revival, 167
  making Home Rule his main political platform in 1886, 169
  and Home Rule, 170
  and South Africa, 176
  lack of imperial direction, 177
  proud of British mission in 1892, 192
  second administration and Africa in 1885, 180
  second administration, 196
  and Egypt, 197
  against increasing the Zululand protectorate, 198
  reserved about expansionism in Africa, 201
  entrusted Rosebery with the Foreign Office, 202
  fourth administration and Ireland, 205
  and Carnegie, 238
Gladstone Ministry, 95
Global struggles now in progress, xvii
Glubb, Sir John B., British officer, 305
Gobineau, Alexandre de, inventor of racist theory, 87, 258

409

Index

Index

Index

Index

Index

Schumpeter, J. A., economic historian, 273
Schurz, Carl, American statesman, 238, 239, 240
Schwab, American financier, 253
Salisbury, Lord, 124, 145, 168, 187, 193, 207
  on Empire, 142–3
  responsible for the acquisition of Cyprus, 143
  and Egypt, 197
  rejects Niger monopoly, 200
  colonial treaties, 201
  African policy, 202
  his reserved attitude towards imperial federation, 190
Scientific history, as comment on popular consciousness, xx, xxi
Scientific historian, the service of, xxi
Scotland, 184
Sea of Marmara, 135
Secession, right of, 284
Security and national sovereignty, 339
Sedan, battle of, 26, 155, 157
Seebohm, Frederic, banker and historian, 162–4
Seeley, John Robert, 173–5, 177, 179, 182, 183, 184, 187, 188
Self-determination, 161, 230, 283, 284, 325, 327–40
  and imperialism, 265
  a fraud, 277
  in the Soviet Union, 285
Self-governing colonies, 44, 133
Self-governing dominions, 209, 215
Self-government, 27, 40, 51, 54, 55, 56, 57, 62, 67, 69, 70, 71, 78, 79, 80, 82, 85, 86, 92, 93, 101, 102, 109, 110, 118, 136, 137, 154, 161, 168, 171, 172, 175, 176, 184, 206, 240, 242, 243, 315, 323
  suppressed in France, 17
  aim of British rule, 42, 44
  and Empire vision, 105
Self-interest, as imperial tie, 72
Semantic approach to history, xiii, xv, xvi, xx
Semantic delusion, 316, 322
Semitic Federation, 320
Semmel, Bernard, 264
Sentiment, as political factor, 74
  and theory, 250

Separation of the Colonies from Britain, 24, 27, 53, 55, 56, 65, 69, 70, 71, 72, 73, 76, 79, 80, 82, 83, 87, 89, 90, 91, 93, 94, 97, 98, 100, 101, 103, 105, 109, 131, 132, 133, 138, 142, 146, 151, 160, 168, 170, 177, 182, 184
  See also Imperial connexion
Serbs, in the first World War, 327
Service interest, and empire, 224
Shaw, Bernard, English playwright and Fabian, 232
Shelley, Percy B., English poet, 229
Shigetomo Sayegusa, 298
Singapore, 321
Sino-Soviet friendship, 312
Sketches of Imperial Paris (Theodor Mundt), 15
Slav sympathies in England, 126
Slave trade, 194, 204, 205
Slavery, 252
  abolition of, 65, 86
  fight against, 203
Slogans, xiii, xiv, xv, xvi, xvii, 170
  retroactive application, 29
  losing effect in 1880, 162
  their study, 166
  when overworked, 302
Slovaks, 330
Slovenes, 330
Smith, Adam, economist, 45, 59, 76, 179, 258
Smith, Goldwin, historian and publicist, 20, 30, 32, 33, 34, 37, 45, 47–8, 91, 97, 144, 169, 171, 175, 237
  candidate for the House of Commons, 1868, 24, 25
  influencing Dilke, 90
  his ideas fading, 95
  his ideas attacked, 100
Smith, W. H., 178
Smuts, General J. C., and national self-determination, 330
Social Democrats, 287
Social motives, xvi
Social problems, and expansion in Africa, 203
Social reform, 261
Socialism, 163
  denounced, 237
  the remedy for imperialism, 253

Index

Date Due